# Natural Language Processing with TensorFlow

Teach language to machines using Python's deep learning library

**Thushan Ganegedara**

BIRMINGHAM - MUMBAI

# Natural Language Processing with TensorFlow

**Acquisition Editor:** Frank Pohlmann
**Project Editor:** Radhika Atitkar
**Content Development Editor:** Chris Nelson
**Technical Editor:** Bhagyashree Rai
**Copy Editor:** Tom Jacob
**Proofreader:** Safis Editing
**Indexer:** Rekha Nair
**Graphics:** Tom Scaria
**Production Coordinator:** Nilesh Mohite

First published: May 2018

Production reference: 2310518

Published by Packt Publishing Ltd.
Livery Place
35 Livery Street
Birmingham B3 2PB, UK.

ISBN 978-1-78847-831-1

www.packtpub.com

`mapt.io`

Mapt is an online digital library that gives you full access to over 5,000 books and videos, as well as industry leading tools to help you plan your personal development and advance your career. For more information, please visit our website.

## Why subscribe?

- Spend less time learning and more time coding with practical eBooks and Videos from over 4,000 industry professionals

- Learn better with Skill Plans built especially for you

- Get a free eBook or video every month

- Mapt is fully searchable

- Copy and paste, print, and bookmark content

## PacktPub.com

Did you know that Packt offers eBook versions of every book published, with PDF and ePub files available? You can upgrade to the eBook version at `www.PacktPub.com` and as a print book customer, you are entitled to a discount on the eBook copy. Get in touch with us at `service@packtpub.com` for more details.

At `www.PacktPub.com`, you can also read a collection of free technical articles, sign up for a range of free newsletters, and receive exclusive discounts and offers on Packt books and eBooks.

# Contributors

## About the author

**Thushan Ganegedara** is currently a third year Ph.D. student at the University of Sydney, Australia. He is specializing in machine learning and has a liking for deep learning. He lives dangerously and runs algorithms on untested data. He also works as the chief data scientist for AssessThreat, an Australian start-up. He got his BSc. (Hons) from the University of Moratuwa, Sri Lanka. He frequently writes technical articles and tutorials about machine learning. Additionally, he also strives for a healthy lifestyle by including swimming in his daily schedule.

I would like to thank my parents, my siblings, and my wife for the faith they had in me and the support they have given, also all my teachers and my Ph.D advisor for the guidance he provided me with.

# About the reviewers

**Motaz Saad** holds a Ph.D. in computer science from the University of Lorraine. He loves data and he likes to play with it. He has over 10 years, professional experience in NLP, computational linguistics, data science, and machine learning. He currently works as an assistant professor at the faculty of information technology, IUG.

**Dr Joseph O'Connor** is a data scientist with a deep passion for deep learning. His company, Deep Learn Analytics, a UK-based data science consultancy, works with businesses to develop machine learning applications and infrastructure from concept to deployment. He was awarded a Ph.D. from University College London for his work analyzing data on the MINOS high-energy physics experiment. Since then, he has developed ML products for a number of companies in the private sector, specializing in NLP and time series forecasting. You can find him at http://deeplearnanalytics.com/.

# Packt is searching for authors like you

If you're interested in becoming an author for Packt, please visit authors.packtpub.com and apply today. We have worked with thousands of developers and tech professionals, just like you, to help them share their insight with the global tech community. You can make a general application, apply for a specific hot topic that we are recruiting an author for, or submit your own idea.

# Table of Contents

# Preface

In the digital information age that we live in, the amount of data has grown exponentially, and it is growing at an unprecedented rate as we read this. Most of this data is language-related data (textual or verbal), such as emails, social media posts, phone calls, and web articles. Natural Language Processing (NLP) leverages this data efficiently to help humans in their businesses or day-to-day tasks. NLP has already revolutionized the way we use data to improve both businesses and our lives, and will continue to do so in the future.

One of the most ubiquitous use cases of NLP is Virtual Assistants (VAs), such as Apple's Siri, Google Assistant, and Amazon Alexa. Whenever you ask your VA for "the cheapest rates for hotels in Switzerland," a complex series of NLP tasks are triggered. First, your VA needs to understand (parse) your request (for example, learn that it needs to retrieve hotel rates, not the dog parks). Another decision the VA needs to make is "what is cheap?". Next, the VA needs to rank the cities in Switzerland (perhaps based on your past traveling history). Then, the VA might crawl websites such as Booking.com and Agoda.com to fetch the hotel rates in Switzerland and rank them by analyzing both the rates and reviews for each hotel. As you can see, the results you see in a few seconds are a result of a very intricate series of complex NLP tasks.

So, what makes such NLP tasks so versatile and accurate for our everyday tasks? The underpinning elements are "deep learning" algorithms. Deep learning algorithms are essentially complex neural networks that can map raw data to a desired output without requiring any sort of task-specific feature engineering. This means that you can provide a hotel review of a customer and the algorithm can answer the question "How positive is the customer about this hotel?", directly. Also, deep learning has already reached, and even exceeded, human-level performance in a variety of NLP tasks (for example, speech recognition and machine translation).

By reading this book, you will learn how to solve many interesting NLP problems using deep learning. So, if you want to be an influencer who changes the world, studying NLP is critical. These tasks range from learning the semantics of words, to generating fresh new stories, to performing language translation just by looking at bilingual sentence pairs. All of the technical chapters are accompanied by exercises, including step-by-step guidance for readers to implement these systems. For all of the exercises in the book, we will be using Python with TensorFlow—a popular distributed computation library that makes implementing deep neural networks very convenient.

# Who this book is for

This book is for aspiring beginners who are seeking to transform the world by leveraging linguistic data. This book will provide you with a solid practical foundation for solving NLP tasks. In this book, we will cover various aspects of NLP, focusing more on the practical implementation than the theoretical foundation. Having sound practical knowledge of solving various NLP tasks will help you to have a smoother transition when learning the more advanced theoretical aspects of these methods. In addition, a solid practical understanding will help when performing more domain-specific tuning of your algorithms, to get the most out of a particular domain.

# What this book covers

*Chapter 1, Introduction to Natural Language Processing*, embarks us on our journey with a gentle introduction to NLP. In this chapter, we will first look at the reasons we need NLP. Next, we will discuss some of the common subtasks found in NLP. Thereafter, we will discuss the two main eras of NLP—the traditional era and the deep learning era. We will gain an understanding of the characteristics of the traditional era by working through how a language modeling task might have been solved with traditional algorithms. Then, we will discuss the deep learning era, where deep learning algorithms are heavily utilized for NLP. We will also discuss the main families of deep learning algorithms. We will then discuss the fundamentals of one of the most basic deep learning algorithms—a fully connected neural network. We will conclude the chapter with a road map that provides a brief introduction to the coming chapters.

*Chapter 2, Understanding TensorFlow*, introduces you to the Python TensorFlow library — the primary platform we will implement our solutions on. We will start by writing code to perform a simple calculation in TensorFlow. We will then discuss how things are executed, starting from running the code to getting results. Thereby, we will understand the underlying components of TensorFlow in detail. We will further strengthen our understanding of TensorFlow with a colorful analogy of a restaurant and see how orders are fulfilled. Later, we will discuss more technical details of TensorFlow, such as the data structures and operations (mostly related to neural networks) defined in TensorFlow. Finally, we will implement a fully connected neural network to recognize handwritten digits. This will help us to understand how an end-to-end solution might be implemented with TensorFlow.

*Chapter 3, Word2vec – Learning Word Embeddings*, begins by discussing how to solve NLP tasks with TensorFlow. In this chapter, we will see how neural networks can be used to learn word vectors or word representations. Word vectors are also known as word embeddings. Word vectors are numerical representations of words that have similar values for similar words and different values for different words. First, we will discuss several traditional approaches to achieving this, which include using a large human-built knowledge base known as WordNet. Then, we will discuss the modern neural network-based approach known as Word2vec, which learns word vectors without any human intervention. We will first understand the mechanics of Word2vec by working through a hands-on example. Then, we will discuss two algorithmic variants for achieving this — the skip-gram and continuous bag-of-words (CBOW) model. We will discuss the conceptual details of the algorithms, as well as how to implement them in TensorFlow.

*Chapter 4, Advance Word2vec*, takes us on to more advanced topics related to word vectors. First, we will compare skip-gram and CBOW to see whether a winner exists. Next, we will discuss several improvements that can be used to improve the performance of the Word2vec algorithms. Then, we will discuss a more recent and powerful word embedding learning algorithm — the GloVe (global vectors) algorithm. Finally, we will look at word vectors in action, in a document classification task. In that exercise, we will see that word vectors are powerful enough to represent the topic (for example, entertainment and sport) that the document belongs to.

*Chapter 5, Sentence Classification with Convolutional Neural Networks*, discusses convolution neural networks (CNN) — a family of neural networks that excels at processing spatial data such as images or sentences. First, we will develop a solid high-level understanding of CNNs by discussing how they process data and what sort of operations are involved. Next, we will dive deep into each of the operations involved in the computations of a CNN to understand the underpinning mathematics of a CNN. Finally, we will walk through two exercises. First, we will classify hand written digit images with a CNN. We will see that CNNs are is capable of reaching a very high accuracy quickly for this task. Next, we will explore how CNNs can be used to classify sentences. Particularly, we will ask a CNN to predict whether a sentence is about an object, person, location, and so on.

*Chapter 6, Recurrent Neural Networks*, is about a powerful family of neural networks that can model sequences of data, known as recurrent neural networks (RNNs). We will first discuss the mathematics behind the RNNs and the update rules that are used to update the RNNs over time during learning. Then, we will discuss section different variants of RNNs and their applications (for example, one-to-one RNNs and one-to-many RNNs). Finally, we will go through an exercise where RNNs are used for a text generation task. In this, we will train the RNN on folk stories and ask the RNN to produce a new story. We will see that RNNs are poor at persisting long-term memory. Finally, we will discuss a more advanced variant of RNNs, which we will call RNN-CF, which is able to persist memory for longer.

*Chapter 7, Long Short-Term Memory Networks*, allows us to explore more powerful techniques that are able to remember for a longer period of time, having found out that RNNs are poor at retaining long-term memory. We will discuss one such technique in this chapter — Long Short-Term Memory Networks (LSTMs). LSTMs are more powerful and have been shown to outperform other sequential models in many time-series tasks. We will first investigate the underlying mathematics and update the rules of the LSTM, along with a colorful example that illustrates why each computation matters. Then, we will look at how LSTMs can persist memory for longer. Next, we will discuss how we can improve LSTMs prediction capabilities further. Finally, we will discuss several variants of LSTMs that have a more complex structure (LSTMs with peephole connections), as well as a method that tries to simplify the LSTMs gated recurrent units (GRUs).

*Chapter 8, Applications of LSTM – Generating Text*, extensively evaluates how LSTMs perform in a text generation task. We will qualitatively and quantitatively measure how good the text generated by LSTMs is. We will also conduct comparisons between LSTMs, LSTMs with peephole connections, and GRUs. Finally, we will see how we can bring word embeddings into the model to improve the text generated by LSTMs.

*Chapter 9*, *Applications of LSTM – Image Caption Generation*, moves us on to multimodal data (that is, images and text) after coping with textual data. In this chapter, we will investigate how we can automatically generate descriptions for a given image. This involves combining a feed-forward model (that is, a CNN) with a word embedding layer and a sequential model (that is, an LSTM) in a way that forms an end-to-end machine learning pipeline.

*Chapter 10*, *Sequence to Sequence Learning – Neural Machine Translation*, is about the implementing neural machine translation (NMT) model. Machine translation is where we translate a sentence/phrase from a source language into a target language. We will first briefly discuss what machine translation is. This will be followed by a section about the history of machine translation. Then, we will discuss the architecture of modern neural machine translation models in detail, including the training and inference procedures. Next, we will look at how to implement an NMT system from scratch. Finally, we will explore ways to improve standard NMT systems.

*Chapter 11*, *Current Trends and Future of Natural Language Processing*, the final chapter, focuses on the current and future trends of NLP. We will discuss the latest discoveries related to the systems and tasks we discussed in the previous chapters. This chapter will cover most of the exciting novel innovations, as well as giving you in-depth intuition to implement some of the technologies.

*Appendix*, *Mathematical Foundations and Advanced TensorFlow*, will introduce the reader to various mathematical data structures (for example, matrices) and operations (for example, matrix inverse). We will also discuss several important concepts in probability. We will then introduce Keras—a high-level library that uses TensorFlow underneath. Keras makes the implementing of neural networks simpler by hiding some of the details in TensorFlow, which some might find challenging. Concretely, we will see how we can implement a CNN with Keras, to get a feel of how to use Keras. Next, we will discuss how we can use the seq2seq library in TensorFlow to implement a neural machine translation system with much less code that we used in Chapter 11, Current Trends and the Future of Natural Language Processing. Finally, we will walk you through a guide aimed at teaching to use the TensorBoard to visualize word embeddings. TensorBoard is a handy visualization tool that is shipped with TensorFlow. This can be used to visualize and monitor various variables in your TensorFlow client.

# To get the most out of this book

To get the most out of this book, we assume the following from the reader:

- A solid will and an ambition to learn the modern ways of NLP

- Familiarity with basic Python syntax and data structures (for example, lists and dictionaries)

- A good understanding of basic mathematics (for example, matrix/vector multiplication)

- (Optional) Advance mathematics knowledge (for example, derivative calculation) to understand a handful of subsections that cover the details of how certain learning models overcome potential practical issues faced during training

- (Optional) Read research papers to refer to advances/details in systems, beyond what the book covers

# Download the example code files

You can download the example code files for this book from your account at `http://www.packtpub.com`. If you purchased this book elsewhere, you can visit `http://www.packtpub.com/support` and register to have the files emailed directly to you.

You can download the code files by following these steps:

1. Log in or register at `http://www.packtpub.com`.
2. Select the **SUPPORT** tab.
3. Click on **Code Downloads & Errata**.
4. Enter the name of the book in the **Search** box and follow the on-screen instructions.

Once the file is downloaded, please make sure that you unzip or extract the folder using the latest version of one of these:

- WinRAR / 7-Zip for Windows
- Zipeg / iZip / UnRarX for macOS
- 7-Zip / PeaZip for Linux

The code bundle for the book is also hosted on GitHub at `https://github.com/PacktPublishing/Natural-Language-Processing-with-TensorFlow`. We also have other code bundles from our rich catalog of books and videos available at `https://github.com/PacktPublishing/`. Check them out!

# Download the color images

We also provide a PDF file that has color images of the screenshots/diagrams used in this book. You can download it here: `https://www.packtpub.com/sites/default/files/downloads/NaturalLanguageProcessingwithTensorFlow_ColorImages.pdf`.

# Conventions used

There are a number of text conventions used throughout this book.

`CodeInText`: Indicates code words in text, database table names, folder names, filenames, file extensions, pathnames, dummy URLs, user input, and Twitter handles. For example; "Mount the downloaded `WebStorm-10*.dmg` disk image file as another disk in your system."

A block of code is set as follows:

```
graph = tf.Graph() # Creates a graph
session = tf.InteractiveSession(graph=graph) # Creates a session
```

When we wish to draw your attention to a particular part of a code block, the relevant lines or items are set in bold:

```
graph = tf.Graph() # Creates a graph
session = tf.InteractiveSession(graph=graph) # Creates a session
```

Any command-line input or output is written as follows:

```
conda --version
```

**Bold**: Indicates a new term, an important word, or words that you see on the screen, for example, in menus or dialog boxes, also appear in the text like this. For example: "Select **System info** from the **Administration** panel."

*References*: In *Chapter 11*, *Current Trends and the Future of Natural Language Processing*, in-text references include a bracketed number (for example, [1]) that correlates with the numbering in the *References* section at the end of the chapter.

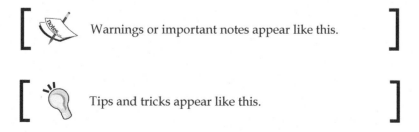

Warnings or important notes appear like this.

Tips and tricks appear like this.

# Get in touch

Feedback from our readers is always welcome.

**General feedback**: Email feedback@packtpub.com, and mention the book's title in the subject of your message. If you have questions about any aspect of this book, please email us at questions@packtpub.com.

**Errata**: Although we have taken every care to ensure the accuracy of our content, mistakes do happen. If you have found a mistake in this book we would be grateful if you would report this to us. Please visit, http://www.packtpub.com/submit-errata, selecting your book, clicking on the Errata Submission Form link, and entering the details.

**Piracy**: If you come across any illegal copies of our works in any form on the Internet, we would be grateful if you would provide us with the location address or website name. Please contact us at copyright@packtpub.com with a link to the material.

**If you are interested in becoming an author**: If there is a topic that you have expertise in and you are interested in either writing or contributing to a book, please visit http://authors.packtpub.com.

# Reviews

Please leave a review. Once you have read and used this book, why not leave a review on the site that you purchased it from? Potential readers can then see and use your unbiased opinion to make purchase decisions, we at Packt can understand what you think about our products, and our authors can see your feedback on their book. Thank you!

For more information about Packt, please visit packtpub.com.

# 1
# Introduction to Natural Language Processing

**Natural Language Processing** (**NLP**) is an important tool for understanding and processing the immense volume of unstructured data in today's world. Recently, deep learning has been widely adopted for many NLP tasks because of the remarkable performance that deep learning algorithms have shown in a plethora of challenging tasks, such as, image classification, speech recognition, and realistic text generation. TensorFlow, in turn, is one of the most intuitive and efficient deep learning frameworks currently in existence. This book will enable aspiring deep learning developers to handle massive amounts of data using NLP and TensorFlow.

In this chapter, we will provide an introduction to NLP and to the rest of the book. We will answer the question, "What is Natural Language Processing?" Also, we'll look at some of its most important uses. We will also consider the traditional approaches and the more recent deep learning-based approaches to NLP, including a **Fully-Connected Neural Network** (**FCNN**). Finally, we will conclude with an overview of the rest of the book and the technical tools we will be using.

## What is Natural Language Processing?

According to IBM, 2.5 exabytes (1 exabyte = 1,000,000,000 gigabytes) of data were generated every day in 2017, and this is growing as this book is being written. To put that into perspective, if all the human beings in the world were to process that data, it would be roughly 300 MB for each of us every day to process. Of all this data, a large fraction is unstructured text and speech as there are millions of emails and social media content created and phone calls made every day.

These statistics provide a good basis for us to define what NLP is. Simply put, the goal of NLP is to make machines understand our spoken and written languages. Moreover, NLP is ubiquitous and is already a large part of human life. **Virtual Assistants (VAs)**, such as Google Assistant, Cortana, and Apple Siri, are largely NLP systems. Numerous NLP tasks take place when one asks a VA, "Can you show me a good Italian restaurant nearby?". First, the VA needs to convert the utterance to text (that is, speech-to-text). Next, it must understand the semantics of the request (for example, the user is looking for a good restaurant with an Italian cuisine) and formulate a structured request (for example, cuisine = Italian, rating = 3-5, distance < 10 km). Then, the VA must search for restaurants filtering by the location and cuisine, and then, sort the restaurants by the ratings received. To calculate an overall rating for a restaurant, a good NLP system may look at both the rating and text description provided by each user. Finally, once the user is at the restaurant, the VA might assist the user by translating various menu items from Italian to English. This example shows that NLP has become an integral part of human life.

It should be understood that NLP is an extremely challenging field of research as words and semantics have a highly complex nonlinear relationship, and it is even more difficult to capture this information as a robust numerical representation. To make matters worse, each language has its own grammar, syntax, and vocabulary. Therefore, processing textual data involves various complex tasks such as text parsing (for example, tokenization and stemming), morphological analysis, word sense disambiguation, and understanding the underlying grammatical structure of a language. For example, in these two sentences, *I went to the bank* and *I walked along the river bank*, the word *bank* has two entirely different meanings. To distinguish or (disambiguate) the word *bank*, we need to understand the context in which the word is being used. Machine learning has become a key enabler for NLP, helping to accomplish the aforementioned tasks through machines.

# Tasks of Natural Language Processing

NLP has a multitude of real-world applications. A good NLP system is that which performs many NLP tasks. When you search for today's weather on Google or use *Google Translate* to find out how to say, "How are you?" in French, you rely on a subset of such tasks in NLP. We will list some of the most ubiquitous tasks here, and this book covers most of these tasks:

- **Tokenization**: Tokenization is the task of separating a text corpus into atomic units (for example, words). Although it may seem trivial, tokenization is an important task. For example, in the Japanese language, words are not delimited by spaces nor punctuation marks.

- **Word-sense Disambiguation (WSD)**: WSD is the task of identifying the correct meaning of a word. For example, in the sentences, *The dog barked at the mailman,* and *Tree bark is sometimes used as a medicine,* the word *bark* has two different meanings. WSD is critical for tasks such as question answering.

- **Named Entity Recognition (NER)**: NER attempts to extract entities (for example, person, location, and organization) from a given body of text or a text corpus. For example, the sentence, *John gave Mary two apples at school on Monday* will be transformed to *[John]$_{name}$ gave [Mary]$_{name}$ [two]$_{number}$ apples at [school]$_{organization}$ on [Monday.]$_{time}$*. NER is an imperative topic in fields such as information retrieval and knowledge representation.

- **Part-of-Speech (PoS) tagging**: PoS tagging is the task of assigning words to their respective parts of speech. It can either be basic tags such as noun, verb, adjective, adverb, and preposition, or it can be granular such as proper noun, common noun, phrasal verb, verb, and so on.

- **Sentence/Synopsis classification**: Sentence or synopsis (for example, movie reviews) classification has many use cases such as spam detection, news article classification (for example, political, technology, and sport), and product review ratings (that is, positive or negative). This is achieved by training a classification model with labeled data (that is, reviews annotated by humans, with either a positive or negative label).

- **Language generation**: In language generation, a learning model (for example, neural network) is trained with text corpora (a large collection of textual documents), which predict new text that follows. For example, language generation can output an entirely new science fiction story by using existing science fiction stories for training.

- **Question Answering (QA)**: QA techniques possess a high commercial value, and such techniques are found at the foundation of chatbots and VA (for example, Google Assistant and Apple Siri). Chatbots have been adopted by many companies for customer support. Chatbots can be used to answer and resolve straightforward customer concerns (for example, changing a customer's monthly mobile plan), which can be solved without human intervention. QA touches upon many other aspects of NLP such as information retrieval, and knowledge representation. Consequently, all this makes developing a QA system very difficult.

- **Machine Translation (MT)**: MT is the task of transforming a sentence/phrase from a source language (for example, German) to a target language (for example, English). This is a very challenging task as, different languages have highly different morphological structures, which means that it is not a one-to-one transformation. Furthermore, word-to-word relationships between languages can be one-to-many, one-to-one, many-to-one, or many-to-many. This is known as the **word alignment problem** in MT literature.

Finally, to develop a system that can assist a human in day-to-day tasks (for example, VA or a chatbot) many of these tasks need to be performed together. As we saw in the previous example where the user asks, "Can you show me a good Italian restaurant nearby?" several different NLP tasks, such as speech-to-text conversion, semantic and sentiment analyses, question answering, and machine translation, need to be completed. In *Figure 1.1*, we provide a hierarchical taxonomy of different NLP tasks categorized into several different types. We first have two broad categories: analysis (analyzing existing text) and generation (generating new text) tasks. Then we divide analysis into three different categories: syntactic (language structure-based tasks), semantic (meaning-based tasks), and pragmatic (open problems difficult to solve):

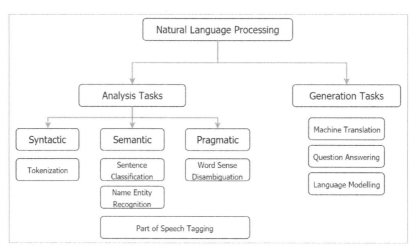

Figure 1.1: A taxonomy of the popular tasks of NLP categorized under broader categories

Having understood the various tasks in NLP, let us now move on to understand how we can solve these tasks with the help of machines.

# The traditional approach to Natural Language Processing

The traditional or classical approach to solving NLP is a sequential flow of several key steps, and it is a statistical approach. When we take a closer look at a traditional NLP learning model, we will be able to see a set of distinct tasks taking place, such as preprocessing data by removing unwanted data, feature engineering to get good numerical representations of textual data, learning to use machine learning algorithms with the aid of training data, and predicting outputs for novel unfamiliar data. Of these, feature engineering was the most time-consuming and crucial step for obtaining good performance on a given NLP task.

# Understanding the traditional approach

The traditional approach to solving NLP tasks involves a collection of distinct subtasks. First, the text corpora need to be preprocessed focusing on reducing the vocabulary and *distractions*. By *distractions*, I refer to the things that distract the algorithm (for example, punctuation marks and stop word removal) from capturing the vital linguistic information required for the task.

Next, comes several feature engineering steps. The main objective of feature engineering is to make the learning easier for the algorithms. Often the features are hand-engineered and biased toward the human understanding of a language. Feature engineering was of utter importance for classical NLP algorithms, and consequently, the best performing systems often had the best engineered features. For example, for a sentiment classification task, you can represent a sentence with a parse tree and assign positive, negative, or neutral labels to each node/subtree in the tree to classify that sentence as positive or negative. Additionally, the feature engineering phase can use external resources such as WordNet (a lexical database) to develop better features. We will soon look at a simple feature engineering technique known as *bag-of-words*.

Next, the learning algorithm learns to perform well at the given task using the obtained features and optionally, the external resources. For example, for a text summarization task, a thesaurus that contains synonyms of words can be a good external resource. Finally, prediction occurs. Prediction is straightforward, where you will feed a new input and obtain the predicted label by forwarding the input through the learning model. The entire process of the traditional approach is depicted in *Figure 1.2*:

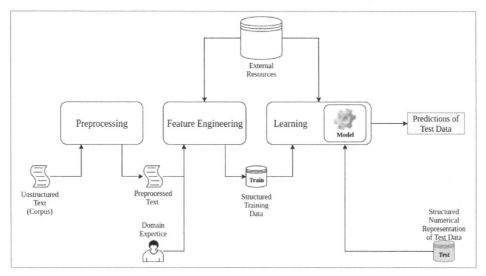

Figure 1.2: The general approach of classical NLP

# Example – generating football game summaries

To gain an in-depth understanding of the traditional approach to NLP, let's consider a task of automatic text generation from the statistics of a game of football. We have several sets of game statistics (for example, score, penalties, and yellow cards) and the corresponding articles generated for that game by a journalist, as the training data. Let's also assume that for a given game, we have a mapping from each statistical parameter to the most relevant phrase of the summary for that parameter. Our task here is that, given a new game, we need to generate a natural looking summary about the game. Of course, this can be as simple as finding the best-matching statistics for the new game from the training data and retrieving the corresponding summary. However, there are more sophisticated and elegant ways of generating text.

If we were to incorporate machine learning to generate natural language, a sequence of operations such as preprocessing the text, tokenization, feature engineering, learning, and prediction are likely to be performed.

**Preprocessing** the text involves operations, such as stemming (for example, converting *listened* to *listen*) and removing punctuation (for example, ! and ;), in order to reduce the vocabulary (that is, features), thus reducing the memory requirement. It is important to understand that stemming is not a trivial operation. It might appear that stemming is a simple operation that relies on a simple set of rules such as removing *ed* from a verb (for example, the stemmed result of *listened* is *listen*); however, it requires more than a simple rule base to develop a good stemming algorithm, as stemming certain words can be tricky (for example, the stemmed result of *argued* is *argue*). In addition, the effort required for proper stemming can vary in complexity for other languages.

**Tokenization** is another preprocessing step that might need to be performed. Tokenization is the process of dividing a corpus into small entities (for example, words). This might appear trivial for a language such as English, as the words are isolated; however, this is not the case for certain languages such as Thai, Japanese, and Chinese, as these languages are not consistently delimited.

**Feature engineering** is used to transform raw text data into an appealing numerical format so that a model can be trained on that data, for example, converting text into a bag-of-words representation or using the n-gram representation which we will discuss later. However, remember that state-of-the-art classical models rely on much more sophisticated feature engineering techniques.

The following are some of the feature engineering techniques:

**Bag-of-words**: This is a feature engineering technique that creates feature representations based on the word occurrence frequency. For example, let's consider the following sentences:

- *Bob went to the market to buy some flowers*
- *Bob bought the flowers to give to Mary*

The vocabulary for these two sentences would be:

["Bob", "went", "to", "the", "market", "buy", "some", "flowers", "bought", "give", "Mary"]

Next, we will create a feature vector of size $V$ (vocabulary size) for each sentence showing how many times each word in the vocabulary appears in the sentence. In this example, the feature vectors for the sentences would respectively be as follows:

[1, 1, 2, 1, 1, 1, 1, 1, 0, 0, 0]

[1, 0, 2, 1, 0, 0, 0, 1, 1, 1, 1]

A crucial limitation of the bag-of-words method is that it loses contextual information as the order of words is no longer preserved.

**n-gram**: This is another feature engineering technique that breaks down text into smaller components consisting of *n* letters (or words). For example, 2-gram would break the text into two-letter (or two-word) entities. For example, consider this sentence:

*Bob went to the market to buy some flowers*

The letter level n-gram decomposition for this sentence is as follows:

["Bo", "ob", "b ", " w", "we", "en", ..., "me", "e "," f", "fl", "lo", "ow", "we", "er", "rs"]

The word-based n-gram decomposition is this:

["Bob went", "went to", "to the", "the market", ..., "to buy", "buy some", "some flowers"]

The advantage in this representation (letter, level) is that the vocabulary will be significantly smaller than if we were to use words as features for large corpora.

Next, we need to structure our data to be able to feed it into a learning model. For example, we will have data tuples of the form, *(statistic, a phrase explaining the statistic)* as follows:

Total goals = 4, "The game was tied with 2 goals for each team at the end of the first half"

Team 1 = Manchester United, "The game was between Manchester United and Barcelona"

Team 1 goals = 5, "Manchester United managed to get 5 goals"

**The learning process** may comprise three sub modules: a **Hidden Markov Model (HMM)**, a sentence planner, and a discourse planner. In our example, a HMM might learn the morphological structure and grammatical properties of the language by analyzing the corpus of related phrases. More specifically, we will concatenate each phrase in our dataset to form a sequence, where the first element is the statistic followed by the phrase explaining it. Then, we will train a HMM by asking it to predict the next word, given the current sequence. Concretely, we will first input the statistic to the HMM and then get the prediction made by the HMM; then, we will concatenate the last prediction to the current sequence and ask the HMM to give another prediction, and so on. This will enable the HMM to output meaningful phrases, given statistics.

Next, we can have a sentence planner that corrects any linguistic mistakes (for example, morphological or grammar), which we might have in the phrases. For examples, a sentence planner outputs the phrase, *I go house* as *I go home*; it can use a database of rules, which contains the correct way of conveying meanings (for example, the need of a preposition between a verb and the word *house*).

Now we can generate a set of phrases for a given set of statistics using a HMM. Then, we need to aggregate these phrases in such a way that an essay made from the collection of phrases is human readable and flows correctly. For example, consider the three phrases, *Player 10 of the Barcelona team scored a goal in the second half*, *Barcelona played against Manchester United*, and *Player 3 from Manchester United got a yellow card in the first half*; having these sentences in this order does not make much sense. We like to have them in this order: *Barcelona played against Manchester United*, *Player 3 from Manchester United got a yellow card in the first half*, and *Player 10 of the Barcelona team scored a goal in the second half*. To do this, we use a discourse planner; discourse planners can order and structure a set of messages that need to be conveyed.

Now we can get a set of arbitrary test statistics and obtain an essay explaining the statistics by following the preceding workflow, which is depicted in *Figure 1.3*:

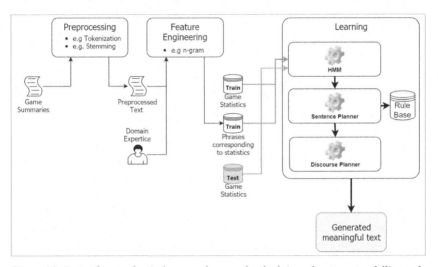

Figure 1.3: A step from a classical approach example of solving a language modelling task

Here, it is important to note that this is a very high level explanation that only covers the main general-purpose components that are most likely to be included in the traditional way of NLP. The details can largely vary according to the particular application we are interested in solving. For example, additional application-specific crucial components might be needed for certain tasks (a rule base and an alignment model in machine translation). However, in this book, we do not stress about such details as the main objective here is to discuss more modern ways of natural language processing.

# Drawbacks of the traditional approach

Let's list several key drawbacks of the traditional approach as this would lay a good foundation for discussing the motivation for deep learning:

- The preprocessing steps used in traditional NLP forces a trade-off of potentially useful information embedded in the text (for example, punctuation and tense information) in order to make the learning feasible by reducing the vocabulary. Though preprocessing is still used in modern deep-learning-based solutions, it is not as crucial as for the traditional NLP workflow due to the large representational capacity of deep networks.

- Feature engineering needs to be performed manually by hand. In order to design a reliable system, good features need to be devised. This process can be very tedious as different feature spaces need to be extensively explored. Additionally, in order to effectively explore robust features, domain expertise is required, which can be scarce for certain NLP tasks.

- Various external resources are needed for it to perform well, and there are not many freely available ones. Such external resources often consist of manually created information stored in large databases. Creating one for a particular task can take several years, depending on the severity of the task (for example, a machine translation rule base).

# The deep learning approach to Natural Language Processing

I think it is safe to assume that deep learning revolutionized machine learning, especially in fields such as computer vision, speech recognition, and of course, NLP. Deep models created a wave of paradigm shifts in many of the fields in machine learning, as deep models learned rich features from raw data instead of using limited human-engineered features. This consequentially caused the pesky and expensive feature engineering to be obsolete. With this, deep models made the traditional workflow more efficient, as deep models perform feature learning and task learning, simultaneously. Moreover, due to the massive number of parameters (that is, weights) in a deep model, it can encompass significantly more features than a human would've engineered. However, deep models are considered a black box due to the poor interpretability of the model. For example, understanding the "how" and "what" features learnt by deep models for a given problem still remains an open problem.

A deep model is essentially an artificial neural network that has an input layer, many interconnected hidden layers in the middle, and finally, an output layer (for example, a classifier or a regressor). As you can see, this forms an end-to-end model from raw data to predictions. These hidden layers in the middle give the power to deep models as they are responsible for learning the *good* features from raw data, eventually succeeding at the task at hand.

# History of deep learning

Let's briefly discuss the roots of deep learning and how the field evolved to be a very promising technique for machine learning. In 1960, Hubel and Weisel performed an interesting experiment and discovered that a cat's visual cortex is made of simple and complex cells, and that these cells are organized in a hierarchical form. Also, these cells react differently to different stimuli. For example, simple cells are activated by variously oriented edges while complex cells are insensitive to spatial variations (for example, the orientation of the edge). This kindled the motivation for replicating a similar behavior in machines, giving rise to the concept of deep learning.

In the years that followed, neural networks gained the attention of many researchers. In 1965, a neural network trained by a method known as the **Group Method of Data Handling** (**GMDH**) and based on the famous *Perceptron* by Rosenblatt, was introduced by Ivakhnenko and others. Later, in 1979, Fukushima introduced the *Neocognitron*, which laid the base for one of the most famous variants of deep models—Convolution Neural Networks. Unlike the perceptrons, which always took in a 1D input, a neocognitron was able to process 2D inputs using convolution operations.

Artificial neural networks used to backpropagate the error signal to optimize the network parameters by computing a Jacobian matrix from one layer to the layer before it. Furthermore, the problem of vanishing gradients strictly limited the potential number of layers (depth) of the neural network. The gradients of layers closer to the inputs, being very small, is known as the **vanishing gradients phenomenon**. This transpired due to the application of the chain rule to compute gradients (the Jacobian matrix) of lower layer weights. This in turn limited the plausible maximum depth of classical neural networks.

Then in 2006, it was found that *pretraining* a deep neural network by minimizing the *reconstruction error* (obtained by trying to compress the input to a lower dimensionality and then reconstructing it back into the original dimensionality) for each layer of the network, provides a good initial starting point for the weight of the neural network; this allows a consistent flow of gradients from the output layer to the input layer. This essentially allowed neural network models to have more layers without the ill-effects of the vanishing gradient. Also, these deeper models were able to surpass traditional machine learning models in many tasks, mostly in computer vision (for example, test accuracy for the MNIST hand-written digit dataset). With this breakthrough, deep learning became the buzzword in the machine learning community.

Things started gaining a progressive momentum, when in 2012, AlexNet (a deep convolution neural network created by Alex Krizhevsky (http://www.cs.toronto.edu/~kriz/), Ilya Sutskever (http://www.cs.toronto.edu/~ilya/), and Geoff Hinton) won the **Large Scale Visual Recognition Challenge** (**LSVRC**) 2012 with an error decrease of 10% from the previous best. During this time, advances were made in speech recognition, wherein state-of-the-art speech recognition accuracies were reported using deep neural networks. Furthermore, people began realizing that **Graphical Processing Units** (**GPUs**) enable more parallelism, which allows for faster training of larger and deeper networks compared with **Central Processing Units** (**CPUs**).

Deep models were further improved with better model initialization techniques (for example, Xavier initialization), making the time-consuming pretraining redundant. Also, better nonlinear activation functions, such as **Rectified Linear Units** (**ReLUs**), were introduced, which alleviated the ill-effects of the vanishing gradient in deeper models. Better optimization (or learning) techniques, such as Adam, automatically tweaked individual learning rates of each parameter among the millions of parameters that we have in the neural network model, which rewrote the state-of-the-art performance in many different fields of machine learning, such as object classification and speech recognition. These advancements also allowed neural network models to have large numbers of hidden layers. The ability to increase the number of hidden layers (that is, to make the neural networks deep) is one of the primary contributors to the significantly better performance of neural network models compared with other machine learning models. Furthermore, better intermediate regularizers, such as batch normalization layers, have improved the performance of deep nets for many tasks.

Later, even deeper models such as ResNets, Highway Nets, and Ladder Nets were introduced, which had hundreds of layers and billions of parameters. It was possible to have such an enormous number of layers with the help of various empirically and theoretically inspired techniques. For example, ResNets use shortcut connections to connect layers that are far apart, which minimizes the diminishing of gradients, layer to layer, as discussed earlier.

# The current state of deep learning and NLP

Many different deep models have seen the light since their inception in early 2000. Even though they share a resemblance, such as all of them using nonlinear transformation of the inputs and parameters, the details can vary vastly. For example, a **Convolution Neural Network (CNN)** can learn from two-dimensional data (for example, RGB images) as it is, while a multilayer perceptron model requires the input to be unwrapped to a one-dimensional vector, causing loss of important spatial information.

When processing text, as one of the most intuitive interpretations of text is to perceive it as a sequence of characters, the learning model should be able to do time-series modelling, thus requiring the *memory* of the past. To understand this, think of a language modelling task; the next word for the word *cat* should be different from the next word for the word *climbed*. One such popular model that encompasses this ability is known as a **Recurrent Neural Network (RNN)**. We will see in *Chapter 6, Recurrent Neural Networks* how exactly RNNs achieve this by going through interactive exercises.

It should be noted that *memory* is not a trivial operation that is inherent to a learning model. Conversely, ways of persisting memory should be carefully designed. Also, the term *memory* should not be confused with the learned weights of a non-sequential deep network that only looks at the current input, where a sequential model (for example, RNN) will look at both the learned weights and the previous element of the sequence to predict the next output.

One prominent drawback of RNNs is that they cannot remember more than few (approximately 7) time steps, thus lacking long-term memory. **Long Short-Term Memory (LSTM)** networks are an extension of RNNs that encapsulate long-term memory. Therefore, often LSTMs are preferred over standard RNNs, nowadays. We will peek under the hood in *Chapter 7, Long Short-Term Memory Networks* to understand them better.

In summary, we can mainly separate deep networks into two categories: the non-sequential models that deal with only a single input at a time for both training and prediction (for example, image classification) and the sequential models that cope with sequences of inputs of arbitrary length (for example, text generation where a single word is a single input). Then we can categorize non-sequential (also called feed-forward) models into deep (approximately less than 20 layers) and very deep networks (can be greater than hundreds of layers). The sequential models are categorized into short-term memory models (for example, RNNs), which can only memorize short-term patterns and long-term memory models, which can memorize longer patterns. In *Figure 1.4*, we outline the discussed taxonomy. It is not expected that you understand these different deep learning models fully at this point, but it only illustrates the diversity of the deep learning models:

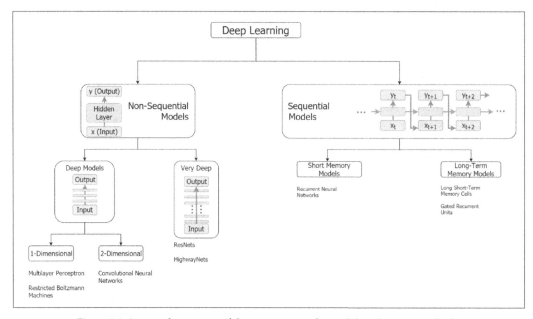

Figure 1.4: A general taxonomy of the most commonly used deep learning methods, categorized into several classes

# Understanding a simple deep model – a Fully-Connected Neural Network

Now let's have a closer look at a deep neural network in order to gain a better understanding. Although there are numerous different variants of deep models, let's look at one of the earliest models (dating back to 1950-60), known as a **Fully-Connected Neural Network (FCNN)**, or sometimes called a multilayer perceptron. The *Figure 1.5* depicts a standard three-layered FCNN.

The goal of a FCNN is to map an input (for example, an image or a sentence) to a certain label or annotation (for example, the object category for images). This is achieved by using an input $x$ to compute $h$—a hidden representation of $x$—using a transformation such as $h = sigma\ (W * x + b)$; here, $W$ and $b$ are the weights and bias of the FCNN, respectively, and *sigma* is the sigmoid activation function. Next, a classifier (for example, a softmax classifier) is placed on top of the FCNN that gives the ability to leverage the learned features in hidden layers to classify inputs. Classifier, essentially is a part of the FCNN and yet another hidden layer with some weights, $W_s$ and a bias, $b_s$. Also, we can calculate the final output of the FCNN as, $output = softmax\ (W_s * h + b_s)$. For example, a softmax classifier provides a normalized representation of the scores output by the classifier layer; the label is considered to be the output node with the highest softmax value. Then, with this, we can define a classification loss that is calculated as the difference between the predicted output label and the actual output label. An example of such a loss function is the mean squared loss. You don't have to worry if you don't understand the actual intricacies of the loss function. We will discuss quite a few of them in later chapters. Next, the neural network parameters, $W, b, W_s,$ and $b_s,$ are optimized using a standard stochastic optimizer (for example, the stochastic gradient descent) to reduce the classification loss all the inputs. *Figure 1.5* depicts the process explained in this paragraph for a three-layer FCNN. We will walk-through the details on how to use such a model for NLP tasks, step by step in *Chapter 3, Word2vec – Learning Word Embeddings*.

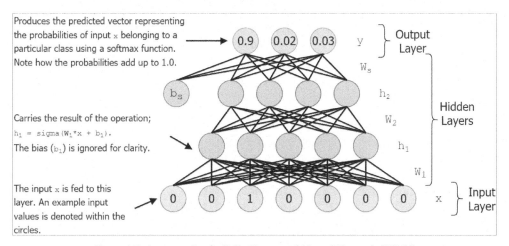

Figure 1.5: An example of a Fully Connected Neural Network (FCNN)

Let's look at an example of how to use a neural network for a sentiment analysis task. Consider that we have a dataset where the input is a sentence expressing a positive or negative opinion about a movie and a corresponding label saying if the sentence is actually positive (1) or negative (0). Then, we are given a test data set, where we have single sentence movie reviews, and our task is to classify these new sentences as positive or negative.

It is possible to use a neural network (which can be deep or shallow, depending on the difficulty of the task) for this task by adhering to the following workflow:

1. Tokenize the sentence by words
2. Pad the sentences with a special token if necessary, to bring all sentences to a fixed length
3. Convert the sentences into a numerical representation (for example, Bag-of-Words representation)
4. Feed the numerical inputs to the neural network and predict the output (positive or negative)
5. Optimize the neural network using a desired loss function

# The roadmap – beyond this chapter

This section delineates the details of the rest of the book; it's brief, but has informative details about what each chapter of the book covers. In this book, we will be looking at numerous exciting fields of NLP, from algorithms that find word similarities without any sort of annotated data, to algorithms that can write a story by themselves.

Starting from the next chapter, we will dive into the details about several popular and interesting NLP tasks. In order to gain an in-depth knowledge and to make the learning interactive, various exercises are also provided. We will use Python and TensorFlow, an open-source library for distributed numerical computations, for all the implementations. TensorFlow encapsulates advance technicalities such as optimizing your code for GPUs using **Compute Unified Device Architecture (CUDA)**, which can be challenging. Furthermore, TensorFlow provides built-in functions for implementing deep learning algorithms, for example, activations, stochastic optimization methods, and convolutions, making everyone's life easier.

We will embark on a journey that covers many hot topics of NLP and how they perform, while using TensorFlow to see the state-of-the-art algorithms in action. This is what we will look at in this book:

- *Chapter 2, Understanding TensorFlow*, provides you with a sound guide to understand how to write client programs and run them in TensorFlow. This is important especially if you are new to TensorFlow, because TensorFlow behaves differently from a traditional coding language such as Python. This chapter will first offer an in-depth explanation about how TensorFlow executes a client. This will help you to understand the TensorFlow execution workflow and feel comfortable around TensorFlow terminology. Next, the chapter will walk you through various elements of a TensorFlow client such as defining variables, defining operations/functions, feeding inputs to an algorithm, and obtaining the results. We will finally discuss how all this knowledge of TensorFlow can be used to implement a moderately complex neural network to classify images of hand-written images.

- *Chapter 3, Word2vec – Learning Word Embeddings*. The objective of this chapter is to introduce Word2vec—a method to learn numerical representations of words that reflects semantic of the words. But before diving straight into the Word2vec techniques, we will first discuss some classical approaches used to represent word semantics. One of the early approach was to rely on WordNet—a large lexical database. WordNet can be used to measure the semantic similarity between different words. However, maintaining such a large lexical database is costly. Therefore, there exist other simpler representation techniques, such as one-hot-encoded representations, and the term-frequency inverse document frequency method, that doesn't rely on external resources. Following this, we will move onto the modern way of learning word vectors known as Word2vec, where we use a neural network to learn word representations. We will discuss two popular Word2vec techniques: skip-gram and continuous bag-of-words (CBOW) model.

- *Chapter 4, Advanced Word2vec*. We will start this chapter with several comparisons including a comparison between the skip-gram and CBOW algorithms to see if there is a clear-cut winner. Then we will discuss several extensions that have been introduced to the original Word2vec techniques over the course of the past few years. For example, ignoring common words in the text, such as "the" and "a", that have a high probability, improves the performance of the Word2vec models. On the other hand, the Word2vec model only considers the local context of a word and ignores the global statistics of the entire corpus. Consequently, a word embedding learning technique known as GloVe, which incorporates both global and local statistics in finding word vectors will be discussed.

- *Chapter 5, Sentence Classification with Convolution Neural Networks*, introduces you to convolution neural networks (CNNs). Convolution networks are a powerful family of deep models that can leverage the spatial structure of an input to learn from data. In other words, a CNN can process images in their two-dimensional form, where a multilayer perceptron needs the image to be unwrapped to a one-dimensional vector. We will first discuss various operations that undergoes in CNNs, such as the convolution and pooling operations, in detail. Then we will see an example where we will learn to classify hand-written digit images with a CNN. Then we will transition into an application of CNNs in NLP. Precisely, we will be investigating how to apply a CNN to classify sentences, where the task is to classify if a sentence is about a person, location, object, and so on.

- *Chapter 6, Recurrent Neural Networks*, focuses on introducing recurrent neural networks (RNNs) and using RNNs for language generation. RNNs are different from feed-forward neural networks (for example, CNNs) as RNNs have memory. The memory is stored as a continuously updated system state. We will start with a representation of a feed-forward neural network and modify that representation to learn from sequences of data instead of individual data points. This process will transform the feed-forward network to a RNN. This will be followed by a technical description about the exact equations used for computations within the RNN. Next, we will discuss the optimization process of RNNs that is used to update the RNN's weights. Thereafter we will iterate through different types of RNNs such as one-to-one RNNs and one-to-many RNNs. We will then walkthrough an exciting application of RNNs, where the RNN will learn to tell new stories by learning from a corpus of existing stories. We achieve this by training the RNN to predict the next word given the preceding sequence of words of the story. Finally, we will discuss a variant of standard RNNs, which we call RNN-CF (RNN with contextual features), and will compare it with the standard RNN to see which one performs better.

- *Chapter 7, Long Short-Term Memory Networks*, discusses LSTMs by initially providing a solid intuition to how these models work and progressively diving into the technical details adequate to implement them on your own. Standard RNNs suffer from the crucial limitation of the inability to persist long-term memory. However, advanced RNN models (for example, long short-term memory cells (LSTMs) and gated recurrent units (GRUs)) have been proposed, which can remember sequences for large number of time steps. We will also examine how exactly does the LSTMs alleviate the problem of persisting long-term memory (this is known as the vanishing gradient problem). We will then discuss several improvements that can be used to improve LSTM models further such as predicting for several time steps ahead at once and reading sequences both forward and backward. Finally, we will discuss several variants of LSTM models such as GRUs and LSTMs with peephole connections.

- *Chapter 8, Applications of LSTM – Generating Text*, explains how to implement LSTMs, GRUs, and LSTMs with peephole connections discussed in *Chapter 7, Long Short-Term Memory Networks*. Furthermore, we will compare the performance of these extensions both qualitatively and quantitatively. We will also discuss how to implement some of the extensions examined in *Chapter 7, Long Short-Term Memory Networks* such as predicting several time steps ahead (known as beam search) and using word vectors as inputs instead of one-hot-encoded representations. Finally, we will discuss how we can use the RNN API, which is a sub library of TensorFlow that simplifies the implementation of recurrent models.

- *Chapter 9, Applications of LSTM – Image Caption Generation*, looks at another exciting application, where the model learns how to generate captions (that is, descriptions) for images using an LSTM and a CNN. This application is interesting because it shows us how to combine two different types of models as well as how to learn with multimodal data (for example, images and text). The specific way to achieve this is to first learn image representations (similar to word vectors) with the CNN and train the LSTM by feeding that image vector followed by the words of the description of the image as a sequence. We will first discuss how we can use a pretrained CNN to obtain the image representations. Then we will discuss how to learn the word embeddings. Next we will discuss how to feed the image vectors along with word embeddings to train the LSTM. This is followed by a description of different evaluation metrics that exist for evaluating image captioning systems. Afterwards, we will evaluate the captions generated by our model, both qualitatively and quantitatively. We will conclude the chapter with a guide of how to implement the same system using the TensorFlow RNN API.

- *Chapter 10, Sequence-to-Sequence Learning – Neural Machine Translation.*
  Machine Translation has gained a lot of attention both due to the necessity of
  automating translation and the inherent difficulty of the task. We will start
  the chapter with a brief historical flashback of how machine translation was
  implemented in the early days. This discussion ends with an introduction
  to neural machine translation (NMT) systems. We will see how well current
  NMT systems are doing compared to old systems (such as statistical machine
  translation systems), which will motivate us to learn about NMT systems.
  Afterwards, we will discuss the intuition behind the design of NMT systems
  and continue with the technical details. Then we will discuss the evaluation
  metric we use to evaluate our system. Following this, we will investigate
  how we can implement a German to English translator from scratch. Next,
  we will learn about ways to improve NMT systems. We will look at one of
  those extensions in detail, called attention mechanism. Attention mechanism
  has become an essential in sequence to sequence learning problems. Finally,
  we will compare the performance improvement obtained with attention
  mechanism and analyze reasons behind the performance gain. This chapter
  concludes with a section on how the same concept of NMT systems can be
  extended to implement chatbots. Chatbots are systems that can communicate
  with humans and are used to fulfill various customer requests.

- *Chapter 11, Current Trends and the Future of Natural Language Processing.*
  Natural language processing has branched out to a vast spectrum of
  different tasks. Here we will discuss some of the current trends and future
  developments of NLP we can expect in the future. We will first discuss
  various word embedding extensions that have emerged recently. We will
  also look at the implementation of one such embedding learning technique,
  known as tv-embeddings. Next, we will examine various trends growing
  in the field of neural machine translation. Then we will look at how NLP
  is combined with other fields such as computer vision and reinforcement
  learning to solve some interesting problems such as teaching computer
  agents to communicate by devising their own language. Another booming
  area these days is artificial general intelligence, which is about developing
  systems that can do multiple tasks (classify images, translate text, caption
  images, and so on) with a single system. We will investigate several such
  systems. Afterwards, we will talk about the introduction of NLP into mining
  social media. We will conclude this chapter with some of the new tasks
  emerging (for example, language grounding – developing common sense
  NLP systems) and new models (for example, phased LSTMs).

- *Appendix*, *Mathematical Foundations and Advanced TensorFlow*, will introduce the reader to various mathematical data structures (for example, matrices) and operations (for example, matrix inverse). We will also discuss several important concepts in probability. We will then introduce Keras—a high-level library that uses TensorFlow underneath. Keras makes the implementing of neural networks simpler by hiding some of the details in TensorFlow, which some might find challenging. Concretely, we will see how we can implement a CNN with Keras, to get a feel of how to use Keras. Next, we will discuss how we can use the seq2seq library in TensorFlow to implement a neural machine translation system with much less code that we used in *Chapter 11*, *Current Trends and the Future of Natural Language Processing*. Finally, we will walk you through a guide aimed at teaching to use the TensorBoard to visualize word embeddings. TensorBoard is a handy visualization tool that is shipped with TensorFlow. This can be used to visualize and monitor various variables in your TensorFlow client.

# Introduction to the technical tools

In this section, you will be introduced to the technical tools that will be used in the exercises of the following chapters. First, we will present a brief introduction to the main tools provided. Next, we will present a coarse guide on how to install each tool along with hyperlinks to detailed guides provided by the official websites. Additionally, we will share tips on how to make sure that the tools were installed properly.

# Description of the tools

We will use Python as the coding/scripting language. Python is a very versatile easy-to-set-up coding language that is heavily used by the scientific community. Additionally, there are numerous scientific libraries floating around Python, catering to areas ranging from deep learning to probabilistic inference to data visualization. TensorFlow is one such library that is well-known among the deep learning community, providing many basic and advanced operations that are useful for deep learning. Next, we will use Jupyter notebooks in all our exercises as it provides a more interactive environment for coding compared to using an IDE. We will also use scikit-learn—another popular machine learning toolkit for Python—for various miscellaneous purposes such as data preprocessing. Another library we will be using for various text related operations is NLTK—Python natural language toolkit. Finally, we will use matplotlib for data visualization.

# Installing Python and scikit-learn

Python is hassle-free to install in any of the commonly used operating systems such as Windows, macOS, or Linux. We will use Anaconda to set up Python, as it does all the laborious work for setting up Python as well as the essential libraries.

To install Anaconda, follow these steps:

1. Download Anaconda from `https://www.continuum.io/downloads`
2. Select the appropriate OS and download Python 3.5
3. Install Anaconda by following the instructions at `https://docs.continuum.io/anaconda/install/`

To check whether Anaconda was properly installed, follow these steps:

1. Open a Terminal window (Command Prompt in Windows)
2. Now, run the following command:

```
conda --version
```

If installed properly, the version of the current Anaconda distribution should be shown in Terminal.

Next, install scikit-learn by following the instructions at `http://scikit-learn.org/stable/install.html`, NLTK from `https://www.nltk.org/install.html` and Matplotlib from `https://matplotlib.org/users/installing.html`.

# Installing Jupyter Notebook

You can install Jupyter Notebook by following the instruction at `http://jupyter.readthedocs.io/en/latest/install.html`.

To check whether Jupyter Notebook is properly installed, follow these steps:

1. Open a Terminal window
2. Run this command:

```
jupyter notebook
```

You should be presented with a new browser window that looks like *Figure 1.6*:

Figure 1.6. Jupyter Notebook installed successfully

# Installing TensorFlow

Follow the instructions given at `https://www.tensorflow.org/install/` under the *Installing with Anaconda* subsection to install TensorFlow. We will use TensorFlow 1.8.x throughout all the exercises.

When providing the tfBinaryURL as asked in the instruction, make sure that you provide a TensorFlow 1.8.x version. We stress this as the API has undergone many changes compared to the previous TensorFlow versions.

To check whether TensorFlow installed properly, follow these steps:

1. Open Command Prompt in Windows or Terminal in Linux or macOS.

2. Type `python` to enter the Python environment. You should now see the Python version right below. Make sure that you are using Python 3.

3. Next, enter the following commands:

```
import tensorflow as tf
print(tf.__version__)
```

If all went well, you should not have any errors (there might be warnings if your computer does not have a dedicated GPU, but you can ignore them) and the TensorFlow version 1.8.x should be shown.

Many cloud-based computational platforms are also available, where you can set up your own machine with various customization (operating system, GPU card type, number of GPU cards, and so on). Many are migrating to such cloud-based services due to the following benefits:

- More customization options
- Less maintenance effort
- No infrastructure requirements

Several popular cloud-based computational platforms are as follows:

- **Google Cloud Platform (GCP)**: `https://cloud.google.com/`
- **Amazon Web Services (AWS)**: `https://aws.amazon.com/`
- **TensorFlow Research Cloud (TFRC)**: `https://www.tensorflow.org/tfrc/`

# Summary

In this chapter, we broadly explored NLP to get an impression of the kind of tasks involved in building a good NLP-based system. First, we explained why we need NLP and then discussed various tasks of NLP to generally understand the objective of each task and how difficult it is to succeed at these tasks.

Next, we looked at the classical approach of solving NLP and went into the details of the workflow using an example of generating sport summaries for football games. We saw that the traditional approach usually involves cumbersome and tedious feature engineering. For example, in order to check the correctness of a generated phrase, we might need to generate a parse tree for that phrase. Next, we discussed the paradigm shift that transpired with deep learning and saw how deep learning made the feature engineering step obsolete. We started with a bit of time-travelling to go back to the inception of deep learning and artificial neural networks and worked our way to the massive modern networks with hundreds of hidden layers. Afterward, we walked through a simple example illustrating a deep model—a multilayer perceptron model—to understand the mathematical wizardry taking place in such a model (on the surface of course!).

With a nice foundation to both traditional and modern ways of approaching NLP, we then discussed the roadmap to understand the topics we will be covering in the book, from learning word embeddings to mighty LSTMs, generating captions for images to neural machine translators! Finally, we set up our environment by installing Python, scikit-learn, Jupyter Notebook, and TensorFlow.

In the next chapter, you will learn the basics of TensorFlow. By the end of the chapter, you should be comfortable with writing a simple algorithm that can take some input, transform the input through a defined function and output the result.

# 2
# Understanding TensorFlow

In this chapter, you will get an in-depth understanding of TensorFlow. This is an open source distributed numerical computation framework, and it will be the main platform on which we will be implementing all our exercises.

We will get started with TensorFlow by defining a simple calculation and trying to compute it using TensorFlow. After we successfully complete this, we will investigate how TensorFlow executes this computation. This will help us to understand how the framework creates a computational graph to compute the outputs and execute this graph through something known as a **session**. Then we will gain a hands-on experience of the TensorFlow architecture by relating how TensorFlow executes things, with the help of an analogy of how a restaurant might operate.

Having gained a good conceptual and technical understanding of how TensorFlow operates, we will look at some of the important computational operations that the framework offers. First, we will look at defining various data structures in TensorFlow, such as variables, placeholders and tensors, and we'll also see how to read inputs. Then we will work through some neural-network related operations (for example, convolution operation, defining losses, and optimization). Following this, we will learn how to reuse and efficiently manage TensorFlow variables using scoping. Finally, we will apply this knowledge in an exciting exercise, where we will implement a neural network that can recognize images of handwritten digits.

# What is TensorFlow?

In *Chapter 1*, *Introduction to Natural Language Processing*, we briefly discussed what TensorFlow is. Now let's take a closer look at it. TensorFlow is an open source distributed numerical computation framework released by Google that is mainly intended to alleviate the painful details of implementing a neural network (for example, computing derivatives of the weights of the neural network). TensorFlow takes this even a step further by providing efficient implementations of such numerical computations using **Compute Unified Device Architecture (CUDA)**, which is a parallel computational platform introduced by NVIDIA. The **Application Programming Interface (API)** of TensorFlow at `https://www.tensorflow.org/api_docs/python/` shows that TensorFlow provides thousands of operations that make our lives easier.

TensorFlow was not developed overnight. This is a result of the persistence of talented, good-hearted individuals who wanted to make a difference by bringing deep learning to a wider audience. If you are interested, you can take a look at the TensorFlow code at `https://github.com/tensorflow/tensorflow`. Currently, TensorFlow has around 1,000 contributors, and it sits on top of more than 25,000 commits, evolving to be better and better every day.

# Getting started with TensorFlow

Now let's learn about a few essential components in the TensorFlow framework by working through a code example. Let's write an example to perform the following computation, which is very common for neural networks:

```
h = sigmoid(W * x + b)
```

Here `W` and `x` are matrices and `b` is a vector. Then, * denotes the dot product. `sigmoid` is a non-linear transformation given by the following equation:

$$\text{sigmoid}(x) = \frac{1}{1 + e^{-x}}$$

We will discuss how to do this computation through TensorFlow step by step.

First, we will need to import TensorFlow and NumPy. Importing them is essential before you run any type of TensorFlow- or NumPy-related operation, in Python:

```
import tensorflow as tf
import numpy as np
```

Next, we'll define a graph object, which we will populate with operations and variables later:

```
graph = tf.Graph() # Creates a graph
session = tf.InteractiveSession(graph=graph) # Creates a session
```

The `graph` object contains the computational graph that connects the various inputs and outputs we define in our program to get the final desired output (that is, it defines how `W`, `x`, and `b` are connected to produce `h` in terms of a graph). For example, if you think of the output as a *cake*, then the *graph* would be the recipe to make that cake using *ingredients* (that is, inputs). Also, we'll define a `session` object that takes the defined graph as the input, which executes the graph. We will talk about these elements in detail in the next section.

To create a new `graph` object, you can either use the following, as we did in the preceding example:

```
graph = tf.Graph()
```

Alternatively, you can use the following to get the TensorFlow default computational graph:

```
graph = tf.get_default_graph()
```

We show exercises using both these methods.

Now we'll define a few tensors, namely x, W, b, and h. A tensor is essentially an *n*-dimensional array in TensorFlow. For example, a one-dimensional vector or a two-dimensional matrix is called a **tensor**. There are several different ways in TensorFlow that you can define tensors. Here we will look at three such different approaches:

1. First, x is a placeholder. Placeholders, as the name suggests, are not initialized with some value. Rather, we will provide the value on-the-fly at the time of the graph execution.

2. Next, we have variables W and b. Variables are mutable, meaning that their values can change over time.

3. Finally, we have h, which is an immutable tensor produced by performing some operations on x, W, and b:

```
x = tf.placeholder(shape=[1,10],dtype=tf.float32,name='x')
W = tf.Variable(tf.random_uniform(shape=[10,5], minval=-0.1,
maxval=0.1, dtype=tf.float32),name='W')
b = tf.Variable(tf.zeros(shape=[5],dtype=tf.float32),name='b')
h = tf.nn.sigmoid(tf.matmul(x,W) + b)
```

Also, notice that for `W` and `b` we provide some important arguments such as the following:

```
tf.random_uniform(shape=[10,5], minval=-0.1, maxval=0.1,
dtype=tf.float32)
tf.zeros(shape=[5],dtype=tf.float32)
```

These are called variable initializers and are the tensors that will be assigned to the `W` and `b` variables initially. Variables cannot float without an initial value as placeholders and need to have some value assigned to them all the time. Here, `tf.random_uniform` means that we uniformly sample values between `minval` (`-0.1`) and `maxval` (`0.1`) to assign values to the tensors, and `tf.zeros` initializes the tensor with zeros. It is also very important to define the *shape* of your tensor when you are defining it. The `shape` property defines the size of each dimension of a tensor. For example, if `shape` is `[10, 5]`, this means that it will be a two-dimensional structure and will have `10` elements on axis 0 and `5` elements on axis 1.

Next, we'll run an initialization operation that initializes the variables in the graph, `W` and `b`:

```
tf.global_variables_initializer().run()
```

Now, we will execute the graph to obtain the final output we need, `h`. This is done by running `session.run(...)`, where we provide the value to the placeholder as an argument of the `session.run()` command:

```
h_eval = session.run(h,feed_dict={x: np.random.rand(1,10)})
```

Finally, we close the session, releasing any resources held by the `session` object.

```
session.close()
```

Here is the full code of this TensorFlow example. All the code examples in this chapter will be available in the `tensorflow_introduction.ipynb` file in the `ch2` folder:

```
import tensorflow as tf
import numpy as np

# Defining the graph and session
graph = tf.Graph() # Creates a graph
session = tf.InteractiveSession(graph=graph) # Creates a session

# Building the graph
# A placeholder is an symbolic input
x = tf.placeholder(shape=[1,10],dtype=tf.float32,name='x')
W = tf.Variable(tf.random_uniform(shape=[10,5], minval=-0.1,
maxval=0.1, dtype=tf.float32),name='W') # Variable
```

```
# Variable
b = tf.Variable(tf.zeros(shape=[5],dtype=tf.float32),name='b')

h = tf.nn.sigmoid(tf.matmul(x,W) + b) # Operation to be performed

# Executing operations and evaluating nodes in the graph
tf.global_variables_initializer().run() # Initialize the variables

# Run the operation by providing a value to the symbolic input x
h_eval = session.run(h,feed_dict={x: np.random.rand(1,10)})
# Closes the session to free any held resources by the session
session.close()
```

When you run this code, you might encounter a warning, as shown here:

```
... tensorflow/core/platform/cpu_feature_guard.cc:137] Your CPU
supports instructions that this TensorFlow binary was not compiled to
use: ...
```

Don't worry about this. This is a warning saying that you used an off-the-shelf precompiled version of TensorFlow without compiling it on your computer. This is totally fine. It is just that you will get a slightly better performance if you compile it on your computer, as TensorFlow will be optimized for that particular hardware.

In the following sections we will explain how TensorFlow executes this code to produce the final output. Also note that the next two sections will be somewhat complex and technical. However, you don't have to worry if you don't understand everything completely, because after this, we will go through a nice, thorough real-world example, where the same execution is explained in terms of how an order is fulfilled in a restaurant, our own *Café Le TensorFlow*.

# TensorFlow client in detail

The preceding example program is called a TensorFlow client. In any client program you write with TensorFlow, there will be two main types of objects: *operations* and *tensors*. In the preceding example, `tf.nn.sigmoid` is an operation and h is a tensor.

Then we have a `graph` object, which is the computational graph that stores the dataflow of our program. When we add the subsequent lines defining x, W, b, and h in the code, TensorFlow automatically adds these tensors and any operations (for example, `tf.matmul()`) to the graph as nodes. The graph will store vital information such as the tensor dependencies and which operation to perform where. In our example, the graph will know that to calculate h, tensors x, W, and b are required. So, if you haven't properly initialized one of them during runtime, TensorFlow can point you to the exact initialization error that needs to be fixed.

Next, the session plays the role of executing the graph by dividing the graph into subgraphs and subsequently to even finer pieces which will then be assigned to workers that will perform the assigned task. This is done with the `session.run(...)` function. We will talk about this soon. For future reference, let's call our example *the sigmoid example*.

# TensorFlow architecture – what happens when you execute the client?

We know that TensorFlow is skillful at creating a nice computational graph with all the dependencies and operations so that it knows exactly how, when, and where the data flows. But there should be one more element to this to make TensorFlow great: the effective execution of the defined computational graph. This is where the session comes in. Now let's peek under the hood of the session to understand how the graph is executed.

First, the TensorFlow client holds a graph and session. When you create a session, it sends the computational graph as a `tf.GraphDef` protocol buffer to the distributed master. `tf.GraphDef` is a standardized representation of the graph. The distributed master sees all computations in the graph and divides the computations to different devices (for example, different GPUs and CPUs). The graph in our sigmoid example looks like *Figure 2.1*. A single element of the graph is called a **node**:

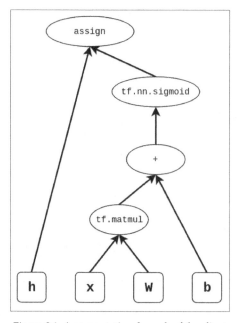

Figure 2.1: A computational graph of the client

Next, the computational graph will be broken into subgraphs and further into finer pieces by the distributed master. Though decomposing the computational graph appears too trivial in our example, the computational graph can exponentially grow in real-world solutions with many hidden layers. Additionally, it becomes important to break the computational graph into multiple pieces in order to execute things in parallel (for example, multiple devices). Executing this graph (or a subgraph if the graph is divided to subgraphs) is called a single *task*, where a task is allocated to a single TensorFlow server.

However, in reality, each task will be executed by breaking this down into two pieces, where each piece is executed by a single worker:

- One worker executes the TensorFlow operations using the current values of the parameters (operation executor)
- The other worker stores the parameters and updates them with new values obtained after executing the operations (parameter server)

This general workflow of a TensorFlow client is depicted in *Figure 2.2*:

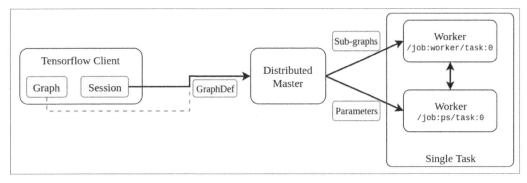

Figure 2.2: The generic execution of a TensorFlow client

*Figure 2.3* illustrates the decomposition of the graph. In addition to breaking the graph down, TensorFlow inserts send and receive nodes to help with the communication between the parameter server and the operation executor. You can understand send nodes to be sending data whenever data is available, where the receive nodes keep listening and capture data when the corresponding send node sends data:

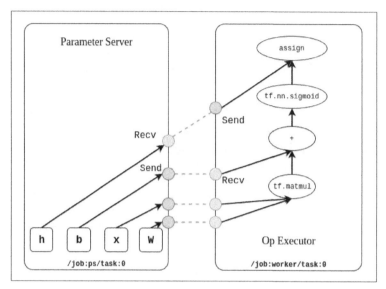

Figure 2.3: Decomposition of the TensorFlow graph

Finally, the session brings back the updated data to the client from the parameter server once the calculation is done. The architecture of TensorFlow is shown in *Figure 2.4*. This explanation is based on the official TensorFlow documentation found at `https://www.tensorflow.org/extend/architecture`.

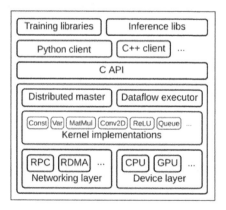

Figure 2.4: TensorFlow framework architecture (https://www.tensorflow.org/extend/architecture)

# Cafe Le TensorFlow – understanding TensorFlow with an analogy

If you were overwhelmed with the information contained in the technical explanation, we'll try to grasp the concept from a different perspective. Let's say that a new cafe just opened and you've been dying to try it. So you go there and grab a seat by a window.

Next, the waiter comes to take your order, and you order a *chicken burger with extra cheese and no tomatoes*. Think of yourself as the client and your order as defining the graph. The graph defines what you need and how you need it. The waiter is analogous to the session, where his responsibility is to carry the order to the kitchen so the order can be made. When taking the order, the waiter uses a certain format to convey your order, for example, table number, menu item ID, quantity, and special requirements. Think of this formatted order written in the waiter's notebook as `GraphDef`. Then the waiter takes the order to the kitchen and gives it to the kitchen manager. From this point, the kitchen manager assumes the responsibility of fulfilling the order. Here, the kitchen manager represents the distributed master. The kitchen manager makes decisions, such as how many chefs are required to make the dish and which chefs are the best candidates for the job. Let's also assume that each chef has a cook, whose responsibility is to provide the chef with the right ingredients, equipment, and so forth. So the kitchen manager takes the order to a single chef and a cook (a burger is not that hard to prepare) and asks them to prepare the dish. In our example, the chef is the operation executor, and the cook is the parameter server.

The chef looks at the order and tells the cook what is needed. So the cook first finds the things that will be required (for example, buns, patties, and onions) and keeps them close to fulfill the chef's requests as soon as possible. Moreover, the chef might also ask to keep the intermediate results (for example, cut vegetables) of the dish temporarily until the chef needs it back again.

When the order is ready, the kitchen manager receives the burger from the chef and the cook and notifies the waiter. At this point, the waiter takes the burger from the kitchen manager and brings it to you. You will finally be able to enjoy the delicious burger made according to your specifications. This process is shown in *Figure 2.5*:

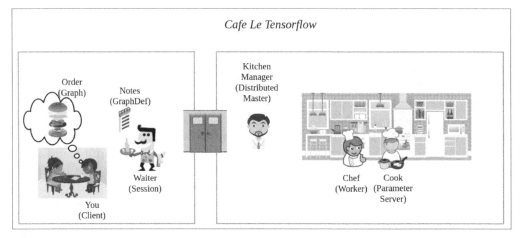

Figure 2.5: The restaurant analogy illustrated

# Inputs, variables, outputs, and operations

Now with an understanding of the underlying architecture let's proceed to the most common elements that comprise a TensorFlow client. If you read any of the millions of TensorFlow clients available on the internet, they all (the TensorFlow-related code) fall into one of these buckets:

- **Inputs**: Data used to train and test our algorithms
- **Variables**: Mutable tensors, mostly defining the parameters of our algorithms
- **Outputs**: Immutable tensors storing both terminal and intermediate outputs
- **Operations**: Various transformations for inputs to produce the desired outputs

In our earlier example, in the sigmoid example, we can find instances of all these categories. We list the elements in *Table 2.1*:

| TensorFlow element | Value from example client |
|---|---|
| Inputs | x |
| Variables | W and b |
| Outputs | h |
| Operations | tf.matmul(...), tf.nn.sigmoid(...) |

The following subsections explain each of these TensorFlow elements in more detail.

# Defining inputs in TensorFlow

The client can mainly receive data in three different ways:

- Feeding data at every step of the algorithm with Python code
- Preloading and storing data as TensorFlow tensors
- Building an input pipeline

Let's look at each of these ways.

## Feeding data with Python code

In the first method, data can be fed to the TensorFlow client using conventional Python code. In our earlier example, x is an example of this method. To feed data into the client from external data structures (for example, `numpy.ndarray`), the TensorFlow library provides an elegant symbolic data structure known as a **placeholder** defined as `tf.placeholder(...)`. As the name suggests, a placeholder does not require actual data at the graph building stage. Rather, the data is fed only for graph executions invoked with `session.run(...,feed_dict={placeholder: value})` by passing the external data to the `feed_dict` argument in the form of a Python dictionary where the key is the `tf.placeholder` variable and the corresponding value is the actual data (for example, `numpy.ndarray`). The placeholder definition takes the following form:

```
tf.placeholder(dtype, shape=None, name=None)
```

The arguments are as follows:

- `dtype`: This is the data type for the data fed into the placeholder
- `shape`: This is the shape of the placeholder, given as a 1D vector
- `name`: This is the name of the placeholder, and it is important for debugging

# Preloading and storing data as tensors

The second method is similar to the first one, but with one less thing to worry about. We do not have to feed data during the graph execution as the data is preloaded. To see this in action, let's modify our sigmoid example. Remember that we defined x as a placeholder:

```
x = tf.placeholder(shape=[1,10],dtype=tf.float32,name='x')
```

Instead, let's define this as a tensor that contains specific values:

```
x = tf.constant(value=[[0.1,0.2,0.3,0.4,0.5,0.6,0.7,0.8,0.9,1.0]],
dtype=tf.float32,name='x')
```

Also, the full code would become as follows:

```
import tensorflow as tf
# Defining the graph and session
graph = tf.Graph() # Creates a graph
session = tf.InteractiveSession(graph=graph) # Creates a session

# Building the graph

# x - A pre-loaded input
x = tf.constant(value=[[0.1,0.2,0.3,0.4,0.5,0.6,0.7,0.8,0.9,1.0]],
dtype=tf.float32,name='x')

W = tf.Variable(tf.random_uniform(shape=[10,5], minval=-0.1,
maxval=0.1, dtype=tf.float32),name='W') # Variable
# Variable
b = tf.Variable(tf.zeros(shape=[5],dtype=tf.float32),name='b')

h = tf.nn.sigmoid(tf.matmul(x,W) + b) # Operation to be performed

# Executing operations and evaluating nodes in the graph
tf.global_variables_initializer().run() # Initialize the variables

# Run the operation without feed_dict
h_eval = session.run(h)
print(h_eval)
session.close()
```

You will notice there are two main differences from our original sigmoid example. We have defined x in a different way. Instead of using a placeholder object and feeding in the actual value at graph execution, we now assign a specific value straightaway and define x as a tensor. Also, as you can see, we do not feed in any extra arguments at session.run(...). However, on the downside, now you cannot feed different values to x at session.run(...) and see how the output changes.

# Building an input pipeline

Input pipelines are designed for more heavy-duty clients that need to process a lot of data quickly. This essentially creates a queue that holds data until it is needed. TensorFlow also provides various preprocessing steps (for example, for adjusting image contrast/brightness or standardization) that can be performed before feeding data to the algorithm. To make things even more efficient, it is possible to have multiple threads reading and processing data in parallel.

A typical pipeline will consist of the following components:

- The list of filenames
- A filename queue producing filenames for an input (record) reader
- A record reader for reading the inputs (records)
- A decoder to decode the read records (for example, JPEG image decoding)
- Preprocessing steps (optional)
- An example (that is, decoded inputs) queue

Let's write a quick example input pipeline using TensorFlow. In this example, we have three text files (`text1.txt`, `text2.txt`, and `text3.txt`) in CSV format, each with five lines and each line having 10 numbers separated by commas (an example line: `0.1,0.2,0.3,0.4,0.5,0.6,0.7,0.8,0.9,1.0`). We need to read this data as batches (multiple rows of data vectors) by forming an input pipeline from the files all the way to a tensor representing those inputs in the files. We will go step by step to see what is going on.

> For more information, refer to the official TensorFlow page on *Importing Data* at https://www.tensorflow.org/programmers_guide/reading_data.

First, let's import a few important libraries as before:

```
import tensorflow as tf
import numpy as np
```

Next, we'll define the `graph` and `session` objects:

```
graph = tf.Graph() # Creates a graph
session = tf.InteractiveSession(graph=graph) # Creates a session
```

Then we'll define a filename queue, a queue data structure containing filenames. This will be passed as an argument to a reader (soon to be defined). The queue will produce filenames as requested by the reader, so that the reader can fetch the files with these filenames to read data:

```
filenames = ['test%d.txt'%i for i in range(1,4)]
filename_queue = tf.train.string_input_producer(filenames, capacity=3,
shuffle=True, name='string_input_producer')
```

Here, `capacity` is the amount of data held in the queue at a given time, and `shuffle` tells the queue if the data should be shuffled before spitting out.

TensorFlow has several different types of readers (a list of available readers is available at https://www.tensorflow.org/api_guides/python/io_ops#Readers). As we have a few separate text files where a single line represents a single data point, `TextLineReader` suits us the best:

```
reader = tf.TextLineReader()
```

After defining the reader, we can use the `read()` function to read data from the files. It outputs *(key,value)* pairs. The key identifies the file and the record (that is, the line of text) being read within the file. We can omit this. The value returns the actual value of the line read by the reader:

```
key, value = reader.read(filename_queue, name='text_read_op')
```

Next, we'll define `record_defaults`, which will be output if any faulty records are found:

```
record_defaults = [[-1.0], [-1.0], [-1.0], [-1.0], [-1.0], [-1.0],
[-1.0], [-1.0], [-1.0], [-1.0]]
```

Now we decode the read line of text into numerical columns (as we have CSV files). For this we use the `decode_csv()` method. You will see that we have 10 columns in a single line if you open a file (for example, `test1.txt`) with a text editor:

```
col1, col2, col3, col4, col5, col6, col7, col8, col9, col10 =
tf.decode_csv(value, record_defaults=record_defaults)
```

Then we'll concatenate these columns to form a single tensor (we call this features) that will be passed to another method, `tf.train.shuffle_batch()`. The `tf.train.shuffle_batch()` method takes the previously defined tensor (features), and outputs a batch of a given batch size by randomly shuffling the tensor:

```
features = tf.stack([col1, col2, col3, col4, col5, col6, col7, col8,
col9, col10])

x = tf.train.shuffle_batch([features], batch_size=3, capacity=5,
name='data_batch', min_after_dequeue=1, num_threads=1)
```

The `batch_size` argument is the size of the data batch we'll be sampling at a given step, `capacity` is the capacity of the data queue (more memory required for large queues), and `min_after_dequeue` represents the minimum number of elements to be left in the queue after dequeue. Finally, `num_threads` defines how many threads are used to produce a batch of data. If there is lot of preprocessing taking place in the pipeline, you can increase this number. Also, if you need to read data without shuffling (as with `tf.train.shuffle_batch`), you can use the `tf.train.batch` operation. Then we'll start this pipeline by calling the following:

```
coord = tf.train.Coordinator()
threads = tf.train.start_queue_runners(coord=coord, sess=session)
```

The `tf.train.Coordinator()` class can be seen as a thread manager. It implements various mechanisms for managing threads (for example, starting threads and joining threads to the main thread once the task is finished). The `tf.train.Coordinator()` class is needed because, the input pipeline spawns many threads for filling in (that is, enqueue) queues, dequeuing queues, and many other tasks. Next, we will execute `tf.train.start_queue_runners(...)` using the thread manager we created before. `QueueRunner()` holds enqueue operations for a queue and they are automatically created during the definition of the input pipeline. So, to fill in the defined queues, we need to start these queue runners with the `tf.train.start_queue_runners` function.

Next, after the task we're interested in is completed, we explicitly need to stop the threads and join them to the main thread, otherwise the program will hang indefinitely. This is achieved by `coord.request_stop()` and `coord.join(threads)`. This input pipeline combined with our sigmoid example—so that it reads data from the file directly—would look like the following:

```
import tensorflow as tf
import numpy as np
import os

# Defining the graph and session
graph = tf.Graph() # Creates a graph
session = tf.InteractiveSession(graph=graph) # Creates a session

### Building the Input Pipeline ###
# The filename queue
filenames = ['test%d.txt'%i for i in range(1,4)]
filename_queue = tf.train.string_input_producer(filenames, capacity=3,
shuffle=True,name='string_input_producer')

# check if all files are there
for f in filenames:
    if not tf.gfile.Exists(f):
        raise ValueError('Failed to find file: ' + f)
```

```
    else:
        print('File %s found.'%f)

# Reader which takes a filename queue and
# read() which outputs data one by one
reader = tf.TextLineReader()

# ready the data of the file and output as key,value pairs
# We're discarding the key
key, value = reader.read(filename_queue, name='text_read_op')

# if any problems encountered with reading file
# this is the value returned
record_defaults = [[-1.0], [-1.0], [-1.0], [-1.0], [-1.0], [-1.0],
[-1.0], [-1.0], [-1.0], [-1.0]]

# decoding the read value to columns
col1, col2, col3, col4, col5, col6, col7, col8, col9, col10 =
tf.decode_csv(value, record_defaults=record_defaults)
# Now we stack the columns together to form a single tensor containing
# all the columns
features = tf.stack([col1, col2, col3, col4, col5, col6, col7, col8,
col9, col10])

# output x is randomly assigned a batch of data of batch_size
# where the data is read from the .txt files
x = tf.train.shuffle_batch([features], batch_size=3,
                            capacity=5, name='data_batch',
                            min_after_dequeue=1,num_threads=1)

# QueueRunner retrieve data from queues and we need to explicitly
start them
# Coordinator coordinates multiple QueueRunners
# Coordinator coordinates multiple QueueRunners
coord = tf.train.Coordinator()
threads = tf.train.start_queue_runners(coord=coord, sess=session)

# Building the graph by defining the variables and calculations
W = tf.Variable(tf.random_uniform(shape=[10,5], minval=-0.1,
maxval=0.1, dtype=tf.float32),name='W') # Variable
# Variable
b = tf.Variable(tf.zeros(shape=[5],dtype=tf.float32),name='b')

h = tf.nn.sigmoid(tf.matmul(x,W) + b) # Operation to be performed

# Executing operations and evaluating nodes in the graph
tf.global_variables_initializer().run() # Initialize the variables

# Calculate h with x and print the results for 5 steps
for step in range(5):
```

```
    x_eval, h_eval = session.run([x,h])
    print('========== Step %d =========='%step)
    print('Evaluated data (x)')
    print(x_eval)
    print('Evaluated data (h)')
    print(h_eval)
    print('')

# We also need to explicitly stop the coordinator
# otherwise the process will hang indefinitely
coord.request_stop()
coord.join(threads)
session.close()
```

# Defining variables in TensorFlow

Variables play an important role in TensorFlow. A variable is essentially a tensor with a specific shape defining how many dimensions the variable will have and the size of each dimension. However, unlike a regular tensor, variables are *mutable*; meaning that the value of the variables can change after they are defined. This is an ideal property to have to implement parameters of a learning model (for example, neural network weights), where the weights change slightly after each step of learning. For example, if you define a variable with x = tf.Variable(0,dtype=tf.int32), you can change the value of that variable using a TensorFlow operation such as tf.assign(x,x+1). However, if you define a tensor such as x = tf.constant(0,dtype=tf.int32), you cannot change the value of the tensor, as for a variable. It should stay 0 until the end of the program execution.

Variable creation is quite simple. In our example, we already created two variables, w and b. When creating a variable, a few things are of high importance. We list them here and discuss each in detail in the following paragraphs:

- Variable shape
- Data type
- Initial value
- Name (optional)

The variable shape is a 1D vector of the [x,y,z,...] format. Each value in the list indicates how large the corresponding dimension or axis is. For instance, if you require a 2D tensor with 50 rows and 10 columns as the variable, the shape would be equal to [50,10].

The dimensionality of the variable (that is, the length of the shape vector) is recognized as the rank of the tensor in TensorFlow. Do not confuse this with the rank of a matrix.

Tensor rank in TensorFlow indicates the dimensionality of the tensor; for a two-dimensional matrix, *rank* = 2.

The data type plays an important role in determining the size of a variable. There are many different data types including the commonly used `tf.bool`, `tf.uint8`, `tf.float32`, and `tf.int32`. Each data type has a number of bits required to represent a single value with that type. For example, `tf.uint8` requires 8 bits, whereas `tf.float32` requires 32 bits. It is common practice to use the same data types for computations as doing otherwise can lead to data type mismatches. So if you have two different data types for two tensors that you need to transform, you have to explicitly convert one tensor to the other tensor's type using the `tf.cast(...)` operation. The `tf.cast(...)` operation is designed to cope with such situations. For example, if you have an x variable with the `tf.int32` type, which needs to be converted to `tf.float32`, employ `tf.cast(x,dtype=tf.float32)` to convert x to `tf.float32`.

Next, a variable requires an *initial* value to be initialized with. TensorFlow provides several different initializers for our convenience, including constant intializers and normal distribution intializers. Here are a few popular TensorFlow intializers you can use to initialize variables:

- `tf.zeros`
- `tf.constant_initializer`
- `tf.random_uniform`
- `tf.truncated_normal`

Finally, the *name* of the variable will be used as an ID to identify that variable in the graph. So if you ever visualize the computational graph, the variable will appear by the argument passed to the `name` keyword. If you do not specify a name, TensorFlow will use the default naming scheme.

 Note that the Python variable `tf.Variable` is assigned to, is not known by the computational graph and is not a part of TensorFlow variable naming. Consider this example where you specify a TensorFlow variable as follows:

```
a = tf.Variable(tf.zeros([5]),name='b')
```

Here, the TensorFlow graph will know this variable by the name b and not a.

# Defining TensorFlow outputs

TensorFlow outputs are usually tensors and a result of a transformation to either an input or a variable or both. In our example, h is an output, where `h = tf.nn.sigmoid(tf.matmul(x,W) + b)`. It is also possible to give such outputs to other operations, forming a chained set of operations. Furthermore, it does not necessarily have to be TensorFlow operations. You also can use standard Python arithmetic with TensorFlow. Here is an example:

```
x = tf.matmul(w,A)
y = x + B
z = tf.add(y,C)
```

# Defining TensorFlow operations

If you take a look at the TensorFlow API at `https://www.tensorflow.org/api_docs/python/`, you will see that TensorFlow has a massive collection of operations available. Here we will take a look at a selected few of the myriad TensorFlow operations.

## Comparison operations

Comparison operations are useful for comparing two tensors. The following code example includes a few useful comparison operations. You can find the comprehensive list of comparison operators in the *Comparison Operators* section at `https://www.tensorflow.org/api_guides/python/control_flow_ops`. Furthermore, to understand the working of these operations, let's consider two example tensors, x and y:

```
# Let's assume the following values for x and y
# x (2-D tensor) => [[1,2],[3,4]]
# y (2-D tensor) => [[4,3],[3,2]]
x = tf.constant([[1,2],[3,4]], dtype=tf.int32)
y = tf.constant([[4,3],[3,2]], dtype=tf.int32)

# Checks if two tensors are equal element-wise and returns a boolean
tensor
# x_equal_y => [[False,False],[True,False]]
x_equal_y = tf.equal(x, y, name=None)

# Checks if x is less than y element-wise and returns a boolean tensor
# x_less_y => [[True,True],[False,False]]
x_less_y = tf.less(x, y, name=None)

# Checks if x is greater or equal than y element-wise and returns a
boolean tensor
# x_great_equal_y => [[False,False],[True,True]]
```

```
x_great_equal_y = tf.greater_equal(x, y, name=None)

# Selects elements from x and y depending on whether,
# the condition is satisfied (select elements from x)
# or the condition failed (select elements from y)
condition = tf.constant([[True,False],[True,False]],dtype=tf.bool)
# x_cond_y => [[1,3],[3,2]]
x_cond_y = tf.where(condition, x, y, name=None)
```

# Mathematical operations

TensorFlow allows you to perform math operations on tensors that range from the simple to the complex. We will discuss a few of the mathematical operations made available in TensorFlow. The complete set of operations is available at `https://www.tensorflow.org/api_guides/python/math_ops`.

```
# Let's assume the following values for x and y
# x (2-D tensor) => [[1,2],[3,4]]
# y (2-D tensor) => [[4,3],[3,2]]
x = tf.constant([[1,2],[3,4]], dtype=tf.float32)
y = tf.constant([[4,3],[3,2]], dtype=tf.float32)

# Add two tensors x and y in an element-wise fashion
# x_add_y => [[5,5],[6,6]]
x_add_y = tf.add(x, y)

# Performs matrix multiplication (not element-wise)
# x_mul_y => [[10,7],[24,17]]
x_mul_y = tf.matmul(x, y)

# Compute natural logarithm of x element-wise
# equivalent to computing ln(x)
# log_x => [[0,0.6931],[1.0986,1.3863]]
log_x = tf.log(x)

# Performs reduction operation across the specified axis
# x_sum_1 => [3,7]
x_sum_1 = tf.reduce_sum(x, axis=[1], keepdims=False)

# x_sum_2 => [[4],[6]]
x_sum_2 = tf.reduce_sum(x, axis=[0], keepdims=True)
```

```
# Segments the tensor according to segment_ids (items with same id in
# the same segment) and computes a segmented sum of the data

data = tf.constant([1,2,3,4,5,6,7,8,9,10], dtype=tf.float32)
segment_ids = tf.constant([0,0,0,1,1,2,2,2,2,2 ], dtype=tf.int32)
# x_seg_sum => [6,9,40]
x_seg_sum = tf.segment_sum(data, segment_ids)
```

# Scatter and gather operations

Scatter and gather operations play a vital role in matrix manipulation tasks, as these
two variants are the only way (until recent times) to index tensors in TensorFlow. In
other words, you cannot access elements of tensors in TensorFlow as you would in
NumPy (for example, x[1,0], where x is a 2D numpy.ndarray). A **scatter** operation
allows you to assign values to specific indices of a given tensor, whereas the **gather**
operation allows you to extract a slice (or individual elements) of a given tensor. The
following code shows a few variations of the scatter and gather operations:

```
# 1-D scatter operation
ref = tf.Variable(tf.constant([1,9,3,10,5],dtype=tf.
float32),name='scatter_update')
indices = [1,3]
updates = tf.constant([2,4],dtype=tf.float32)
tf_scatter_update = tf.scatter_update(ref, indices, updates, use_
locking=None, name=None)


# n-D scatter operation
indices = [[1],[3]]
updates = tf.constant([[1,1,1],[2,2,2]])
shape = [4,3]
tf_scatter_nd_1 = tf.scatter_nd(indices, updates, shape, name=None)


# n-D scatter operation
indices = [[1,0],[3,1]] # 2 x 2
updates = tf.constant([1,2]) # 2 x 1
shape = [4,3] # 2
tf_scatter_nd_2 = tf.scatter_nd(indices, updates, shape, name=None)


# 1-D gather operation
params = tf.constant([1,2,3,4,5],dtype=tf.float32)
indices = [1,4]
```

```
tf_gather = tf.gather(params, indices, validate_indices=True,
name=None) #=> [2,5]


# n-D gather operation
params = tf.constant([[0,0,0],[1,1,1],[2,2,2],[3,3,3]],dtype=tf.
float32)
indices = [[0],[2]]
tf_gather_nd = tf.gather_nd(params, indices, name=None) #=>
[[0,0,0],[2,2,2]]


params = tf.constant([[0,0,0],[1,1,1],[2,2,2],[3,3,3]],dtype=tf.
float32)
indices = [[0,1],[2,2]]
tf_gather_nd_2 = tf.gather_nd(params, indices, name=None) #=>
[[0,0,0],[2,2,2]]
```

# Neural network-related operations

Now let's look at several useful neural network-related operations that we will use heavily in the following chapters. The operations we will discuss here range from simple element-wise transformations (that is, activations) to computing partial derivatives of a set of parameters with respect to another value. We will also implement a simple neural network as an exercise.

## Nonlinear activations used by neural networks

Nonlinear activations enable neural networks to perform well at numerous tasks. Typically, there is a nonlinear activation transformation (that is, activation layer) after each layer output in a neural network (except for the last layer). A nonlinear transformation helps a neural network to learn various nonlinear patterns that are present in data. This is very useful for complex real-world problems, where data often has more complex nonlinear patterns, in contrast to linear patterns. If not for the nonlinear activations between layers, a deep neural network will be a bunch of linear layers stacked on top of each other. Also, a set of linear layers can essentially be compressed to a single bigger linear layer. In conclusion, if not for the nonlinear activations, we cannot create a neural network with more than one layer.

Let's observe the importance of nonlinear activation through an example. First, recall the computation for the neural networks we saw in *the sigmoid example*. If we disregard b, it will be this:

```
h = sigmoid(W*x)
```

Assume a three-layer neural network (having W1, W2, and W3 as layer weights) where each layer does the preceding computation; we can summarize the full computation as follows:

```
h = sigmoid(W3*sigmoid(W2*sigmoid(W1*x)))
```

However, if we remove the nonlinear activation (that is, sigmoid), we get this:

```
h = (W3 * (W2 * (W1 *x))) = (W3*W2*W1)*x
```

So, without the nonlinear activations, the three layers can be brought down to a single linear layer.

Now we'll list two commonly used nonlinear activations in neural networks and how they can be implemented in TensorFlow:

```
# Sigmoid activation of x is given by 1 / (1 + exp(-x))
tf.nn.sigmoid(x,name=None)
# ReLU activation of x is given by max(0,x)
tf.nn.relu(x, name=None)
```

# The convolution operation

A convolution operation is a widely used signal-processing technique. For images, convolution is used to produce different effects of an image. An example of edge detection using convolution is shown in *Figure 2.6*. This is achieved by shifting a convolution filter on top of an image to produce a different output at each location (see *Figure 2.7* later in this section). Specifically, at each location we do element-wise multiplication of the elements in the convolution filter with the image patch (same size as the convolution filter) that overlaps with the convolution filter and takes the sum of the multiplication:

$$* \begin{bmatrix} -1 & -1 & -1 \\ -1 & 8 & -1 \\ -1 & -1 & -1 \end{bmatrix} =$$

Figure 2.6: Using the convolution operation for edge detection in an image
(Source: https://en.wikipedia.org/wiki/Kernel_(image_processing))

The following is the implementation of the convolution operation:

```
x = tf.constant(
    [[
        [[1],[2],[3],[4]],
        [[4],[3],[2],[1]],
        [[5],[6],[7],[8]],
        [[8],[7],[6],[5]]
    ]],
    dtype=tf.float32)

x_filter = tf.constant(
    [
        [
            [[0.5]],[[1]]
        ],
        [
            [[0.5]],[[1]]
        ]
    ],
    dtype=tf.float32)

x_stride = [1,1,1,1]
x_padding = 'VALID'

x_conv = tf.nn.conv2d(
    input=x, filter=x_filter,
    strides=x_stride, padding=x_padding
)
```

Here, the apparently excessive number of square brackets used might make you think that the example can be made easy to follow by getting rid of these redundant brackets. Unfortunately, that is not the case. For the `tf.conv2d(...)` operation, TensorFlow requires `input`, `filter`, and `stride` to be of an exact format. We will now go through each argument in `tf.conv2d(input, filter, strides, padding)` in more detail:

- **input**: This is typically a 4D tensor where the dimensions should be ordered as `[batch_size, height, width, channels]`.

- **batch_size**: This is the amount of data (for example, inputs such as, images, and words) in a single batch of data. We normally process data in batches as often large datasets are used for learning. At a given training step, we randomly sample a small batch of data that approximately represents the full dataset. And doing this for many steps allows us to approximate the full dataset quite well. This `batch_size` parameter is the same as the one we discussed in the TensorFlow input pipeline example.
  - **height and width**: This is the height and the width of the input.
  - **channels**: This is the depth of an input (for example, for a RGB image, channels will be 3 — a channel for each color).

- **filter**: This is a 4D tensor that represents the convolution window of the convolution operation. The filter dimensions should be [height, width, in_channels, out_channels]:
  - **height and width**: This is the height and the width of the filter (often smaller than that of the input)
  - **in_channels**: This is the number of channels of the input to the layer
  - **out_channels**: This is the number of channels to be produced in the output of the layer

- **strides**: This is a list with four elements, where the elements are [batch_stride, height_stride, width_stride, channels_stride]. The `strides` argument denotes how many elements to skip during a single shift of the convolution window on the input. If you do not completely understand what `strides` is, you can use the default value of 1.

- **padding**: This can be one of ['SAME', 'VALID']. It decides how to handle the convolution operation near the boundaries of the input. The VALID operation performs the convolution without padding. If we were to convolve an input of $n$ length with a convolution window of size $h$, this will result in an output of size $(n-h+1 < n)$. The diminishing of the output size can severely limit the depth of neural networks. SAME pads zeros to the boundary such that the output will have the same height and width as the input.

To gain a better understanding of what filter size, stride, and padding are, refer to *Figure 2.7*:

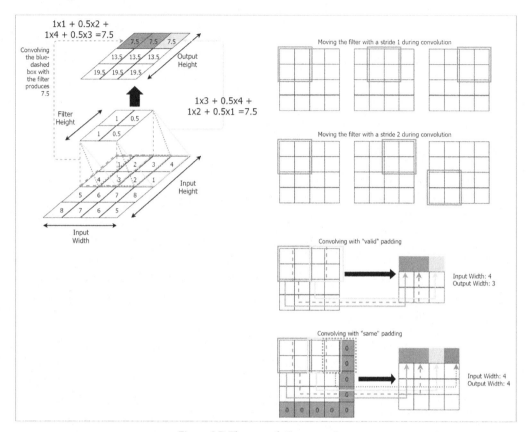

Figure 2.7: The convolution operation

# The pooling operation

A pooling operation behaves similar to the convolution operation, but the final output is different. Instead of outputting the sum of the element-wise multiplication of the filter and the image patch, we now take the maximum element of the image patch for that location (see *Figure 2.8*):

```
x = tf.constant(
    [[
        [[1],[2],[3],[4]],
        [[4],[3],[2],[1]],
        [[5],[6],[7],[8]],
        [[8],[7],[6],[5]]
    ]],
    dtype=tf.float32)
```

```
x_ksize = [1,2,2,1]
x_stride = [1,2,2,1]
x_padding = 'VALID'

x_pool = tf.nn.max_pool(
    value=x, ksize=x_ksize,
    strides=x_stride, padding=x_padding
)
# Returns (out) =>
[[[[ 4.]
   [ 4.]],
  [[ 8.]
   [ 8.]]]]
```

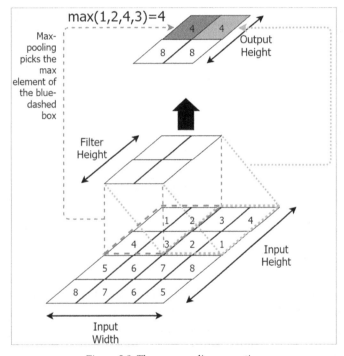

Figure 2.8: The max-pooling operation

## Defining loss

We know that in order for a neural network to learn something useful, a loss needs to be defined. There are several functions for automatically calculating the loss in TensorFlow, two of which are shown in the following code. The `tf.nn.l2_loss` function is the mean squared error loss, and `tf.nn.softmax_cross_entropy_with_logits_v2` is another type of loss, which actually gives better performance in classification tasks. And by logits here, we mean the unnormalized output of the neural network (that is, the linear output of the last layer of the neural network):

```
# Returns half of L2 norm of t given by sum(t**2)/2
x = tf.constant([[2,4],[6,8]],dtype=tf.float32)
x_hat = tf.constant([[1,2],[3,4]],dtype=tf.float32)
# MSE = (1**2 + 2**2 + 3**2 + 4**2)/2 = 15
MSE = tf.nn.l2_loss(x-x_hat)


# A common loss function used in neural networks to optimize the
network
# Calculating the cross_entropy with logits (unnormalized outputs of
the last layer)
# instead of outputs leads to better numerical stabilities

y = tf.constant([[1,0],[0,1]],dtype=tf.float32)
y_hat = tf.constant([[3,1],[2,5]],dtype=tf.float32)
# This function alone doesnt average the cross entropy losses of all
data points,
# You need to do that manually using reduce_mean function
CE = tf.reduce_mean(tf.nn.softmax_cross_entropy_with_logits_
v2(logits=y_hat,labels=y))
```

## Optimization of neural networks

After defining the loss of a neural network, our objective is to minimize that loss over time. Optimization is the procedure used for this. In other words, the objective of the optimizer is to find the neural network parameters (that is, weights and bias values) that give the minimum loss for all the inputs. Again, our beloved TensorFlow provides us with several different optimizers, so we don't have to worry about implementing them from scratch.

*Figure 2.9* illustrates a simple optimization problem and shows how the optimization happens over time. The curve can be imagined as the *loss curve* (for high dimensions, we say *loss surface*), where *x* can be thought of as the parameters of the neural network (in this case a neural network with a single weight), and *y* can be thought of as the loss. We have an initial guess of *x=2*. From this point, we use the optimizer to reach the minimum *y* (that is, loss), which is obtained at *x=0*. More specifically, we take small steps in the direction opposite to the gradient at a given point and continue for several steps in this manner. However, in real-world problems, the loss surface will not be as nice as in the illustration, but it will be more complex:

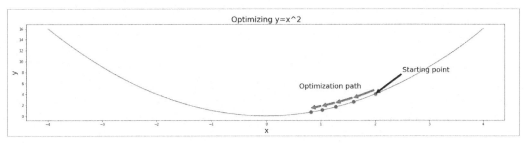

Figure 2.9: The optimization process

In this example, we use `GradientDescentOptimizer`. The `learning_rate` parameter denotes the step size you take in the direction of minimization (distance between two red dots):

```
# Optimizers play the role of tuning neural network parameters so that
# their task error is minimal
# For example task error can be the cross_entropy error
# for a classification task
tf_x = tf.Variable(tf.constant(2.0,dtype=tf.float32),name='x')
tf_y = tf_x**2
minimize_op = tf.train.GradientDescentOptimizer(learning_rate=0.1).
minimize(tf_y)
```

Everytime you execute the loss minimize operation with `session.run(minimize_op)`, you will get close to the `tf_x` value that gives the minimum of `tf_y`.

## The control flow operations

Control flow operations, as the name implies, controls the order of execution in the graph. For example, let's say we need to perform the following computation, in this order:

$x = x+5$

$z = x*2$

Precisely, if *x* = *2*, we should get *z* = *14*. Let's first try to achieve this in the simplest possible way:

```
session = tf.InteractiveSession()

x = tf.Variable(tf.constant(2.0), name='x')
x_assign_op = tf.assign(x, x+5)
z = x*2

tf.global_variables_initializer().run()
print('z=',session.run(z))
print('x=',session.run(x))
session.close()
```

Ideally, we would want *x* = *7* and *z* = *14*, instead, TensorFlow produced *x*=2 and *z*=4. This is not the answer you were expecting. This is because TensorFlow does not care about the order of execution of things unless you explicitly specify it. Control flow operations enable you to exactly do this. To fix the preceding code, we do the following:

```
session = tf.InteractiveSession()

x = tf.Variable(tf.constant(2.0), name='x')
with tf.control_dependencies([tf.assign(x, x+5)]):
  z = x*2

tf.global_variables_initializer().run()
print('z=',session.run(z))
print('x=',session.run(x))
session.close()
```

Now this should give us *x*=7 and *z*=14. The `tf.control_dependencies(...)` operation makes sure that the operations passed to it as arguments will be performed before performing the nested operation.

# Reusing variables with scoping

Until now, we have looked at the architecture of TensorFlow and the essentials required to implement a basic TensorFlow client. However, there is much more to TensorFlow than this. As we already saw, TensorFlow behaves quite differently from a typical Python script. For example, you cannot debug TensorFlow code in real time (as you would do a simple Python script using a Python IDE), as the computations do not happen in real time in TensorFlow (unless you are using the Eager Execution method, which was only recently in TensorFlow 1.7: `https://research.googleblog.com/2017/10/eager-execution-imperative-define-by.html`). In other words, TensorFlow first defines the full computational graph, does all computations on a device, and finally fetches results. Consequently, it can be quite tedious and painful to debug a TensorFlow client. This emphasizes the importance of *attention to detail* when implementing a TensorFlow client. Therefore, it is advised to adhere to proper coding practices introduced for TensorFlow. One such practice is known as **scoping** and allows easier variable reusing.

Reusing TensorFlow variables is a common scenario that occurs frequently in TensorFlow clients. To understand the value of an answer, we must first understand the question. Also, what better way to understand the question than erroneous code. Let's say that we want a function that performs a certain computation; given w, we need to compute x*w + y**2. Let's write a TensorFlow client, which has a function that performs this:

```
import tensorflow as tf
session = tf.InteractiveSession()
def very_simple_computation(w):
  x = tf.Variable(tf.constant(5.0, shape=None, dtype=tf.float32),
  name='x')
  y = tf.Variable(tf.constant(2.0, shape=None, dtype=tf.float32),
  name='y')
  z = x*w + y**2
  return z
```

Say that you want to compute this for a single step. Then, you can call `session.run(very_simple_computation(2))` (of course, after calling `tf.global_variables_initializer().run()`), and you will have the answer and feel good about writing code that actually works. However, don't get too comfortable, because an issue arises if you want to run this function several times. Each time you call this method, two TensorFlow variables will be created. Remember that we discussed that TensorFlow is different to Python? This is one such instance. The x and y variables will not get replaced in the graph when you call this method multiple times. Rather, the old variables will be retained and new variables will be created in the graph until you run out of memory. But of course, the answer will be correct. To see this in action, run `session.run(very_simple_computation(2))` in a `for` loop, and if you print the names of the variables in the graph, you will see more than two variables. This is the output when you run it 10 times:

```
'x:0', 'y:0', 'x_1:0', 'y_1:0', 'x_2:0', 'y_2:0', 'x_3:0', 'y_3:0',
'x_4:0', 'y_4:0', 'x_5:0', 'y_5:0', 'x_6:0', 'y_6:0', 'x_7:0',
'y_7:0', 'x_8:0', 'y_8:0', 'x_9:0', 'y_9:0', 'x_10:0', 'y_10:0'
```

Each time you run the function, a pair of variables is created. Let's make this explicit: if you run this function for 100 times, you will have 198 obsolete variables in your graph (99 x variables and 99 y variables).

This is where *scoping* comes to the rescue. Scoping allows you to reuse the variables instead of creating one each time a function is invoked. Now to add reusability to our little example, we will be changing the code to the following:

```
def not_so_simple_computation(w):
  x = tf.get_variable('x', initializer=tf.constant (5.0, shape=None,
                      dtype=tf.float32))
  y = tf.get_variable('y', initializer=tf.constant(2.0, shape=None,
                      dtype=tf.float32))
  z = x*w + y**2
  return z


def another_not_so_simple_computation(w):
  x = tf.get_variable('x', initializer=tf.constant(5.0, shape=None,
                      dtype=tf.float32))
  y = tf.get_variable('y', initializer=tf.constant(2.0, shape=None,
                      dtype=tf.float32))
  z = w*x*y
  return z


# Since this is the first call, the variables will
# be created with following names
# x => scopeA/x, y => scopeA/y
with tf.variable_scope('scopeA'):
```

```
  z1 = not_so_simple_computation(tf.constant(1.0,dtype=tf.float32))
# scopeA/x and scopeA/y alread created we reuse them
with tf.variable_scope('scopeA',reuse=True):
  z2 = another_not_so_simple_computation(z1)


# Since this is the first call, the variables will be created with
# be created with
# following names x => scopeB/x, y => scopeB/y
with tf.variable_scope('scopeB'):
  a1 = not_so_simple_computation(tf.constant(1.0,dtype=tf.float32))
# scopeB/x and scopeB/y alread created we reuse them
with tf.variable_scope('scopeB',reuse=True):
  a2 = another_not_so_simple_computation(a1)


# Say we want to reuse the "scopeA" again, since variables are already
# created we should set "reuse" argument to True when invoking the
scope
with tf.variable_scope('scopeA',reuse=True):
  zz1 = not_so_simple_computation(tf.constant(1.0,dtype=tf.float32))
  zz2 = another_not_so_simple_computation(z1)
```

In this example, if you do `session.run([z1,z2,a1,a2,zz1,zz2])`, you should see z1, z2, a1, a2, zz1, zz2 has 9.0, 90.0, 9.0, 90.0, 9.0, 90.0 values in that order. Now if you print variables, you should see only four different variables: `scopeA/x`, `scopeA/y`, `scopeB/x`, and `scopeB/y`. We can now run it as many times as we want in a loop without worrying about creating redundant variables and running out of memory.

Now you might wonder why you cannot just create four variables at the beginning of the code and use them within the methods. However, this breaks the *encapsulation* of your code, because now you are explicitly depending on something outside your code.

Finally, scoping enables reusability while preserving the encapsulation of the code. Furthermore, scoping makes the flow of the code more intuitive and reduces the chance of errors as we are explicitly getting the variable by the scope and name instead of using the Python variable the TensorFlow variable was assigned to.

# Implementing our first neural network

Great! Now that you've learned the architecture, basics, and scoping mechanism of TensorFlow, it's high time that we move on and implement something moderately complex. Let's implement a neural network. Precisely, we will implement a fully connected neural network model that we discussed in *Chapter 1, Introduction to Natural Language Processing*.

One of the stepping stones to the introduction of neural networks is to implement a neural network that is able to classify digits. For this task, we will be using the famous MNIST dataset made available at http://yann.lecun.com/exdb/mnist/. You might feel a bit skeptical regarding our using a computer vision task rather than a NLP task. However, vision tasks can be implemented with less preprocessing and are easy to understand.

As this is our first encounter with neural networks, we will walk through the main parts of the example. However, note that I will only walk through the crucial bits of the exercise. To run the example end to end, you can find the full exercise in the tensorflow_introduction.ipynb file in the ch2 folder.

# Preparing the data

First, we need to download the dataset with the maybe_download(...) function and preprocess it with the read_mnist(...) function. These two functions are defined in the exercise file. The read_mnist(...) function performs two main steps:

- Reading the byte stream of the dataset and forming it into a proper numpy.ndarray object

- Standardizing the images to have a zero-mean and unit-variance (also known as **whitening**)

The following code shows the read_mnist(...) function. The read_mnist(...) function takes the filename of the file containing images and the filename of the file containing labels, as input. Then the read_mnist(...) function produces two NumPy matrices containing all the images and their corresponding labels:

```
def read_mnist(fname_img, fname_lbl):
  print('\nReading files %s and %s'%(fname_img, fname_lbl))

  with gzip.open(fname_img) as fimg:
    magic, num, rows, cols = struct.unpack(">IIII", fimg.read(16))
    print(num,rows,cols)
    img = (np.frombuffer(fimg.read(num*rows*cols), dtype=np.uint8).
        reshape(num, rows * cols)).astype(np.float32)
    print('(Images) Returned a tensor of shape ',img.shape)
    # Standardizing the images
    img = (img - np.mean(img))/np.std(img)

  with gzip.open(fname_lbl) as flbl:
    # flbl.read(8) reads upto 8 bytes
    magic, num = struct.unpack(">II", flbl.read(8))
    lbl = np.frombuffer(flbl.read(num), dtype=np.int8)
```

```
print('(Labels) Returned a tensor of shape: %s'%lbl.shape)
print('Sample labels: ',lbl[:10])

return img, lbl
```

# Defining the TensorFlow graph

To define the TensorFlow graph, we'll first define placeholders for the input images (`tf_inputs`) and the corresponding labels (`tf_labels`):

```
# Defining inputs and outputs
tf_inputs = tf.placeholder(shape=[batch_size, input_size], dtype=tf.
float32, name = 'inputs')
tf_labels = tf.placeholder(shape=[batch_size, num_labels], dtype=tf.
float32, name = 'labels')
```

Next, we'll write a Python function that will create the variables for the first time. Note that we are using scoping to ensure the reusability, and make sure that our variables are named properly:

```
# Defining the TensorFlow variables
def define_net_parameters():
  with tf.variable_scope('layer1'):
    tf.get_variable(WEIGHTS_STRING,shape=[input_size,500],
    initializer=tf.random_normal_initializer(0,0.02))
    tf.get_variable(BIAS_STRING, shape=[500],
    initializer=tf.random_uniform_initializer(0,0.01))

  with tf.variable_scope('layer2'):
    tf.get_variable(WEIGHTS_STRING,shape=[500,250],
    initializer=tf.random_normal_initializer(0,0.02))
    tf.get_variable(BIAS_STRING, shape=[250],
    initializer=tf.random_uniform_initializer(0,0.01))

  with tf.variable_scope('output'):
    tf.get_variable(WEIGHTS_STRING,shape=[250,10], initializer=tf.
    random_normal_initializer(0,0.02))
    tf.get_variable(BIAS_STRING, shape=[10], initializer=tf.random_
    uniform_initializer(0,0.01))
```

Next, we'll define the inference process for the neural network. Note how the scoping has given a very intuitive flow to the code in the function, compared with using variables without scoping. So, in this network we have three layers:

- A fully-connected layer with ReLU activation (`layer1`)
- A fully-connected layer with ReLU activation (`layer2`)
- A fully-connected softmax layer (`output`)

By means of scoping, we name variables (weights and biases) for each layer as, `layer1/weights`, `layer1/bias`, `layer2/weights`, `layer2/bias`, `output/weights`, and `output/bias`. Note that in the code, all of them have the same name, but different scopes:

```
# Defining calcutations in the neural network
# starting from inputs to logits
# logits are the values before applying softmax to the final output

def inference(x):
  # calculations for layer 1
  with tf.variable_scope('layer1',reuse=True):
    w,b = tf.get_variable(WEIGHTS_STRING),
                          tf.get_variable(BIAS_STRING)
    tf_h1 = tf.nn.relu(tf.matmul(x,w) + b, name = 'hidden1')

  # calculations for layer 2
  with tf.variable_scope('layer2',reuse=True):
    w,b = tf.get_variable(WEIGHTS_STRING),
                          tf.get_variable(BIAS_STRING)
    tf_h2 = tf.nn.relu(tf.matmul(tf_h1,w) + b, name = 'hidden1')

  # calculations for output layer
  with tf.variable_scope('output',reuse=True):
    w,b = tf.get_variable(WEIGHTS_STRING),
                          tf.get_variable(BIAS_STRING)
    tf_logits = tf.nn.bias_add(tf.matmul(tf_h2,w), b, name = 'logits')

  return tf_logits
```

Now we'll define a loss function and then a loss minimize operation. The loss minimize operation minimizes the loss by nudging the network parameters in the direction that minimizes the loss. There is a diverse collection of optimizers available in TensorFlow. Here, we will be using `MomentumOptimizer`, which gives better final accuracy and convergence than `GradientDescentOptimizer`:

```
# defining the loss
tf_loss = tf.reduce_mean(tf.nn.softmax_cross_entropy_with_logits_
v2(logits=inference(tf_inputs), labels=tf_labels))
# defining the optimize function
tf_loss_minimize = tf.train.MomentumOptimizer(momentum=0.9,learning_
rate=0.01).minimize(tf_loss)
```

Finally, we'll define an operation to retrieve the predicted softmax probabilities for a given batch of inputs. This in turn will be used to calculate the accuracy of your neural network:

```
# defining predictions
tf_predictions = tf.nn.softmax(inference(tf_inputs))
```

# Running the neural network

Now we have all the essential operations required to run the neural network and examine whether it's capable of learning to successfully classify digits:

```
for epoch in range(NUM_EPOCHS):
  train_loss = []

  # Training Phase
  for step in range(train_inputs.shape[0]//batch_size):
    # Creating one-hot encoded labels with labels
    # One-hot encoding digit 3 for 10-class MNIST dataset
    # will result in
    # [0,0,0,1,0,0,0,0,0,0]
    labels_one_hot = np.zeros((batch_size, num_labels),
                              dtype=np.float32)
    labels_one_hot[np.arange(batch_size),train_labels[
    step*batch_size:(step+1)*batch_size]] = 1.0


    # Running the optimization process
    loss, _ = session.run([tf_loss,tf_loss_minimize],feed_dict={
    tf_inputs: train_inputs[step*batch_size: (step+1)*batch_size,:],
    tf_labels: labels_one_hot})
```

```
    train_loss.append(loss)
# Used to average the loss for a single epoch

    test_accuracy = []
    # Testing Phase
    for step in range(test_inputs.shape[0]//batch_size):
        test_predictions = session.run(tf_predictions,feed_dict={tf_
inputs: test_inputs[step*batch_size: (step+1)*batch_size,:]})
        batch_test_accuracy = accuracy(test_predictions,test_
labels[step*batch_size: (step+1)*batch_size])
        test_accuracy.append(batch_test_accuracy)

    print('Average train loss for the %d epoch: %.3f\n'%(epoch+1,np.
mean(train_loss)))
    print('\tAverage test accuracy for the %d epoch:
%.2f\n'%(epoch+1,np.mean(test_accuracy)*100.0))
```

In this code, `accuracy(test_predictions,test_labels)` is a function that takes some predictions and labels as inputs and provides the accuracy (how many predictions matched the actual label). It is defined in the exercise file.

If successful, you should be able to see a behavior similar to the ones shown in *Figure 2.10*. After 50 epochs, the test accuracy should reach approximately 98%:

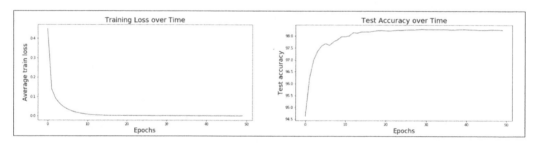

Figure 2.10: Training loss and test accuracy for the MNIST digit classification task

# Summary

In this chapter, you took your first steps to solving NLP tasks by understanding the primary underlying platform (TensorFlow) on which we will be implementing our algorithms. First, we discussed the underlying details of TensorFlow architecture. Next, we discussed the essential ingredients of a meaningful TensorFlow client. Then we discussed a general coding practice widely used in TensorFlow known as scoping. Later, we brought all these elements together to implement a neural network to classify an MNIST dataset.

Specifically, we discussed the TensorFlow architecture lining up the explanation with an example TensorFlow client. In the TensorFlow client, we defined the TensorFlow graph. Then, when we created a session, it looked at the graph, created a `GraphDef` object representing the graph, and sent it to the distributed master. The distributed master looked at the graph, decided which components to use for the relevant computation, and divided it into several subgraphs to make the computations faster. Finally, workers executed subgraphs and returned the result through the session.

Next, we discussed various elements that composes a typical TensorFlow client: inputs, variables, outputs, and operations. Inputs are the data we feed to the algorithm for training and testing purposes. We discussed three different ways of feeding inputs: using placeholders, preloading data and storing data as TensorFlow tensors, and using an input pipeline. Then we discussed TensorFlow variables, how they differ from other tensors, and how to create and initialize them. Following this, we discussed how variables can be used to create intermediate and terminal outputs. Finally, we discussed several available TensorFlow operations, such as mathematical operations, matrix operations, neural-network related operations, and control-flow operations, that will be used later in the book.

Then we discussed how scoping can be used to avoid certain pitfalls when implementing a TensorFlow client. Scoping allows variables to be used with ease, while maintaining the encapsulation of the code.

Finally, we implemented a neural network using all the previously learned concepts. We used a three-layer neural network to classify an MNIST digit dataset.

In the next chapter, we will see how to use the fully connected neural network we implemented in this chapter, for learning the semantic numerical word representation of words.

# 3

# Word2vec – Learning Word Embeddings

In this chapter, we will discuss a topic of paramount importance in NLP—Word2vec, a technique to learn word embeddings or distributed numerical feature representations (that is, vectors) of words. Learning word representations lies at the very foundation of many NLP tasks because many NLP tasks rely on good feature representations for words that preserve their semantics as well as their context in a language. For example, the feature representation of the word *forest* should be very different from *oven* as these words are rarely used in similar contexts, whereas the representations of *forest* and *jungle* should be very similar.

Word2vec is called a *distributed representation*, as the semantics of the word is captured by the activation pattern of the full representation vector, in contrast to a single element of the representation vector (for example, setting a single element in the vector to 1 and rest to 0 for a single word).

We will go step by step from the classical approach to solving this problem to modern neural network-based methods that deliver state-of-the-art performance in finding good word representations. We visualize (using t-SNE, a visualization technique for high-dimensional data) such learned word embeddings for a set of words on a 2D canvas in *Figure 3.1*. If you take a closer look, you will see that similar things are placed close to each other (for example, numbers in the cluster in the middle):

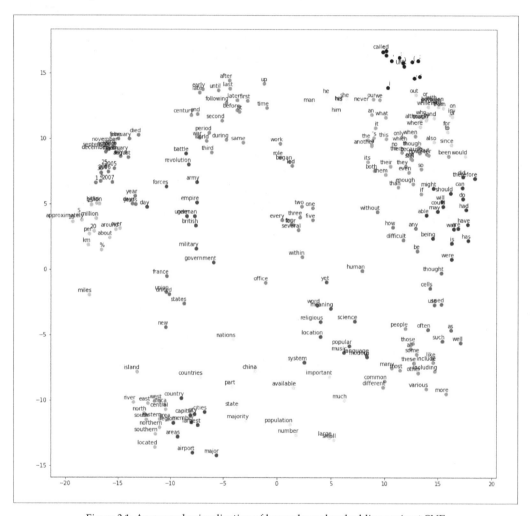

Figure 3.1: An example visualization of learned word embeddings using t-SNE

**t-Distributed Stochastic Neighbor Embedding (t-SNE)**

This is a dimensionality reduction technique that projects high-dimensional data to a two-dimensional space. This allows us to imagine how high-dimensional data is distributed in space, and it is quite useful as we cannot visualize beyond three dimensions easily. You will learn about t-SNE in more detail in the next chapter.

# What is a word representation or meaning?

What is meant by the word *meaning*? This is more of a philosophical question than a technical one. So, we will not try to discern the most proper answer for this question, but accept a more modest answer, that is, *meaning* is the idea or the representation conveyed by a word. Since the primary objective of NLP is to achieve human-like performance in linguistic tasks, it is sensible to explore principled ways of representing words for machines. To achieve this, we will use algorithms that can analyze a given text corpus and come up with good numerical representations of words (that is, word embeddings), such that words that fall within similar contexts (for example, *one* and *two*, *I* and *we*) will have similar numerical representations compared with words that are irrelevant (for example, *cat* and *volcano*).

First, we will discuss some classical approaches to achieve this and then move on to understanding more sophisticated recent methods that use neural networks to learn such feature representations and deliver state-of-the-art performance.

# Classical approaches to learning word representation

In this section, we will discuss some of the classical approaches used for numerically representing words. These approaches mainly can be categorized into two classes: approaches that use external resources for representing words and approaches that do not. First, we will discuss WordNet—one of the most popular external resource-based approaches for representing words. Then we will proceed to more localized methods (that is, those that do not rely on external resources), such as **one-hot encoding** and **Term Frequency-Inverse Document Frequency (TF-IDF)**.

# WordNet – using an external lexical knowledge base for learning word representations

WordNet is one of the most popular classical approaches or statistical NLP that deals with word representations. It relies on an external lexical knowledge base that encodes the information about the definition, synonyms, ancestors, descendants, and so forth of a given word. WordNet allows a user to infer various information for a given word, such as the aspects of a word discussed in the preceding sentence and the similarity between two words.

## Tour of WordNet

As already mentioned, WordNet is a lexical database, encoding part-of-speech tag relationships between words including nouns, verbs, adjectives, and adverbs. WordNet was pioneered by the Department of Psychology of Princeton University, United States, and it is currently hosted at the Department of Computer Science of Princeton University. WordNet considers the synonymy between words to evaluate the relationship between words. The English WordNet currently hosts more than 150,000 words and more than 100,000 synonym groups (that is, synsets). Also, WordNet is not just restricted to English. A multitude of different wordnets have been founded since its inception and can be viewed at `http://globalwordnet.org/wordnets-in-the-world/`.

In order to understand how to leverage WordNet, it is important to lay a solid ground on the terminology used in WordNet. First, WordNet uses the term **synset** to denote a group or set of synonyms. Next, each synset has a **definition** that explains what the synset represents. Synonyms contained within a synset are called **lemmas**.

In WordNet, the word representations are modeled hierarchically, which forms a complex graph between a given synset and the associations to another synset. These associations can be of two different categories: an *is-a* relationship or an *is-made-of* relationship. First, we will discuss the *is-a* association.

For a given synset, there exist two categories of relations: hypernyms and hyponyms. **Hypernyms** of a synset are the synsets that carry a general (high-level) meaning of the considered synset. For example, *vehicle* is a hypernym of the synset *car*. Next, **hyponyms** are synsets that are more specific than the corresponding synset. For example, *Toyota car* is a hyponym of the synset *car*.

Now let's discuss the *is-made-of* relationships for a synset. **Holonyms** of a synset are the group of synsets that represents the whole entity of the considered synset. For example, a holonym of *tires* is the *cars* synset. **Meronyms** are an *is-made-of* category and represent the opposite of holonyms, where meronyms are the parts or substances synset that makes the corresponding synset. We can visualize this in *Figure 3.2*:

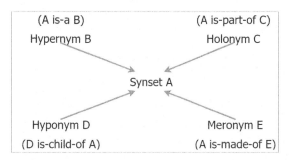

Figure 3.2: The various associations that exist for a synset

The NLTK library, a Python natural language processing library, can be used to understand WordNet and its mechanisms. The full example is available as an exercise in the `ch3_wordnet.ipynb` file located in the `ch3` folder.

**Installing the NLTK Library**

To install the NLTK library to Python, you can use the following Python `pip` command:

**pip install nltk**

Alternatively, you can use an IDE (such as PyCharm) to install the library through the **Graphical User Interface (GUI)**. You can find more detailed instructions at `http://www.nltk.org/install.html`.

To import NLTK into Python and download the WordNet corpus, first import the `nltk` library:

```
import nltk
```

Then you can download the WordNet corpus by running the following command:

```
nltk.download('wordnet')
```

After the `nltk` library is installed and imported, we need to import the WordNet corpus with this command:

```
from nltk.corpus import wordnet as wn
```

Then we can query the WordNet corpus as follows:

```
# retrieves all the available synsets
word = 'car'
car_syns = wn.synsets(word)

# The definition of each synset of car synsets
syns_defs = [car_syns[i].definition() for i in range(len(car_syns))]

# Get the lemmas for the first Synset
car_lemmas = car_syns[0].lemmas()[:3]

# Let's get hypernyms for a Synset (general superclass)
syn = car_syns[0]
print('\t',syn.hypernyms()[0].name(),'\n')

# Let's get hyponyms for a Synset (specific subclass)
syn = car_syns[0]
print('\t',[hypo.name() for hypo in syn.hyponyms()[:3]],'\n')

# Let's get part-holonyms for the third "car"
# Synset (specific subclass)
syn = car_syns[2]
print('\t',[holo.name() for holo in syn.part_holonyms()],'\n')

# Let's get meronyms for a Synset (specific subclass)
syn = car_syns[0]
print('\t',[mero.name() for mero in syn.part_meronyms()[:3]],'\n')
```

After running the example, the results will look like this:

```
All the available Synsets for car
[Synset('car.n.01'), Synset('car.n.02'), Synset('car.n.03'),
Synset('car.n.04'), Synset('cable_car.n.01')]

Example definitions of available synsets:
car.n.01 :  a motor vehicle with four wheels; usually propelled by an
internal combustion engine
car.n.02 :  a wheeled vehicle adapted to the rails of railroad
car.n.03 :  the compartment that is suspended from an airship and that
carries personnel and the cargo and the power plant

Example lemmas for the Synset  car.n.03
['car', 'auto', 'automobile']

Hypernyms of the Synset  car.n.01
motor_vehicle.n.01
```

```
Hyponyms of the Synset  car.n.01
['ambulance.n.01', 'beach_wagon.n.01', 'bus.n.04']

Holonyms (Part) of the Synset  car.n.03
['airship.n.01']

Meronyms (Part) of the Synset  car.n.01
['accelerator.n.01', 'air_bag.n.01', 'auto_accessory.n.01']
```

We can also obtain the similarities between two synsets in the following way. There are several different similarity metrics implemented in NLTK, and you can see them in action on the official website (www.nltk.org/howto/wordnet.html). Here, we use the Wu-Palmer similarity, which measures the similarity between two synsets based on their depth in the hierarchical organization of the synsets:

```
sim = wn.wup_similarity(w1_syns[0], w2_syns[0])
```

# Problems with WordNet

Though WordNet is an amazing resource that anyone can use to learn meanings of word in the NLP tasks, there are quite a few drawbacks in using WordNet for this. They are as follows:

- Missing nuances is a key problem in WordNet. There are both theoretical and practical reasons why this is not viable for WordNet. From a theoretical perspective, it is not well-posed or direct to model the definition of the subtle difference between two entities. Practically speaking, defining nuances is subjective. For example, the words *want* and *need* have similar meanings, but one of them (*need*) is more assertive. This is considered to be a nuance.

- Next, WordNet is subjective in itself as WordNet was designed by a relatively small community. Therefore, depending on what you are trying to solve, WordNet might be suitable or you might be able to perform better with a loose definition of words.

- There also exists the issue of maintaining WordNet, which is labor-intensive. Maintaining and adding new synsets, definitions, lemmas, and so on, can be very expensive. This adversely affects the scalability of WordNet, as human labor is essential to keep WordNet up to date.

- Developing WordNet for other languages can be costly. There are also some efforts to build WordNet for other languages and link it with the English WordNet as **MultiWordNet** (**MWN**), but they are yet incomplete.

Next, we will discuss several word representation techniques that do not rely on external resources.

# One-hot encoded representation

A simpler way of representing words is to use the one-hot encoded representation. This means that if we have a vocabulary of $V$ size, for each $i^{th}$ word $w_i$, we will represent the word $w_i$ with a $V$-long vector $[0, 0, 0, ..., 0, 1, 0, ..., 0, 0, 0]$ where the $i^{th}$ element is 1 and other elements are zero. As an example, consider this sentence:

*Bob and Mary are good friends.*

The one-hot encoded representation for each word might look like this:

*Bob: [1,0,0,0,0,0]*

*and: [0,1,0,0,0,0]*

*Mary: [0,0,1,0,0,0]*

*are: [0,0,0,1,0,0]*

*good: [0,0,0,0,1,0]*

*friends: [0,0,0,0,0,1]*

However, as you might have already figured out, this representation has many drawbacks.

This representation does not encode the similarity between words in any way and completely ignores the context in which the words are used. Let's consider the dot product between the word vectors as the similarity measure. The more similar two vectors are, the higher the dot product is for those two vectors. For example, the representation of the words *car* and *automobile* will have a similarity distance of 0, where *car* and *pencil* will also have the same value.

This method becomes extremely ineffective for large vocabularies. Also, for a typical NLP task, the vocabulary easily can exceed 50,000 words. Therefore, the word representation matrix for 50,000 words will result in a very sparse 50,000 × 50,000 matrix.

However, one-hot encoding plays an important role even in the state-of-the-art word embedding learning algorithms. We use one-hot encoding to represent words numerically and feed them into neural networks so that the neural networks can learn better and smaller numerical feature representations of the words.

One-hot encoding is also known as a localist representation (opposite of the distributed representation), as the feature representation is decided by the activation of a single element in the vector.

# The TF-IDF method

TF-IDF is a frequency-based method that takes into account the frequency with which a word appears in a corpus. This is a word representation in the sense that it represents the importance of a specific word in a given document. Intuitively, the higher the frequency of the word, the more important that word is in the document. For example, in a document about cats, the word *cats* will appear more. However, just calculating the frequency would not work, because words such as *this* and *is* are very frequent but do not carry that much information. TF-IDF takes this into consideration and gives a value of zero for such common words.

Again, *TF* stands for term frequency and *IDF* stands for inverse document frequency:

$$TF(w_i) = number\ of\ times\ w_i\ appear\ /\ total\ number\ of\ words$$

$$IDF(w_i) = log(total\ number\ of\ documents\ /\ number\ of\ documents\ with\ w_i\ in\ it)$$

$$TF\text{-}IDF(w_i) = TF(w_i)\ x\ IDF(w_i)$$

Let's do a quick exercise. Consider two documents:

- Document 1: *This is about cats. Cats are great companions.*
- Document 2: *This is about dogs. Dogs are very loyal.*

Now let's crunch some numbers:

*TF-IDF (cats, doc1) = (2/8) \* log(2/1) = 0.075*

*TF-IDF (this, doc2) = (1/8) \* log(2/2) = 0.0*

Therefore, the word *cats* is informative while *this* is not. This is the desired behavior we needed in terms of measuring the importance of words.

# Co-occurrence matrix

Co-occurrence matrices, unlike one-hot-encoded representation, encodes the context information of words, but requires maintaining a V × V matrix. To understand the co-occurrence matrix, let's take two example sentences:

- *Jerry and Mary are friends.*
- *Jerry buys flowers for Mary.*

The co-occurrence matrix will look like the following matrix. We only show one triangle of the matrix, as the matrix is symmetric:

|         | Jerry | and | Mary | are | friends | buys | flowers | for |
|---------|-------|-----|------|-----|---------|------|---------|-----|
| **Jerry**   | 0     | 1   | 0    | 0   | 0       | 1    | 0       | 0   |
| **and**     |       | 0   | 1    | 0   | 0       | 0    | 0       | 0   |
| **Mary**    |       |     | 0    | 1   | 0       | 0    | 0       | 1   |
| **are**     |       |     |      | 0   | 1       | 0    | 0       | 0   |
| **friends** |       |     |      |     | 0       | 0    | 0       | 0   |
| **buys**    |       |     |      |     |         | 0    | 1       | 0   |
| **flowers** |       |     |      |     |         |      | 0       | 1   |
| **for**     |       |     |      |     |         |      |         | 0   |

However, it is not hard to see that maintaining such a co-occurrence matrix comes at a cost as the size of the matrix grows polynomially with the size of the vocabulary. Furthermore, it is not straightforward to incorporate a context window size larger than 1. One option is to have a weighted count, where the weight for a word in the context deteriorates with the distance from the word of interest.

All these drawbacks motivate us to investigate more principled, robust, and scalable ways of learning and inferring meanings (that is, representations) of words.

Word2vec is a recently-introduced distributed word representation learning technique that is currently being used as a feature engineering technique for many NLP tasks (for example, machine translation, chatbots, and image caption generators). Essentially, Word2vec learns word representations by looking at the surrounding words (that is, context) in which the word is used. More specifically, we attempt to predict the context, given some words (or vice versa), through a neural network, which leads the neural network to be forced to learn good word embeddings. We will discuss this method in detail in the next section. The Word2vec approach has many advantages over the previously-described methods. They are as follows:

- The Word2vec approach is not subjective to the human knowledge of language as in the WordNet-based approach.

- Word2vec representation vector size is <u>independent of the vocabulary size</u> <u>unlike one-hot encoded representation</u> or the <u>word co-occurrence matrix.</u>
- Word2vec is <u>a distributed representation</u>. Unlike localist representation, where the representation depends on the activation of a single element of the representation vector (for example, one-hot encoding), the distributed representation depends on the activation pattern of all the elements in the vector. This <u>gives more expressive power to Word2vec</u> than produced by the one-hot encoded representation.

In the following section, we will first develop some intuitive feeling about learning word embeddings by working through an example. Then we will define a loss function so that we can use machine learning to learn word embeddings. Also, we will discuss two Word2vec algorithms, namely, the **skip-gram** and **Continuous Bag-of-Words** (CBOW) algorithms.

# Word2vec – a neural network-based approach to learning word representation

*"You shall know a word by the company it keeps."*

*– J.R. Firth*

This statement, uttered by J.R. Firth in 1957, lies at the very foundation of Word2vec, as Word2vec techniques use the context of a given word to learn its semantics. Word2vec is a groundbreaking approach that allows to learn the meaning of words without any human intervention. Also, Word2vec learns numerical representations of words by looking at the words surrounding a given word.

We can test the correctness of the preceding quote by imagining a real-world scenario. Imagine you are sitting for an exam and you find this sentence in your first question: "Mary is a very stubborn child. Her pervicacious nature always gets her in trouble." Now, unless you are very clever, you might not know what *pervicacious* means. In such a situation, you automatically will be compelled to look at the phrases surrounding the word of interest. In our example, *pervicacious* is surrounded by *stubborn*, *nature*, and *trouble*. Looking at these three words is enough to determine that pervicacious in fact means a state of being stubborn. I think this is adequate evidence to observe the importance of context for a word's meaning.

Now let's discuss the basics of Word2vec. As already mentioned, Word2vec learns the meaning of a given word by looking at its context and representing it numerically. By *context*, we refer to a fixed number of words in front of and behind the word of interest. Let's take a hypothetical corpus with $N$ words. Mathematically, this can be represented by a sequence of words denoted by $w_0, w_1, ..., w_i,$ and $w_N,$ where $w_i$ is the $i^{th}$ word in the corpus.

Next, if we want to find a good algorithm that is capable of learning word meanings, given a word, our algorithm should be able to predict the context words correctly. This means that the following probability should be high for any given word $w_i$:

$$P\left(w_{i-m}, ..., w_{i-1}, w_{i+1}, ..., w_{i+m} \mid w_i\right) = \prod_{j \neq i \wedge j = i-m}^{i+m} P\left(w_j \mid w_i\right)$$

To arrive at the right-hand side of the equation, we need to assume that given the target word ($w_i$), the context words are independent of each other (for example, $w_{i-2}$ and $w_{i-1}$ are independent). Though not entirely true, this approximation makes the learning problem practical and works well in practice.

# Exercise: is queen = king – he + she?

Before proceeding further, let's do a small exercise to understand how maximizing the previously-mentioned probability leads to finding good meaning (or representations) of words. Consider the following very small corpus:

*There was a very rich king. He had a beautiful queen. She was very kind.*

Now let's do some manual preprocessing and remove the punctuation and the uninformative words:

*was rich king he had beautiful queen she was kind*

Now let's form a set of tuples for each word with their context words in the format (*target word → context word 1, context word 2*). We will assume a context window size of 1 on either side:

*was → rich*

**rich → was, king**

**king → rich, he**

*he → king, had*

*had → he, beautiful*

*beautiful* → *had, queen*

**queen** → **beautiful, she**

**she** → **queen, was**

*was* → *she, kind*

*kind* → *was*

Remember, our goal is to be able to predict the words on the right, provided the word at the left is given. To do this, for a given word, the words on the right-side context should share a high numerical or geometrical similarity with the words on the left-side context. In other words, the word of interest should be conveyed by the surrounding word. Now let's assume actual numerical vectors to understand how this works. For simplicity, let's only consider the tuples highlighted in bold. Let's begin by assuming the following for the word *rich*:

*rich* → *[0,0]*

To be able to correctly predict *was* and *king* from *rich*, *was* and *king* should have high similarity with the word *rich*. Let's assume the Euclidean distance between vectors as the similarity product.

Let's try the following values for the words *king* and *rich*:

*king* → *[0,1]*

*was* → *[-1,0]*

This works out fine as the following:

*Dist(rich,king) = 1.0*

*Dist(rich,was) = 1.0*

Here, *Dist* is the Euclidean distance between two words. This is illustrated in *Figure 3.3*:

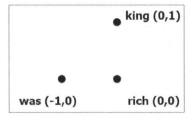

Figure 3.3: The positioning of word vectors for the words "rich", "was" and "king"

Now let's consider the following tuple:

*king → rich, he*

We have established the relationship between *king* and *rich* already. However, it is not done yet; the more we see a relationship, the closer these two words should be. So, let's first adjust the vector of *king* so that it is a bit closer to *rich*:

*king → [0,0.8]*

Next, we will need to add the word *he* to the picture. The word *he* should be closer to *king*. This is all the information that we have right now about the word *he*:

*he → [0.5,0.8]*

At this moment, the graph with the words looks like *Figure 3.4*:

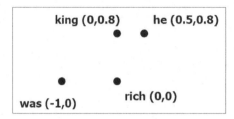

Figure 3.4: The positioning of word vectors for the words "rich", "was", "king," and "he"

Now let's proceed with the next two tuples: *queen → beautiful, she* and *she → queen, was*. Note that I have swapped the order of the tuples as this makes it easier for us to understand the example:

*she → queen, was*

Now, we will have to use our prior knowledge about English to proceed further. It is a reasonable decision to place the word *she*, which has the same distance as *he* from the word *was* because their usage in the context of the word *was* is equivalent. Therefore, let's use this:

*she → [0.5,0.6]*

Next, we will use the word *queen* close to the word *she*:

*queen → [0.0,0.6]*

This is illustrated in *Figure 3.5*:

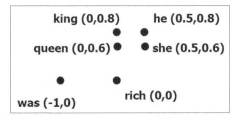

Figure 3.5: The positioning of word vectors for the words "rich," "was," "king," "he," "she," and "queen"

Next, we only have the following tuple:

*queen → beautiful, she*

Here, the word *beautiful* is found. It should have approximately the same distance from the words *queen* and *she*. Let's use the following:

*beautiful → [0.25,0]*

Now we have the following graph depicting the relationships between words. When we observe *Figure 3.6*, it seems to be a very intuitive representation of the meanings of words:

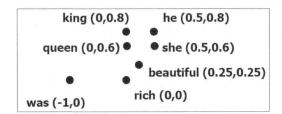

Figure 3.6: The positioning of word vectors for the words
"rich," "was," "king," "he," "she," "queen," and "beautiful"

Now, let's look at the question that has been lurking in our minds since the beginning of this exercise. Are the quantities in this equation equivalent: *queen = king – he + she*? Well, we've got all the resources that we'll need to solve this mystery now. Let's try the right-hand side of the equation first:

*= king – he + she*

*= [0,0.8] – [0.5,0.8] + [0.5,0.6]*

*= [0,0.6]*

It all works out at the end. If you look at the word vector we obtained for the word *queen*, you see that this is exactly similar to the answer we deduced earlier.

Note that this is a crude working to show how word embeddings are learned, and this might differ from the exact positions of word embeddings if learned using an algorithm.

However, keep in mind that this is an unrealistically scaled down exercise with regard to what a real-world corpus might look like. So, you will not be able to work out these values by hand just by crunching a dozen numbers. This is where sophisticated function approximators such as neural networks do the job for us. But, to use neural networks, we need to formulate our problem in a mathematically assertive way. However, this is a good exercise that actually shows the power of word vectors.

# Designing a loss function for learning word embeddings

The vocabulary for even a simple real-world task can easily exceed 10,000 words. Therefore, we cannot develop word vectors by hand for large text corpora and need to devise a way to automatically find good word embeddings using some machine learning algorithms (for example, neural networks) to perform this laborious task efficiently. Also, to use any sort of machine learning algorithm for any sort of task, we need to define a loss, so completing the task becomes minimizing the loss. Let's define the loss for finding good word embedding vectors.

First, let's recall the equation we discussed at the beginning of this section:

$$P\left(w_{i-m},\ldots,w_{i-1},w_{i+1},\ldots,w_{i+m}\mid w_i\right)=\prod_{j\neq i\wedge j=i-m}^{i+m} P\left(w_j\mid w_i\right)$$

With this equation in mind, we can define a cost function for the neural network:

$$J\left(\theta\right)=-\left(1/N-2m\right)\sum_{i=m+1}^{N-m}\prod_{j\neq i\wedge j=i-m}^{i+m} P\left(w_j\mid w_i\right)$$

Remember, $J(\theta)$ is a loss (that is, cost), not a reward. Also, we want to maximize $P(w_j\mid w_i)$. Thus, we need a minus sign in front of the expression to convert it into a cost function.

Now, instead of working with the product operator, let's convert this to log space. Converting the equation to log space will introduce consistency and numerical stability. This gives us the following equation:

$$J(\theta) = -(1/N - 2m) \sum_{i=m+1}^{N-m} \sum_{j \neq i \wedge j=i-m}^{i+m} log P(w_j \mid w_i)$$

This formulation of the cost function is known as the **negative log-likelihood**.

Now, as we have a well-formulated cost function, a neural network can be used to optimize this cost function. Doing so will force the word vectors or word embeddings to organize themselves well according to their meaning. Now, it is time to learn about the existing algorithms that use this cost function to find good word embeddings.

# The skip-gram algorithm

The first algorithm we will talk about is known as the **skip-gram algorithm**. The skip-gram algorithm, introduced by Mikolov and others in 2013, is an algorithm that exploits the context of the words of written text to learn good word embeddings. Let's go through step by step to understand the skip-gram algorithm.

First, we will discuss the data preparation process, followed by an introduction to the notation required to understand the algorithm. Finally, we will discuss the algorithm itself.

As we discussed in numerous places, the meaning of the word can be elicited from the contextual words surrounding that particular word. However, it is not entirely straightforward to develop a model that exploits this property to learning word meanings.

# From raw text to structured data

First, we need to design a mechanism to extract a dataset that can be fed to our learning model. Such a dataset should be a set of tuples of the format *(input, output)*. Moreover, this needs to be created in an unsupervised manner. That is, a human should not have to manually engineer the labels for the data. In summary, the data preparation process should do the following:

- Capture the surrounding words of a given word
- Perform in an unsupervised manner

The skip-gram model uses the following approach to design such a dataset:

1. For a given word $w_i$, a context window size $m$ is assumed. By *context window size*, we mean the number of words considered as context on a single side. Therefore, for $w_i$, the context window (including the target word $w_i$) will be of size $2m+1$ and will look like this: $[w_{i-m}, ..., w_{i-1}, w_i, w_{i+1}, ..., w_{i+m}]$.

2. Next, input-output tuples are formed as $[..., (w_i, w_{i-m}), ...,(w_i, w_{i-1}), (w_i, w_{i+1}), ..., (w_i, w_{i+m}), ...]$; here, $m+1 \leq i \leq N-m$ and $N$ is the number of words in the text to get a practical insight. Let's assume the following sentence and context window size ($m$) of 1:

*The dog barked at the mailman.*

For this example, the dataset would be as follows:

*[(dog, The), (dog, barked), (barked, dog), (barked, at), ..., (the, at), (the, mailman)]*

# Learning the word embeddings with a neural network

Once the data is in the *(input, output)* format, we can use a neural network to learn the word embeddings. First, let's identify the variables we need to learn the word embeddings. To store the word embeddings, we need a V × D matrix, where $V$ is the vocabulary size and $D$ is the dimensionality of the word embeddings (that is, the number of elements in the vector that represents a single word). $D$ is a user-defined hyperparameter. The higher $D$ is, the more expressive the word embeddings learned will be. This matrix will be referred to as the *embedding space* or the *embedding layer*. Next, we have a softmax layer with weights of size D × V, a bias of size $V$.

Each word will be represented as a one-hot encoded vector of size $V$ with one element being 1 and all the others being 0. Therefore, an input word and the corresponding output words would each be of size $V$. Let's refer to the $i^{th}$ input as $x_i$, the corresponding embedding of $x_i$ as $z_i$, and the corresponding output as $y_i$.

At this point, we have the necessary variables defined. Next, for each input $x_i$, we will look up the embedding vectors from the embedding layer corresponding to the input. This operation provides us with $z_i$, which is a $D$-sized vector (that is, a $D$-long embedding vector). Afterwards, we calculate the prediction output for $x_i$ using the following transformation:

$$logit(x_i) = z_i W + b$$

$$\hat{y}_i = softmax(logit(x_i))$$

Here, $logit(x_i)$ represents the unnormalized scores (that is, logits), $\hat{y}_i$ is the $V$-sized predicted output (representing the probability of output being a word from the $V$-sized vocabulary), $W$ is the D × V weight matrix, $b$ is the V × 1 bias-vector, and *softmax* is the softmax activation. We will visualize both the conceptual (*Figure 3.7*) and implementation (*Figure 3.8*) views of the skip-gram model. Here is a summary of the notation:

- $V$: This is the size of the vocabulary
- $D$: This is the dimensionality of the embedding layer
- $x_i$: This is the $i^{th}$ input word represented as a one-hot-encoded vector
- $z_i$: This is the embedding (that is, representation) vector corresponding to the $i^{th}$ input word
- $y_i$: This is the one-hot-encoded output word corresponding to $x_i$
- $\hat{y}_i$: This is the predicted output for $x_i$
- $logit(x_i)$: This is the unnormalized score for the input $x_i$
- $\mathbb{I}_{w_j}$: This is the one-hot-encoded representation for word $w_j$
- $W$: This is the softmax weight matrix
- $b$: This is the bias of the softmax

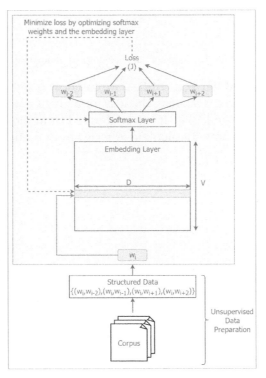

Figure 3.7: The conceptual skip-gram model

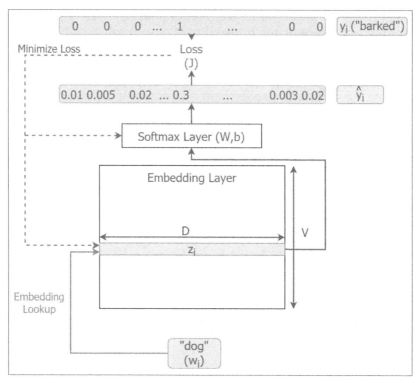

Figure 3.8: The implementation of the skip-gram model

Using both the existing and derived entities, we can now use the negative log-likelihood loss function to calculate the loss for a given data point $(x_i, y_i)$. If you are wondering what $P(w_j \mid w_i)$ is, it can be derived from the already defined entities. Next, let's discuss how to calculate $P(w_j \mid w_i)$ from $\hat{y}_i$ and also derive a formal definition for that.

**Why does the original word embeddings paper use two embedding layers?**

The original paper (by Mikolov, and others, 2013) uses two distinct V × D embedding spaces to denote words in the target space (words when used as the target) and words in the contextual space (words used as context words). One motivation to do this is that the same word does not occur in the context of itself often. So, we want to minimize the probability of such things happening. For example, for the target word *dog*, it is highly unlikely that the word *dog* is also found in its context (*P(dog | dog)*  ~ 0). Intuitively, if we feed the ($x_i$=*dog* and $y_i$=*dog*) data point to the neural network, we are asking the neural network to give a higher loss if the neural network predicts *dog* as a context word of *dog*. In other words, we are asking the word embedding of the word *dog* to have a very high distance to the word embedding of the word *dog*. This creates a strong contradiction as the distance between the embedding of the same word will be 0. Therefore, we cannot achieve this if we only have a single embedding space. However, having two separate embedding spaces for target words and contextual words allows us to have this property because this way we have two separate embedding vectors for the same word. However, in practice, as long as you avoid feeding input-output tuples, having the same word as input and output allows us to work with a single embedding space and eliminate the need of two distinct embedding layers.

# Formulating a practical loss function

Let's inspect our loss function more closely. We have derived that the loss should be as follows:

$$J(\theta) = -(1/N - 2m) \sum_{i=m+1}^{N-m} \sum_{j \neq i \wedge j=i-m}^{i+m} log P(w_j \mid w_i)$$

However, calculating this particular loss from the entities we have at hand at the moment is not entirely straightforward.

First, let's understand what the $P(w_j | w_i)$ entity represents. To do this, we will move from individual words notation to an individual data points notation. That is, we will say that $P(w_j, w_i)$ is given by the $n^{th}$ data point, which has the one-hot encoded vector of $w_i$ as the input $(x_n)$ and the one-hot encoded representation of $w_j$ as the true output $(y_n)$. This is given by the following equation:

$$P\left(w_j \mid w_i\right) = \frac{exp\left(logit\left(x_n\right)_{w_j}\right)}{\sum_{w_k \in vocabulary} exp\left(logit\left(x_n\right)_{w_k}\right)}$$

The $logit(x_n)$ term denotes the unnormalized prediction score (that is, logit) vector ($V$-sized) obtained for a given input $x_n$ and $logit(x_n)_{w_j}$ is the score value corresponding to the non-zeroth index of the one-hot encoded representation of $w_j$ (we call this, the index of $w_j$ from now onwards). Then, we normalize the logit value at the index of $w_j$ with respect to all the logit values corresponding to all the words in the entire vocabulary. This particular type of normalization is known as the softmax activation (or normalization). Now, by converting this to log space, we get the following equation:

$$J\left(\theta\right) = -\left(1/N - 2m\right) \sum_{i=m+1}^{N-m} \sum_{j \neq i \, j=i-m}^{i+m} logit\left(x_n\right)_{w_j} - log\left(\sum_{w_k \in vocabulary} exp\left(logit\left(x_n\right)_{w_k}\right)\right)$$

To calculate the *logit* function effectively, we can fiddle with variables and come up with the following notation:

$$logit\left(x_n\right)_{w_j} = \sum_{l=1}^{V} \mathbb{I}_{w_j} logit\left(x_n\right)$$

Here, $\mathbb{I}_{w_j}$ is the one-hot encoded vector of $w_j$. Now the *logit* operation has reduced to a sum and product operation. Since $\mathbb{I}_{w_j}$ only has a single nonzero element corresponding to the word $w_j$, only that index of the vector will be used in the computation. This is more computationally efficient than finding the value in the logit vector that corresponds to the index of the nonzero element by sweeping through a vector of the size of the vocabulary.

Now, by assigning the logit calculation we obtained, for the loss, we get the following:

$$J\left(\theta\right) = -\left(1/N - 2m\right) \sum_{i=m+1}^{N-m} \sum_{j \neq i \, j=i-m}^{i+m} \sum_{l=1}^{V} \mathbb{I}_{w_j} logit\left(x_n\right) - log\left(\sum_{w_k \in vocabulary} exp\left(\sum_{l=1}^{V} \mathbb{I}_{w_k} logit\left(x_n\right)\right)\right)$$

Let's consider an example to understand this calculation:

*I like NLP*

We can create input-output tuples as follows:

*(like, I)*

*(like, NLP)*

Now let's assume the following one-hot-encoded representations for the preceding words:

*like – 1,0,0*

*I – 0,1,0*

*NLP – 0,0,1*

Next, let's consider the input-output tuple *(like, I)*. When we propagated the input *like* through the skip-gram learning model, let's assume that we obtained the following logits for the words *like*, *I*, and *NLP* in that order:

2,10,5

Now softmax outputs for each word in the vocabulary will be as follows:

*P(like | like) = exp(2)/(exp(2)+exp(10)+exp(5)) = 0.118*

*P(I | like) = exp(10)/ (exp(2)+exp(10)+exp(5)) = 0.588*

*P(NLP | like) = exp(5)/ (exp(2)+exp(10)+exp(5)) = 0.294*

The preceding loss function says that we need to maximize *P(I | like)* to minimize the loss. Now let's apply our example to this loss function:

*=- ( [0,1,0] \* ([2, 10, 5]) - log(exp([1,0,0]\*[2, 10, 5]) + exp([0,1,0]\*[2, 10, 5]) + exp([0,0,1]\*[2, 10, 5])))*

*=- (10 - log(exp(2)+exp(10)+exp(5))) = 0.007*

With this loss function, for the term before the minus sign, there is only a single nonzero element in the *y* vector corresponding to the word *I*. Therefore, we will only be considering the probability *P(I | like)*, which is exactly what we wanted.

However, this is not the ideal solution we were looking for. The objective of this loss function from a practical perspective, we want to maximize the probability of predicting a contextual word given a word, while minimizing the probability of "all" the noncontextual words, given a word. We will soon see that having a well-defined loss function will not solve our problem effectively in practice. We will need to devise a more clever approximate loss function to learn good word embeddings in a feasible time duration.

# Efficiently approximating the loss function

We are fortunate to have a loss function that is solid both mathematically and intuitively. However, hard work does not end here. If we try to calculate the loss function in closed form as we discussed earlier, we will face an inevitable tremendous slowness of our algorithm.

This slowness is due to the large vocabulary causing a performance bottleneck. Let's have a look at our cost function:

$$J(\theta) = -(1/N - 2m) \sum_{i=m+1}^{N-m} \sum_{\substack{j \neq i \\ j=i-m}}^{i+m} logit(x_n)_{w_j} - log\left( \sum_{w_k \in vocabulary} exp\left( logit(x_n)_{w_k} \right) \right)$$

You will see that computing the loss for a single example requires computing logits for all the words in the vocabulary. Unlike computer vision problems, where a few hundreds of output classes is more than adequate to solve most of the existing real-world problems, skip-gram does not boast such properties. Therefore, we need to turn our heads towards efficient approximations of the loss without losing efficacy of our model.

We will discuss two popular choices of approximations:

* Negative sampling
* Hierarchical softmax

## Negative sampling of the softmax layer

Here we will discuss our first approach: negative sampling the softmax layer. Negative sampling is an approximation of the **Noise-Contrastive Estimation (NCE)** method. NCE says that a good model should differentiate data from noise by means of logistic regression.

With this property in mind, let's reformulate our objective of learning word embeddings. We do not require a full-probabilistic model, which has the exact probabilities of all words in the vocabulary for a given word. What we need are high-quality word vectors. Therefore, we can simplify our problem to differentiating actual data (that is, input-output pairs) from noise (that is, K-many imaginary noise input-output pairs). By *noise*, we refer to false input-output pairs created using words that do not fall within the context of a given word. We will also get rid of the softmax activation and replace it with a sigmoid activation (also known as the logistic function). This allows us to remove the dependency of the cost function, on the full vocabulary while keeping output between [0,1]. We can visualize the negative sample process in *Figure 3.9*.

Precisely, our original loss function is given by the following equation:

$$J(\theta) = -(1/N - 2m) \sum_{i=m+1}^{N-m} \sum_{j \neq i \, j=i-m}^{i+m} log\left( exp\left( logit(x_n)_{w_j} \right) \right) - log\left( \sum_{w_k \in vocabulary} exp\left( logit(x_n)_{w_k} \right) \right)$$

The preceding formula becomes this:

$$J(\theta) = -(1/N - 2m) \sum_{i=m+1}^{N-m} \sum_{j \neq i \, j=i-m}^{i+m} log\left( \sigma\left( logit(x_n)_{w_j} \right) \right) + \sum_{q=1}^{k} \mathbb{E}_{w_q \sim vocabulary - (w_i, w_j)} log\left( 1 - \sigma\left( logit(x_n)_{w_q} \right) \right)$$

Here, σ denotes the sigmoid activation, where *σ(x)=1/(1+exp(-x))*. Note that I have replaced *logit(x_n)_{wj}* with a $log\left( exp\left( logit(x_n)_{w_j} \right) \right)$ in the original loss function, for clarity. You can see that the new loss function depends only on the calculations related to *k* items from the vocabulary.

After some simplification, we arrive at the following equation:

$$J(\theta) = -(1/N - 2m) \sum_{i=m+1}^{N-m} \sum_{j \neq i \, j=i-m}^{i+m} log\left( \sigma\left( logit(x_n)_{w_j} \right) \right) + \sum_{q=1}^{k} \mathbb{E}_{w_q \sim vocabulary - (w_i, w_j)} log\left( \sigma\left( -logit(x_n)_{w_q} \right) \right)$$

Let's take a moment to understand what this equation says. To simplify things let's assume *k=1*. This gives us the following equation:

$$J(\theta) = -(1/N - 2m) \sum_{i=m+1}^{N-m} \sum_{j \neq i \, j=i-m}^{i+m} log\left( \sigma\left( logit(x_n)_{w_j} \right) \right) + log\left( \sigma\left( -logit(x_n)_{w_q} \right) \right)$$

Here, $w_j$ represents a context word of $w_i$ and $w_q$ represents a noncontext word of $w_i$. What this equation essentially says is that, to minimize $J(\theta)$, we should make $\sigma\left(logit\left(x_n\right)_{w_j}\right) \approx 1$, which means $logit\left(x_n\right)_{w_j}$ needs to be a large positive value. Then, $\sigma\left(-logit\left(x_n\right)_{w_q}\right) \approx 1$ means that $logit\left(x_n\right)w_q$ needs to be a large negative value. In other words, for true data points representing true target words and context words should get large positive values and fake data points representing target words and noise should get large negative values. This is the same behavior you would get with a softmax function, but with more computational efficiency.

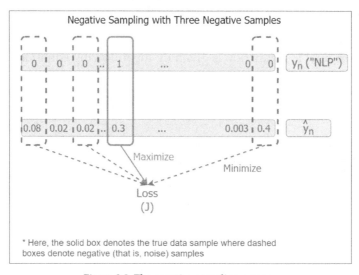

Figure 3.9: The negative sampling process

Here, $\sigma$ is the sigmoid activation. Intuitively, we do the following two steps in our loss function calculation:

- Calculating the loss for the nonzero column of $w_j$ (pushing towards positive)
- Calculating the loss for K-many noise samples (pulling towards negative)

# Hierarchical softmax

Hierarchical softmax is slightly more complex than negative sampling, but serves the same objective as the negative sampling; that is, approximating the softmax without having to calculate activations for all the words in the vocabulary for all the training samples. However, unlike negative sampling, hierarchical softmax uses only the actual data and does not need noise samples. We can visualize the hierarchical softmax model in *Figure 3.10*.

To understand hierarchical softmax, let's consider an example:

*I like NLP. Deep learning is amazing.*

The vocabulary for this is as follows:

*I, like, NLP, Deep, learning, is, amazing*

With this vocabulary, we will build a binary tree, where all the words in the vocabulary are present as leaf nodes. We will also add a special token **PAD** to make sure that all the tree leaves have two members:

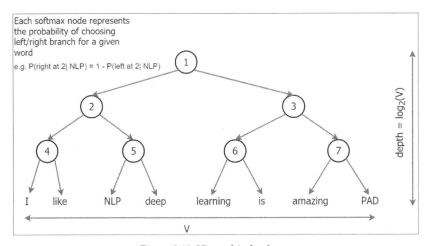

Figure 3.10: Hierarchical softmax

Then, our last hidden layer will be fully connected to all the nodes in the hierarchy (see *Figure 3.11*). Note that this model has similar amount of total weights compared with a classical softmax layer; however, it uses only a subset of them for a given calculation:

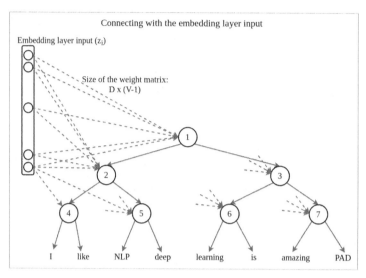

Figure 3.11: How the hierarchical softmax connects to the embedding layer

Let's say that we need to infer the probability of *P(NLP | like)*, where *like* is the input word. Then we only need a subset of the weights to calculate the probability, as shown in *Figure 3.12*:

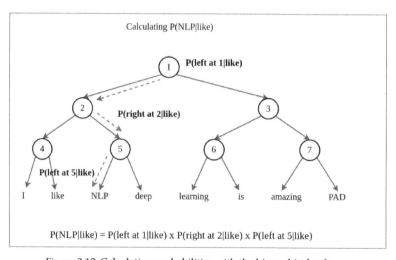

Figure 3.12: Calculating probabilities with the hierarchical softmax

Concretely, here is how the probability is calculated:

$$(NLP \mid like) = P(left \, at \, 1 \mid like) \times P(right \, at \, 2 \mid like) \times P(left \, at \, 5 \mid like)$$

Since now we know how to calculate $P(w_i \mid w_j)$, we can use the original loss function. Note that this method uses only the weights connected to the nodes in the path for calculation, resulting in a high computational efficiency.

## Learning the hierarchy

Though hierarchical softmax is efficient, an important question remains unanswered. How do we determine the decomposition of the tree? More precisely, which word will follow which branch? There are a few options to achieve this:

- **Initialize the hierarchy randomly**: This method does have some performance degradations as the random placement cannot be guaranteed to have the best branching possible among words.
- **Use WordNet to determine the hierarchy**: WordNet can be utilized to determine a suitable order for the words in the tree. This method has shown to perform significantly better than the random initialization.

## Optimizing the learning model

Since we own a well-formulated loss function, the optimization is a matter of calling the correct function from the TensorFlow library. The optimization process that will be used is a stochastic optimization process, meaning that we do not feed the full dataset at once, but only a random batch of data for many steps.

# Implementing skip-gram with TensorFlow

We will now walk through an implementation of the skip-gram algorithm that uses the TensorFlow library. Here we will only be discussing the essential parts of defining the required TensorFlow operations to learn the embeddings, not running the operations. The full exercise is available in `ch3_word2vec.ipynb` in the `ch3` exercise directory.

First let's define the hyperparameters of the model. You are free to change these hyperparameters to see how they affect final performance (for example, `batch_size = 16` or `batch_size = 256`). However, since this is a simple problem compared with the more complex real-word problems, you might not see any significant differences (unless you change them to extremes, for example, `batch_size = 1` or `num_sampled = 1`):

```
batch_size = 128
embedding_size = 128 # Dimension of the embedding vector.
window_size = 4 # How many words to consider left and right.
valid_size = 16 # Random set of words to evaluate similarity on.
# Only pick dev samples in the head of the distribution.
valid_window = 100
valid_examples = get_common_and_rare_word_ids(valid_size//2,valid_
size//2)
num_sampled = 32 # Number of negative examples to sample.
```

Next, define TensorFlow placeholders for training inputs, labels, and valid inputs:

```
train_dataset = tf.placeholder(tf.int32, shape=[batch_size])
train_labels = tf.placeholder(tf.int32, shape=[batch_size, 1])
valid_dataset = tf.constant(valid_examples, dtype=tf.int32)
```

Then, define the TensorFlow variables for the embedding layer and softmax weights and bias:

```
embeddings = tf.Variable(
  tf.random_uniform([vocabulary_size, embedding_size], -1.0, 1.0))
softmax_weights = tf.Variable(
  tf.truncated_normal([vocabulary_size, embedding_size],
stddev=0.5 / math.sqrt(embedding_size)))
softmax_biases =
  tf.Variable(tf.random_uniform([vocabulary_size],0.0,0.01))
```

Next, we will define an embedding lookup operation that gathers the corresponding embeddings of a given batch of training inputs:

```
embed = tf.nn.embedding_lookup(embeddings, train_dataset)
```

Afterwards, we will define the softmax loss, using a negative sampling:

```
loss = tf.reduce_mean(
  tf.nn.sampled_softmax_loss(weights=softmax_weights,
  biases=softmax_biases, inputs=embed,
  labels=train_labels, num_sampled=num_sampled,
  num_classes=vocabulary_size))
```

Here we define an optimizer to optimize (minimize) the preceding defined `loss` function. Feel free to experiment with other optimizers listed at `https://www.tensorflow.org/api_guides/python/train`:

```
optimizer = tf.train.AdagradOptimizer(1.0).minimize(loss)
```

Compute the similarity between validation input examples and all embeddings. The cosine distance is used:

```
norm = tf.sqrt(tf.reduce_sum(tf.square(embeddings), 1, keepdims=True))
normalized_embeddings = embeddings / norm
valid_embeddings = tf.nn.embedding_lookup(
  normalized_embeddings, valid_dataset)
similarity = tf.matmul(valid_embeddings,
  tf.transpose(normalized_embeddings))
```

With all the TensorFlow variables and operations defined, we can now move onto executing the operations to get some results. Here we will outline the basic procedure for executing these operations. You can refer to the exercise file for a complete view of the execution.

- First initialize the TensorFlow variables with `tf.global_variables_initializer().run()`

- For each step (for a predefined number of total steps), do the following:

    ◦ Generate a batch of data (`batch_data` – inputs, `batch_labels` – outputs) using the data generator

    ◦ Create a dictionary called `feed_dict` that maps train input/output placeholders to data generated by the data generator:
    ```
    feed_dict = {train_dataset : batch_data, train_labels : batch_labels}
    ```

    ◦ Execute an optimization step and obtain the loss value as follows:
    ```
    _, l = session.run([optimizer, loss], feed_dict=feed_dict)
    ```

We will now discuss another popular Word2vec algorithm known as the **Continuous Bag-of-Words (CBOW)** model.

# The Continuous Bag-of-Words algorithm

The CBOW model has a working similar to the skip-gram algorithm with one significant change in the problem formulation. In the skip-gram model, we predicted the context words from the target word. However, in the CBOW model, we will predict the target from contextual words. Let's compare what data looks like for skip-gram and CBOW by taking the previous example sentence:

*The dog barked at the mailman.*

For skip-gram, data tuples — *(input word, output word)* — might look like this:

*(dog, the)*, *(dog, barked)*, *(barked, dog)*, and so on.

For CBOW, data tuples would look like the following:

*([the, barked], dog)*, *([dog, at], barked)*, and so on.

Consequently, the input of the CBOW has a dimensionality of $2 \times m \times D$, where $m$ is the context window size and $D$ is the dimensionality of the embeddings. The conceptual model of CBOW is shown in *Figure 3.13*:

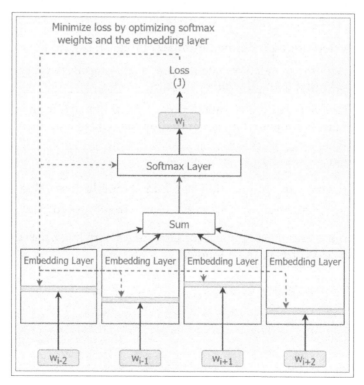

Figure 3.13: The CBOW model

We will not go into great details about the intricacies of CBOW as they are quite similar to those of skip-gram. However, we will discuss the algorithm implementation (though not in depth, as it shares a lot of similarities with skip-gram) to get a clear understanding of how to properly implement CBOW. The full implementation of CBOW is available at `ch3_word2vec.ipynb` in the `ch3` exercise folder.

# Implementing CBOW in TensorFlow

First, we define the variables; this is same as in the case of the skip-gram model:

```
embeddings = tf.Variable(tf.random_uniform([vocabulary_size,
  embedding_size], -1.0, 1.0, dtype=tf.float32))
softmax_weights = tf.Variable(
  tf.truncated_normal([vocabulary_size, embedding_size],
  stddev=1.0 / math.sqrt(embedding_size),
  dtype=tf.float32))
softmax_biases =
  tf.Variable(tf.zeros([vocabulary_size],dtype=tf.float32))
```

Here, we are creating a stacked set of embeddings, representing each position of the context. So we will have a matrix of size *[batch_size, embeddings_size, 2*context_window_size]*. Then, we will use a reduction operator to reduce the stacked matrix to that of size *[batch_size, embedding size]* by averaging the stacked embeddings over the last axis:

```
stacked_embedings = None
for i in range(2*window_size):
  embedding_i = tf.nn.embedding_lookup(embeddings,
  train_dataset[:,i])
  x_size,y_size = embedding_i.get_shape().as_list()
  if stacked_embedings is None:
    stacked_embedings = tf.reshape(embedding_i, [x_size,y_size,1])
  else:
    stacked_embedings =
    tf.concat(axis=2,
      values=[stacked_embedings,
      tf.reshape(embedding_i,[x_size,y_size,1])]
    )

assert stacked_embedings.get_shape().as_list()[2]==2*window_size
mean_embedings = tf.reduce_mean(stacked_embedings,2,keepdims=False)
```

Thereafter, `loss` and `optimizer` are defined as in the skip-gram model:

```
loss = tf.reduce_mean(
    tf.nn.sampled_softmax_loss(weights=softmax_weights,
        biases=softmax_biases,
        inputs=mean_embeddings,
        labels=train_labels,
        num_sampled=num_sampled,
        num_classes=vocabulary_size))
optimizer = tf.train.AdagradOptimizer(1.0).minimize(loss)
```

# Summary

Word embeddings have become an integral part of many NLP tasks and are widely used for tasks such as machine translation, chatbots, image caption generation, and language modeling. Not only do word embeddings act as a dimensionality reduction technique (compared to one-hot encoding) but they also give a richer feature representation than other existing techniques. In this chapter, we discussed two popular neural network-based methods for learning word representations, namely the skip-gram model and the CBOW model.

First, we discussed the classical approaches to develop an understanding about how word representations were learned in the past. We discussed various methods such as using WordNet, building a co-occurrence matrix of the words, and calculating TF-IDF. Later, we discussed the limitations of these approaches.

This motivated us to explore neural network-based word representation learning methods. First, we worked out an example by hand to understand how word embeddings or word vectors can be calculated and one use case of word vectors to learn the interesting things that can be done with word vectors.

Next, we discussed the first word-embedding learning algorithm—the skip-gram model. We then learned how to prepare the data to be used for learning. Later, we examined how to design a loss function that allows us to use word embeddings using the context words of a given word. Afterwards, we discussed a crucial limitation of the close-form loss function we developed. The loss function is not scalable for large vocabularies. Later we analyzed two popular approximations of the close-form loss that allowed us to calculate the loss efficiently and effectively—negative sampling and hierarchical softmax. Finally, we discussed how to implement the skip-gram algorithm using TensorFlow.

Then we reviewed the next choice for learning word embeddings—the CBOW model. We also discussed how CBOW differs from the skip-gram model. Finally, we discussed a TensorFlow implementation of CBOW as well.

In the next chapter, we will analyze the performance of the Word2vec techniques we learned and also learn several extensions that significantly improve their performance. Furthermore, we will learn another word embedding learning technique known as Global Vectors or GloVe.

# 4
# Advanced Word2vec

In *Chapter 3*, *Word2vec – Learning Word Embeddings*, we introduced you to Word2vec, the basics of learning word embeddings, and the two common Word2vec algorithms: skip-gram and CBOW. In this chapter, we will discuss several topics related to Word2vec, focusing on these two algorithms and extensions.

First, we will explore how the original skip-gram algorithm was implemented and how it compares to its more modern variant, which we used in *Chapter 3*, *Word2vec – Learning Word Embeddings*. We will examine the differences between skip-gram and CBOW and look at the behavior of the loss over time of the two approaches. We will also discuss which method works better, using both our observation and the available literature.

We will discuss several extensions to the existing Word2vec methods that boost performance. These extensions include using more effective sampling techniques to sample negative examples for negative sampling and ignoring uninformative words in the learning process, among others. You will also learn a novel word embedding learning technique known as **Global Vectors (GloVe)** and the specific advantages that GloVe has over skip-gram and CBOW.

Finally, you will learn how to use Word2vec to solve a real-world problem: document classification. We will see this with a simple trick of obtaining document embeddings from word embeddings.

# The original skip-gram algorithm

The skip-gram algorithm discussed up to this point in the book is actually an improvement over the original skip-gram algorithm proposed in the original paper by Mikolov and others, published in 2013. In this paper, the algorithm did not use an intermediate hidden layer to learn the representations. In contrast, the original algorithm used two different embedding or projection layers (the input and output embeddings in *Figure 4.1*) and defined a cost function derived from the embeddings themselves:

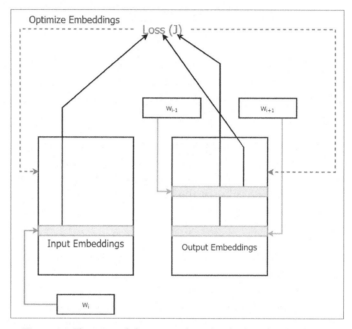

Figure 4.1: The original skip-gram algorithm without hidden layers

The original negative sampled loss was defined as follows:

$$J(\theta) = -\left(\frac{1}{N-2m}\right)\sum_{i=m+1}^{N-m}\sum_{j\neq i \wedge j=i-m}^{i+m} log\left(\sigma\left(v'_{w_j}{}^T v_{w_i}\right)\right) + kE_{w_q \sim P_n(w)}\left[log\sigma\left(-v'_{w_q}{}^T v_{w_i}\right)\right]$$

Here, $v$ is the input embeddings layer, $v'$ is the output word embeddings layer, $v_{w_i}$ corresponds to the embedding vector for the word $w_i$ in the input embeddings layer and $v'_{w_i}$ corresponds to the word vector for the word $w_i$ in the output embeddings layer. $P_n(w)$ is the noise distribution, from which we sample noise samples (for example, it can be as simple as uniformly sampling from vocabulary — $\{w_i, w_j\}$, as we saw in *Chapter 3, Word2vec – Learning Word Embeddings*). Finally, $E$ denotes the expectation (average) of the loss obtained from k-negative samples. As you can see, there are no weights and bias in this equation except for the word embeddings themselves.

# Implementing the original skip-gram algorithm

Implementing the original skip-gram algorithm is not as straightforward as the version we have already implemented. This is because the loss function needs to be handcrafted using TensorFlow functions as there is no built-in function for calculating the loss as we had for the other algorithms.

First, let's define placeholders for the following:

- **Input data**: This is a placeholder containing a batch of target words of the `[batch_size]` shape

- **Output data**: This is a placeholder containing the corresponding context words for the batch of target words and is of size, `[batch_size, 1]`

```
train_dataset = tf.placeholder(tf.int32, shape=[batch_size])
train_labels = tf.placeholder(tf.int64, shape=[batch_size, 1])
```

With the input and output placeholders defined, we can use a TensorFlow built-in `candidate_sampler` to sample negative samples as shown in the following code:

```
negative_samples, _, _ = tf.nn.log_uniform_candidate_sampler(
                                train_labels, num_true=1,
                                num_sampled=num_sampled,
                                unique=True,
                                range_max=vocabulary_size)
```

Here we sample negative words uniformly without any special preference for different words. `train_labels` are the true samples, so TensorFlow can avoid producing them as negative samples. Then we have the number of `num_true`, which denotes number of true classes for a given data point, which is 1. Next comes the number of negative samples we want for a batch of data (`num_sampled`). `unique` defines whether the negative samples should be unique. Finally, `range` defines the maximum ID a word has, so that the sampler doesn't produce any invalid word IDs.

We get rid of the softmax weights and biases. Then, we introduce two embedding layers, one for the input data and the other for the output data.

Two embedding layers are needed because if we had only one embedding layer, the cost function would not work, as discussed in *Chapter 3, Word2vec – Learning Word Embeddings*.

Let's embed lookups for the input data, output data, and negative samples:

```
in_embed = tf.nn.embedding_lookup(in_embeddings, train_dataset)
out_embed = tf.nn.embedding_lookup(out_embeddings, tf.reshape(
                                    train_labels,[-1]))
negative_embed = tf.nn.embedding_lookup(out_embeddings,
                                        negative_samples)
```

Next, we will define the loss function, and it is the most important part of the code. This code implements the loss function we discussed earlier. However, as we defined in the loss function $J(\theta)$, we do not calculate the loss for all the words in a document at once. This is due to the fact that a document can be too large to fit into the memory fully. Therefore, we calculate the loss for small batches of data at a single time step. The full code is available in the ch4_word2vec_improvements.ipynb exercise book located in the ch4 folder:

```
# Computing the loss for the positive sample
loss = tf.reduce_mean(
    tf.log(
        tf.nn.sigmoid(
            tf.reduce_sum(
                tf.diag([1.0 for _ in range(batch_size)])*
                tf.matmul(out_embed,tf.transpose(in_embed)),
            axis=0)
        )
    )
)


# Computing loss for the negative samples
loss += tf.reduce_mean(
    tf.reduce_sum(
        tf.log(tf.nn.sigmoid(
            -tf.matmul(negative_embed,tf.transpose(in_embed))))),
        axis=0
    )
)
```

Tensorflow implements `sampled_softmax_loss` by defining a smaller subset of weights and biases that are only required to process the current batch of data, from the full softmax weights and biases. Thereafter, TensorFlow computes the loss similar to the standard softmax cross entropy calculation. However, we cannot directly translate that approach to calculate the original skip-gram loss as there are no softmax weights and biases.

# Comparing the original skip-gram with the improved skip-gram

We should have a good reason to use a hidden layer in contrast to the original skip-gram algorithm which does not use one. Therefore, we will observe the loss function behavior of the original skip-gram algorithm and the hidden-layer-including skip-gram algorithm in *Figure 4.2*:

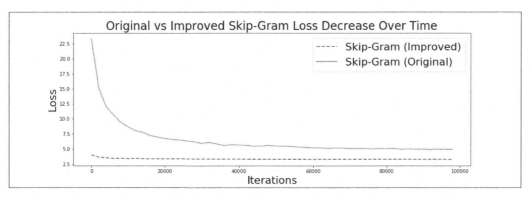

Figure 4.2: The original skip-gram algorithm versus the improved skip-gram algorithm

We can clearly see that having a hidden layer leads to better performance compared with not having one. This also suggest that deeper Word2vec models tend to perform better.

# Comparing skip-gram with CBOW

Before looking at the performance differences and investigating reasons, let's remind ourselves about the fundamental difference between the skip-gram and CBOW methods.

As shown in the following figures, given a context and a target word, skip-gram observes only the target word and a single word of the context in a single input/output tuple. However, CBOW observes the target word and all the words in the context in a single sample. For example, if we assume the phrase *dog barked at the mailman*, skip-gram sees an input-output tuple such as *["dog", "at"]* at a single time step, whereas CBOW sees an input-output tuple *[["dog","barked","the","mailman"], "at"]*. Therefore, in a given batch of data, CBOW receives more information than skip-gram about the context of a given word. Let's next see how this difference affects the performance of the two algorithms.

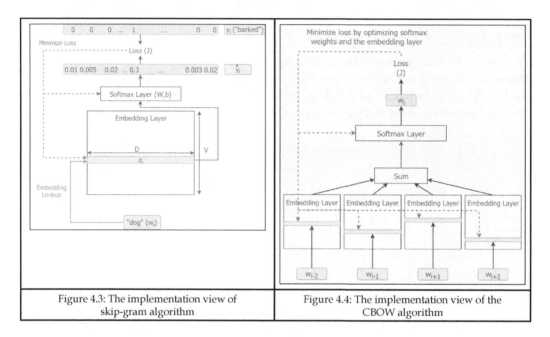

| Figure 4.3: The implementation view of skip-gram algorithm | Figure 4.4: The implementation view of the CBOW algorithm |
|---|---|

As shown in the preceding figures, the CBOW model has access to more information (inputs) at a given time compared to the skip-gram algorithm, allowing CBOW to perform perform better in certain conditions.

# Performance comparison

Now let's plot the loss over time for both skip-gram and CBOW in the task we trained the models earlier in *Chapter 3, Word2vec – Learning Word Embeddings* (see *Figure 4.4*):

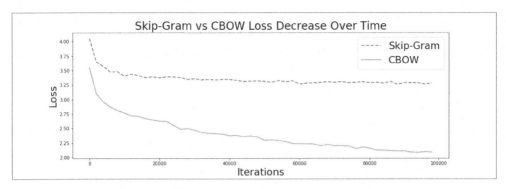

Figure 4.5: Loss decrease: skip-gram versus CBOW

We discussed that, compared to the skip-gram algorithm, CBOW has access to more information about the context of a given target word for a given input-output tuple. We can see that CBOW shows a rapid decrease of the loss compared to the skip-gram model. However, loss itself is an inadequate measure of performance, as the loss can be rapidly dwindling due to overfitting to the training data. Though there are benchmark tasks that are used to evaluate the quality of word embeddings (for example, word analogy tasks), we will use a simpler way of inspection. Let's visually inspect the learned embeddings in order to make sure that skip-gram and CBOW show a significant semantic difference between them. For this, we use a popular visualization technique known as **t-Distributed Stochastic Neighbor Embedding (t-SNE)**.

It should be noted that the reduction of loss is not a very convincing metric to evaluate the performance of a word embedding system, because the sampled softmax we use to measure loss is a significant underestimate of the full softmax loss. Performances of word embeddings are often evaluated in terms of word analogy tasks. A typical word analogy task might ask this:

Aware to unaware is like impressive to _____.

So, a good embedding set should answer this with *unimpressive*. This can be computed with a simple arithmetic operation given by embedding(impressive) - [embedding(aware) - embedding(unaware)]. If the resulting vector has the embedding of the word unimpressive as its nearest neighbor, then you have obtained the correct answer.

There are several word analogy testing datasets available, such as the following:

- **Google analogy dataset**: http://download.tensorflow.org/data/questions-words.txt
- **Bigger Analogy Test Set (BATS)**: http://vsm.blackbird.pw/bats

In *Figure 4.6*, we can see that CBOW tends to cluster the words together more than skip-gram, where words seem to be distributed across the full space sparsely. Therefore, we can say that CBOW looks visually appealing compared to skip-gram, in this particular example:

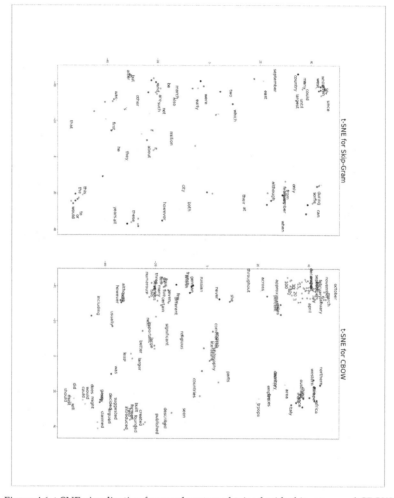

Figure 4.6: t-SNE visualization for word vectors obtained with skip-gram and CBOW

We will use the scikit-learn provided t-SNE algorithm to compute the low-dimensional representation and then visualize it through Matplotlib. However, TensorFlow provides a much more convenient embedding visualization option through its visualization framework TensorBoard. You can find an exercise of this in `tensorboard_word_embeddings.ipynb` located in the `appendix` folder.

**t-SNE – a brief tour**

t-SNE is a visualization technique that can visualize high-dimensional data (for example, images and word embeddings) in lower two-dimensional space. We will not dive into all the complex mathematics behind the technique, but only understand how the algorithm works on a more intuitive level.

Let's define the notations first. $x_i \in R^D$ denotes a $D$-dimensional data point and $X = \{x_i\}$ is the input space. For example, this can be a word-embedding vector similar to the ones we covered in *Chapter 3, Word2vec – Learning Word Embeddings*, and $D$ is the embedding size. Next, let's imagine a hypothetical two-dimensional space $Y = \{y_i\}$, where $y_i$ denotes a two-dimensional vector corresponding to the $x_i$ data point; $X$ and $Y$ have a one-to-one mapping. We will refer to $Y$ as the map space and $y_i$ as the map points.

Now let's define a conditional probability $P_{j|i}$ that defines the probability that the $x_i$ data point will pick $x_j$ as its neighbor. $P_{j|i}$ needs to be low when point $x_j$ is far from $x_i$ and vise versa. An intuitive choice for $P_{j|i}$ is a Gaussian centered at the $x_i$ data point with the $\sigma^2_i$ variance. The variance will be low for data points with dense neighborhoods and high for data points with sparse neighborhoods. Concretely, the formula for the conditional probability is given by:

$$p_{j|i} = \frac{exp\left(-\|x_i - x_j\|^2 / 2\sigma_i^2\right)}{\sum_{k \neq i} exp\left(-\|x_i - x_k\|^2 / 2\sigma_i^2\right)}$$

Similarly, we can define a similar conditional probability for map points $y_i$ in space $Y$, $q_{j|i}$.

Now, in order to obtain a good low-dimensional representation $Y$ of the high-dimensional space $X$, $p_{j|i}$ and $q_{j|i}$ should demonstrate similar behaviors. That is, if two data points are similar in the $X$ space, they should be similar in space $Y$ as well, and vice versa. Therefore, the problem of getting a good two-dimensional representation of the data boils down to minimizing the mismatch between $p_{j|i}$ and $q_{j|i}$ for all $i = 1, \ldots, N$.

This problem can be formally formulated as minimizing the Kullback-Leibler divergence between $p_{j|i}$ and $q_{j|i}$ denoted by $KL\left(p_{j|i} \| q_{j|i}\right)$. Therefore, the cost function for our problem is:

$$C = \sum_{i=1}^{N} KL\left(p_{j|i} \| q_{j|i}\right) == \sum_{i=1}^{N} \sum_{j \neq i} p_{j|i} log\left(\frac{p_{j|i}}{q_{j|i}}\right)$$

Also, by minimizing this $C$ cost by means of stochastic gradient descent, we can find an optimal representation $Y$ that matches closely with $X$.

Intuitively, this process can be thought of as an equilibrium reached by a collection of springs attached between all the pairs of data points. $p_{j|i}$ is the stiffness of the spring between the $x_i$ and $x_j$ data points. Therefore, when $x_i$ and $x_j$ are similar, they will remain close to each other and far apart when they are dissimilar. Therefore, $C$ for a particular data point acts as the total force acting on that data point and will cause it to either attract or repel for all the other data points according to the total force.

# Which is the winner, skip-gram or CBOW?

There is no clear-cut winner between skip-gram and CBOW when it comes to performance. For example, the paper *Distributed Representations of Words and Phrases and their Compositionality, Mikolov and others, 2013* suggests that skip-gram works better in semantic tasks, whereas CBOW works better in syntactic tasks. However, skip-gram appears to perform better than CBOW in most tasks, which contradicts our findings.

Various empirical evidence suggests that skip-gram works well with large datasets compared to CBOW, and that is supported in *Distributed Representations of Words and Phrases and their Compositionality, Mikolov and others, 2013* and *GloVe: Global Vectors for Word Representation, Pennington and others, 2014*, which usually use corpora of billions of words. However, our task involved a few hundred thousand words, which is comparatively small. For this reason, CBOW might be performing better.

Now let me explain why I believe this is the case. Consider the following two sentences:

- *It is a nice day*
- *It is a brilliant day*

For CBOW, input-output tuples would look like this:

*[[It, is, nice, day], a]*

*[[It, is, brilliant, day],a]*

And input output tuples for skip-gram would look like this:

*[It, a], [is, a], [nice, a], [day, a]*

*[It, a], [is, a], [brilliant, a], [day, a]*

We would like our model to understand that *nice* and *brilliant* are slightly different things (that is, brilliant means nicer than nice). Such words having subtle differences in meaning are called *nuances*. We can see that, for CBOW, there is a high chance that it would see *brilliant* and *nice* as the same thing, because their semantics get averaged by the surrounding words (*It*, *is*, and *day*) as these words are also a part of the input. By contrast, for skip-gram, the words *nice* and *brilliant* appear separated from *It*, *is*, and *day*, allowing skip-gram to pay more attention to subtle differences between words (such as *brilliant* and *nice*) than CBOW.

However, note that there are millions of parameters in our model. To train such models, a lot of data is needed. CBOW somehow circumvents this problem by trying not to focus learning subtle differences in words, but by just an averaging of all the words in a given context (for example, average semantic of *It is nice day* or *It is brilliant day*). However, skip-gram would learn more meticulous representations because there is no averaging effect as in CBOW. To learn meticulous representations, skip-gram would require more data. But once more data is provided, skip-gram will most likely outperform the CBOW algorithm.

In addition, note that a single input to the CBOW model is approximately equal to $2 \times m$ many inputs for the skip-gram model, where $m$ is the context window size. This is because a single input to the skip-gram consists only of a single word, where a single input to CBOW has $2 \times m$ many words. So, to make this a fairer comparison, if we run CBOW for $L$ steps, we should run the skip-gram algorithm for $2m \times L$ steps.

So far, you have learned how skip-gram was initially implemented — it had two embedding layers (one to look up input words and the other to look up output words). We discussed how the skip-gram algorithm discussed in *Chapter 3, Word2vec – Learning Word Embeddings*, actually is an improvement of the original skip-gram algorithm. We saw that the improved skip-gram in fact outperforms the original algorithm. Then, we compared performances of skip-gram and CBOW and saw that, in our example, CBOW performs better. Finally, we discussed some of the reasons why CBOW might be performing better than skip-gram.

# Extensions to the word embeddings algorithms

The original paper by Mikolov and others, published in 2013, discusses several extensions that can improve the performance of the word embedding learning algorithms even further. Though they are initially introduced to be used for skip-gram, they are extendable to CBOW as well. Also, as we already saw that CBOW outperforms the skip-gram algorithm in our example, we will use CBOW for understanding all the extensions.

## Using the unigram distribution for negative sampling

It has been found that the performance results of negative sampling are better when performed by sampling from certain distributions rather than from the uniform distribution. One such distribution is the **unigram distribution**. The unigram probability of a word $w_i$ is given by the following equation:

$$U(w_i) = \frac{count(w_i)}{\sum_{j \in Corpus} count(w_j)}$$

Here, *count(w_i)* is the number of times $w_i$ appears in the document. When the unigram distribution is distorted as $U(w_i)^{(3/4)} / Z$ for some constant $Z$, it has shown to provide better performance than the uniform distribution or the standard unigram distribution.

Let's use an example to understand the unigram distribution better. Consider the following sentences:

*Bob is a football fan. He is on the school football team.*

Here, the unigram probability of the word *football* would be as follows:

Similar to tf/idf

$$U(football) = 2/12 = 1/6$$

It can be seen that the unigram probability for common words will be higher. These common words tend to be very uninformative words, such as *the*, *a*, and *is*. Therefore, such frequent words will be negatively sampled more during the cost optimization, leading to more informative words being less negatively sampled. Consequently, this creates a balance between the common words and rare words during the optimization, leading to better performance.

# Implementing unigram-based negative sampling

Here, we will see how we can implement unigram-based negative sampling with TensorFlow:

```
unigrams = [0 for _ in range(vocabulary_size)]
for word,w_count in count:
    w_idx = dictionary[word]
    unigrams[w_idx] = w_count*1.0/token_count
    word_count_dictionary[w_idx] = w_count
```

Here, `count` is a list of tuples, where each tuple is made of (`word ID`, `frequency`). This algorithm computes the unigram probabilities of each word and returns them as a list ordered by the index of the word. (This is a specific format for the unigrams stipulated by TensorFlow). This is available as an exercise in `ch4_word2vec_improvements.ipynb`, located in the `ch4` folder.

Next, we calculate up to the embedding lookups as we normally did for CBOW:

```
train_dataset = tf.placeholder(tf.int32, shape=[batch_size,
    window_size*2])
train_labels = tf.placeholder(tf.int32, shape=[batch_size, 1])
valid_dataset = tf.constant(valid_examples, dtype=tf.int32)

# Variables.
# embedding, vector for each word in the vocabulary
embeddings = tf.Variable(tf.random_uniform([vocabulary_size,
    embedding_size], -1.0, 1.0, dtype=tf.float32))
softmax_weights =
    tf.Variable(tf.truncated_normal([vocabulary_size,
    embedding_size],
    stddev=1.0 / math.sqrt(embedding_size), dtype=tf.float32))
softmax_biases =
    tf.Variable(tf.zeros([vocabulary_size], dtype=tf.float32))

stacked_embedings = None

for i in range(2*window_size):
    embedding_i = tf.nn.embedding_lookup(embeddings,
    train_dataset[:,i])
    x_size,y_size = embedding_i.get_shape().as_list()
    if stacked_embedings is None:
        stacked_embedings =
            tf.reshape(embedding_i, [x_size,y_size,1])
    else:
```

```
        stacked_embedings =
            tf.concat(axis=2,values=[stacked_embedings,
            tf.reshape(embedding_i,[x_size,y_size,1])])
    mean_embeddings = tf.reduce_mean(stacked_embedings,2,keepdims=False)
```

Next, we'll sample negative examples based on the unigram distribution. To do this, we'll use the TensorFlow built-in function `tf.nn.fixed_unigram_candidate_sampler`:

```
candidate_sampler = tf.nn.fixed_unigram_candidate_sampler(
    true_classes = tf.cast(train_labels, dtype=tf.int64),
    num_true = 1, num_sampled = num_sampled, unique = True,
    range_max = vocabulary_size, distortion=0.75,
    num_reserved_ids=0, unigrams=unigrams, name='unigram_sampler')


loss = tf.reduce_mean(
    tf.nn.sampled_softmax_loss(weights=softmax_weights,
    biases=softmax_biases, inputs=mean_embeddings,
    labels=train_labels, num_sampled=num_sampled,
    num_classes=vocabulary_size, sampled_values=candidate_sampler))
```

This code snippet provides the general flow of implementing the word-embedding learning with unigram-based negative sampling. Generally, the following steps take place:

1. Defining the variables, placeholders, and hyperparameters.
2. For each batch of data, the following occurs:
    1. Computing the mean input embedding matrix by looking up the embeddings for each index of the context window and averaging them
    2. Calculating the loss by means of negative sampling, sampled according to the unigram distribution
    3. Optimizing the neural network using stochastic gradient descent

The following one-liner code extracted from the preceding code snippet plays the most important role in this algorithm by producing negative samples generated according to the distorted unigram distribution:

```
candidate_sampler = tf.nn.fixed_unigram_candidate_sampler(
    true_classes = tf.cast(train_labels,dtype=tf.int64),
    num_true = 1, num_sampled = num_sampled, unique = True,
    range_max = vocabulary_size, distortion=0.75,
    num_reserved_ids=0, unigrams=unigrams, name='unigram_sampler')
```

We will go through each argument in this function in detail:

- `true_classes`: This is a vector of the `batch_size` size that provides the target word ID (an integer) for a given batch of context words corresponding to that target word.

- `num_true`: This is the number of true elements for a given word (often 1).

- `num_sampled`: This is the number of negative elements to sample for a single input.

- `unique`: This says to sample unique negative samples (no replacement).

- `range_max`: This is the size of the vocabulary.

- `distortion`: This returns the unigram sample raised to the power given by the value distortion. In our example it is 3/4 = (0.75).

- `num_reserved_ids`: This is a list of indices indicating words from the vocabulary. The IDs in `num_reserved_ids` will not be sampled as negative samples.

- `unigrams`: These are unigram probabilities ordered by the ID of the word.

# Subsampling – probabilistically ignoring the common words

Subsampling, or ignoring common words, also has proved to provide better performance. This can be understood intuitively as follows—the input-output words extracted from a finite context (*"The"*, *"France"*) provide less information than the tuple (*"Paris"*, *"France"*). Therefore, it is a better choice to ignore such uninformative words (or stop words), such as *the*, being sampled frequently from the corpus. Mathematically, this is achieved by ignoring the word $w_i$ in the sequence of words in the corpus with a probability:

$$1 - \sqrt{\frac{t}{f(w_i)}}$$

Here, *t* is a constant that controls the threshold of the word frequency that causes to ignore words and $f(w_i)$ is the frequency of $w_i$ in the corpus. This effectively reduces the frequency of stop words (for example, "the", "a", "of", ".", and ","), thus creating more balance in the dataset.

# Implementing subsampling

Implementing subsampling is quite simple, as shown in the following example code snippet. We'll create a new word sequence from the original sequence by dropping words from the sequence with the probability obtained as we just saw, and use this new word sequence for learning the word embeddings. Here we have chosen $t$ as 10,000:

```
subsampled_data = []
for w_i in data:
    p_w_i = 1 - np.sqrt(1e5/word_count_dictionary[w_i])

    if np.random.random() < p_w_i:
        drop_count += 1
        drop_examples.append(reverse_dictionary[w_i])
    else:
        subsampled_data.append(w_i)
```

# Comparing the CBOW and its extensions

In *Figure 4.6*, we'll see the different loss decreases of CBOW, the CBOW with unigram-based negative sampling—**CBOW(Unigram)**—and CBOW with unigram-based negative sampling and subsampling—**CBOW (Unigram+Subsampling)**:

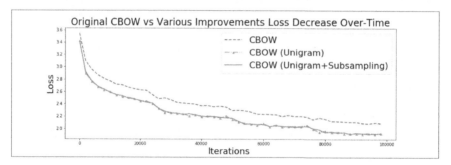

Figure 4.6: Loss behavior with original CBOW and two extensions to CBOW

It is quite interesting to see that having both unigram and subsampling improvements gives a similar looking loss value overall compared to having only unigram-based negative sampling. However, this should not be misunderstood as a lack of advantage of subsampling on the learning problem. The reason for this particular behavior can be understood as follows. As with subsampling, we get rid of many uninformative words, so the quality of the text increases (in terms of information quality). This in turn makes the learning problem more difficult. In the previous problem setting, the word vectors had the opportunity to exploit the abundance of uninformative words in the optimization process, whereas in the new problem setting, such chances are rare. This results in a higher loss, but semantically sound word vectors.

# More recent algorithms extending skip-gram and CBOW

We already saw that the Word2vec techniques are quite powerful in capturing semantics of words. However, they are not without their limitations. For example, they do not pay attention to the distance between a context word and the target word. However, if the context word is further away from the target word, its impact on the target word should be less. Therefore, we will discuss techniques that pay separate attention to different positions in the context. Another limitation of Word2vec is that it only pays attention to a very small window around a given word when computing the word vector. However, in reality, the way the word co-occurs throughout a corpus should be considered to compute good word vectors. So, we will look at a technique that not only looks at the context of a word, but also at the global co-occurrence information of the word.

# A limitation of the skip-gram algorithm

The previously-discussed skip-gram algorithm and all its variants ignore the localization of contextual words within a given context. In other words, skip-gram does not exploit the exact position of a context word within the context, but treats all the words within a given context equally. For example, let's consider a sentence:

*The dog barked at the mailman.*

Let's consider a window size of 2 and the target word, *barked*. Then the context for the word *barked* would be *the*, *dog*, *at*, and *the*. Also, we will compose four data points *("barked", "the")*, *("barked", "dog")*, *("barked", "at")*, and *("barked", "the")*, where the first element of the tuple is the input word and the second is the output word. If we consider two data points from this collection, *("barked", "the")* and *("barked, "dog")*, the original skip-gram algorithm will treat both these tuples equally during the optimization. In other words, skip-gram ignores the actual position of a context word in the context. However, from a linguistic perspective, clearly the tuple *("barked", "dog")* carries more information than *("barked", "the")*. Essentially, the structured skip-gram algorithm attempts to address this limitation. Let's see how this is solved in the next section.

# The structured skip-gram algorithm

The structured skip-gram algorithm uses the architecture shown in *Figure 4.7* to tackle the limitation of the original skip-gram algorithm discussed in the preceding section:

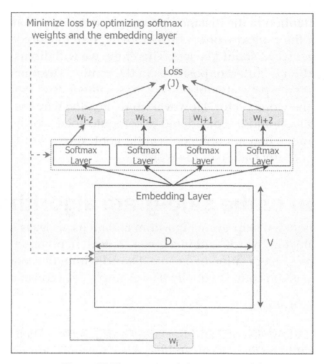

Figure 4.7. The structured skip-gram model

As shown here, structured skip-gram preserves the structure or localization of the context words during the optimization. However, it poses a higher memory requirement, as the number of parameters is linearly dependent on the window size. More precisely, for a window size $m$ (that is, on one side), if the original skip-gram model had $P$ parameters in the softmax layer, the structured skip-gram algorithm will have $2mP$ parameters, as we have a set of $P$ parameters for each position in the context window.

# The loss function

The original negative sampled softmax loss for the skip-gram model looked like this:

$$J(\theta) = -\left(1/N - 2m\right) \sum_{i=m+1}^{N-m} \sum_{j \neq i\, j=i-m}^{i+m} log\left(\sigma\left(logit\left(x_n\right)_{w_j}\right)\right) + \sum_{q=1}^{k} \mathbb{E}_{w_q \sim vocabulary - \{w_i, w_j\}} log\left(\sigma\left(-logit\left(x_n\right)_{w_q}\right)\right)$$

For structured skip-gram, we use the following loss:

$$J(\theta) = \sum_{p=1}^{2m} -(1/N-2m) \sum_{i=m+1}^{N-m} \sum_{j \neq i\, j=i-m}^{i+m} log\left(\sigma\left(logit_k\left(x_n\right)_{w_j}\right)\right) + \sum_{q=1}^{k} \mathbb{E}_{w_q \sim vocabulary - \{w_i, w_j\}} log\left(\sigma\left(-logit_p\left(x_n\right)_{w_q}\right)\right)$$

Here, $logit_p\left(x_n\right)_{w_j}$ is calculated using the $p^{th}$ set of softmax weights and softmax bias corresponding to the index of $w_j$ position.

This is implemented as shown in the following code, which is available in `ch4_word2vec_extended.ipynb` in the `ch4` folder. As we can see, we now have $2 \times m$ softmax weights and biases, and the embedding vectors corresponding to each context position are propagated through their corresponding softmax weight and bias.

First, we'll define input and output placeholders:

```
train_dataset = tf.placeholder(tf.int32, shape=[batch_size])
train_labels = [tf.placeholder(tf.int32, shape=[batch_size, 1]) for _
in range(2*window_size)]
```

Then we'll define the calculations required to calculate loss, starting from the training inputs and labels:

```
# Variables.
embeddings = tf.Variable(
    tf.random_uniform([vocabulary_size, embedding_size],
    -1.0, 1.0))
softmax_weights = [tf.Variable(
    tf.truncated_normal([vocabulary_size, embedding_size],
    stddev=0.5 / math.sqrt(embedding_size))) for _ in range(2*window_
size)]
softmax_biases =
    [tf.Variable(tf.random_uniform([vocabulary_size],0.0,0.01)) for _
in range(2*window_size)]

# Model.
# Look up embeddings for inputs.
embed = tf.nn.embedding_lookup(embeddings, train_dataset)
# Compute the softmax loss, using a sample of
# the negative labels each time.
loss = tf.reduce_sum(
    [
        tf.reduce_mean(tf.nn.sampled_softmax_loss(
            weights=softmax_weights[wi],
            biases=softmax_biases[wi], inputs=embed,
            labels=train_labels[wi], num_sampled=num_sampled,
```

```
            num_classes=vocabulary_size))
      for wi in range(window_size*2)
   ]
 )
```

Structured skip-gram addresses an important limitation of the standard skip-gram algorithm, which is paying attention to the position of context words during learning. This is achieved by introducing a separate set of softmax weights and a bias for each position of the context. This leads to an improved performance, which however possesses a high memory requirement due to the increased amount of parameters. Next, we will see a similar extension to the CBOW model.

# The continuous window model

The continuous window model extends the CBOW algorithm in a way similar to the one in the structured skip-gram algorithm. In the original CBOW algorithm, the embeddings found for all the context words are averaged before propagating through the softmax layer. However, in the continuous window model, instead of averaging the embeddings, they are concatenated, resulting in $m \times D_{emb}$-long embedding vectors, where $D_{emb}$ is the original embedding size of the CBOW algorithm. *Figure 4.8* illustrates the continuous window model:

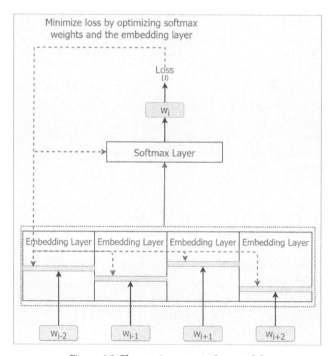

Figure 4.8: The continuous window model

In this section, we discussed two extended algorithms of skip-gram and CBOW. These two variants essentially employ the position of the words in the context instead of treating all words in a given context equally. Next, we will discuss a newly-introduced word embedding learning algorithm called GloVe. We will see that GloVe overcomes certain limitations of skip-gram and CBOW.

# GloVe – Global Vectors representation

Methods for learning word vectors fall into either of two categories: global matrix factorization-based methods or local context window-based methods. **Latent Semantic Analysis (LSA)** is an example of a global matrix factorization-based method, and skip-gram and CBOW are local context window-based methods. LSA is used as a document analysis technique that maps words in the documents to something known as a **concept**, a common pattern of words that appears in a document. Global matrix factorization-based methods efficiently exploit the global statistics of a corpus (for example, co-occurrence of words in a global scope), but have shown to perform poorly at word analogy tasks. On the other hand, context window-based methods have been shown to perform well at word analogy tasks, but do not utilize global statistics of the corpus, leaving space for improvement. GloVe attempts to get the best of both worlds — an approach that efficiently leverages global corpus statistics while optimizing the learning model in a context window-based manner similar to skip-gram or CBOW.

# Understanding GloVe

Before looking at the implementation details of GloVe, let's take time to understand the basic idea behind GloVe. To do so, let's consider an example:

1. Consider word $i =$ "$dog$" and $j =$ "$cat$"
2. Define an arbitrary probe word $k$
3. Define $P_{ik}$ to be the probability of words $i$ and $k$ occurring close to each other, and $P_{jk}$ to be the words $j$ and $k$ occurring together

Now let's look at how the $P_{ik}/P_{jk}$ entity behaves with different values for $k$.

For $k =$ "$bark$", it is highly likely to appear with $i$ thus, $P_{ik}$ will be high. However, $k$ would not often appear along with $j$ causing a low $P_{jk}$. Therefore, we get the following expression:

$$P_{ik} / P_{jk} >> 1$$

Next, for $k = "purr"$, it is unlikely to appear in the close proximity of $i$ and therefore will have a low $P_{ik}$; however, since $k$ highly correlates with $j$, the value of $P_{jk}$ will be high. This leads to the following:

$$P_{ik}/P_{jk} \approx 0$$

Now, for words such as $k = "pet"$, which has a strong relationship with both $i$ and $j$, or $k = "politics"$, where $i$ and $j$, both have a minimal relevance to, we get this:

$$P_{ik}/P_{jk} \approx 1$$

It can be seen that the $P_{ik}/P_{jk}$ entity, which is calculated by measuring the frequency of two words appearing close to each other, is a good means for measuring the relationship between words. As a result, it becomes a good candidate for learning word vectors. Therefore, a good starting point for defining the loss function will be as shown here:

$$F\left(w_i, w_j, \tilde{w}_k\right) = P_{ik}/P_{jk}$$

Here, $F$ is some function. From this point, the original paper goes through the derivation meticulously to reach the following loss function:

$$J = \sum_{i,j=1}^{V} f\left(X_{ij}\right)\left(w_i^T \tilde{w}_j + b_i + \tilde{b}_j - log\left(X_{ij}\right)\right)^2$$

Here, $f(x) = (x/x_{max})^{(3/4)}$ if $x < x_{max}$ else $1$, $X_{ij}$ is the frequency with which the word $j$ appeared in the context of the word $i$. Also, $w_i$ and $b_i$ represent the word embedding and the bias embedding for the word $i$ obtained from input embeddings, respectively. And, $\tilde{w}_j$ and $\tilde{b}_j$ represents the word embedding and bias embedding for word $j$ obtained from output embeddings, respectively. $x_{max}$ is a hypeparameter we set. Both these embeddings behave similarly except for the randomization at the initialization. At the evaluation phase, these two embeddings are added together, leading to an improved performance.

# Implementing GloVe

In this subsection, we will discuss the steps for implementing GloVe. The full code is available in the `ch4_glove.ipynb` exercise file located in the `ch4` folder.

First, we'll define the inputs and outputs:

```
train_dataset = tf.placeholder(tf.int32, shape=[batch_
size],name='train_dataset')
train_labels = tf.placeholder(tf.int32, shape=[batch_
size],name='train_labels')
```

Next, we'll define the embedding layers. We have two different embedding layers, one to look up input words and the other to look up output words. In addition, we'll define a *bias* embedding, like the bias we had for the softmax layer:

```
in_embeddings = tf.Variable(
    tf.random_uniform([vocabulary_size, embedding_size],
    -1.0, 1.0), name='embeddings')
in_bias_embeddings = tf.Variable(
    tf.random_uniform([vocabulary_size],0.0,0.01,
    dtype=tf.float32), name='embeddings_bias')

out_embeddings = tf.Variable(
    tf.random_uniform([vocabulary_size, embedding_size],
    -1.0, 1.0), name='embeddings')
out_bias_embeddings = tf.Variable(
    tf.random_uniform([vocabulary_size],0.0,0.01,
    dtype=tf.float32), name='embeddings_bias')
```

Now, we'll look up the corresponding embeddings for given inputs and outputs (labels):

```
embed_in = tf.nn.embedding_lookup(in_embeddings, train_dataset)
embed_out = tf.nn.embedding_lookup(out_embeddings, train_labels)
embed_bias_in = tf.nn.embedding_lookup(in_bias_embeddings, train_
dataset)
embed_bias_out = tf.nn.embedding_lookup(out_bias_embeddings, train_
labels)
```

Also, we'll define placeholders for $f(X_{ij})$ (`weights_x`) and $X_{ij}$ (`x_ij`) in the cost function:

```
weights_x = tf.placeholder(tf.float32, shape=[batch_size],
name='weights_x')
x_ij = tf.placeholder(tf.float32, shape=[batch_size], name='x_ij')
```

Finally, we'll define the full loss function with the preceding defined entities, which is as follows:

```
loss = tf.reduce_mean(
    weights_x * (tf.reduce_sum(embed_in*embed_out,axis=1) +
    embed_bias_in + embed_bias_out - tf.log(epsilon+x_ij))**2)
```

In this section, we looked at GloVe, another word embedding learning technique. The main advantage of GloVe over the previously described Word2vec techniques is that it pays attention to both global and local statistics of the corpus to learn embeddings. As GloVe are able to capture the global information about words, they tend to give better performance, especially when the corpus size increases. Another advantage is that unlike in Word2vec techniques, GloVe does not approximate the cost function (for example, Word2vec using negative sampling), but calculates the true cost. This leads to better and easier optimization of the loss.

# Document classification with Word2vec

Although Word2vec gives a very elegant way of learning numerical representations of words, as we saw quantitatively (loss value) and qualitatively (t-SNE embeddings), learning word representations alone is not convincing enough to realize the power of word vectors in real-world applications. Word embeddings are used as the feature representation of words for many tasks, such as image caption generation and machine translation. However, these tasks involve combining different learning models (such as **Convolution Neural Networks** (**CNNs**) and **Long Short-Term Memory** (**LSTM**) models or two LSTM models). These will be discussed in later chapters. To understand a real-world usage of word embeddings let's stick to a simpler task—document classification.

Document classification is one of the most popular tasks in NLP. Document classification is extremely useful for anyone who is handling massive collections of data such as those for news websites, publishers, and universities. Therefore, it is interesting to see how learning word vectors can be adapted to a real-world task such as document classification by means of embedding entire documents instead of words.

This exercise is available in the ch4 folder (ch4_document_embedding.ipynb).

# Dataset

For this task, we will use an already-organized set of text files. These are news articles from the BBC. Every document in this collection belongs to one of the following categories: *Business*, *Entertainment*, *Politics*, *Sports*, or *Technology*. We use 250 documents from each category. Our vocabulary will be of size 25,000. Also, each document will be represented by a `<type of document>-<id>` tag for visualization purposes. For example, the 50th document of the *Entertainment* section will be represented as `entertainment-50`. It should be noted that this is a very small dataset compared to the large text corpora that is being analyzed in real-world applications. However, this small example is adequate at the moment to see the power of word embeddings.

Here are a couple brief snippets from the actual data:

*Business*

*Japan narrowly escapes recession*

*Japan's economy teetered on the brink of a technical recession in the three months to September, figures show.*

*Revised figures indicated growth of just 0.1% - and a similar-sized contraction in the previous quarter. On an annual basis, the data suggests annual growth of just 0.2%,...*

*Technology*

*UK net users leading TV downloads*

*British TV viewers lead the trend of illegally downloading US shows from the net, according to research.*

*New episodes of 24, Desperate Housewives and Six Feet Under, appear on the web hours after they are shown in the US, said a report. Web tracking company Envisional said 18% of downloaders were from within the UK and that downloads of TV programmers had increased by 150% in the last year....*

# Classifying documents with word embeddings

The problem broadly is to see if word embedding methods such as skip-gram or CBOW can be extended to classify/cluster documents. In this example, we will use the CBOW algorithm, as it has been shown to perform better with smaller datasets than skip-gram.

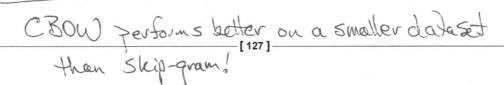
CBOW performs better on a smaller dataset than skip-gram!

We will take the following approach:

1.  Extracting data from all the text files and learning word embeddings as we did already.

2.  Extracting a random set of documents from the already trained documents.

3.  Extending the learned embeddings to embed these selected documents. More specifically, we'll represent a document by the mean value of the embeddings belonging to all the words found in the document.

4.  Visualizing the found document embeddings with the t-SNE visualization technique to see whether word embeddings can be useful for document clustering or classification.

5.  Finally, a clustering algorithm such as K-means can be used to assign a label for each document. We will briefly discuss what K-means is while discussing the implementation.

# Implementation – learning word embeddings

First, we will define several placeholders for train data, train labels, and valid data (used to monitor word embeddings) and test data (used to compute mean embeddings of the test documents):

```
# Input data.
train_dataset = tf.placeholder(tf.int32,
    shape=[batch_size, 2*window_size])
train_labels = tf.placeholder(tf.int32, shape=[batch_size, 1])
valid_dataset = tf.constant(valid_examples, dtype=tf.int32)

test_labels = tf.placeholder(tf.int32,
    shape=[batch_size], name='test_dataset')
```

Next, we'll define the variables for embeddings for the vocabulary and softmax weights and biases (used to compute mean embeddings of the test documents):

```
# Variables.
# embedding, vector for each word in the vocabulary
embeddings = tf.Variable(tf.random_uniform([vocabulary_size,
    embedding_size], -1.0, 1.0, dtype=tf.float32))
softmax_weights = tf.Variable(
    tf.truncated_normal([vocabulary_size, embedding_size],
    stddev=1.0 / math.sqrt(embedding_size), dtype=tf.float32))
softmax_biases = tf.Variable(
    tf.zeros([vocabulary_size], dtype=tf.float32))
```

Then we define the sampled negative softmax loss function as we did before:

```
loss = tf.reduce_mean(
    tf.nn.sampled_softmax_loss(weights=softmax_weights,
    biases=softmax_biases, inputs=mean_embeddings,
    labels=train_labels, num_sampled=num_sampled,
    num_classes=vocabulary_size))
```

# Implementation – word embeddings to document embeddings

In order to obtain good document embeddings from word embeddings, we will take the average embedding of all the words found in a document as the document embedding. However, we will be processing data in batches. So, we will use the following to achieve this.

For each document, do the following:

1. Creating a dataset where each data point is a word belonging to the document

2. For a mini-batch sampled from the dataset, returning the mean embedding vector by averaging the embedding vectors for all the words in the mini-batch

3. Traversing the test document in batches and obtaining the document embedding by averaging the mini-batch mean embeddings

We'll get the mean batch embeddings as follows:

```
mean_batch_embedding = tf.reduce_mean(tf.nn.embedding_
lookup(embeddings, test_labels), axis=0)
mean_embeddings = tf.reduce_mean(stacked_embeddings, 2,
keepdims=False)
```

Then, we'll collect such mean embeddings in a list for all the batches in a document and obtain the average embedding as the document embedding. This is a very simple method for obtaining document embeddings, but very powerful, as we will see soon.

# Document clustering and t-SNE visualization of embedded documents

In *Figure 4.9*, we can visualize the document embeddings learned by the CBOW algorithm. We can see that the algorithm has learned reasonably well to cluster documents with the same topic. We employed the prefix of the documents (different colors for different document categories) to add colors to data points so that the separation is more obvious. As we discussed before, this simple method has proved to be a very effective way to classify/cluster documents in an unsupervised manner:

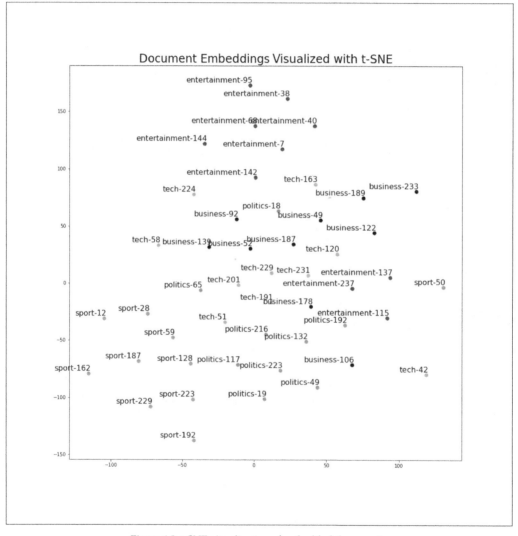

Figure 4.9: t-SNE visualization of embedded documents

# Inspecting several outliers

We can see from *Figure 4.9* that very few documents appear to be outliers (for example, `tech-42` and `sport-50`). It is interesting to see the content of these documents so we can investigate the likely reasons for such a behavior.

The following is a snippet from the `tech-42` document:

> *Tech-42*
>
> *Hotspot users gain free net calls*
>
> *People using wireless net hotspots will soon be able to make free phone calls as well as surf the net.*
>
> *Users of the system can also make calls to landlines and mobiles for a fee. The system is gaining in popularity and now has 28 million users around the world. Its paid service - dubbed Skype Out - has so far attracted 940,000 users....*

This document has been written in a way that emphasizes the value of Skype to people, rather than diving into technical details of Skype. This in turn can lead the document to be clustered close to topics more related to people, such as entertainment or politics.

The following is a snippet from the `sport-50` document:

> *Sport-50*
>
> *IAAF awaits Greek pair's response*
>
> *Kostas Kenteris and Katerina Thanou are yet to respond to doping charges from the International Association of Athletics Federations (IAAF).*
>
> *The Greek pair were charged after missing a series of routine drugs tests in Tel Aviv, Chicago and Athens. They have until midnight on 16 December and an IAAF spokesman said: "We're sure their responses are on their way." If they do not respond or their explanations are rejected, they will be provisionally banned from competition. They will then face a hearing in front of the Greek Federation,...*

We can shed some light as to why `sport-50` has been clustered far away from the other sports-related articles. Let's closely look at another document close to *sport-50*, which is, `entertainment-115`:

> *Entertainment-115*
>
> *Rapper Snoop Dogg sued for 'rape'*
>
> *US rapper Snoop Dogg has been sued for $25m (£13m) by a make-up artist who claimed he and his entourage drugged and raped her two years ago.*
>
> *The woman said she was assaulted after a recording of the Jimmy Kimmel Live TV show on the ABC network in 2003. The rapper's spokesman said the allegations were "untrue" and the woman was "misusing the legal system as a means of extracting financial gain". ABC said the claims had "no merit". The star has not been charged by police.*

So, the documents around this area seem to be related to various criminal or illicit charges instead of being about sports or entertainment. This causes these documents to be clustered far away from other typical sports or entertainment-related documents.

# Implementation – clustering/classification of documents with K-means

So far, we have been able to visually inspect clusters of documents. However, this is not enough, because if we have 1,000 more documents that we would like to cluster/classify, we will have to visually inspect things for 1,000 times. So we need more automated ways for achieving this.

We can use K-means to cluster these documents. K-means is a simple but powerful technique used to break data into groups (clusters) based on the similarity of data, so that similar data will be in the same group and different data will be in different groups. K-means works in the following way:

1. Define $K$, the number of clusters to be formed. We will set that to 5 since we already know that there are five categories.
2. Form $K$ random centroids, which are the centers of the clusters.
3. Then we'll assign each data point to the nearest cluster centroid.
4. After assigning all the data points to some cluster, we'll recompute the cluster centroids (that is, mean of the data points).

5. We'll continue in this fashion until the centroid movement becomes smaller than some threshold.

We'll use scikit-learn library to get the K-means algorithm. In code, this looks like the following:

```
kmeans = KMeans(n_clusters=5, random_state=43643, max_iter=10000,
                n_init=100, algorithm='elkan')
```

The most important hyperparameter is `n_clusters`, which is the number of clusters we want to form. You can play around with the other hyperparameters to see what sort of effect they have on the performance. An explanation of the possible hyperparameters is available at `http://scikit-learn.org/stable/modules/generated/sklearn.cluster.KMeans.html`.

Then we can classify the documents we used to train (or any other document) into classes. We will obtain the following:

| Label | Documents |
|-------|-----------|
| 0 | 'entertainment-207', 'entertainment-14', 'entertainment-232', 'entertainment-49', 'entertainment-191', 'entertainment-243', 'entertainment-240' |
| 1 | 'sport-145', 'sport-228', 'sport-141', 'sport-249' |
| 2 | 'sport-4', 'sport-43', 'entertainment-54', 'politics-214', 'politics-12', 'politics-165', 'sport-42', 'politics-203', 'politics-87', 'sport-33', 'politics-81', 'politics-247', 'entertainment-245', 'entertainment-22', 'tech-102', 'sport-50', 'politics-33', 'politics-28' |
| 3 | 'business-220', 'business-208', 'business-51', 'business-30', 'business-130', 'business-190', 'business-34', 'business-206' |
| 4 | 'business-185', 'business-238', 'tech-105', 'tech-99', 'tech-239', 'tech-227', 'tech-31', 'tech-131', 'tech-118', 'politics-10', 'tech-150', 'tech-165' |

It's not perfect, but it does a decent job of classifying documents belonging to different categories to different labels. We can see that the entertainment-related documents have the 0 label, the sports-related documents the 1 label, the business-related documents the 3 label, and so on.

In this section, you learned how we can extend word embeddings to classify/cluster documents. First, you learned word embeddings, as we normally did. Then we created document embeddings by averaging the word embeddings of all the words found in that document. Later we used these document embeddings to cluster/classify some BBC news articles which fall into these categories: entertainment, tech, politics, business, and sports. After clustering the documents, we saw that documents were reasonably clustered such that documents belonging to one category were clustered close to each other. However, there were a few outlier documents. But after analyzing the textual content of these documents, we saw that there were certain valid reasons behind these documents behaving in this particular way.

# Summary

In this chapter, we examined the performance difference between the skip-gram and CBOW algorithms. For the comparison, we used a popular two-dimensional visualization technique, t-SNE, which we also briefly introduced to you, touching on the fundamental intuition and mathematics behind the method.

Next, we introduced you to the several extensions to Word2vec algorithms that boost their performance, followed by several novel algorithms that were based on the skip-gram and CBOW algorithms. Structured skip-gram extends the skip-gram algorithm by preserving the position of the context word during optimization, allowing the algorithm to treat input-output based on the distance between them. The same extension can be applied to the CBOW algorithm, and this results in the continuous window algorithm.

Then we discussed GloVe—another word embedding learning technique. GloVe takes the current Word2vec algorithms a step further by incorporating global statistics into the optimization, thus increasing the performance. Finally, we discussed a real-world application of using word embeddings—document clustering/classification. We showed that word embeddings are very powerful and allow us to cluster related documents together reasonably well.

In the next chapter, we will move onto discuss a different family of deep networks that are more powerful in exploiting spatial information present in data known as **Convolutional Neural Networks (CNNs)**. Precisely, we will see how CNNs can be used to exploit the spatial structure of sentences to classify them into different classes.

# 5
# Sentence Classification with Convolutional Neural Networks

In this chapter, we will discuss a type of neural networks known as **Convolutional Neural Networks (CNNs)**. CNNs are quite different from fully connected neural networks and have achieved state-of-the-art performance in numerous tasks. These tasks include image classification, object detection, speech recognition, and of course, sentence classification. One of the main advantages of CNNs is that compared to a fully connected layer, a convolution layer in a CNN has a much smaller number of parameters. This allows us to build deeper models without worrying about memory overflow. Also, deeper models usually lead to better performance.

We will introduce you to what a CNN is in detail by discussing different components found in a CNN and what makes CNNs different from their fully connected counterparts. Then we will discuss the various operations used in CNNs, such as the convolution and pooling operations, and certain hyperparameters related to these operations, such as filter size, padding, and stride. We will also look at some of the mathematics behind the actual operations. After establishing a good understanding of CNNs, we will look at the practical side of implementing a CNN with TensorFlow. First, we will implement a CNN to classify objects and then use a CNN for sentence classification.

# Introducing Convolution Neural Networks

In this section, you will learn about CNNs. Specifically, you will first get an understanding of the sort of operations present in a CNN, such as convolution layers, pooling layers, and fully connected layers. Next, we will briefly see how all of these are connected to form an end-to-end model. Then we will dive into the details of each of these operations, define them mathematically, and learn how the various hyperparameters involved with these operations change the output produced by them.

## CNN fundamentals

Now, let's explore the fundamental idea behind a CNN without delving into too much technical detail. As noted in the preceding paragraph, a CNN is a stack of layers, such as convolution layers, pooling layers, and fully connected layers. We will discuss each of these to understand their role in the CNN.

Initially, the input is connected to a set of convolution layers. These convolution layers slide a patch of weights (sometimes called the convolution window or filter) over the input and produce an output by means of the convolution operation. Convolution layers use a small number of weights organized to cover only a small patch of input in each layer, unlike fully connected neural networks, and these weights are shared across certain dimensions (for example, the width and height dimensions of an image). Also, CNNs use the convolution operations to share the weights form the output by sliding this small set of weights along the desired dimension. What we ultimately get from this convolution operation is illustrated in *Figure 5.1*. If the pattern present in a convolution filter is present in a patch of image, the convolution will output a high value for that location; if not, it will output a low value. Also, by convolving the full image, we get a matrix indicating whether a pattern was present or not in a given location. Finally, we will get a matrix as the convolution output:

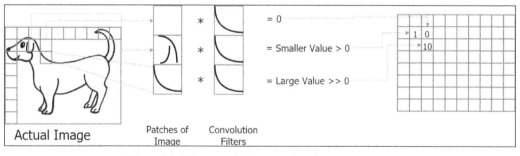

Figure 5.1: What convolution operation does to an image

Also, these convolution layers are optionally interleaved with pooling/subsampling layers, which reduces the dimensionality of the input. While reducing the dimensionality, we make the translation of CNNs invariant as well as force the CNN to learn with less information, leading to better generalization and regularization of the model. The dimensionality is reduced by dividing the input into several patches and transforming each patch to a single element. For example, such transformations include picking the maximum element of a patch or averaging all the values in a patch. We will illustrate how pooling can make the translation of CNNs invariant in *Figure 5.2*:

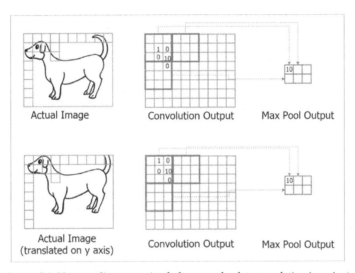

Figure 5.2: How pooling operation helps to make data translation invariant

Here, we have the original image and an image slightly translated on the $y$ axis. We have convolution output for both images, and you can see that the value **10** appears at slightly different places in the convolution output. However, using max pooling (which takes the maximum value of each thick square), we can get the same output at the end. We will discuss these operations in detail later.

Finally, the output is fed to a set of fully connected layers, which then forward the output to the final classification/regression layer (for example, sentence/image classification). Fully connected layers contain a significant fraction of the total number of weights of the CNN as convolution layers have a small number of weights. However, it has been found that CNNs perform better with fully connected layers than without them. This could be because convolution layers learn more localized features due to small size, whereas fully connected layers provide a global picture about how these localized features should be connected together to produce a desirable final output. *Figure 5.3* shows a typical CNN used to classify images:

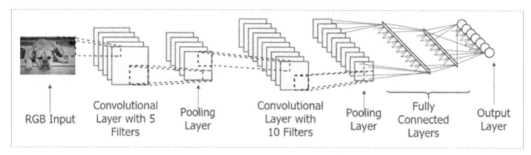

Figure 5.3: A typical CNN architecture

As is evident from the figure, CNNs, by design, preserve the spatial structure of the inputs during the learning. In other words, for a two-dimensional input, a CNN will have most of the layers two-dimensional, whereas we have fully connected layers only close to the output layer. Preserving the spatial structure allows CNNs to exploit valuable spatial information of the inputs and learn about inputs with fewer parameters. The value of spatial information is illustrated in *Figure 5.4*:

Figure 5.4: Unwrapping an image into a one-dimensional vector loses some of the important spatial information

As you can see, when a two-dimensional image of a cat is unwrapped to be a one-dimensional vector, ears are no longer close to the eyes, and the nose is far away from the eyes as well. This means we have destroyed some of useful spatial information during the unwrapping.

# The power of Convolution Neural Networks

CNNs are a very versatile family of models and have shown a remarkable performance in many types of tasks. Such versatility is attributed to the ability of CNNs to perform feature extraction and learning simultaneously, leading to greater efficiency and generalizability. Let's discuss a few examples of the utility of CNNs.

In the **ImageNet Large Scale Visual Recognition Challenge (ILSVRC)** 2016, which involved classifying images, detecting objects, and localizing objects in the image, CNNs were used to achieve incredible test accuracies. For example, for image-classification tasks, its test accuracy was approximately 98% for 1,000 different object classes, which means that the CNN was able to correctly identify around 980 different objects correctly.

CNNs also have been used for image segmentation. Image segmentation involves segmenting an image into different areas. For example, in an urbanscape image that includes buildings, a road, vehicles, and passengers, isolating the road from the buildings is a segmentation task. Moreover, CNNs have made incredible strides, demonstrating their performance in NLP tasks such as sentence classification, text generation, and machine translation.

# Understanding Convolution Neural Networks

Now let's walk through the technical details of a CNN. First, we will discuss the convolution operation and introduce some terminology, such as filter size, stride, and padding. In brief, **filter size** refers to the window size of the convolution operation, **stride** refers to the distance between two movements of the convolution window, and **padding** refers to the way you handle boundaries of the input. We will also discuss an operation that is known as deconvolution or transposed convolution. Then we will discuss the details of the pooling operation. Finally, we will discuss how to connect fully connected layers and the two-dimensional outputs produced by the convolution and pooling layers and how to use the output for classification or regression.

# Convolution operation

In this section, we will discuss the convolution operation in detail. First we will discuss the convolution operation without stride and padding, next we will describe the convolution operation with stride, and then we will discuss the convolution operation with padding. Finally, we will discuss something called transposed convolution. For all the operations in this chapter, we consider index starting from one, and not from zero.

## Standard convolution operation

The convolution operation is a central part of CNNs. For an input of size $n \times n$ and a weight patch (also known as a *filter*) of $m \times m$, where $n \geq m$, the convolution operation slides the patch of weights over the input. Let's denote the input by $X$, the patch of weights by $W$, and the output by $H$. Also, at each location $i, j$; the output is calculated as follows:

$$h_{i,j} = \sum_{k=1}^{m} \sum_{l=1}^{m} w_{k,l} \cdot x_{i+k-1, j+l-1} \ where\ 1 \leq i, j \leq n-m+1$$

Here, $x_{i,j}$, $w_{i,j}$, and $h_{i,j}$ denote the value at the $(i,j)^{th}$ location of $X$, $W$, and $H$, respectively. As already shown by the equation, though the input size is $n \times n$, the output in this case will be $n-m+1 \times n-m+1$. Also, $m$ is known as the filter size. Let's look at this through a visualization (see *Figure 5.5*):

 The output produced by the convolution operation (the rectangle on the top in *Figure 5.5*) is sometimes called a **features map**.

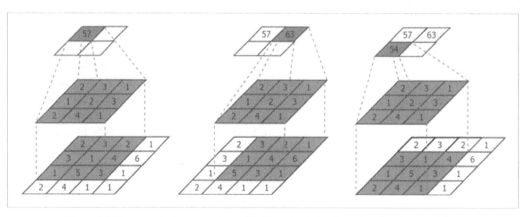

Figure 5.5: The convolution operation with filter size (m) = 3 stride = 1 and no padding

# Convolving with stride

In the preceding example, we shifted the filter by a single step. However, this is not mandatory; we can take large steps or strides while convolving the input. Therefore, the size of the step is known as the stride. Let's modify the previous equation to include the $s_i$ and $s_j$ strides:

$$h_{i,j} = \sum_{k=1}^{m}\sum_{l=1}^{m} w_{k,l} x_{(i-1)\times s_i+k,(j-1)\times s_j+l} \; where \; 1 \leq i \leq floor\left[(n-m)/s_i\right]+1 \; and \; floor\left[(n-m)/s_j\right]+1$$

In this case, the output will be smaller as the size of $s_i$ and $s_j$ increases. Comparing *Figure 5.5* (*stride = 1*) and *Figure 5.6* (*stride = 2*) illustrates the effect of different strides:

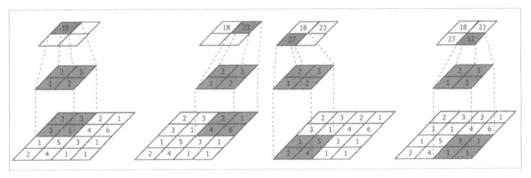

Figure 5.6: The convolution operation with a filter size (m) = 2 stride = 2 and no padding

 As you can see, doing convolution with stride helps to reduce the dimensionality of the input similar to a pooling layer. Therefore, sometimes convolution with strides are used instead of pooling in the CNNs as it reduces the computational complexity.

# Convolving with padding

The inevitable output size reduction resulting from each convolution (without stride) is an undesirable property. This greatly limits the number of layers we can have in a network. Also, it is known that deeper networks perform better than shallow networks. This should not be confused with the dimensionality reduction achieved by stride, as this is a design choice and we can decide to have a stride of 1 if necessary. Therefore, padding is used to circumvent this issue. This is achieved by padding zeros to the boundary of the input so that the output size and the input size are equal. Let's assume a stride of 1:

$$h_{i,j} = \sum_{k=1}^{m} \sum_{l=1}^{m} w_{k,l} x_{i+k-(m-1),j+l-(m-1)} \; where \, 1 \le i, j \le n$$

Here:

$$x_{i,j} = 0 \, if \, i, j < 1 \, or \, i, j > n$$

*Figure 5.7* depicts the result of the padding:

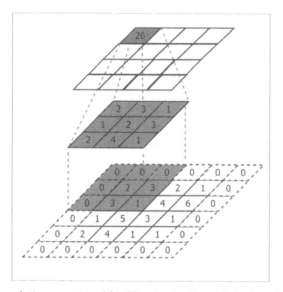

Figure 5.7: Convolution operation with a filter size (m=3), stride (s=1), and zero padding

# Transposed convolution

Though the convolution operation looks complicated in terms of mathematics, it can be simplified to a matrix multiplication. For this reason, we can define the transpose of the convolution operation or **deconvolution**, as it is sometimes called. However, we will use the term **transposed convolution** as it sounds more natural. In addition, deconvolution refers to a different mathematical concept. The transposed convolution operation plays an important role in CNNs for the reverse accumulation of the gradients during backpropagation. Let's go through an example.

For an input of size $n \times n$ and a weight patch, or filter, $m \times m$, where $n \geq m$, the convolution operation slides the patch of weights over the input. Let's denote the input by $X$, the patch of weights by $W$, and the output by $H$. The output $h$ can be calculated as a matrix multiplication as follows.

Let's assume $n = 4$ and $m = 3$ for clarity and unwrap the input $X$ from left to right, top to bottom, resulting in this:

$$x^{(16,1)} = x_{1,1}, x_{1,2}, x_{1,3}, x_{1,4}, x_{2,1}, x_{2,2}, x_{2,3}, x_{2,4}, \ldots, x_{4,1}, x_{4,2}, x_{4,3}, x_{4,4}$$

Let's define a new matrix $A$ from $W$:

$$A^{(4,16)} = \begin{bmatrix} w_{1,1} & w_{1,2} & w_{1,3} & 0 & w_{2,1} & w_{2,2} & w_{2,3} & 0 & w_{3,1} & w_{3,2} & w_{3,3} & 0 & 0 & 0 & 0 & 0 \\ 0 & w_{1,1} & w_{1,2} & w_{1,3} & 0 & w_{2,1} & w_{2,2} & w_{2,3} & 0 & w_{3,1} & w_{3,2} & w_{3,3} & 0 & 0 & 0 & 0 \\ 0 & 0 & 0 & 0 & w_{1,1} & w_{1,2} & w_{1,3} & 0 & w_{2,1} & w_{2,2} & w_{2,3} & 0 & w_{3,1} & w_{3,2} & w_{3,3} & 0 \\ 0 & 0 & 0 & 0 & 0 & w_{1,1} & w_{1,2} & w_{1,3} & 0 & w_{2,1} & w_{2,2} & w_{2,3} & 0 & w_{3,1} & w_{3,2} & w_{3,3} \end{bmatrix}$$

Then, if we perform the following matrix multiplication, we obtain $H$:

$$H^{(4,1)} = A^{(4,16)} X^{(16,1)}$$

Now, by reshaping the output $H^{(4,1)}$ to $H^{(2,2)}$ we obtain the convolved output. Now let's project this result back to $n$ and $m$:

By unwrapping the input $X^{(n,n)}$ to $X^{(n^2,1)}$ and by creating a matrix $A^{\left((n-m+1)^2,n^2\right)}$ from $w$, as we showed earlier, we obtain $H^{\left((n-m+1)^2,1\right)}$, which will then be reshaped to $H^{(n-m+1,n-m+1)}$.

Next, to obtain the transposed convolution, we simply transpose $A$ and arrive at the following:

$$\hat{X}^{\left(n^2,1\right)} = \left(A^T\right)^{\left(n^2,(n-m+1)^2\right)} H^{\left((n-m+1)^2,1\right)}$$

Here, $\hat{x}$ is the resultant output of the transposed convolution.

We end our discussion about the convolution operation here. We discussed the convolution operation, convolution operation with stride, convolution operation with padding, and how to calculate the transposed convolution. Next we will discuss the pooling operation in more detail.

# Pooling operation

The pooling operation, which is sometimes known as the subsampling operation, was introduced to CNNs mainly for reducing the size of the intermediate outputs as well as for making the translation of CNNs invariant. This is preferred over the natural dimensionality reduction caused by convolution without padding, as we can decide where to reduce the size of the output with the pooling layer, in contrast to forcing it to happen every time. Forcing the dimensionality to decrease without padding would strictly limit the number of layers we can have in our CNN models.

We define the pooling operation mathematically in the following sections. More precisely, we will discuss two types of pooling: max pooling and average pooling. First, however, we will define the notation. For an input of size $n \times n$ and a kernel (analogous to the filter of convolution layer) of size $m \times m$, where $n \geq m$, the convolution operation slides the patch of weights over the input. Let's denote the input by $x$, the patch of weights by $w$ and the output by $h$.

# Max pooling

The max pooling operation picks the maximum element within the defined kernel of an input to produce the output. The max pooling operation shifts are windows over the input (the middle squares in *Figure 5.8*) and take the maximum at each time. Mathematically, we define the pooling equation as follows:

$$h_{i,j} = \max\left(\left\{x_{i,j}, x_{i,j+1}, \ldots, x_{i,j+m-1}, x_{i+1,j}, \ldots, x_{i+1,j+m-1}, \ldots, x_{i+m-1,j}, \ldots, x_{i+m-1,j+m-1}\right\}\right) where\, 1 \le i,j \le n-m+1$$

*Figure 5.8* shows this operation:

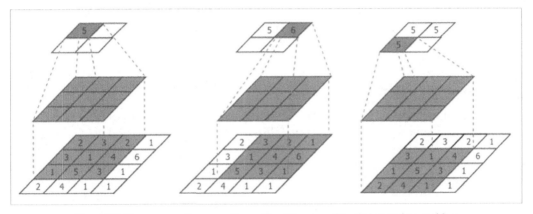

Figure 5.8: The max pooling operation with a filter size of 3, stride 1 and no padding

# Max pooling with stride

Max pooling with stride is similar to convolution with stride. Here is the equation:

$$h_{i,j} = max\left(\left\{x_{(i-1)\times s_i+1,(j-1)\times s_j+1}, x_{(i-1)\times s_i+1,(j-1)\times s_j+2}, \ldots, x_{(i-1)\times s_i+1,(j-1)\times s_j+m}, x_{(i-1)\times s_i+2,(j-1)\times s_j+1}, \ldots, x_{(i-1)\times s_i+2,(j-1)\times s_j+m}, \ldots, x_{(i-1)\times s_i+m,(j-1)\times s_j+1}, \ldots, x_{(i-1)\times s_i+m,(j-1)\times s_j+m}\right\}\right)$$

$$where\, 1 \le i \le floor\left[(n-m)/s_i\right]+1 \, and \, 1 \le j \le floor\left[(n-m)/s_i\right]+1$$

*Figure 5.9* shows the result:

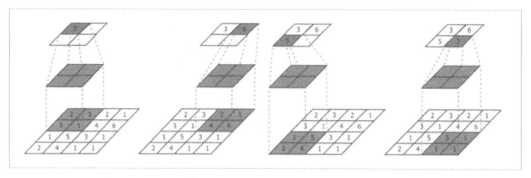

Figure 5.9: Max pooling operation for an input of size (n=4) with a filter
size of (m=2), stride (s=2) and no padding

# Average pooling

Average pooling works similar to max pooling, except that instead of only taking the
maximum, the average of all the inputs falling within the kernel is taken. Consider
the following equation:

$$h_{i,j} = \frac{x_{i,j}, x_{i,j+1}, \ldots, x_{i,j+m-1}, x_{i+1,j}, \ldots, x_{i+1,j+m-1}, \ldots, x_{i+m-1,j}, \ldots, x_{i+m-1,j+m-1}}{m \times m} \forall i \geq 1, j \leq n-m+1$$

The average pooling operation is shown in *Figure 5.10*:

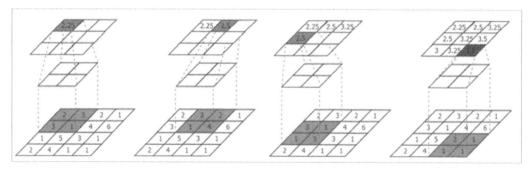

Figure 5.10: Average pooling operation for an input of size (n=4) with
a filter size of (m=2), stride (s=1) and no padding

# Fully connected layers

Fully connected layers are a fully connected set of weights from the input to the output. These fully connected weights are able to learn global information as they are connected from each input to each output. Also, having such layers of full connectedness allows us to combine features learned by the convolution layers preceding the fully connected layers, globally, to produce meaningful outputs.

Let's define the output of the last convolution or pooling layer to be of size $p \times o \times d$, where $p$ is the height of the input, $o$ is the width of the input, and $d$ is the depth of the input. As an example, think of an RGB image, which will have a fixed height, fixed width, and a depth of 3 (one depth channel for each RGB component).

Then, for the initial fully connected layer found immediately after the last convolution or pooling layer, the weight matrix will be $w^{(m, p \times o \times d)}$, where *height x width x depth* of the layer output is the number of output units produced by that last layer and $m$ is the number of hidden units in the fully connected layer. Then, during inference (or prediction), we reshape the output of the last convolution/pooling layer to be of size $(p \times o \times d, 1)$ and perform the following matrix multiplication to obtain $h$:

$$h^{(m \times 1)} = w^{(m, p \times o \times d)} x^{(p \times o \times d, 1)}$$

The resultant fully connected layers will behave as in a fully connected neural network, where you have several fully connected layers and an output layer. The output layer can be a softmax classification layer for a classification problem or a linear layer for a regression problem.

# Putting everything together

Now we will discuss how the convolutional, pooling, and fully connected layers come together to form a complete CNN.

As shown in *Figure 5.11*, the convolution, pooling, and fully connected layers come together to form an end-to-end learning model that takes raw data, which can be high-dimensional (for example, RGB images) and produce meaningful output (for example, class of the object). First, the convolution layers learn spatial features of the images. The lower convolution layers learn low-level features such as differently oriented edges present in the images, and the higher layers learn more high-level features such as shapes present in the images (for example, circles and triangles) or bigger parts of an object (for example, the face of a dog, tail of a dog, and front section of a car). The pooling layers in the middle make each of these learned features slightly translation invariant. This means that in a new image even if the feature appears a bit offset compared to the location in which the feature appeared in the learned images, the CNN will still recognize that feature. Finally, the fully connected layers combine the high-level features learned by the CNN to produce global representations that will be used by the final output layer to determine the class the object belongs to:

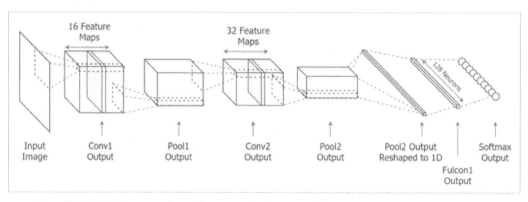

Figure 5.11: Combining convolution layers, pooling layers, and fully connected layers to form a CNN

# Exercise – image classification on MNIST with CNN

This will be our first example of using a CNN for a real-world machine learning task. We will classify images using a CNN. The reason for not starting with an NLP task is that applying CNNs to NLP tasks (for example, sentence classification) is not very straightforward. There are several tricks involved in using CNNs for such a task. However, originally, CNNs were designed to cope with image data. Therefore, let's start there and then find our way through to see how CNNs apply to NLP tasks.

# About the data

In this exercise, we will use a dataset well-known in the computer vision community: the MNIST dataset. The MNIST dataset is a database of labeled images of handwritten digits from 0 to 9. The dataset contains three different subdatasets: the training, validation, and test sets. We will train on the training set and evaluate the performance of our model on the unseen test dataset. We will use the validation dataset to improve the performance of the model and use this as a monitoring mechanism for our model. We will discuss the details later. This is one of the easiest tasks in image classification and can be solved fairly well with a simple CNN. We will see that we can reach up to approximately 98% test accuracy without any special regularization or tricks.

# Implementing the CNN

In this subsection, we will look at some important code snippets from the TensorFlow implementation of the CNN. The full code is available in `image_classification_mnist.ipynb` in the `ch5` folder. First, we will define the TensorFlow placeholders for feeding inputs (images) and outputs (labels). Then we will define a global step, which will then be used to decay the learning rate:

```
# Inputs and Outputs Placeholders
tf_inputs = tf.placeholder(shape=[batch_size, image_size, image_size,
n_channels],dtype=tf.float32,name='tf_mnist_images')
tf_labels = tf.placeholder(shape=[batch_size, n_classes],dtype=tf.
float32,name='tf_mnist_labels')

# Global step for decaying the learning rate
global_step = tf.Variable(0,trainable=False)
```

Next, we will define the TensorFlow variables, which are the convolution weights and biases and fully connected weights. We will define the filter size, stride, and padding for each convolution layer, kernel size, stride and padding for each pooling layer, and the number of output units for each fully connected layer in a Python dictionary called `layer_hyperparameters`:

```
# Initializing the variables
layer_weights = {}
layer_biases = {}
for layer_id in cnn_layer_ids:
    if 'pool' not in layer_id:
        layer_weights[layer_id] =
tf.Variable(initial_value=tf.random_normal(shape=layer_
hyperparameters[layer_id]['weight_shape'],
stddev=0.02,dtype=tf.float32),name=layer_id+'_weights')
```

```
layer_biases[layer_id] = tf.Variable(initial_value=tf.random_
normal(shape=[layer_hyperparameters[layer_id]['weight_shape'][-1]],
stddev=0.01,dtype=tf.float32), name=layer_id+'_bias')
```

We will also define the logit calculation. **Logits** are the value of the output layer before applying the softmax activation. To calculate this, we will iterate through each layer.

For each convolution layer, we will convolve the input using this:

```
h = tf.nn.conv2d(h,layer_weights[layer_id],layer_
hyperparameters[layer_id]['stride'],
layer_hyperparameters[layer_id]['padding']) + layer_biases[layer_id]
```

Here, the input `h` to `tf.nn.conv2d` is replaced with `tf_inputs` for the very first convolution. Remember that we discussed each of the arguments we feed to `tf.nn.conv2d` in detail in *Chapter 2, Understanding TensorFlow*. However, we will briefly revisit the arguments of `tf.nn.conv2d`. Also, `tf.nn.conv2d(input, filter, strides, padding)` takes the following argument values in that order:

- `input`: This is the input to convolve, having the shape `[batch size, input height, input width, input depth]`
- `filter`: This is the convolution filter we convolve the input with and has the shape `[filter height, filter width, input depth, output depth]`
- `strides`: This denotes the stride on each dimension of the input and has the shape `[batch stride, height stride, width stride, depth stride]`
- `padding`: This denotes the type of padding (can be `'SAME'` or `'VALID'`)

We also apply a nonlinear activation as follows:

```
h = tf.nn.relu(h)
```

Then, for each pooling layer, we subsample the input with this:

```
h = tf.nn.max_pool(h, layer_hyperparameters[layer_id]['kernel_
shape'],layer_hyperparameters[layer_id]['stride'],
layer_hyperparameters[layer_id]['padding'])
```

The `tf.nn.max_pool(input, ksize, strides, padding)` function takes the following arguments in that order:

- `input`: This is the input to subsample, having the shape `[batch size, input height, input width, input depth]`
- `ksize`: This is the kernel size on each dimension for the max pooling operation `[batch kernel size, height kernel size, width kernel size, depth kernel size]`

- `strides`: This is the stride on each dimension of the input [batch stride, height stride, width stride, depth stride]
- `padding`: This can be `'SAME'` or `'VALID'`

Next, for the first fully connected layer, we reshape the output:

```
h = tf.reshape(h,[batch_size,-1])
```

Then we will perform the weight multiplication and the bias addition followed by the nonlinear activation:

```
h = tf.matmul(h,layer_weights[layer_id]) + layer_biases[layer_id]
h = tf.nn.relu(h)
```

Now, we can calculate the logits:

```
h = tf.matmul(h,layer_weights[layer_id]) + layer_biases[layer_id]
```

We will assign the very last value of h (output of the very last layer) to `tf_logits` using this:

```
tf_logits = h
```

Next, we will define the softmax cross-entropy loss, which is a popular loss function for supervised classification tasks:

```
tf_loss = tf.nn.softmax_cross_entropy_with_logits_v2(logits=tf_
logits,labels=tf_labels)
```

We also need to define a learning rate where we will decrease the learning rate by a factor of `0.5` whenever the validation accuracy has not increased for a predefined number of epochs (an epoch is a single traverse through the full dataset). This is known as the **learning rate decay**:

```
tf_learning_rate = tf.train.exponential_decay(learning_
rate=0.001,global_step=global_step,decay_rate=0.5,decay_
steps=1,staircase=True)
```

Next, we will define the loss minimization using an optimizer known as `RMSPropOptimizer`, which has been found to perform better than the conventional **Stochastic Gradient Descent (SGD)**, especially in compute vision:

```
tf_loss_minimize = tf.train.RMSPropOptimizer(learning_rate=tf_
learning_rate, momentum=0.9).minimize(tf_loss)
```

Finally, to calculate the accuracy of the predictions by comparing the predicted labels to actual labels, we will define the following prediction calculation function:

```
tf_predictions = tf.nn.softmax(tf_logits)
```

You just finished learning about the functions that we used to create our first CNN. You learned to use the functions to implement the CNN structure as well as define the loss, minimizing the loss, and getting the predictions to unseen data. We used a simple CNN to see if it could learn to classify handwritten images. Also, we were able to achieve an accuracy above 98% with a reasonabley simple CNN. Next we will analyze some of the results produced by the CNN. We will see why the CNN couldn't recognize some of the images correctly.

# Analyzing the predictions produced with a CNN

Here, we can randomly pick some correctly and incorrectly classified samples from the test set to evaluate the learning power of CNNs (see *Figure 5.12*). We can see that for the correctly classified instances, the CNN is very confident about the output, which can be seen as a good property of a learning algorithm. However, when we evaluate the incorrectly classified examples, we can see that they are in fact difficult, and even a human can get some of them wrong (for example, the third image from the left in the second row). For the incorrect samples, the CNN often is not as confident as it is for the correct samples, which again is a good characteristic. Also, even though the highest confidence answer is wrong for the misclassified ones, the correct label is often not completely ignored and given some recognition in terms of the value of the prediction:

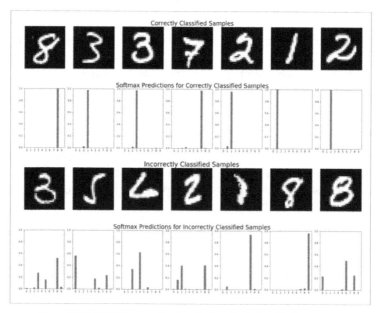

Figure 5.12: MNIST correctly classified and misclassified instances

# Using CNNs for sentence classification

Though CNNs have mostly been used for computer vision tasks, nothing stops them from being used in NLP applications. One such application for which CNNs have been used effectively is sentence classification.

In sentence classification, a given sentence should be classified to a class. We will use a question database, where each question is labeled by what the question is about. For example, the question "Who was Abraham Lincoln?" will be a question and its label will be *Person*. For this we will use a sentence classification dataset available at `http://cogcomp.org/Data/QA/QC/;` here you will find 1,000 training sentences and their respective labels and 500 testing sentences.

We will use the CNN network introduced in the paper by Yoon Kim, *Convolutional Neural Networks for Sentence Classification*, to understand the value of CNNs for NLP tasks. However, using CNNs for sentence classification is somewhat different from the MNIST example we discussed, because operations (for example, convolution and pooling) now happen in one dimension rather than two dimensions. Furthermore, the pooling operations will also have certain differences from the normal pooling operation, as we will see soon. You can find the code for this exercise in the `cnn_sentence_classification.ipynb` file in the `ch5` folder.

# CNN structure

Now we will discuss the technical details of the CNN used for sentence classification. First, we will discuss how data or sentences are transformed to a preferred format that can easily be dealt with by CNNs. Next, we will discuss how the convolution and pooling operations are adapted for sentence classification, and finally, we will discuss how all these components are connected.

# Data transformation

Let's assume a sentence of $p$ words. First, we will pad the sentence with some special word (if the length of the sentence is $< n$) to set the sentence length to $n$ words, where $n \geq p$. Next, we will represent each word in the sentence by a vector of size $k$, where this vector can either be a one-hot-encoded representation, or Word2vec word vectors learnt using skip-gram, CBOW, or GloVe. Then a batch of sentences of size $b$ can be represented by a $b \times n \times k$ matrix.

Let's walk through an example. Let's consider the following three sentences:

- *Bob and Mary are friends.*
- *Bob plays soccer.*
- *Mary likes to sing in the choir.*

In this example, the third sentence has the most words, so let's set $n = 7$, which is the number of words in the third sentence. Next, let's look at the one-hot-encoded representation for each word. In this case, there are 13 distinct words. Therefore, we get this:

*Bob: 1,0,0,0,0,0,0,0,0,0,0,0,0*

*and: 0,1,0,0,0,0,0,0,0,0,0,0,0*

*Mary: 0,0,1,0,0,0,0,0,0,0,0,0,0*

Also, $k = 13$ for the same reason. With this representation, we can represent the three sentences as a three-dimensional matrix of size $3 \times 7 \times 13$, as shown in *Figure 5.13*:

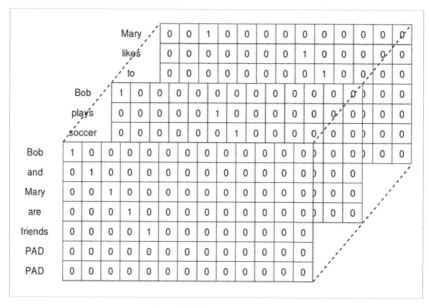

Figure 5.13: A sentence matrix

# The convolution operation

If we ignore the batch size, that is, if we assume that we are only processing a single sentence at a time, our data is a $n \times k$ matrix, where $n$ is the number of words per sentence after padding, and $k$ is the dimension of a single word vector. In our example, this would be $7 \times 13$.

Now we will define our convolution weight matrix to be of size $m \times k$, where $m$ is the filter size for a one-dimensional convolution operation. By convolving the input $x$ of size $n \times k$ with a weight matrix $W$ of size $m \times k$, we will produce an output of $h$ of size $1 \times n$ as follows:

$$h_{i,1} = \sum_{j=1}^{m} \sum_{l=1}^{k} w_{j,l} x_{i+j-1,l}$$

Here, $w_{i,j}$ is the $(i,j)^{th}$ element of $W$ and we will pad $x$ with zeros so that $h$ is of size $1 \times n$. Also, we will define this operation more simply, as shown here:

$$h = W * x + b$$

Here, * defines the convolution operation (with padding) and we will add an additional scalar bias $b$. *Figure 5.14* illustrates this operation:

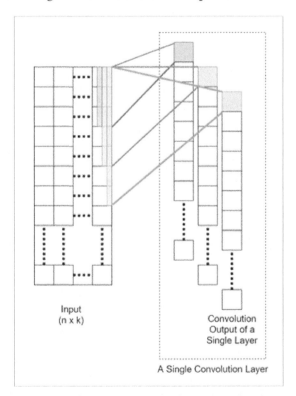

Figure 5.14: A convolution operation for sentence classification

Then, to learn a rich set of features, we have parallel layers with different convolution filter sizes. Each convolution layer outputs a hidden vector of size $1 \times n$, and we will concatenate these outputs to form the input to the next layer of size $q \times n$, where $q$ is the number of parallel layers we will use. The larger $q$ is, the better the performance of the model.

The value of convolving can be understood in the following manner. Think about the movie rating learning problem (with two classes, positive or negative), and we have the following sentences:

- *I like the movie, not too bad*
- *I did not like the movie, bad*

Now imagine a convolution window of size 5. Let's bin the words according to the movement of the convolution window.

The sentence *I like the movie, not too bad* gives:

*[I, like, the, movie, ',']*

*[like, the, movie, ',', not]*

*[the, movie, ',', not, too]*

*[movie, ',', not, too, bad]*

The sentence *I did not like the movie, bad* gives the following:

*[I, did, not, like, the]*

*[did, not ,like, the, movie]*

*[not, like, the, movie, ',']*

*[like, the, movie, ',', bad]*

For the first sentence, windows such as the following convey that the rating is positive:

*[I, like, the, movie, ',']*

*[movie, ',', not, too, bad]*

However, for the second sentence, windows such as the following convey negativity in the rating:

*[did, not, like, the, movie]*

We are able to see such patterns that help to classify ratings thanks to the preserved spatiality. For example, if you use a technique such as *bag-of-words* to calculate sentence representations that lose spatial information, the sentence representations would be highly similar. The convolution operation plays an important role in preserving spatial information of the sentences.

Having $q$ different layers with different filter sizes, the network learns to extract the rating with different size phrases, leading to an improved performance.

# Pooling over time

The pooling operation is designed to subsample the outputs produced by the previously discussed parallel convolution layers. This is achieved as follows.

Let's assume the output of the last layer $h$ is of size $q \times n$. The pooling over time layer would produce an output $h'$ of size $q \times 1$ output. The precise calculation would be as follows:

$$h_{i,1}' = \left\{ max\left(h^{(i)}\right) where 1 \leq i \leq q \right\}$$

Here, $h^{(i)} = W^{(i)} * x + b$ and $h^{(i)}$ is the output produced by the $i^{th}$ convolution layer and $W^{(i)}$ is the set of weights belonging to that layer. Simply put, the pooling over time operation creates a vector by concatenating the maximum element of each convolution layer. We will illustrate this operation in *Figure 5.15*:

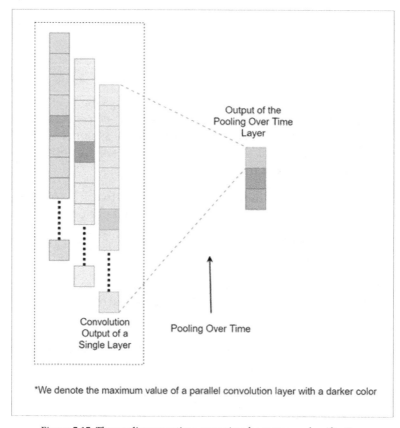

Figure 5.15: The pooling over time operation for sentence classification

By combining these operations, we finally arrive at the architecture shown in *Figure 5.16*:

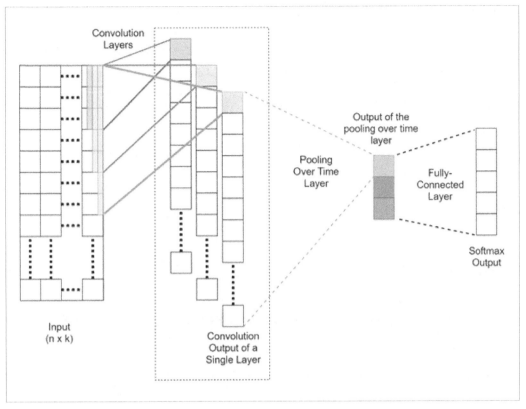

5.16: A sentence classification CNN architecture

# Implementation – sentence classification with CNNs

First, we will define the inputs and outputs. The input will be a batch of sentences, where the words are represented by one-hot-encoded word vectors — word embeddings will deliver even better performance than the one-hot-encoded representations; however, we will use the one-hot-encoded representation for simplicity:

```
sent_inputs = tf.placeholder(shape=[batch_size,sent_length,vocabulary_
size],dtype=tf.float32,name='sentence_inputs')
sent_labels = tf.placeholder(shape=[batch_size,num_classes],dtype=tf.
float32,name='sentence_labels')
```

Here, we will define three different one-dimensional convolution layers with three different filter sizes of 3, 5, and 7 (provided as a list in `filter_sizes`) and their respective biases:

```
w1 = tf.Variable(tf.truncated_normal([filter_sizes[0],vocabulary_
size,1],stddev=0.02,dtype=tf.float32),name='weights_1')
b1 = tf.Variable(tf.random_uniform([1],0,0.01,dtype=tf.
float32),name='bias_1')

w2 = tf.Variable(tf.truncated_normal([filter_sizes[1],vocabulary_
size,1],stddev=0.02,dtype=tf.float32),name='weights_2')
b2 = tf.Variable(tf.random_uniform([1],0,0.01,dtype=tf.
float32),name='bias_2')

w3 = tf.Variable(tf.truncated_normal([filter_sizes[2],vocabulary_
size,1],stddev=0.02,dtype=tf.float32),name='weights_3')
b3 = tf.Variable(tf.random_uniform([1],0,0.01,dtype=tf.
float32),name='bias_3')
```

Now we will calculate three outputs, each belonging to a single convolution layer, as we just defined. This can easily be calculated with the `tf.nn.conv1d` function provided in TensorFlow. We use a stride of 1 and zero padding to ensure that the outputs will have the same size as the input:

```
h1_1 = tf.nn.relu(tf.nn.conv1d(sent_inputs,w1,stride=1,padding='SAME'
) + b1)
h1_2 = tf.nn.relu(tf.nn.conv1d(sent_inputs,w2,stride=1,padding='SAME'
) + b2)
h1_3 = tf.nn.relu(tf.nn.conv1d(sent_inputs,w3,stride=1,padding='SAME'
) + b3)
```

For calculating max pooling over time, we need to write the elementary functions to do that in TensorFlow, as TensorFlow does not have a native function that does this for us. However, it is quite easy to write these functions.

First, we will calculate the maximum value of each hidden output produced by each convolution layer. This results in a single scalar for each layer:

```
h2_1 = tf.reduce_max(h1_1,axis=1)
h2_2 = tf.reduce_max(h1_2,axis=1)
h2_3 = tf.reduce_max(h1_3,axis=1)
```

Then we will concatenate the produced outputs on axis 1 (width) to produce an output of size $batchsize \times q$:

```
h2 = tf.concat([h2_1,h2_2,h2_3],axis=1)
```

Next, we will define the fully connected layers, which will be fully connected to the output *batchsize*×*q* produced by the pooling over time layer. There is only one fully connected layer in this case and this will also be our output layer:

```
w_fc1 = tf.Variable(tf.truncated_normal([len(filter_sizes),num_
classes],stddev=0.5,dtype=tf.float32),name='weights_fulcon_1')
b_fc1 = tf.Variable(tf.random_uniform([num_classes],0,0.01,dtype=tf.
float32),name='bias_fulcon_1')
```

The function defined here will produce the logits that are then used to calculate the loss of the network:

```
logits = tf.matmul(h2,w_fc1) + b_fc1
```

Here, by applying the softmax activation to the logits, we will obtain the predictions:

```
predictions = tf.argmax(tf.nn.softmax(logits),axis=1)
```

Also, we will define the `loss` function, which is the cross-entropy loss:

```
loss = tf.reduce_mean(tf.nn.softmax_cross_entropy_with_logits_
v2(labels=sent_labels,logits=logits))
```

To optimize the network, we will use a TensorFlow built-in optimizer called `MomentumOptimizer`:

```
optimizer = tf.train.MomentumOptimizer(learning_
rate=0.01,momentum=0.9).minimize(loss)
```

Running these preceding defined operations to optimize the CNN and evaluate the test data as given in the exercise, gives us a test accuracy close to 90% (500 test sentences) in this sentence classification task.

Here we end our discussion about using CNNs for sentence classification. We first discussed how one-dimensional convolution operations combined with a special pooling operation called *pooling over time* can be used to implement a sentence classifier based on the CNN architecture. Finally, we discussed how to use TensorFlow to implement such a CNN and saw that it in fact performs well in sentence classification.

It can be useful to know how the problem we just solved can be useful in the real world. Assume that you have a large document about the history of Rome in your hand, and you want to find out about Julius Caesar without reading the whole document. In this situation, the sentence classifier we just implemented can be used as a handy tool to summarize the sentences that only correspond to a person, so you don't have to read the whole document.

Sentence classification can be used for many other tasks as well; one common use of this is classifying movie reviews as positive or negative, which is useful for automating computation of movie ratings. Another important application of sentence classification can be seen in the medical domain, which is extracting clinically useful sentences from large documents containing large amounts of text.

# Summary

In this chapter, we discussed CNNs and their various applications. First, we went through a detailed explanation about what CNNs are and their ability to excel at machine learning tasks. Next we decomposed the CNN into several components, such as convolution and pooling layers, and discussed in detail how these operators work. Furthermore, we discussed several hyperparameters that are related to these operators such as filter size, stride, and padding. Then, to illustrate the functionality of CNNs, we walked through a simple example of classifying images of handwritten digits to the corresponding image. We also did a bit of analysis to see why the CNN fails to recognize some images correctly. Finally, we started talking about how CNNs are applied for NLP tasks. Concretely, we discussed an altered architecture of CNNs that can be used to classify sentences. We then implemented this particular CNN architecture and tested it on an actual sentence classification task.

In the next chapter, we will move on to one of the most popular types of neural networks used for many NLP tasks — **Recurrent Neural Networks (RNNs)**.

# 6

# Recurrent Neural Networks

**Recurrent Neural Networks (RNNs)** are a special family of neural networks that are designed to cope with sequential data (that is, time series data), such as a sequence of texts (for example, variable length sentence or a document) or stock market prices. RNNs maintain a state variable that captures the various patterns present in sequential data; therefore, they are able to model sequential data. For example, conventional feed-forward neural networks do not have this ability unless the data is represented with a feature representation that captures the important patterns present in the sequence. However, coming up with such feature representations is extremely difficult. Another alternative for feed-forward models to model sequential data is to have a separate set of parameters for each position in time/sequence. So that the set of parameters assigned to a certain position learns about the patterns that occur at that position. This will greatly increase the memory requirement for your model.

However, as opposed to having a separate set of parameters for each position like feed-forward networks, RNNs share the same set of parameters over time. Sharing parameters over time is an important part of RNNs and in fact is one of the main enablers for learning temporal patterns. Then the state variable is updated over time for each input we observe in the sequence. These parameters shared over time, combined with the state vector, are able to predict the next value of a sequence, given the previously observed values of the sequence. Furthermore, since we process a single element of a sequence at a time (for example, one word in a document at a time), RNNs can process data of arbitrary lengths without padding data with special tokens.

In this chapter, we will dive into the details of RNNs. First, we will discuss how an RNN can be formed by starting with a simple feed-forward model. After this we will discuss the basic functionality of an RNN. We also will delve into the underlying equations, such as output calculation and parameter update rules of RNNs, and discuss several variants of applications of RNNs: one-to-one, one-to-many, and many-to-many RNNs. We will walk through an example of using RNNs to generate new text based on a collection of training data and will also discuss some of the limitations of RNNs. After computing and evaluating the generated text, we will discuss a better extension of RNNs, known as the RNN-CF, that remembers longer compared with conventional RNNs.

# Understanding Recurrent Neural Networks

In this section, we will discuss what an RNN is by starting with a gentle introduction, and then move on to more in-depth technical details. We mentioned earlier that RNNs maintain a state variable which evolves over time as the RNN is seeing more data, thus giving the power to model sequential data. In particular, this state variable is updated over time by a set of recurrent connections. Existence of recurrent connections is the main structural difference between an RNN and a feed-forward network. The recurrent connections can be understood as links between a series of memory RNN learned in the past, connecting to the current state variable of the RNN. In other words, the recurrent connections update the current state variable with respect to the past memory the RNN has, enabling the RNN to make a prediction based on the current input as well as the previous inputs.

In the upcoming section, we will discuss the following things. First, we will discuss how we can start with representing a feed-forward network as a computational graph. Then we will see through an example why a feed-forward network might fail at a sequential task. Then we will adapt that feed-forward graph to model sequential data, which will give us the basic computational graph of an RNN. We will also discuss the technical details (for example, update rules) of an RNN. Finally, we will discuss the details of how we can train RNN models.

# The problem with feed-forward neural networks

To understand the limits of feed-forward neural networks and how RNNs address them, let's imagine a sequence of data:

$$x = \{x_1, x_2, \ldots x_T\}, y = \{y_1, y_2, \ldots y_T\}$$

Next, let's assume that, in the real world, $x$ and $y$ are linked in the following relationship:

$$h_t = g_1\left(x_t, h_{t-1}\right)$$

$$y_t = g_2\left(h_t\right)$$

Here, $g_1$ and $g_2$ are some functions. This means that the current output $y_t$ depends on the current state $h_t$ for some state belonging to the model that outputs $x$ and $y$. Also, $h_t$ is calculated with the current input $x_t$ and previous state $h_{t-1}$. The state encodes information about previous inputs observed in the history by the model.

Now, let's imagine a simple feed-forward neural network, which we will represent by the following:

$$y_t = f\left(x_t; \theta\right)$$

Here, $y_t$ is the predicted output for some input $x_t$.

If we use a feed-forward neural network to solve this task, the network will have to produce $\{y_1, y_2, \ldots, y_T\}$ one at a time, by taking $\{x_1, x_2, \ldots, x_T\}$ as inputs. Now, let's consider the problem we face in this solution for a time-series problem.

The predicted output $y_t$ at time $t$ of a feed-forward neural network depends only on the current input $x_t$. In other words, it does not have any knowledge about the inputs that led to $x_t$ (that is, $\{x_1, x_2, \ldots, x_{t-1}\}$). For this reason, a feed-forward neural network will fail at a task, where the current output not only depends on the current input but also on the previous inputs. Let's understand this through an example.

Say we need to train a neural network to fill missing words. We have the following phrase, and we would like to predict the next word:

*James had a cat and it likes to drink ____.*

If we are to process one word at a time and use a feed-forward neural network, we will only have the input *drink* and this is not enough at all to understand the phrase or even to understand the context (the word *drink* can appear in many different contexts). One can argue that we can achieve good results by processing the full sentence at a single go. Even though this is true, such an approach has limitations, such as it will quickly become impractical for very long sentences.

# Modeling with Recurrent Neural Networks

On the other hand, we can use an RNN to find a solution to this problem. We will start with the data we have:

$$x = \{x_1, x_2, \ldots, x_T\}, y = \{y_1, y_2, \ldots, y_T\}$$

Assume that we have the following relationship:

$$h_t = g_1(x_t, h_{t-1})$$

$$y_t = g_2(h_t)$$

Now, let's replace $g_1$ with a function approximator $f_1(x_t, h_{t-1}; \theta)$ parametrized by $\theta$ that takes the current input $x_t$ and the previous state of the system $h_{t-1}$ as the input and produces the current state $h_t$. Then, we will replace $g_2$ with $f_2(h_t; \varphi)$, which takes the current state of the system $h_t$ to produce $y_t$. This gives us the following:

$$h_t = f_1(x_t, h_{t-1}; \theta)$$

$$y_t = f_2(h_t; \varphi)$$

We can think of $f_1 \circ f_2$ as an approximation of the true model that generates $x$ and $y$. To understand this more clearly, let's now expand the equation as follows:

$$y_t = f_2(f_1(x_t, h_{t-1}; \theta); \varphi)$$

For example, we can represent $y_4$ as follows:

$$y_4 = f_2\left(f_1\left(x_4, h_3; \theta\right); \varphi\right)$$

Also, by expansion we get the following (omitting $\theta$ and $\varphi$ for clarity):

$$y_4 = f_2\left(f_1\left(x_4, f_2\left(f_1\left(x_3, f_2\left(f_1\left(x_2, f_2\left(f_1\left(x_1, h_0\right)\right)\right)\right)\right)\right)\right)\right)$$

This can be illustrated in a graph, as shown in *Figure 6.1*:

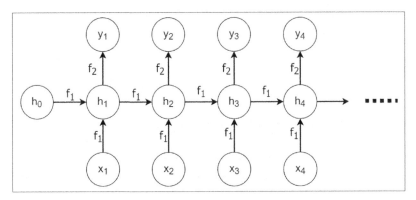

Figure 6.1: The relationship between $x_t$ and $y_t$ expanded

We can generally summarize the diagram, for any given time step $t$, as shown in *Figure 6.2*:

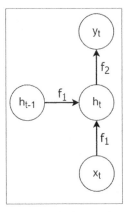

Figure 6.2: A single-step calculation of an RNN structure

However, it should be understood that $h_{t-1}$ in fact is what $h_t$ was before receiving $x_t$. In other words, $h_{t-1}$ is $h_t$ before one time step. Therefore, we can represent the calculation of $h_t$ with a recurrent connection, as shown in *Figure 6.3*:

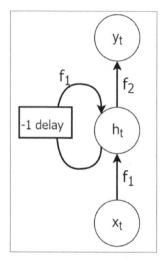

Figure 6.3: A single-step calculation of an RNN with the recurrent connection

The ability to summarize a chain of equations mapping $\{x_1, x_2, \ldots, x_T\}$ to $\{y_1, y_2, \ldots, y_T\}$ as in *Figure 6.3* allows us to write any $y_t$ in terms of $x_t$, $h_{t-1}$, and $h_t$. This is the key idea behind an RNN.

# Technical description of a Recurrent Neural Network

Let's now have an even closer look at what makes an RNN and define the mathematical equations for the calculations taking place within an RNN. Let's start with the two functions we derived as function approximators for learning $y_t$ from $x_t$:

$$h_t = f_1\left(x_t, h_{t-1}; \theta\right)$$

$$y_t = f_2\left(h_t; \varphi\right)$$

As we have seen, a neural network is composed of a set of weights and biases and some nonlinear activation function. Therefore, we can write the preceding relation as shown here:

$$h_t = \tanh\left(Ux_t + Wh_{t-1}\right)$$

Here, *tanh* is the tanh activation function, and $U$ is a weight matrix of size $m \times d$, where $m$ is the number of hidden units and $d$ is the dimensionality of the input. Also, $W$ is a weight matrix of size $m \times m$ that creates the recurrent link from $h_{t-1}$ to $h_t$. The $y_t$ relation is given by the following equation:

$$y_t = \text{softmax}\left(Vh_t\right)$$

Here, $V$ is a weight matrix of size $c \times m$ and $c$ is the dimensionality of the output (can be the number of output classes). In *Figure 6.4*, we illustrate how these weights form an RNN:

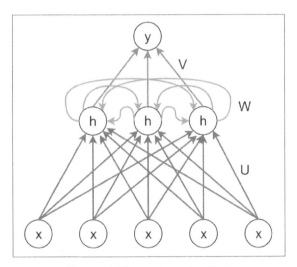

Figure 6.4: The structure of an RNN

So far, we have seen how we can represent an RNN with a graph of computational nodes, with edges denoting computations. Also, we looked at the actual mathematics behind an RNN. Let's now look at how to optimize (or train) the weights of an RNN to learn from sequential data.

# Backpropagation Through Time

For training RNNs, a special form of backpropagation, known as **Backpropagation Through Time** (**BPTT**), is used. To understand BPTT, however, first we need to understand how **backpropagation** (**BP**) works. Then we will discuss why BP cannot be directly applied to RNNs, but how BP can be adapted to RNNs, resulting in BPTT. Finally, we will discuss two major problems present in BPTT.

## How backpropagation works

Backpropagation is the technique that is used to train a feed-forward neural network. In backpropagation, you do the following:

1.  Calculate a prediction for a given input

2.  Calculate an error, $E$, of the prediction by comparing it to the actual label of the input (for example, mean squared error and cross-entropy loss)

3.  Update the weights of the feed-forward network to minimize the loss calculated in step 2, by taking a small step in the opposite direction of the gradient $\partial E / \partial w_{ij}$ for all $w_{ij}$, where $w_{ij}$ is the $j^{th}$ weight of $i^{th}$ layer

To understand more clearly, consider the feed-forward network depicted in *Figure 6.5*. This has two single weights, $w_1$ and $w_2$, and calculates two outputs, $h$ and $y$, as shown in the following figure. We assume no nonlinearities in the model for simplicity:

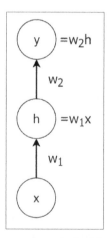

Figure 6.5: Computations of a feed-forward network

We can calculate $\frac{\partial E}{\partial w_1}$ using the chain rule as follows:

$$\frac{\partial E}{\partial w_1} = \frac{\partial L}{\partial y}\frac{\partial y}{\partial h}\frac{\partial h}{\partial w_1}$$

This simplifies to the following:

$$\frac{\partial E}{\partial w_1} = \frac{\partial(y-l)^2}{\partial y}\frac{\partial(w_2 h)}{\partial h}\frac{\partial(w_1 x)}{\partial w_1}$$

Here, $l$ is the correct label for the data point $x$. Also, we are assuming the mean squared error as the loss function. Everything here is defined, and it is quite straightforward to calculate $\frac{\partial E}{\partial w_1}$.

# Why we cannot use BP directly for RNNs

Now, let's try the same for the RNN in *Figure 6.6*. Now we have an additional recurrent weight $w_3$. We have omitted time components of inputs and outputs for the clarity of the problem we are trying to emphasize:

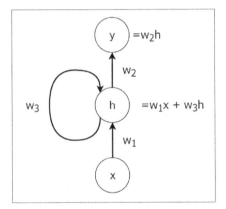

Figure 6.6: Computations of an RNN

Let's see what happens if we apply the chain rule to calculate $\frac{\partial E}{\partial w_3}$:

$$\frac{\partial E}{\partial w_3} = \frac{\partial L}{\partial y}\frac{\partial y}{\partial h}\frac{\partial h}{\partial w_3}$$

This becomes the following:

$$\frac{\partial E}{\partial w_3} = \frac{\partial (y-l)^2}{\partial y} \frac{\partial (w_2 h)}{\partial h} \left( \frac{\partial (w_1 x)}{\partial w_3} + \frac{\partial (w_3 h)}{\partial w_3} \right)$$

The term $\frac{\partial (w_3 h)}{\partial w_3}$ here creates problems because it is a recursive term. You end up with an infinite number of derivative terms, as $h$ is recursive (that is, calculating $h$ includes $h$ itself) and $h$ is not a constant and dependent on $w_3$. This is solved by unrolling the input sequence $x$ over time, creating a copy of RNN for each input $x_t$ and calculating derivatives for each copy separately and rolling them back into, by summing up the gradients, to calculate the weight update. We will discuss the details next.

# Backpropagation Through Time – training RNNs

The trick to calculating backpropagation for RNNs is to consider not a single input, but the full input sequence. Then, if we calculate $\frac{\partial E}{\partial w_3}$ at time step 4, we will get the following:

$$\frac{\partial E}{\partial w_3} = \sum_{j=1}^{3} \frac{\partial L}{\partial y_4} \frac{\partial y_4}{\partial h_4} \frac{\partial h_4}{\partial h_j} \frac{\partial h_j}{\partial w_3}$$

This means that we need to calculate the sum of gradients for all the time steps up to the fourth time step. In other words, we will first unroll the sequence so that we can calculate $\frac{\partial h_4}{\partial h_j}$ and $\frac{\partial h_j}{\partial w_3}$ for each time step $j$. This is done by creating four copies of the RNN. So, to calculate $\frac{\partial h_t}{\partial h_j}$, we need $t$-$j$+1 copies of the RNN. Then we will roll up the copies to a single RNN, by summing up gradients with respect to all previous time steps to get the gradient, and update the RNN with the gradient $\frac{\partial E}{\partial w_3}$. However, this becomes costly as the number of time steps increases. For more computational efficiency, we can use **Truncated Backpropagation Through Time (TBPTT)** to optimize recurrent models, which is an approximation of BPTT.

# Truncated BPTT – training RNNs efficiently

In TBPTT, we only calculate the gradients for a fixed number of $T$ time steps (in contrast to calculating it to the very beginning of the sequence as in BPTT).

More specifically, when calculating $\frac{\partial E}{\partial w_3}$, for time step $t$, we only calculate derivatives down to $t$-$T$ (that is, we do not compute derivatives up to the very beginning):

$$\frac{\partial E}{\partial w_3} = \sum_{j=t-T}^{t-1} \frac{\partial L}{\partial y_t} \frac{\partial y_t}{\partial h_t} \frac{\partial h_t}{\partial h_j} \frac{\partial h_j}{\partial w_3}$$

This is much more computationally efficient than standard BPTT. In standard BPTT, for each time step $t$, we calculate derivatives up to the very beginning of the sequence. But this gets computationally infeasible as the sequence length becomes larger and larger (for example, processing a text document word by word). However, in truncated BPTT, we only calculate the derivatives up for a fixed number of steps backwards, and as you can imagine, the computational cost does not change as the sequence becomes larger.

# Limitations of BPTT – vanishing and exploding gradients

Having a way to calculate gradients for recurrent weights and having a computationally efficient approximation such as TBPTT does not enable us to train RNNs without trouble. Something else can go wrong with the calculations.

To see why, let's expand a single term in $\frac{\partial E}{\partial w_3}$, which is as follows:

$$\frac{\partial L}{\partial y_4} \frac{\partial y_4}{\partial h_4} \frac{\partial h_4}{\partial h_1} \frac{\partial h_1}{\partial w_3} = \frac{\partial L}{\partial y_4} \frac{\partial y_4}{\partial h_4} \frac{\partial \left( w_1 x + w_3 h_3 \right)}{\partial h_1} \frac{\partial \left( w_1 x + w_3 h_0 \right)}{\partial w_3}$$

Since we know that the issues of backpropagation arise from the recurrent connections, let's ignore the $w_1 x$ terms and consider the following:

$$\frac{\partial L}{\partial y_4} \frac{\partial y_4}{\partial h_4} \frac{\partial \left( w_3 h_3 \right)}{\partial h_1} \frac{\partial \left( w_3 h_0 \right)}{\partial w_3}$$

By simply expanding *h3* and doing simple arithmetic operations we can show this:

$$= \frac{\partial L}{\partial y_4} \frac{\partial y_4}{\partial h_4} h_0 w_3^3$$

We see that for just four time steps we have a term $w_3^3$. So at the $n^{th}$ time step, it would become, $w_3^{n-1}$. Say we initialized $w_3$ to be very small (say 0.00001) at *n=100* time step, the gradient would be infinitesimally small (of scale $0.1^{500}$). Also, since computers have limited precision in representing a number, this update would be ignored (that is, arithmetic underflow). This is called the **vanishing gradient**. Solving the vanishing gradient is not very straightforward. There are no easy ways of rescaling the gradients so that they will properly propagate through time. Few techniques to solve the problem of vanishing gradients to some extent is to use careful initialization of weights (for example, the Xavier initialization) or use momentum-based optimization methods (that is, in addition to the current gradient update, we add an additional term, which is the accumulation of all the past gradients, known as the **velocity term**). However, more principled approaches to solving this, such as different structural modifications to the standard RNN, have been introduced, as we will see in *Chapter 7, Long Short-Term Memory Networks*.

On the other hand, say that we initialized $w_3$ to be very large (say 1000.00). Then at the *n=100* time step, the gradients would be massive (of scale $10^{300}$). This leads to numerical instabilities and you will get values such as Inf or NaN (that is, not a number) in Python. This is called the **exploding gradient**.

Gradient explosion also can take place due to the complexity of the loss surface of a problem. Complex nonconvex loss surfaces are very common in deep neural networks due to both the dimensionality of inputs as well as the large number of parameters (weights) present in the models. *Figure 6.7* illustrates the loss surface of an RNN and highlights the presence of walls with very high curvature. If the optimization method comes in contact with such a wall, then the gradients will explode or overshoot, as shown by the solid line in the image. This can either lead to very poor loss minimization or numerical instabilities or both. A simple solution to avoid gradient explosion in such situations is to clip the gradients to a reasonably small value when it is larger than some threshold. The dashed line in the figure shows what happens when we clip the gradient at some small value. (Gradient clipping is covered well in the paper *On the difficulty of training recurrent neural networks, Pascanu, Mikolov,* and *Bengio, International Conference on Machine Learning (2013): 1310-1318.*)

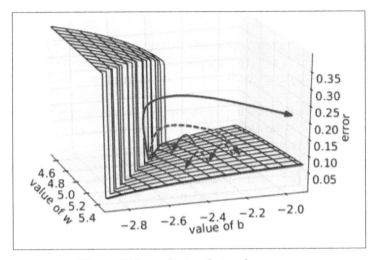

Figure 6.7: The gradient explosion phenomenon
Source: This figure is from the paper, On the difficulty of training recurrent neural
networks by Pascanu, Mikolov, and Bengio

Next we will discuss various ways that RNNs can be used to solve applications. These applications include sentence classification, image captioning, and machine translation. We will categorize the RNNs to several different categories such as one-to-one, one-to-many, many-to-one, and many-to-many.

# Applications of RNNs

So far what we have talked about is a one-to-one mapped RNN, where the current output depends on the current input as well as the previously observed history of inputs. This means that there exists an output for the sequence of previously observed inputs and the current input. However, in the real word, there can be situations where there is only one output for a sequence of inputs, a sequence of outputs for a single input, and a sequence of outputs for a sequence of inputs where the sequence sizes are different. In this section, we will look at a few such applications.

# One-to-one RNNs

In one-to-one RNNs, the current input depends on the previously observed inputs (see *Figure 6.8*). Such RNNs are appropriate for problems where each input has an output, but the output depends both on the current input and the history of inputs that led to the current input. An example of such a task is stock market prediction, where we output a value for the current input, and this output also depends on how the previous inputs have behaved. Another example would be scene classification, where each pixel in an image is labeled (for example, labels such as car, road, and person). Sometimes $x_{t+1}$ can be same as $y_t$ for some problems. For example, in text generation problems, the previously predicted word becomes an input to predict the next word. The following figure depicts a one-to-one RNN:

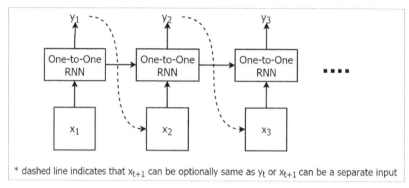

\* dashed line indicates that $x_{t+1}$ can be optionally same as $y_t$ or $x_{t+1}$ can be a separate input

Figure 6.8: One-to-one RNNs having temporal dependencies

# One-to-many RNNs

A one-to-many RNN would take a single input and output a sequence (see *Figure 6.9*). Here, we assume the inputs to be independent of each other. That is, we do not need information about previous inputs to make a prediction about the current input. However, the recurrent connections are needed because, although we process a single input, the output is a sequence of values that depends on the previous output values. An example task where such an RNN would be used is an image captioning task. For example, for a given input image, the text caption can consist of five or ten words. In other words, the RNN will keep predicting words until it outputs a meaningful phrase describing the image. The following figure depicts a one-to-many RNN:

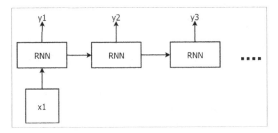

Figure 6.9. A one-to-many RNN

# Many-to-one RNNs

Many-to-one RNNs take an input of arbitrary length as an input and produce a single output for the sequence of inputs (see *Figure 6.10*). Sentence classification is one such task that can benefit from a many-to-one RNN. A sentence is a sequence of words of arbitrary length, which is taken as the input to the network, is used to produce an output classifying the sentence to one of a set of predefined classes. Some specific examples of sentence classification are as follows:

- Classifying movie reviews as positive or negative statements (that is, sentiment analysis)
- Classifying a sentence depending on what the sentence describes (for example, person, object, and location)

Another application of many-to-one RNNs is classifying large-scale images by processing only a patch of images at a time and moving the window over the whole image

The following figure depicts a many-to-one RNN:

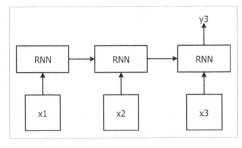

Figure 6.10: A many-to-one RNN

# Many-to-many RNNs

Many-to-many RNNs often produce arbitrary-length outputs from arbitrary-length inputs (see *Figure 6.11*). In other words, inputs and outputs do not have to be of the same length. This is particularly useful in machine translation, where we translate a sentence from one language to another. As you can imagine, one sentence in a certain language does not always align with a sentence from another language. Another such example is chatbots, where the chatbot reads a sequence of words (that is, a user request) and outputs a sequence of words (that is, the answer). The following figure depicts a many-to-many RNN:

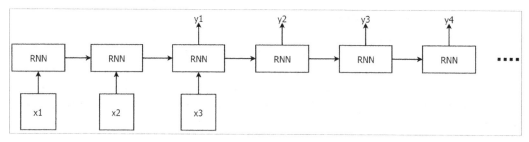

Figure 6.11: A many-to-many RNN

We can summarize the different types of applications of feed-forward networks and RNNs as follows:

| Algorithm | Description | Applications |
|---|---|---|
| One-to-one RNNs | These take a single input and give a single output. Current input depends on the previously observed input(s). | Stock market prediction, scene classification, and text generation |
| One-to-many RNNs | These take a single input and give an output consisting of an arbitrary number of elements | Image captioning |
| Many-to-one RNNs | These take a sequence of inputs and give a single output. | Sentence classification (considering a single word as a single input) |
| Many-to-many RNNs | These take a sequence of arbitrary length as inputs and outputs a sequence of arbitrary length. | Machine translation, chatbots |

# Generating text with RNNs

Now let's look at our first example of using an RNN for an interesting task. In this exercise, we will be using an RNN to generate a fairy tale story! This is a one-to-one RNN problem. We will train a single layer RNN on a collection of fairy tales and ask the RNN to generate a new story. For this task, we will use a small text corpus of 20 different tales (which we will increase later). This example also will highlight one of the crucial limitations of RNNs: the lack of persisting long-term memory. This exercise is available in `rnn_language_bigram.ipynb` in the `ch6` folder.

# Defining hyperparameters

First, we will define several hyperparameters needed for our RNN, as shown here:

- The number of unrolls to perform at one time step. This is the number of steps that the input unrolled for, as discussed in the TBPTT method (*T* in the *Truncated BPTT – training RNNs efficiently* section). The higher this number is, the longer the RNN's memory is. However, due to the vanishing gradient, the effect of this value disappears for very high `num_unroll` values (say, above 50). Note that increasing `num_unroll` increases the memory requirement of the program as well.

- The batch size for training data, validation data, and test data. A higher batch size often leads to better results as we are seeing more data during each optimization step, but just like `num_unroll`, this causes a higher memory requirement.

- The dimensionality of the input, output, and the hidden layer. Increasing dimensionality of the hidden layer usually leads to a better performance. However, note that increasing the size of the hidden layer causes all three sets of weights (that is, *U*, *W*, and *V*) to increase as well, thus resulting in a high computational footprint.

First, we will define our unrolls and batch and test batch sizes:

```
num_unroll = 50
batch_size = 64
test_batch_size = 1
```

We will next define the number of units in a hidden layer (we will be using a single hidden layer RNN), followed by the input and output sizes:

```
hidden = 64
in_size,out_size = vocabulary_size,vocabulary_size
```

# Unrolling the inputs over time for Truncated BPTT

Unrolling the inputs over time is an important part of the RNN optimization process (TBPTT), as we saw earlier. So, this is our next step: defining how the inputs are unrolled over time.

Let's consider an example to understand how unrolling is done:

*Bob and Mary went to buy some flowers.*

Let's assume that we process the data at the granularity level of characters. Also, consider one batch of data and that the number of steps to unroll (num_unroll) is 5.

First, we will break the sentence into characters:

*'B', 'o', 'b', ' ', 'a', 'n', 'd', ' ', 'M', 'a', 'r', 'y', ' ', 'w', 'e', 'n', 't', ' ', 't', 'o', ' ', 'b', 'u', 'y', ' ', 's', 'o', 'm', 'e', ' ', 'f', 'l', 'o', 'w', 'e', 'r', 's'*

If we take the first three batches of inputs and outputs with unrolling, it would look like this:

| Input | Output |
|---|---|
| *'B', 'o', 'b', ' ', 'a'* | *'o', ' ', 'b', 'a', 'n'* |
| *'n', 'd', ' ', 'M', 'a'* | *'d', ' ', 'M', 'a', 'r'* |
| *'r', 'y', ' ', 'w', 'e'* | *'y', ' ', 'w', 'e', 'n'* |

By doing this, the RNN sees a relatively long sequence of data at a time, unlike processing a single character at a time. Therefore, it can retain longer memories of the sequence:

```
train_dataset, train_labels = [],[]
for ui in range(num_unroll):
    train_dataset.append(tf.placeholder(tf.float32,
        shape=[batch_size,in_size],name='train_dataset_%d'%ui))
    train_labels.append(tf.placeholder(tf.float32,
        shape=[batch_size,out_size],name='train_labels_%d'%ui))
```

# Defining the validation dataset

We will define a validation dataset to measure the performance of the RNN over time. We do not train with the data in the validation set. We only observe the predictions given for validation data as an indication of performance of the RNN:

```
valid_dataset = tf.placeholder(tf.float32,
    shape=[1,in_size],name='valid_dataset')
valid_labels = tf.placeholder(tf.float32,
    shape=[1,out_size],name='valid_labels')
```

We collect a validation set by using longer stories and extracting a part of the story from the very end. You can understand the details in the code as the code is documented meticulously.

# Defining weights and biases

Here we will define several weights and bias parameters of the RNN:

- W_xh: Weights between the inputs and the hidden layer
- W_hh: Weights of the recurrent connections of the hidden layer
- W_hy: Weights between the hidden layer and the outputs

```
W_xh = tf.Variable(tf.truncated_normal(
                   [in_size,hidden],stddev=0.02,
                   dtype=tf.float32),name='W_xh')
W_hh = tf.Variable(tf.truncated_normal([hidden,hidden],
                   stddev=0.02,
                   dtype=tf.float32),name='W_hh')
W_hy = tf.Variable(tf.truncated_normal(
                   [hidden,out_size],stddev=0.02,
                   dtype=tf.float32),name='W_hy')
```

# Defining state persisting variables

Here we will define one of the most important entities that differentiate RNNs from feed-forward neural networks: the state of the RNN. The state variables represent the memory of RNNs. Also, these are modeled as untrainable TensorFlow variables.

We will first define variables (training data: `prev_train_h` and validation data: `prev_valid_h`) to persist the previous state of the hidden layer that is used to calculate the current hidden state. We will define two state variables. One state variable maintains the state of the RNN during training and the other maintains the state of the RNN during validation:

```
prev_train_h = tf.Variable(tf.zeros([batch_size,hidden],
               dtype=tf.float32),name='train_h',trainable=False)
               name='prev_h1',trainable=False)
prev_valid_h = tf.Variable(tf.zeros([1,hidden],dtype=tf.float32),
               name='valid_h',trainable=False)
```

# Calculating the hidden states and outputs with unrolled inputs

Next we will define the hidden layer calculations per each unrolled input, the unnormalized scores, and the predictions. In order to calculate the output for each hidden layer, we maintain the `num_unroll` hidden state outputs (that is, `outputs` in code) representing each unrolled element. Then the unnormalized predictions (also called logits or scores) and softmax predictions are calculated for all the `num_unroll` steps:

```
# Appending the calculated output of RNN for each step in
# the num_unroll steps
outputs = list()

# This will be iteratively used within num_unroll steps of calculation
output_h = prev_train_h

# Calculating the output of the RNN for num_unroll steps
# (as required by the truncated BPTT)
for ui in range(num_unroll):
        output_h = tf.nn.tanh(
            tf.matmul(tf.concat([train_dataset[ui],output_h],1),
                    tf.concat([W_xh,W_hh],0))
        )
        outputs.append(output_h)
```

Then we will calculate the unnormalized predictions (`y_scores`) and normalized predictions (`y_predictions`) as follows:

```
# Get the scores and predictions for all the RNN outputs
# we produced for num_unroll steps
y_scores = [tf.matmul(outputs[ui],W_hy) for ui in range(num_unroll)]
y_predictions = [tf.nn.softmax(y_scores[ui]) for ui in range(num_
unroll)]
```

# Calculating the loss

After the predictions are calculated, we will calculate `rnn_loss` as follows. The loss is the cross-entropy loss between the predicted and actual outputs. Note that we save the last output of the RNN (`output_h`) into the `prev_train_h` variable, with the `tf.control_dependencies(...)` operation. So that in the next iteration, we can start with the previously saved RNN output as the initial state:

```
# Here we make sure that before calculating the loss,
# the state variable
# is updated with the last RNN output state we obtained
with tf.control_dependencies([tf.assign(prev_train_h,output_h)]):
    # We calculate the softmax cross entropy for all the predictions
    # we obtained in all num_unroll steps at once.
    rnn_loss = tf.reduce_mean(
            tf.nn.softmax_cross_entropy_with_logits_v2(
            logits=tf.concat(y_scores,0),
            labels=tf.concat(train_labels,0)
))
```

# Resetting state at the beginning of a new segment of text

We also need to define hidden state reset operations. The reset is especially used before producing a new chunk of text at test time. Otherwise, the RNN would continue producing text dependent on the previously produced text, leading to highly correlated outputs. This is bad because it eventually will lead the RNN to output the same word over and over again. It is still debatable if resetting the state is practically beneficial during training. Nevertheless, we define the TensorFlow operations for that:

```
# Reset the hidden states
reset_train_h_op = tf.assign(prev_train_h,tf.zeros(
                                [batch_size,hidden],
                                dtype=tf.float32))
reset_valid_h_op = tf.assign(prev_valid_h,tf.zeros(
                                [1,hidden],dtype=tf.float32))
```

# Calculating validation output

Here, similar to the training state, loss and prediction calculation, we define a state, loss and prediction for validation:

```
# Compute the next valid state (only for 1 step)
next_valid_state = tf.nn.tanh(tf.matmul(valid_dataset,W_xh) +
                              tf.matmul(prev_valid_h,W_hh))

# Calculate the prediction using the state output of the RNN
# But before that, assign the latest state output of the RNN
# to the state variable of the validation phase
# So you need to make sure you execute valid_predictions operation
# To update the validation state
with tf.control_dependencies([tf.assign(prev_valid_h,next_valid_
state)]):
    valid_scores = tf.matmul(next_valid_state,W_hy)
    valid_predictions = tf.nn.softmax(valid_scores)
```

# Calculating gradients and optimizing

Since we have the loss for the RNN defined, we will use stochastic gradient methods to calculate gradients and apply them. For this, we use TBPTT. In this method, we will unroll the RNN over time (similar to how we unrolled the inputs over time) and calculate gradients, then roll back the calculated gradients to update the weights of the RNN. Also, we will be using AdamOptimizer, which is a momentum-based optimization method that has shown far better convergence rates than the standard stochastic gradient descent. Moreover, be sure to use a small learning rate when using Adam (for example, between 0.001 and 0.0001). We will also use gradient clipping to prevent any potential gradient explosions:

```
rnn_optimizer = tf.train.AdamOptimizer(learning_rate=0.001)

gradients, v = zip(*rnn_optimizer.compute_gradients(rnn_loss))
gradients, _ = tf.clip_by_global_norm(gradients, 5.0)
rnn_optimizer = rnn_optimizer.apply_gradients(zip(gradients, v))
```

# Outputting a freshly generated chunk of text

Now we will see how we can use the trained model to output new text. Here, we will predict a word and use that word as the next input and predict another word, and continue in this manner for several time steps:

```
# Maintain the previous state of hidden nodes in testing phase
prev_test_h = tf.Variable(tf.zeros([test_batch_size,hidden],
                          dtype=tf.float32),name='test_h')

# Test dataset
test_dataset = tf.placeholder(tf.float32, shape=[test_batch_size,
                          in_size],name='test_dataset')

# Calculating hidden output for test data
next_test_state = tf.nn.tanh(tf.matmul(test_dataset,W_xh) +
                          tf.matmul(prev_test_h,W_hh)
                  )

# Making sure that the test hidden state is updated
# every time we make a prediction
with tf.control_dependencies([tf.assign(prev_test_h,next_test_
state)]):
    test_prediction = tf.nn.softmax(tf.matmul(next_test_state,W_hy))

# Note that we are using small imputations when resetting
# the test state
# As this helps to add more variation to the generated text
reset_test_h_op = tf.assign(prev_test_h,tf.truncated_normal(
                          [test_batch_size,hidden],stddev=0.01,
                          dtype=tf.float32))
```

# Evaluating text results output from the RNN

Here we will display a segment of text we generated using our RNN. We will show results of when we do not use input unrolling as well as when we use input unrolling.

Without input unrolling, we get the following after 10 epochs:

```
    he the the the the the the the the the the the the the the the the the
the the the the the the the the the the the the the the the the the the the
the the the the the the the the the the the the the the the the the the the
the the the the the the the the the the the the the
    o the the the the the the the the the the the the the the the the the the
the the the the the the the the the the the the the the the the the the the
the the the the the the the the the the the the the the the the the the the
the the the the the the the the the the the the the t
```

With input unrolling, we get the following after 10 epochs:

```
... god grant that our sister may be here, and then we shall be free.
when the maiden,who was standing behind the door watching, heard that
wish,
she came forth, and on this all the ravens were restored to their
human form again.  and they embraced and kissed each other,
and went joyfully home whome, and wanted to eat and drink, and
looked for their little plates and glasses.  then said one after
the other, who has eaten something from my plate.  who has drunk
out of my little glass.  it was a human mouth.  and when the
seventh came to the bottom of the glass, the ring rolled against
his mouth.  then he looked at it, and saw that it was a ring
belonging to his father and mother, and said, god grant that our
sister may be here, and then we shall be free. ...
```

The first thing we can note from these results is that it in fact helps to do input unrolling over time, compared to processing a single input at a time. However, even with unrolling the input, there are some grammatical mistakes and rare spelling mistakes. (This is acceptable as we are processing two characters at a time.)

The other noticeable observation is that our RNN tries to produce a new story by combining different stories that it has previously seen. You can see that it first talks about ravens, and then it moves the story to something similar to *Goldilocks and the Three Bears*, by talking about plates and someone eating from plates. Next the story brings up a ring.

This means that the RNN has learned to combine stories and come up with a new one. However, we can further improve these results by introducing better learning models (for example, LSTM) and better search techniques (for example, beam-search), as we will see in later chapters.

Due to the complexity of the language and the smaller representational power of RNNs, it is unlikely you will get outputs as nice-looking as the text shown here, throughout the learning process. Therefore we have cherry-picked some generated text to get our point across.

Note that this is a cherry-picked generated sample and, if you pay attention, over time you will see that the RNN tries to repeat the same chunk of text over and over again if you keep predicting for many iterations. You can already see that this is already present in the preceding chunk, where the first sentence is identical to the last sentence. This issue becomes more prominent as we increase the size of the dataset as we will see soon. This is due to limited memory capabilities of the RNNs caused by the *vanishing gradient problem*, and we would like to reduce this effect. So we will soon talk about one variant of RNNs, called the **RNNs with Context Features (RNN-CF)**, which reduces this effect.

# Perplexity – measuring the quality of the text result

It is not just enough to produce text; we also need a way to measure the quality of the produced text. One such way is to measure how *surprised* or *perplexed* the RNN was to see the output given the input. That is, if the cross-entropy loss for an input $x_i$ and its corresponding output $y_i$ is $l(x_i, y_i)$, then the perplexity would be as follows:

$$p(x_i, y_i) = e^{l(x_i, y_i)}$$

Using this, we can compute the average perplexity for a training dataset of size $N$ with the following:

$$p(D_{train}) = (1/N) \sum_{i=1}^{N} p(x_i, y_i)$$

In *Figure 6.12*, we show the behavior of the training and validation perplexities over time. We can see that the train perplexity goes down over time steadily, where the validation perplexity is fluctuating significantly. This is expected because what we are essentially evaluating in the validation perplexity is our RNN's ability to predict a unseen text based on our learning on training data. Since language can be quite difficult to model, this is a very difficult task, and these fluctuations are natural:

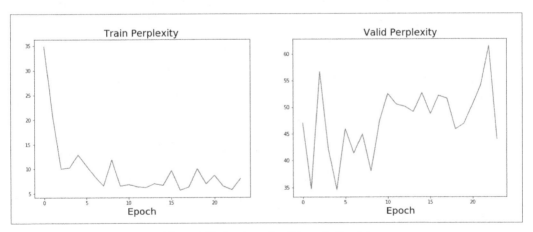

Figure 6.12: A train and valid perplexity plot

One way to improve the results is to add more hidden layers to the RNN, as often deeper models deliver better results. We have implemented a three-layer RNN in `rnn_language_bigram_multilayer.ipynb` in the `ch6` folder. We leave this for the reader to explore.

Now we come to the question, are there better variants of RNNs that work even better? For example, are there variants of RNNs that solve the problem of the vanishing gradient more effectively? Let's talk about one such variant called the RNN-CF in the next section.

# Recurrent Neural Networks with Context Features – RNNs with longer memory

Earlier, we discussed two important challenges in training a simple RNN: the exploding gradient and the vanishing gradient. We also know that we can prevent gradient explosion with a simple trick such as gradient clipping, leading to more stable training. However, solving the vanishing gradient takes much more effort, because there is no simple scaling/clipping mechanism to solve the gradient vanishing, as we did for gradient explosion. Therefore, we need to modify the structure of the RNN itself, giving explicitly the ability for it to remember longer patterns in sequences of data .The RNN-CF proposed in the paper, *Learning Longer Memory in Recurrent Neural Networks, Tomas Mikolov and others, International Conference on Learning Representations (2015)*, is one such modification to the standard RNN, helping RNNs to memorize patterns in sequences of data for longer.

An RNN-CF provides an improvement to reduce the vanishing gradient by introducing a new state and a new set of forward and recurrent connections. In other words, an RNN-CF will have two state vectors, compared to a standard RNN which has only a single state vector. The idea is that one state vector changes slowly, retaining longer memory, while the other state vector can change rapidly, working as short-term memory.

# Technical description of the RNN-CF

Here we modify the conventional RNN with several more parameters to help persisting memory for a longer time. These modifications include introducing a new state vector, in addition to the conventional state vector present in a standard RNN model. As a result of this, several forward and recurrent sets of weights are also introduced. On an abstract level, *Figure 6.13* compares an RNN-CF and its modifications with a simple RNN:

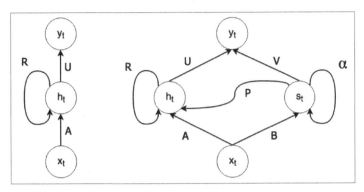

Figure 6.13: Comparing an RNN and an RNN-CF side by side

As we can see from the preceding figure, an RNN-CF has a few additional weights compared to a conventional RNN. Now let's have a close look at what each of these layers and weights do.

First, the input is received by two hidden layers, like the conventional hidden layer also found in RNNs. We have seen that using just this hidden layer is not effective in retaining long-term memory. However, we can force the hidden layer to retain memory for longer by forcing the recurrent matrix to be close to identity and removing the nonlinearity. When the recurrent matrix is close to identity, without nonlinearities, any change that happens to $h$ should always come from a change in the input. In other words, the previous state will have less effect on changing the current state. This leads to the state changing slower than with dense weight matrix and nonlinearities. Thus, this state helps to retain the memory longer. Another reason to favor the recurrent matrix to be close to 1 is that when weights are close to 1, terms such as $w^{n-1}$ that appear in the derivations will not either vanish or explode. However, if we use only this without the hidden layer with nonlinearity, the gradient would never diminish. Here, by diminishing gradient, we refer to the fact that gradients produced by older inputs should have a lesser impact than the more recent inputs. We then will need to propagate the gradients through time to the beginning of the input. This is expensive. Therefore, to get the best of both worlds, we keep both these layers: the standard RNN state layer ($h_t$) that can change rapidly, as well as the context feature layer ($s_t$) that changes more slowly. This new layer is called the **context layer** and is a novel layer that helps with keeping long-term memory. The update rules for the RNN-CF are as follows. Note that you do not see $s_{t-1}$ being multiplied by an identity matrix as discussed because $Is_{t-1} = s_{t-1}$:

$$s_t = (1-\alpha)Bx_t + \alpha s_{t-1}$$

$$h_t = \sigma\left(Ps_t + Ax_t + Rh_{t-1}\right)$$

$$y_t = softmax\left(Uh_t + Vs_t\right)$$

The notation related to the RNN-CF is summarized in the following table:

| Notation | Description |
|---|---|
| $x_t$ | Current input |
| $h_t$ | Current state vector |
| $y_t$ | Current output |
| $s_t$ | Current context feature vector |
| $A$ | Weight matrix between $x_t$ and $h_t$ |
| $B$ | Weight matrix between $x_t$ and $s_t$ |
| $R$ | Recurrent connections of $h_t$ |
| $\alpha$ | Constant that controls the contribution of $s_{t-1}$ to $s_t$ |
| $P$ | Weights connecting $h_t$ and $s_t$ |
| $U$ | Weight matrix between $h_t$ and $y_t$ |
| $V$ | Weight matrix between $s_t$ and $y_t$ |

# Implementing the RNN-CF

We have discussed how the RNN-CF contains an additional state vector and how that helps to prevent vanishing of the gradients. Here we will discuss the implementation of the RNN-CF. In addition to hidden ($h_t$), W_xh ($A$ in the table), W_hh ($R$ in the table), and W_hy ($U$ in the table), which were in the conventional RNN implementation, we now need three more additional sets of weights; namely, we will define B, P, and V. Furthermore we will define a new variable to contain $s_t$ (hidden_context) as well (in addition to $h_t$)

## Defining the RNN-CF hyperparameters

First, we will define the hyperparameters including the ones we defined previously and new ones. One new hyperparameter defines the number of neurons in the context feature layer, $s_t$, where alpha represents the $\alpha$ in the equation.

```
hidden_context = 64
alpha = 0.9
```

# Defining input and output placeholders

As we did for the standard RNN we first define placeholders to contain training inputs and outputs, validation inputs and outputs, and test inputs:

```
# Train dataset
# We use unrolling over time
train_dataset, train_labels = [],[]
for ui in range(num_unroll):
    train_dataset.append(tf.placeholder(tf.float32,
                        shape=[batch_size,in_size],
                        name='train_dataset_%d'%ui))
    train_labels.append(tf.placeholder(tf.float32,
                        shape=[batch_size,out_size],
                        name='train_labels_%d'%ui))


# Validation dataset
valid_dataset = tf.placeholder(tf.float32,
                            shape=[1,in_size],name='valid_dataset')
valid_labels = tf.placeholder(tf.float32,
                            shape=[1,out_size],name='valid_labels')


# Test dataset
test_dataset = tf.placeholder(tf.float32,
                            shape=[test_batch_size,in_size],
                            name='save_test_dataset')
```

# Defining weights of the RNN-CF

Here we define the weights required for the calculations of the RNN-CF. As we saw in the notation table, six sets of weights (*A*, *B*, *R*, *P*, *U*, and *V*) are required. Remember that we only had three sets of weights in the conventional RNN implementation:

```
# Weights between inputs and h
A = tf.Variable(tf.truncated_normal([in_size,hidden],
                stddev=0.02,dtype=tf.float32),name='W_xh')
B = tf.Variable(tf.truncated_normal([in_size,hidden_context],
                stddev=0.02,dtype=tf.float32),name='W_xs')


# Weights between h and h
R = tf.Variable(tf.truncated_normal([hidden,hidden],
                stddev=0.02,dtype=tf.float32),name='W_hh')
P = tf.Variable(tf.truncated_normal([hidden_context,hidden],
```

```
                         stddev=0.02,dtype=tf.float32),name='W_ss')

   # Weights between h and y
   U = tf.Variable(tf.truncated_normal([hidden,out_size],
                   stddev=0.02,dtype=tf.float32),name='W_hy')
   V = tf.Variable(tf.truncated_normal([hidden_context,
                                        out_size],stddev=0.02,
                                        dtype=tf.float32),
                                        name='W_sy')


   # State variables for training data
   prev_train_h = tf.Variable(tf.zeros([batch_size,hidden],
                       dtype=tf.float32),
                       name='train_h',trainable=False)
   prev_train_s = tf.Variable(tf.zeros([batch_size,hidden_context],
                       dtype=tf.float32),name='train_s',
                       trainable=False)


   # State variables for validation data
   prev_valid_h = tf.Variable(tf.zeros([1,hidden],dtype=tf.float32),
                       name='valid_h',trainable=False)
   prev_valid_s = tf.Variable(tf.zeros([1,hidden_context],
                       dtype=tf.float32),
                       name='valid_s',trainable=False)


   # State variables for test data
   prev_test_h = tf.Variable(tf.zeros([test_batch_size,hidden],
                       dtype=tf.float32),
                       name='test_h')
   prev_test_s = tf.Variable(tf.zeros([test_batch_size,hidden_context],
                       dtype=tf.float32),name='test_s')
```

# Variables and operations for maintaining hidden and context states

Here we define state variables of the RNN-CF. In addition to $h_t$ we had in the conventional RNN, we need to have a separate state for context features which is $s_t$. In total, we will have six state variables. Here, three state variables are to maintain state vector $h_t$ during training, validation, and testing, and the other three state variables are to maintain the state vector $s_t$ during training, validation, and testing:

```
# State variables for training data
prev_train_h = tf.Variable(tf.zeros([batch_size,hidden],
                           dtype=tf.float32),
                           name='train_h',trainable=False)
prev_train_s = tf.Variable(tf.zeros([batch_size,hidden_context],
                           dtype=tf.float32),name='train_s',
                           trainable=False)


# State variables for validation data
prev_valid_h = tf.Variable(tf.zeros([1,hidden],dtype=tf.float32),
                           name='valid_h',trainable=False)
prev_valid_s = tf.Variable(tf.zeros([1,hidden_context],
                           dtype=tf.float32),
                           name='valid_s',trainable=False)


# State variables for test data
prev_test_h = tf.Variable(tf.zeros([test_batch_size,hidden],
                          dtype=tf.float32),
                          name='test_h')
prev_test_s = tf.Variable(tf.zeros([test_batch_size,hidden_context],
                          dtype=tf.float32),name='test_s')
```

Next, we define the reset operations required to reset operations required to reset states:

```
reset_prev_train_h_op = tf.assign(prev_train_h,tf.zeros([batch_size,
                          hidden], dtype=tf.float32))
reset_prev_train_s_op = tf.assign(prev_train_s,tf.zeros([batch_size,
                          hidden_context],dtype=tf.float32))

reset_valid_h_op = tf.assign(prev_valid_h,tf.zeros([1,hidden],
                      dtype=tf.float32))
reset_valid_s_op = tf.assign(prev_valid_s,tf.zeros([1,hidden_context],
                      dtype=tf.float32))


# Impute the testing states with noise
reset_test_h_op = tf.assign(prev_test_h,tf.truncated_normal(
                          [test_batch_size,hidden],
                          stddev=0.01,
                          dtype=tf.float32))
reset_test_s_op = tf.assign(prev_test_s,tf.truncated_normal(
                          [test_batch_size,hidden_context],
                          stddev=0.01,dtype=tf.float32))
```

# Calculating output

With all the inputs, variables, and state vectors defined, we now can calculate the output of the RNN-CF according to the equations in the preceding section. In essence, we are doing the following with this code snippet. We first initialize state vectors to be zeros. Then we will unroll our inputs for a fixed set of time steps (as needed by BPTT) and separately calculate unnormalized outputs (sometimes called logits or scores) for each of these unrolled steps. Then we will concatenate all the *y* values belonging to each unrolled time step, and then calculate the mean loss of all these entries, comparing it to the true labels:

```python
# Train score (unnormalized) values and predictions (normalized)
y_scores, y_predictions = [],[]

# These will be iteratively used within num_unroll
# steps of calculation
next_h_state = prev_train_h
next_s_state = prev_train_s

# Appending the calculated state outputs of RNN for
# each step in the num_unroll steps
next_h_states_unrolled, next_s_states_unrolled = [],[]

# Calculating the output of the RNN for num_unroll steps
# (as required by the truncated BPTT)
for ui in range(num_unroll):
    next_h_state = tf.nn.tanh(
        tf.matmul(tf.concat([train_dataset[ui],prev_train_h,
                  prev_train_s],1),
                  tf.concat([A,R,P],0))
    )
    next_s_state = (1-alpha)*tf.matmul(train_dataset[ui],B) +
                  alpha * next_s_state
    next_h_states_unrolled.append(next_h_state)
    next_s_states_unrolled.append(next_s_state)

# Get the scores and predictions for all the RNN outputs
# we produced for num_unroll steps
y_scores = [tf.matmul(next_h_states_unrolled[ui],U) +
            tf.matmul(next_s_states_unrolled[ui],V)
              for ui in range(num_unroll)]
y_predictions = [tf.nn.softmax(y_scores[ui]) for ui in range(num_
unroll)]
```

# Calculating the loss

Here we define the loss calculation of RNN-CF. This operation is identical to the one we defined for the standard RNN and is as follows:

```
# Here we make sure that before calculating the loss,
# the state variables are
# updated with the last RNN output state we obtained
with tf.control_dependencies([tf.assign(prev_train_s, next_s_state),
                             tf.assign(prev_train_h,next_h_state)]):
    rnn_loss = tf.reduce_mean(
            tf.nn.softmax_cross_entropy_with_logits_v2(
            logits=tf.concat(y_scores,0),
            labels=tf.concat(train_labels,0)
    ))
```

# Calculating validation output

Similar to calculating the output at training time, we calculate the output for validation inputs, as well. However, we do not unroll the inputs as we did for training data, as unrolling is not required during prediction, but only for training:

```
# Validation data related inference logic
# (very similar to the training inference logic)

# Compute the next valid state (only for 1 step)
next_valid_s_state = (1-alpha) * tf.matmul(valid_dataset,B) +
                     alpha * prev_valid_s
next_valid_h_state = tf.nn.tanh(tf.matmul(valid_dataset,A)  +
                                tf.matmul(prev_valid_s, P) +
                                tf.matmul(prev_valid_h,R))

# Calculate the prediction using the state output of the RNN
# But before that, assign the latest state output of the RNN
# to the state variable of the validation phase
# So you need to make sure you execute rnn_valid_loss operation
# To update the validation state
with tf.control_dependencies([tf.assign(prev_valid_s,
                             next_valid_s_state),
                             tf.assign(prev_valid_h,next_valid_h_
state)]):
    valid_scores = tf.matmul(prev_valid_h, U) + tf.matmul(
                                             prev_valid_s, V)
    valid_predictions = tf.nn.softmax(valid_scores)
```

# Computing test output

We can now define the output calculations for generating new test data as well:

```
# Test data realted inference logic

# Calculating hidden output for test data
next_test_s = (1-alpha)*tf.matmul(test_dataset,B)+ alpha*prev_test_s

next_test_h = tf.nn.tanh(
    tf.matmul(test_dataset,A) + tf.matmul(prev_test_s,P) +
    tf.matmul(prev_test_h, R)
                        )

# Making sure that the test hidden state is updated
# every time we make a prediction
with tf.control_dependencies([tf.assign(prev_test_s,next_test_s),
                              tf.assign(prev_test_h,next_test_h)]):
    test_prediction = tf.nn.softmax(
        tf.matmul(prev_test_h,U) + tf.matmul(prev_test_s,V)
    )
```

# Computing the gradients and optimizing

Here we use an optimizer to minimize the loss identical to the way we did for the conventional RNN:

```
rnn_optimizer = tf.train.AdamOptimizer(learning_rate=.001)


gradients, v = zip(*rnn_optimizer.compute_gradients(rnn_loss))
gradients, _ = tf.clip_by_global_norm(gradients, 5.0)
rnn_optimizer = rnn_optimizer.apply_gradients(zip(gradients, v))
```

# Text generated with the RNN-CF

Here we will compare the text generated by the RNN and RNN-CF, both qualitatively and quantitatively. We will first compare the results obtained using 20 training documents. Afterwards, we will elevate the number of training documents to 100, to see if the RNN and RNN-CF are able to incorporate large amounts of data, well to output better quality text.

First, we will generate text with the RNN-CF using only 20 documents:

```
the king's daughter, who had
no more excuses left to make.  they cut the could not off, and her his
first rays of life in the garden,
and was amazed to see with the showed to the grown mighted and the
seart the answer to star's brothers, and seeking the golden apple, we
flew over the tree to the seadow where her
heard that he could not have
discome.



emptied him by him.  she himself 'well i ston the fire struck it was
and said the youth, farm of them into the showed to shudder, but here
and said the fire himself 'if i could but the youth, and thought that
is that shudder.'
'then, said he said 'i will by you are you, you.' then the king, who
you are your
wedding-mantle.  you are you are you
bird in wretch me.  ah.  what man caller streep them if i will bed.
the youth
begged for a hearing, and said 'if you will below in you to be your
wedding-mantle.' 'what.' said he,  'i shall said 'if i hall by you are
you

bidden it i could not have
```

In terms of the quality of text, compared to standard RNN, we are not able to see much of a difference. We should think about why the RNN-CF is not performing better than standard RNNs. In their paper, *Learning Longer Memory in Recurrent Neural Networks, Mikolov and others*, mention the following:

> *"When the number of standard hidden units is enough to capture short term patterns, learning the self-recurrent weights does not seem crucial anymore."*

So if the number of hidden units is large enough, the RNN-CF has no significant advantage over standard RNNs. This might be the reason why we are observing this. We are using 64 hidden neurons and a relatively small corpus, and it could be adequate to represent a story, well to a level RNNs are capable of.

Therefore, let's see whether increasing the amount of data actually helps the RNN-CF to perform better. For our example, we will increase the number of documents to 100 documents after training for around 50 epochs.

The following is the output of a standard RNN:

```
they were their dearest and she she told him to stop crying to the
king's son they were their dearest and she she told him to stop crying
to the king's son they were their dearest and she she told him to stop
crying to the king's son they were their dearest and she she told him
to stop crying to the king's son they were their dearest and she she
told him to stop
```

We can see that RNNs have grown worse, compared to how they performed with less data. Having a lot of data and inadequate model capacity affects standard RNNs adversely, leading them to output poor-quality text.

The following is the output of the RNN-CF. You can see that, in terms of variation, the RNN-CF has done a much better job than a standard RNN:

```
then they could be the world.  not was now from the first for a set
out of his pocket, what is the world.  then they were all they were
forest, and the never yet not
rething, and took the
children in themselver to peard, and then the first her.  then the was
in the first, and that he was to the first, and that he was to the
kitchen, and said, and had took the
children in the mountain, and they were hansel of the fire, gretel of
they were all the fire, goggle-eyes and all in the moster.  when she
had took the
changeling the little elves, and now ran into them, and she bridge
away with the witch form,
and their father's daughter was that had neep himselver in the horse,
and now they lived them himselver to them, and they were am the
marriage was all they were and all of the marriage was anger of the
forest, and the manikin was laughing, who had said they had not know,
and took the
children in themselver to themselver and they lived them himselver to
them
```

Therefore, it seems that when data is abundant, the RNN-CF in fact outperforms standard RNNs. We will also plot the training and validation perplexities over time for both these models. As you can see, in terms of training perplexity both RNN-CF and the standard RNN do not show a significant difference. Finally, in the validation perplexity graph (see *Figure 6.14*), we can see that the RNN-CF shows fewer fluctuations compared to the standard RNN.

One important conclusion we can make here is that when we had smaller amounts of data, the standard RNN was probably *overfitting* data. That is, the RNN probably memorized data as it is, rather than trying to learn more general patterns present in data. When RNN is overwhelmed by the amount of data and trained for longer (say around 50 epochs), this weakness becomes more prominent. The quality of the text produced decreases, and there are larger fluctuations of the validation perplexity. However, the RNN-CF shows somewhat consistent behavior with both small and large amounts of data:

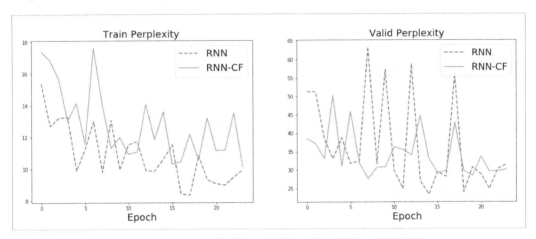

Figure 6.14: Train and valid perplexities of the RNN and RNN-CF

# Summary

In this chapter, we looked at RNNs, which are different from conventional feed-forward neural networks and more powerful in terms of solving temporal tasks. Furthermore, RNNs can manifest in many different forms: one-to-one (text generation), many-to-one (sequential image classification), one-to-many (image captioning), and many-to-many (machine translation).

Specifically, we discussed how to arrive at an RNN from a feed-forward neural networks type structure. We assumed a sequence of inputs and outputs, and designed a computational graph that can represent the sequence of inputs and outputs. This computational graph resulted in a series of copies of functions that we applied to each individual input-output tuple in the sequence. Then, by generalizing this model to any given single time step $t$ in the sequence, we were able to arrive at the basic computational graph of an RNN. We discussed the exact equations and update rules used to calculate the hidden state and the output.

Next we discussed how RNNs are trained with data using BPTT. We examined how we can arrive at BPTT with standard backpropagation as well as why we can't use standard backpropagation for RNNs. We also discussed two important practical issues that arise with BPTT — vanishing gradient and exploding gradient — and how these can be solved on the surface level.

Then we moved on to the practical applications of RNNs. We discussed four main categories of RNNs. One-to-one architectures are used for tasks such as text generation, scene classification, and video frame labeling. Many-to-one architectures are used for sentiment analysis, where we process the sentences/phrases word by word (compared to processing a full sentence at a single go, as we saw in the previous chapter). One-to-many architectures are common in image captioning tasks, where we map a single image to an arbitrarily long sentence phrase describing the image. Many-to-many architectures are leveraged for machine translation tasks.

Next we looked at an interesting application of RNNs: text generation. We used a corpus of fairy tales to train an RNN. In particular, we broke the text in the story to bigrams (a bigram contains two characters). We trained the RNN by giving a set of bigrams selected from a story as the input and the following bigrams (from the input) as the output. Then the RNN was optimized by maximizing the accuracy of predicting the next bigram correctly. Following this procedure, we asked the RNN to generate a different story, and we made two important observations of the generated results:

- Unrolling the input over time in fact helps to maintain memory for longer
- RNNs even with unrolling can only store a limited amount of long-term memory

Therefore, we looked at an RNN variant that has the ability to capture even longer memory. This is referred to as the RNN-CF. The RNN-CF has two different layers: the hidden layer (that is, conventional hidden layer, found in simple RNNs) and a context layer (for persisting long-term memory). We saw that having this additional context layer did not help significantly when used with a small dataset, as we had a fairly complex hidden layer in our RNN, but it produced slightly better results when more data was used.

In the next chapter, we will discuss a more powerful RNN model known as **long short-term memory (LSTM)** networks that further reduces the adverse effect of the vanishing gradient, and thus produces much better results.

# 7
# Long Short-Term Memory Networks

In this chapter, we will discuss a more advanced RNN variant known as **Long Short-Term Memory Networks (LSTMs)**. LSTMs are widely used in many sequential tasks (including stock market prediction, language modeling, and machine translation) and have proven to perform better than other sequential models (for example, standard RNNs), especially given the availability of large amounts of data. LSTMs are well-designed to avoid the problem of the vanishing gradient that we discussed in the previous chapter.

The main practical limitation posed by the vanishing gradient is that it prevents the model from learning long-term dependencies. However, by avoiding the vanishing gradient problem, LSTMs have the ability to store memory for longer than ordinary RNNs (for hundreds of time steps). In contrast to those RNNs, which only maintain a single hidden state, LSTMs have many more parameters as well as better control over what memory to store and what to discard at a given training step. For example, RNNs are not able to decide which memory to store and which to discard, as the hidden state is forced to be updated at every training step.

Specifically, we will discuss what an LSTM is at a very high level and how the functionality of LSTMs allows them to store long-term dependencies. Then we will go into the actual underlying mathematical framework governing LSTMs and discuss an example to highlight why each computation matters. We will also compare LSTMs to vanilla RNNs and see that LSTMs have a much more sophisticated architecture that allows them to surpass vanilla RNNs in sequential tasks. Revisiting the problem of the vanishing gradient and illustrating it through an example will lead us to understand how LSTMs solve the problem.

Thereafter, we will discuss several techniques that have been introduced to improve the predictions produced by a standard LSTM (for example, improving the quality/variety of generated text in a text generation task). For example, generating several predictions at once instead of predicting them one-by-one can help to improve the quality of generated predictions. We will also look at **BiLSTMs**, or **bidirectional LSTMs**, which are an extension to the standard LSTM that has greater capabilities for capturing the patterns present in the sequence than a standard LSTM.

Finally, we will discuss two recent LSTM variants. First, we will look at **peephole connections**, which introduce more parameters and information to the LSTM gates allowing LSTMs to perform better. Next, we will discuss **Gated Recurrent Units (GRUs)**, which are gaining increasing popularity as they have a much simpler structure compared to LSTMs and also do not degrade performance.

# Understanding Long Short-Term Memory Networks

In this section, we will first explain what happens within an LSTM cell. We will see that in addition to the states, a gating mechanism to control information flow inside the cell is present. Then we will work through a detailed example and see how each gate and states help at various stages of the example to achieve desired behaviors, finally leading to the desired output. Finally, we will compare an LSTM against a standard RNN to learn how an LSTM differs from a standard RNN.

# What is an LSTM?

LSTMs can be seen as a fancier family of RNNs. An LSTM is composed mainly of five different things:

- **Cell state**: This is the internal cell state (that is, memory) of an LSTM cell
- **Hidden state**: This is the external hidden state used to calculate predictions
- **Input gate**: This determines how much of the current input is read into the cell state
- **Forget gate**: This determines how much of the previous cell state is sent into the current cell state
- **Output gate**: This determines how much of the cell state is output into the hidden state

We can wrap the RNN to a cell architecture as follows. The cell will output some state which is dependent (with a nonlinear activation function) on previous cell state and the current input. However, in RNNs, the cell state is always changed with every incoming input. This leads the cell state of the RNNs to always change. This behavior is quite undesirable for storing long-term dependencies.

LSTMs can decide when to replace, update, or forget information stored in each neuron in the cell state. In other words, LSTMs are equipped with a mechanism to keep the cell state unchanged (if needed) giving them the ability to store long-term dependencies.

This is achieved by introducing a gating mechanism. LSTMs possess gates for each operation the cell needs to perform. The gates are continuous (often sigmoid functions) between 0 and 1, where 0 means no information flows through the gate and 1 means all the information flows through the gate. An LSTM uses one such gate for each neuron in the cell. As explained earlier, these gates control the following:

- How much of the current input is written to the cell state (input gate)
- How much information is forgotten from the previous cell state (forget gate)
- How much information is output into the final hidden state from the cell state (output gate)

*Figure 7.1* illustrates this functionality. Each gate decides how much of various data (for example, current input, previous hidden state, or the previous cell state) flow into the states (that is, the final hidden state or the cell state). The thickness of each line represents how much information is flowing from/to that gate (in some hypothetical scenario). For example, in this figure, you can see that the input gate is allowing more from the current input than from the previous final hidden state, where the forget gate allows more from the previous final hidden state than from the current input:

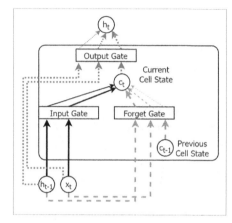

Figure 7.1: An abstract view of the data flow in an LSTM

# LSTMs in more detail

Here we will walk through the actual mechanism of LSTMs. We will first briefly discuss the overall view of an LSTM cell and then start discussing each of the operations taking place within an LSTM cell along with an example of text generation.

As we discussed earlier, the LSTMs are mainly composed of the following three gates:

- **Input gate**: A gate which outputs values between 0 (the current input is not written to the cell state), and 1 (the current input is fully written to the cell state). Sigmoid activation is used to squash the output to between 0 and 1.

- **Forget gate**: A sigmoidal gate which outputs values between 0 (the previous cell state is fully forgotten for calculating the current cell state) and 1 (the previous cell state is fully read in when calculating the current cell state).

- **Output gate**: A sigmoidal gate which outputs values between 0 (the current cell state is fully discarded for calculating the final state) and 1 (the current cell state is fully used when calculating the final hidden state).

This can be shown as in *Figure 7.2*. This is a very high-level diagram, and some details have been hidden in order to avoid clutter. We present LSTMs, both with loops and without loops to improve the understanding. The figure on the right-hand side depicts an LSTM with loops and that on the left-hand side shows the same LSTM with the loops expanded so that no loops are present in the model:

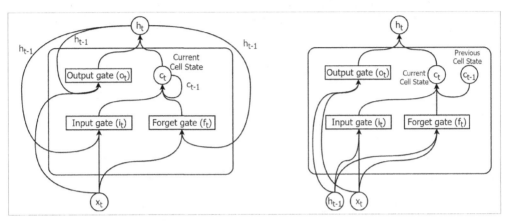

Figure 7.2: LSTM with recurrent links (that is, loops) (right) LSTM with recurrent links expanded (left)

Now, to get a better understanding of LSTMs, let's consider an example. We will discuss the actual update rules and equations along with an example to understand LSTMs better.

Now let's consider an example of generating text starting from the following sentence:

*John gave Mary a puppy.*

The story that we output should be about *John*, *Mary*, and the *puppy*. Let's assume our LSTM to output two sentences following the given sentence:

*John gave Mary a puppy. _____. _____.*

The following is the output given by our LSTM:

*John gave Mary a puppy. It barks very loudly. They named it Luna.*

We are still far from outputting realistic phrases such as these. However, LSTMs can learn relationships such as between nouns and pronouns. For example, *it* is related to the *puppy*, and *they* to *John* and *Mary*. Then, it should learn the relationship between the noun/pronoun and the verb. For example, for *it*, the verb should have an *s* at the end. We illustrate these relationships/dependencies in *Figure 7.3*. As we can see both, long-term (for example, *Luna* → *puppy*) and short-term (for example, *It* → *barks*) dependencies are present in this phrase. The solid arrows depict links between nouns and pronouns and dashed arrows show links between nouns/pronouns and verbs:

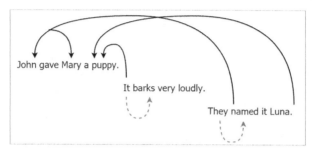

Figure 7.3: Sentences given and predicted by the LSTM with various relationships between words highlighted

Now let's consider how LSTMs, using their various operations, can model such relationships and dependencies to output sensible text, given a starting sentence.

The input gate ($i_t$) takes the current input ($x_t$) and the previous final hidden state ($h_{t-1}$) as the input and calculates $i_t$, as follows:

$$i_t = \sigma \left( W_{ix} x_t + W_{ih} h_{t-1} + b_i \right)$$

The input gate, $i_t$ can be understood as the calculation performed at the hidden layer of a single-hidden-layer standard RNN with the sigmoidal activation. Remember that we calculated the hidden state of a standard RNN as follows:

$$h_t = \tanh \left( U x_t + W h_{t-1} \right)$$

Therefore, the calculation of $i_t$ of the LSTM looks quite analogous to the calculation of $h_t$ of a standard RNN, except for the change in the activation function and the addition of bias.

After the calculation, a value of 0 for $i_t$ will mean that no information from the current input will flow to the cell state, where a value of 1 means that all the information from the current input will flow to the cell state.

Next, another value (which is called **candidate value**) is calculated as follows, which is added to calculate the current cell state later:

$$\tilde{c}_t = tanh\left(W_{cx}x_t + W_{ch}h_{t-1} + b_c\right)$$

We can visualize these calculations in *Figure 7.4*:

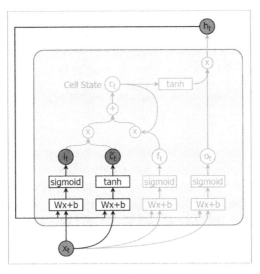

Figure 7.4. Calculation of $i_t$ and $\tilde{c}_t$ (in bold) in the context of all the calculations (grayed out) that take place in an LSTM

In our example, at the very beginning of the learning, the input gate needs to be highly activated. The first word that the LSTM outputs is *it*. Also in order to do so, the LSTM must learn that *puppy* is also referred to as *it*. Let's assume our LSTM has five neurons to store the state. We would like the LSTM to store the information that *it* refers to *puppy*. Another piece of information we would like the LSTM to learn (in a different neuron) is that the present tense verb should have an *s* at the end of the verb, when the pronoun *it* is used. One more thing the LSTM needs to know is that the *puppy barks loud*. *Figure 7.5* illustrates how this knowledge might be encoded in the cell state of the LSTM. Each circle represents a single neuron (that is, hidden unit) of the cell state:

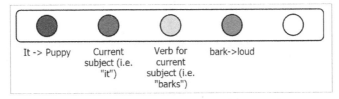

Figure 7.5: The knowledge that should be encoded in the cell state to output the first sentence

With this information, we can output the first new sentence:

*John gave Mary a puppy. It barks very loudly.*

Next, the forget gate is calculated as follows:

$$f_t = \sigma\left(W_{fx}x_t + W_{fh}h_{t-1} + b_f\right)$$

The forget gate does the following. A value of 0 for the forget gate means that no information from $c_{t-1}$ will be passed to calculate $c_t$, and a value of 1 means that all the information of $c_{t-1}$ will propagate into the calculation of $c_t$.

Now we will see how the forget gate helps in predicting the next sentence:

*They named it Luna.*

Now as you can see, the new relationship we are looking at is between *John* and *Mary* and *they*. Therefore, we no longer need information about *it* and how the verb *bark* behaves, as the subjects are *John* and *Mary*. We can use the forget gate in combination with the current subject *they* and the corresponding verb *named* to replace the information stored in the **Current subject** and **Verb for current subject** neurons (see *Figure 7.6*):

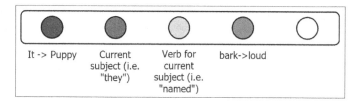

Figure 7.6: The knowledge in the third neuron from left (it $\longrightarrow$ barks)
is replaced with new information (they $\longrightarrow$ named).

In terms of the values of weights, we illustrate this transformation in *Figure 7.7*. We do not change the state of the neuron maintaining the *it* $\rightarrow$ *puppy* relationship, because *puppy* appears as an object in the last sentence. This is done by setting weights connecting *it* $\rightarrow$ *puppy* from $c_{t-1}$ to $c_t$ to 1. Then we will replace the neurons maintaining current subject and current verb information with new subject and verb. This is achieved by setting the forget weights of $f_t$, for that neuron, to 0. Then we will set the weights of $i_t$ connecting the current subject and verb to the corresponding state neurons to 1. We can think of $\tilde{c}_t$ as the entity that contains what new information (such as new information from the current input $x_t$) should be brought to the cell state:

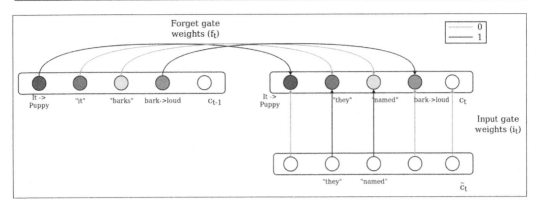

Figure 7.7: How the cell state $c_t$ is calculated with the previous state $c_{t-1}$ and the candidate value $\tilde{c}_t$

The current cell state will be updated as follows:

$$c_t = f_t c_{t-1} + i_t \tilde{c}_t$$

In other words, the current state is the combination of the following:

- What information to forget/remember from the previous cell state
- What information to add/discard to the current input

Next in *Figure 7.8*, we highlight what we have calculated so far with respect to all the calculations that are taking place inside an LSTM:

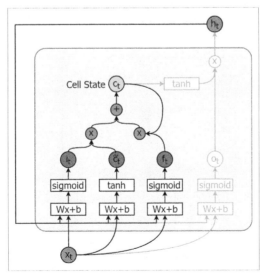

Figure 7.8: Calculations covered so far including $i_t$, $f_t$, $\tilde{c}_t$, and $c_t$

After learning the full state, it would look like *Figure 7.9*:

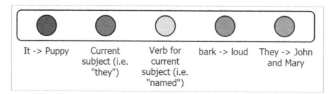

Figure 7.9: The full cell state will look like this after outputting both the sentences

Next, we will look at how the final state of the LSTM cell ($h_t$) is computed:

$$o_t = \sigma\left(W_{ox}x_t + W_{oh}h_{t-1} + b_o\right)$$

$$h_t = o_t tanh\left(c_t\right)$$

In our example, we want to output the following sentence:

*They named it Luna.*

For this we do not need the second to last neuron to compute this sentence, as it contains information about how the puppy barks, where this sentence is about the name of the puppy. Therefore, we can ignore the last neuron (containing *bark -> loud* relationship) during the predictions of the last sentence. This is exactly what $o_t$ does; it will ignore the unnecessary memory and only retrieve the related memory from the cell state when calculating the final output of the LSTM cell. Also, in *Figure 7.10*, we illustrate how an LSTM cell would look like at a full glance:

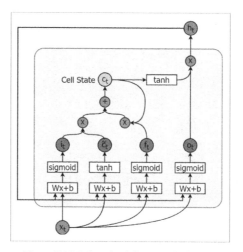

Figure 7.10: What the full LSTM looks like

Here, we summarize all the equations relating to the operations taking place within an LSTM cell.

$$i_t = \sigma\left(W_{ix}x_t + W_{ih}h_{t-1} + b_i\right)$$

$$f_t = \sigma\left(W_{fx}x_t + W_{fh}h_{t-1} + b_f\right)$$

$$\tilde{c}_t = \tanh\left(W_{cx}x_t + W_{ch}h_{t-1} + b_c\right)$$

$$c_t = f_t c_{t-1} + i_t \tilde{c}_t$$

$$o_t = \sigma\left(W_{ox}x_t + W_{oh}h_{t-1} + b_o\right)$$

$$h_t = o_t \tanh\left(c_t\right)$$

Now in the bigger picture, for a sequential learning problem, we can unroll the LSTM cells over time to show how they would link together so they receive the previous state of the cell to compute the next state, as shown in *Figure 7.11*:

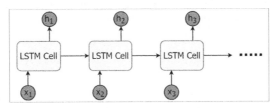

Figure 7.11: How LSTMs will be linked over time

However, this is not adequate to do something useful. As you can see, even though we can create a nice chain of LSTMs that are actually capable of modelling a sequence, we still don't have an output or a prediction. But if we want to use what the LSTM actually learned, we need a way to extract the final output from the LSTM. Therefore, we will fix a softmax layer (with weights $W_s$ and bias $b_s$) on top of the LSTM. The final output is obtained using the following equation:

$$y_t = softmax\left(W_s h_t + b_s\right)$$

Now the final picture of the LSTM with the softmax layer looks like *Figure 7.12*:

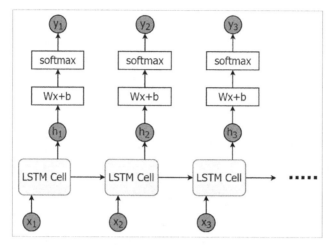

Figure 7.12: LSTMs with a softmax output layer linked over time

# How LSTMs differ from standard RNNs

Let's now investigate how LSTMs compare to standard RNNs. An LSTM has a more intricate structure compared to a standard RNN. One of the primary differences is that an LSTM has two different states: a cell state $c_t$ and a final hidden state $h_t$. However, an RNN only has a single hidden state $h_t$. The next primary difference is that since an LSTM has three different gates, an LSTM has much more control over how the current input and the previous cell state are handled when computing the final hidden state $h_t$.

Having the two different states is quite advantageous. With this mechanism, even when the cell state is changing quickly, the final hidden state will still be changed more slowly. So, while the cell state is learning both short-term and long-term dependencies, the final hidden state can reflect either only the short-term dependencies or only the long-term dependencies or both.

Next, the gating mechanism is composed of three gates: the input, forget, and output gates:

- The *input gate* controls how much of the current input is written to the cell state

- The *forget gate* controls how much of the previous cell state is carried over to the current cell state

- Finally, the *output gate* controls how much from the cell state is propagated to the final hidden state

It is quite evident that this is a much more principled approach (especially, compared to the standard RNNs) that permits better control over how much the current input and the previous cell state contribute to the current cell state. Also, the output gate gives better control over how much the cell state contributes to the final hidden state. In *Figure 7.13*, we compare schematic diagrams of a standard RNN and an LSTM to emphasize the difference in terms of the functionality of the two models.

In summary, with the design of maintaining two different states, an LSTM can learn both short-term and long-term dependencies, which helps solve the problem of the vanishing gradient, which we'll discuss in the following section.

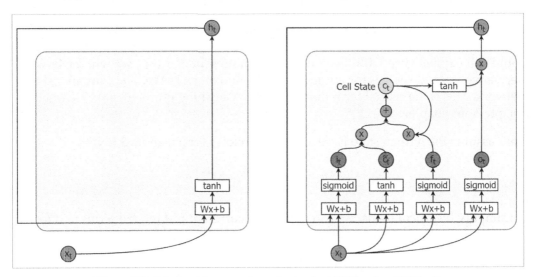

Figure 7.13: Side-by-side comparison of a standard RNN and an LSTM cell

# How LSTMs solve the vanishing gradient problem

As we discussed earlier, even though RNNs are theoretically sound, in practice they suffer from a serious drawback. That is, when the **Backpropagation Through Time (BPTT)** is used, the gradient diminishes quickly, which allows us to propagate the information of only a few time steps. Consequently, we can only store information of very few time steps, thus possessing only short-term memory. This in turn limits the usefulness of RNNs in real-world sequential tasks.

Often useful and interesting sequential tasks (such as stock market predictions or language modeling) require the ability to learn and store long-term dependencies. Think of the following example for predicting the next word:

*John is a talented student. He is an A-grade student and plays rugby and cricket. All the other students envy _____.*

For us, this is a very easy task. The answer would be *John*. However, for an RNN, this is a difficult task. We are trying to predict an answer which lies at the very beginning of the text. Also, to solve this task, we need a way to store long-term dependencies in the state of the RNN. This is exactly the type of tasks LSTMs are designed to solve.

In *Chapter 6, Recurrent Neural Networks,* we discussed how a vanishing/exploding gradient can appear without any nonlinear functions present. We will now see that it could still happen even with the nonlinear term present. For this, we will see how the derivative term $\partial h_t / \partial h_{t-k}$ is for a standard RNN and an LSTM ($\partial c_t / \partial c_{t-k}$ for an LSTM) network. This is the crucial term that causes the vanishing gradient, as we learned in the previous chapter.

Let's assume the hidden state is calculated as follows for a standard RNN:

$$h_t = \sigma\left(W_x x_t + W_h h_{t-1}\right)$$

To simplify the calculations, we can ignore the current input related terms and focus on the recurrent part, which will give us the following equation:

$$h_t = \sigma\left(W_h h_{t-1}\right)$$

If we calculate $\partial h_t / \partial h_{t-k}$ for the preceding equations, we will get the following:

$$\partial h_t / \partial h_{t-k} = \prod_{i=0}^{k-1} W_h \sigma\left(W_h h_{t-k+i}\right)\left(1 - \sigma\left(W_h h_{t-k+i}\right)\right)$$

$$\partial h_t / \partial h_{t-k} = W_h^k \prod_{i=0}^{k-1} \sigma\left(W_h h_{t-k+i}\right)\left(1 - \sigma\left(W_h h_{t-k+i}\right)\right)$$

Now let's see what happens when $W_h h_{t-k+i} << 0$ or $W_h h_{t-k+i} >> 0$ (which will happen as learning continues). In both cases, $\partial h_t / \partial h_{t-k}$ will start to approach 0, giving rise to the vanishing gradient. Even when $W_h h_{t-k+i} = 0$, where the gradient is maximum (0.25) for sigmoid activation, when multiplied for many time steps, the overall gradient becomes quite small. Moreover, the term $W_h^k$ (possibly due to bad initialization) can cause exploding or vanishing of the gradients, as well. However, compared to the gradient vanishing due to $W_h h_{t-k+i} << 0$ or $W_h h_{t-k+i} >> 0$, gradient vanishing/explosion caused by the term $W_h^k$ is relatively easy to solve (with careful initialization of weights and gradient clipping).

Now let's look at an LSTM cell. More specifically, we'll look at the cell state, given by the following equation:

$$c_t = f_t c_{t-1} + i_t \tilde{c}_t$$

This is the product of all the forget gate applications happening in the LSTM. However, if you calculate $\partial c_t / \partial c_{t-k}$ in a similar way for LSTMs (that is, ignoring the $W_{fx} x_t$ terms and $b_f$, as they are non-recurrent), we get the following:

$$\partial c_t / \partial c_{t-k} = \prod_{i=0}^{k-1} \sigma\left(W_{fh} h_{t-k+i}\right)$$

In this case, though the gradient will vanish if $W_h h_{t-k+i} << 0$, on the other hand if $W_h h_{t-k+i} >> 0$, the derivative will decrease much slower than it would in a standard RNN. Therefore, we have one alternative, where the gradient will not vanish. Also, as the squashing function is used, the gradients will not explode due to $\partial c_t / \partial c_{t-k}$ being large (which is the likely thing to happen during a gradient explosion). In addition, when $W_h h_{t-k+i} >> 0$, we get a maximum gradient close to 1, meaning that the gradients will not rapidly decrease as we saw with RNNs (when gradient is at maximum). Finally, there is no term such as $W_h^k$ in the derivation. However, derivations are trickier for $\partial h_t / \partial h_{t-k}$. Let's see if such terms are present in the derivation of $\partial h_t / \partial h_{t-k}$. If you calculate the derivatives of this, you will get something of the following form:

$$\partial h_t / \partial h_{t-k} = \partial\left(o_t \tanh\left(c_t\right)\right) / \partial h_{t-k}$$

Once you solve this, you will get something of this form:

$$\tanh(.)\sigma(.)[1-\sigma(.)]w_{oh} + \sigma(.)[1-\tanh^2(.)]\left\{c_{t-1}\sigma(.)[1-\sigma(.)]w_{fh} + \sigma(.)[1-\tanh^2(.)]w_{ch} + \tanh(.)\sigma(.)[1-\sigma(.)]w_{ih}\right\}$$

We do not care about the content within $\sigma(.)$ or $\tanh(.)$, because no matter what the value, it will be bounded by (0,1) or (-1,1). If we further reduce the notation by replacing the $\sigma(.)$, $[1-\sigma(.)]$, $\tanh(.)$, and $[1-\tanh^2(.)]$ terms with some common notation such as $\gamma(.)$, we get something of this form:

$$\gamma(.)w_{oh} + \gamma(.)\big[c_{t-1}\gamma(.)w_{fh} + \gamma(.)w_{ch} + \gamma(.)w_{ih}\big]$$

Alternatively, we get the following (assuming that the outside $\gamma(.)$ gets absorbed by each $\gamma(.)$ term present within the square brackets):

$$\gamma(.)w_{oh} + c_{t-1}\gamma(.)w_{fh} + \gamma(.)w_{ch} + \gamma(.)w_{ih}$$

This will give the following:

$$\partial h_t / \partial h_{t-k} \approx \prod_{i=0}^{k-1} \gamma(.)w_{oh} + c_{t-1}\gamma(.)w_{fh} + \gamma(.)w_{ch} + \gamma(.)w_{ih}$$

This means that though the term $\partial c_t / \partial c_{t-k}$ is safe from any $W_h^k$ terms, $\partial h_t / \partial h_{t-k}$ is not. Therefore, we must be careful when initializing the weights of the LSTM and we should use gradient clipping as well.

 However, $h_t$ of LSTMs being unsafe from vanishing gradient is not as crucial as for RNNs. Because $c_t$ still can store the long term dependencies without being affected by vanishing gradient, and $h_t$ can retrieve the long-term dependencies from $c_t$, if required to.

# Improving LSTMs

As we have already seen while learning about RNNs, having a solid theoretical foundation does not always guarantee that they will perform the best in practice. This is due to the limitations in numerical precision of the computers. This is also true for LSTMs. Having a sophisticated design—allowing better modeling of long-term dependencies in the data—does not in itself mean the LSTM will output perfectly realistic predictions. Therefore, numerous extensions have been developed to help LSTMs perform better at prediction stage. Here we will discuss several such improvements: greedy sampling, beam search, using word vectors instead of one-hot-encoded representation of words, and using bidirectional LSTMs.

# Greedy sampling

If we try to always predict the word with the highest probability, the LSTM will tend to produce very monotonic results. For example, it will repeat the word *the* many times before switching to another word.

One way to get around this is to use **greedy sampling**, where we pick the predicted best *n* and sample from that set. This helps to break the monotonic nature of the predictions.

Let's consider the first sentence of the previous example:

*John gave Mary a puppy.*

Say, we start with the first word and want to predict the next four words:

*John ____ ____ _ ____.*

If we attempt to choose samples deterministically, the LSTM might tend to output something like the following:

*John gave Mary gave John.*

However, by sampling the next word from a subset of words in the vocabulary (most highly probable ones), the LSTM is forced to vary the prediction and might output the following:

*John gave Mary a puppy.*

Alternatively, it will give the following output:

*John gave puppy a puppy.*

However, even though greedy sampling helps to add more variation to the generated text, this method does not guarantee that the output will always be realistic, especially when outputting longer sequences of text. Now we will see a better search technique that actually looks ahead several steps before predictions.

# Beam search

**Beam search** is a way of helping with the quality of the predictions produced by the LSTM. In this, the predictions are found by solving a search problem. The crucial idea of beam search is to produce the $b$ outputs (that is, $y_t, y_{t+1}, \ldots, y_{t+b}$) at once instead of a single output $y_t$. Here, $b$ is known as the **length** of the beam, and the $b$ outputs produced is known as the **beam**. More technically, we pick the beam that has the highest joint probability $p(y_t, y_{t+1}, \ldots, y_{t+b} \mid x_t)$ instead of picking the highest probable $p(y_t \mid x_t)$. We are looking farther into the future before making a prediction, which usually leads to better results.

Let's understand beam search through the previous example:

*John gave Mary a puppy.*

Say, we are predicting word by word. And initially we have the following:

*John _____ _____ _ _____.*

Let's assume hypothetically that our LSTM produces the example sentence using beam search. Then the probabilities for each word might look like what we see in *Figure 7.13*. Let's assume beam length $b = 2$, and we will consider the $n = 3$ best candidates at each stage of the search. The search tree would look like the following figure:

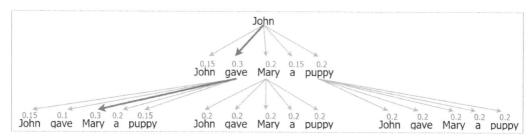

Figure 7.13: The search space of beam search for a b=2 and n=3

We start with the word **John** and get the probabilities for all the words in the vocabulary. In our example, as $n = 2$, we pick the best three candidates for the next level of the tree: **gave**, **Mary**, and **puppy**. (Note that these might not be the candidates found by an actual LSTM and are only used as an example.) Then from these selected candidates, the next level of the tree is grown. And from that, we will pick the best three candidates, and the search will repeat until we reach a depth of $b$ in the tree.

The path that gives the highest joint probability (that is, $P(gave, Mary \mid John) = 0.09$) is highlighted with heavier arrows. Also, this is a better prediction mechanism, as it would return a higher probability, or a reward, for a phrase such as *John gave Mary* than *John Mary John* or *John John gave*.

Note that the outputs produced by both greedy sampling and beam search are identical in our example, which is a simple sentence containing five words. However, this is not the case when we scale this to output a small essay. Then the results produced by beam search will be more realistic and grammatically correct than the ones produced by greedy sampling.

# Using word vectors

Another popular way of improving the performance of LSTMs is to use word vectors instead of using one-hot-encoded vectors as the input to the LSTM. Let's understand the value of this method through an example. Let's assume that we want to generate text starting from some random word. In our case, it would be the following:

*John _____ _____ _ _____.*

We have already trained our LSTM on the following sentences:

*John gave Mary a puppy. Mary has sent Bob a kitten.*

Let's also assume that we have the word vectors positioned as shown in *Figure 7.15*:

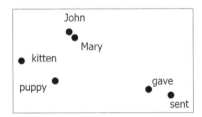

Figure 7.15: Assumed word vectors topology in two-dimensional space

The word embeddings of these words, in their numerical form, might look like the following:

*kitten: [0.5, 0.3, 0.2]*

*puppy: [0.49, 0.31, 0.25]*

*gave: [0.1, 0.8, 0.9]*

It can be seen that $distance(kitten, puppy) < distance(kitten, gave)$. However, if we use one-hot encoding, they would be as follows:

*kitten: [ 1, 0, 0, …]*

*puppy: [0, 1, 0, …]*

*gave: [0, 0, 1, …]*

Then, $distance(kitten, puppy) = distance(kitten, gave)$. As we can already see, one-hot-encoded vectors do not capture the proper relationship between words and see all the words are equally-distanced from each other. However, word vectors are capable of capturing such relationships and are more suitable as features into an LSTM.

Using word vectors, the LSTM will learn to exploit relationships between words better. For example, with word vectors, LSTM will learn the following:

*John gave Mary a kitten.*

This is quite close to the following:

*John gave Mary a puppy.*

Also, it is quite different from the following:

*John gave Mary a gave.*

However, this would not be the case if one-hot-encoded vectors are used.

# Bidirectional LSTMs (BiLSTM)

Making LSTMs bidirectional is another way of improving the quality of the predictions of an LSTM. By this we mean training the LSTM with data read from the beginning to the end and the end to the beginning. So far during the training of the LSTM, we would create a dataset as follows:

Consider the following two sentences:

*John gave Mary a _____. It barks very loudly.*

However, at this stage, there is data missing in the one of the sentences that we would want our LSTM to fill sensibly.

If we read from the beginning up to the missing word, it would be as follows:

*John gave Mary a _____.*

This does not provide enough information about the context of the missing word to fill the word properly. However, if we read in both directions, it would be the following:

*John gave Mary a _____.*

*_____. It barks very loudly.*

If we created data with both these pieces, it is adequate to predict that the missing word should be something like *dog* or *puppy*. Therefore, certain problems can benefit significantly from reading data from both sides. Furthermore, this increases the amount of data available to the neural network and boosts its performance.

Another application of BiLSTMs is neural machine translation, where we translate a sentence of a source language to a target language. As there is no specific alignment between the translation of one language to another, knowing both the past and the future of the source language can greatly help to understand the context better, thus producing better translations. As an example, consider a translation task of translating Filipino to English. In Filipino, sentences are usually written having *verb-object-subject* in that order, whereas in English, it is *subject-verb-object*. In this translation task, it will be extremely helpful to read sentences forward and backward both to make a good translation.

BiLSTM is essentially two separate LSTM networks. One network learns data from the beginning to the end, and the other network learns data from the end to the beginning. In *Figure 7.16*, we illustrate the architecture of a BiLSTM network.

BiLSTM

Training occurs in two phases. First, the solid colored network is trained with data created by reading the text from the beginning to the end. This network represents the normal training procedure used for standard LSTMs. Secondly, the dashed network is trained with data generated by reading the text in the reversed direction. Then, at the inference phase, we use both the solid and dashed states' information (by concatenating both states and creating a vector) to predict the missing word:

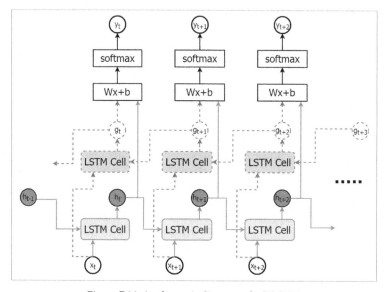

Figure 7.16: A schematic diagram of a BiLSTM

# Other variants of LSTMs

Though we mainly focus on the standard LSTM architecture, many variants have emerged that either simplify the complex architecture found in standard LSTMs or produce better performance or both. We will look at two variants that introduce structural modifications to the cell architecture of LSTM: peephole connections and GRUs.

# Peephole connections

**Peephole connections** allow gates not only to see the current input and the previous final hidden state but also the previous cell state. This increases the number of weights in the LSTM cell. Having such connections have shown to produce better results. The equations would look like these:

$$i_t = \sigma\left(W_{ix}x_t + W_{ih}h_{t-1} + W_{ic}c_{t-1} + b_i\right)$$

$$\tilde{c}_t = tanh\left(W_{cx}x_t + W_{ch}h_{t-1} + b_c\right)$$

$$f_t = \sigma\left(W_{fx}x_t + W_{fh}h_{t-1} + W_{fc}c_{t-1} + b_f\right)$$

$$c_t = f_t c_{t-1} + i_t \tilde{c}_t$$

$$o_t = \sigma\left(W_{ox}x_t + W_{oh}h_{t-1} + W_{oc}c_t + b_o\right)$$

$$h_t = o_t tanh\left(c_t\right)$$

Let's briefly look at how this helps the LSTM perform better. So far, the gates see the current input and final hidden state, but not the cell state. However, in this configuration, if the output gate is close to zero, even when the cell state contains important information crucial for better performance, the final hidden state will be close to zero. Thus, the gates will not take the hidden state into consideration during calculation. Including the cell state directly in the gate calculation equation allows more control over the cell state, and it can perform well even in situations where the output gate is close to zero.

We illustrate the architecture of the LSTM with peephole connections in *Figure 7.17*. We have greyed all the existing connections in a standard LSTM and the newly added connections are shown in black:

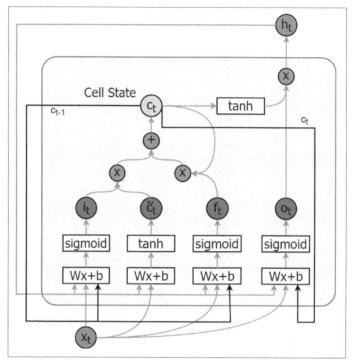

Figure 7.17: An LSTM with peephole connections (the peephole connections are shown in black while the other connections are greyed out)

# Gated Recurrent Units

**GRUs** can be seen as a simplification of the standard LSTM architecture. As we have seen already, an LSTM has three different gates and two different states. This alone requires a large number of parameters even for a small state size. Therefore, scientists have investigated ways to reduce the number of parameters. GRUs are a result of one such endeavor.

There are several main differences in GRUs compared to LSTMs.

First, GRUs combine two states, the cell state and the final hidden state, into a single hidden state $h_t$. Now, as a side effect of this simple modification of not having two different states, we can get rid of the output gate. Remember, the output gate was merely deciding how much of the cell state is read into the final hidden state. This operation greatly reduces the number of parameters in the cell.

Next, GRUs introduce a reset gate which, when it's close to 1, takes the full previous state information in when computing the current state. Also, when the reset gate is close to 0, it ignores the previous state when computing the current state.

$$r_t = \sigma\left(W_{rx}x_t + W_{rh}h_{t-1} + b_r\right)$$

$$\tilde{h}_t = tanh\left(W_{hx}x_t + W_{hh}\left(r_t h_{t-1}\right) + b_h\right)$$

Then, GRUs combine the input and forget gates into one *update gate*. The standard LSTM has two gates known as the input and forget gates. The input gate decides how much of the current input is read into the cell state, and the forget gate determines how much of the previous cell state is read into the current cell state. Mathematically, this can be shown as follows:

$$i_t = \sigma\left(W_{ix}x_t + W_{ih}h_{t-1} + b_i\right)$$

$$f_t = \sigma\left(W_{fx}x_t + W_{fh}h_{t-1} + b_f\right)$$

GRUs combine these two operations into a single gate known as the update gate. If the update gate is 0, then the full state information of the previous cell state is pushed into the current cell state, where none of the current input is read into the state. If the update gate is 1, then the all of the current input is read into the current cell state and none of the previous cell state is propagated into the current cell state. In other words, the input gate $i_t$ becomes inverse of the forget gate, that is, $1 - f_t$:

$$z_t = \sigma\left(W_{zx}x_t + W_{zh}h_{t-1} + b_z\right)$$

$$h_t = z_t \tilde{h}_t + \left(1 - z_t\right)h_{t-1}$$

Now let's bring all the equations into one place. The GRU computations would look like this:

$$r_t = \sigma\left(W_{rx}x_t + W_{rh}h_{t-1} + b_r\right)$$

$$\tilde{h}_t = tanh\left(W_{hx}x_t + W_{hh}\left(r_t h_{t-1}\right) + b_h\right)$$

$$z_t = \sigma\left(W_{zx}x_t + W_{zh}h_{t-1} + b_z\right)$$

$$h_t = z_t \tilde{h}_t + \left(1 - z_t\right)h_{t-1}$$

This is much more compact than LSTMs. In *Figure 7.18*, we can visualize a GRU cell (left) and an LSTM cell (right) side by side:

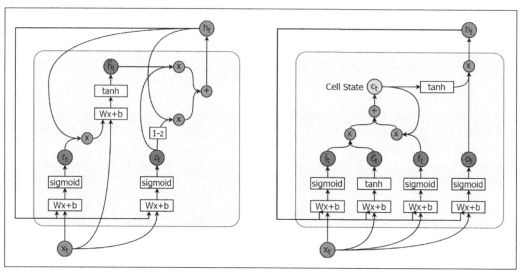

Figure 7.18: A side-by-side comparison of a GRU (left) and the standard LSTM (right)

# Summary

In this chapter, you learned about LSTM networks. First, we discussed what an LSTM is and its high-level architecture. We also delved into the detailed computations that take place in an LSTM and discussed the computations through an example.

We saw that LSTM is composed mainly of five different things:

- **Cell state**: The internal cell state of an LSTM cell
- **Hidden state**: The external hidden state used to calculate predictions
- **Input gate**: This determines how much of the current input is read into the cell state
- **Forget gate**: This determines how much of the previous cell state is sent into the current cell state
- **Output gate**: This determines how much of the cell state is output into the hidden state

Having such a complex structure allows LSTMs to capture both short-term and long-term dependencies quite well.

We compared LSTMs to vanilla RNNs and saw that LSTMs are actually capable of learning long-term dependencies as an inherent part of their structure, whereas RNNs can fail to learn long-term dependencies. Afterwards, we discussed how LSTMs solve the vanishing gradient with its complex structure.

Then we discussed several extensions that improve the performance of LSTMs. First, a very simple technique we called greedy sampling, in which, instead of always outputting the best candidate, we randomly sample a prediction from a set of best candidates. We saw that this improves the diversity of the generated text. Next, we looked at a more complex search technique called beam search. With this, instead of making a prediction for a single time step into the future, we predict several time steps into the future and pick the candidates that produce the best joint probability. Another improvement involved seeing how word vectors can help improve the quality of the predictions of an LSTM. Using word vectors, LSTMs can learn more effectively to replace semantically similar words during prediction (for example, instead of outputting *dog*, LSTM might output *cat*), leading to more realism and correctness of generated text. The final extension we considered was BiLSTMs or bidirectional LSTMs. A popular application of BiLSTMs is filling missing words in a phrase. BiLSTMs read the text in both directions, from the beginning to the end and the end to the beginning. This gives more context as we are looking at both the past and future before predicting.

Finally, we discussed two variants of vanilla LSTMs: peephole connections and GRUs. Vanillan LSTMs, when calculating the gates, only looks at the current input and the hidden state. With peephole connections, we make the gate computations dependent on all: the current input, hidden, and cell states.

GRUs are a much more elegant variant of vanilla LSTMs that simplifies LSTMs without compromising on performance. GRUs have only two gates and a single state, whereas vanilla LSTMs have three gates and two states.

In the next chapter, we will see all these different architectures in action with implementations of each of them and see how well they perform in text generation tasks.

# 8

# Applications of LSTM – Generating Text

Now that we have a good understanding of the underlying mechanisms of LSTMs, such as how they solve the problem of the vanishing gradient and update rules, we can look at how to use them in NLP tasks. LSTMs are heavily employed for tasks such as text generation and image caption generation. For example, language modeling is very useful for text summarization tasks or generating captivating textual advertisements for products, where image caption generation or image annotation is very useful for image retrieval, and where a user might need to retrieve images representing some concept (for example, a cat).

The application that we will cover in this chapter is the use of an LSTM to generate new text. For this task, we will download translations of some folk stories by the Brothers Grimm. We will use these stories to train an LSTM and ask it at the end to output a fresh new story. We will process the text by breaking it into character-level bigrams (n-grams where $n=2$) and make a vocabulary out of the unique bigrams. We will also explore ways to implement previously described techniques such as greedy sampling or beam search for predictions. Afterwards, we will see how we can implement time-series models other than standard LSTMs, such as LSTMs with peepholes and GRUs.

Next, we will see how we can learn to generate text with better input representations beyond character level bigrams, such as individual words. Note that it is very inefficient to have one-hot-encoded word features, as the vocabulary can quickly grow with words, compared to character level bigrams. Therefore, one good technique to deal with this is to first learn the word embeddings (or use pretrained embeddings) and use these as inputs to the LSTM. Using word embeddings allows us to avoid the curse of dimensionality. In an interesting real-world problem, the size of the vocabulary can be between 10,000 and 1,000,000. However, word embeddings have a fixed dimensionality despite the size of the vocabulary.

# Our data

First, we will discuss the data we will use for text generation and various preprocessing steps employed to clean data.

# About the dataset

First, we will understand what the dataset looks like so that when we see the generated text, we can assess whether it makes sense, given the training data. We will download the first 100 books from the website `https://www.cs.cmu.edu/~spok/grimmtmp/`. These are translations of a set of books (from German to English) by the Brothers Grimm. This is the same as the text used in *Chapter 6, Recurrent Neural Networks*, for demonstrating the performance of RNNs.

Initially, we will download the first 100 books from the website with an automated script, as follows:

```
url = 'https://www.cs.cmu.edu/~spok/grimmtmp/'

# Create a directory if needed
dir_name = 'stories'
if not os.path.exists(dir_name):
    os.mkdir(dir_name)

def maybe_download(filename):
  """Download a file if not present"""
  print('Downloading file: ', dir_name+ os.sep+filename)

  if not os.path.exists(dir_name+os.sep+filename):
    filename, _ = urlretrieve(url + filename,
                              dir_name+os.sep+filename)
  else:
    print('File ',filename, ' already exists.')

  return filename

num_files = 100
filenames = [format(i, '03d')+'.txt' for i in range(1,101)]

for fn in filenames:
    maybe_download(fn)
```

We will now show example text snippets extracted from two randomly picked stories.

The following is the first snippet:

*Then she said, my dearest benjamin, your father has had these coffins made for you and for your eleven brothers, for if I bring a little girl into the world, you are all to be killed and buried in them. And as she wept while she was saying this, the son comforted her and said, weep not, dear mother, we will save ourselves, and go hence. But she said, go forth into the forest with your eleven brothers, and let one sit constantly on the highest tree which can be found, and keep watch, looking towards the tower here in the castle. If I give birth to a little son, I will put up a white flag, and then you may venture to come back. But if I bear a daughter, I will hoist a red flag, and then fly hence as quickly as you are able, and may the good God protect you.*

The second text snippet is as follows:

*Red-cap did not know what a wicked creature he was, and was not at all afraid of him.*

*"Good-day, little red-cap," said he.*

*"Thank you kindly, wolf."*

*"Whither away so early, little red-cap?"*

*"To my grandmother's."*

*"What have you got in your apron?"*

*"Cake and wine. Yesterday was baking-day, so poor sick grandmother is to have something good, to make her stronger."*

*"Where does your grandmother live, little red-cap?"*

*"A good quarter of a league farther on in the wood. Her house stands under the three large oak-trees, the nut-trees are just below. You surely must know it," replied little red-cap.*

*The wolf thought to himself, what a tender young creature. What a nice plump mouthful, she will be better to eat than the old woman.*

# Preprocessing data

In terms of preprocessing, we will initially make all the text lowercase and break the text into character n-grams, where *n=2*. Consider the following sentence:

*The king was hunting in the forest.*

This would break down to a sequence of n-grams as follows:

*['th,' 'e ,' 'ki,' 'ng,' ' w,' 'as,' ...]*

We will use character level bigrams because it greatly reduces the size of the vocabulary compared with using individual words. Moreover, we will be replacing all the bigrams that appear fewer than 10 times in the corpus with a special token (that is, *UNK*), representing that bigram as unknown. This helps us to reduce the size of the vocabulary even further.

# Implementing an LSTM

Here we will discuss the details of the LSTM implementation. Though there are sublibraries in TensorFlow that have already implemented ready-to-go LSTMs, we will implement one from scratch. This will be very valuable, as in the real world there might be situations where you cannot use these off-the-shelf components directly. This code is available in the `lstm_for_text_generation.ipynb` exercise located in the `ch8` folder of the exercises. However, we will also include an exercise where we will show how to use the existing TensorFlow RNN API that will be available in `lstm_word2vec_rnn_api.ipynb`, located in the same folder. Here we will discuss the code available in the `lstm_for_text_generation.ipynb` file.

First, we will discuss the hyperparameters and their effects that are used for the LSTM. Thereafter, we will discuss the parameters (weights and biases) required to implement the LSTM. We will then discuss how these parameters are used to write the operations taking place within the LSTM. This will be followed by understanding how we will sequentially feed data to the LSTM. Next, we will discuss how we can implement the optimization of the parameters using gradient clipping. Finally, we will investigate how we can use the learned model to output predictions, which are essentially bigrams that will eventually add up to a meaningful story.

# Defining hyperparameters

First, we will define some hyperparameters required for the LSTM:

```
# Number of neurons in the hidden state variables
num_nodes = 128
```

```
# Number of data points in a batch we process
batch_size = 64

# Number of time steps we unroll for during optimization
num_unrollings = 50

dropout = 0.2 # We use dropout
```

The following list describes each of the hyperparameters:

- num_nodes: This denotes the number of neurons in the cell memory state. When data is abundant, increasing the complexity of the cell memory will give you a better performance; however, at the same time, it slows down the computations.

- batch_size: This is the amount of data processed in a single step. Increasing the size of the batch gives a better performance, but poses higher memory requirements.

- num_unrollings: This is the number of time steps used in truncated-BPTT. The higher the num_unrollings steps, the better the performance, but it will increase both the memory requirement and the computational time.

- dropout: Finally, we will employ dropout (that is, a regularization technique) to reduce overfitting of the model and produce better results; dropout randomly drops information from inputs/outputs/state variables before passing them to their successive operations. This creates redundant features during learning, leading to better performance.

# Defining parameters

Now we will define TensorFlow variables for the actual parameters of the LSTM.

First, we will define the input gate parameters:

- ix: These are weights connecting the input to the input gate
- im: These are weights connecting the hidden state to the input gate
- ib: This is the bias

Here we will define the parameters:

```
# Input gate (it) - How much memory to write to cell state
# Connects the current input to the input gate
ix = tf.Variable(tf.truncated_normal([vocabulary_size, num_nodes],
stddev=0.02))
# Connects the previous hidden state to the input gate
im = tf.Variable(tf.truncated_normal([num_nodes, num_nodes],
```

```
stddev=0.02))
# Bias of the input gate
ib = tf.Variable(tf.random_uniform([1, num_nodes],-0.02, 0.02))
```

Similarly, we will define such weights for the forget gate, candidate value (used for memory cell computations), and output gate.

The forget gate is defined as follows:

```
# Forget gate (ft) - How much memory to discard from cell state
# Connects the current input to the forget gate
fx = tf.Variable(tf.truncated_normal([vocabulary_size, num_nodes],
stddev=0.02))
# Connects the previous hidden state to the forget gate
fm = tf.Variable(tf.truncated_normal([num_nodes, num_nodes],
stddev=0.02))
# Bias of the forget gate
fb = tf.Variable(tf.random_uniform([1, num_nodes],-0.02, 0.02))
```

The candidate value (used to compute the cell state) is defined as follows:

```
# Candidate value (c~t) - Used to compute the current cell state
# Connects the current input to the candidate
cx = tf.Variable(tf.truncated_normal([vocabulary_size, num_nodes],
stddev=0.02))
# Connects the previous hidden state to the candidate
cm = tf.Variable(tf.truncated_normal([num_nodes, num_nodes],
stddev=0.02))
# Bias of the candidate
cb = tf.Variable(tf.random_uniform([1, num_nodes],-0.02,0.02))
```

The output gate is defined as follows:

```
# Output gate - How much memory to output from the cell state
# Connects the current input to the output gate
ox = tf.Variable(tf.truncated_normal([vocabulary_size, num_nodes],
stddev=0.02))
# Connects the previous hidden state to the output gate
om = tf.Variable(tf.truncated_normal([num_nodes, num_nodes],
stddev=0.02))
# Bias of the output gate
ob = tf.Variable(tf.random_uniform([1, num_nodes],-0.02,0.02))
```

Next, we will define variables for the state and output. These are the TensorFlow variables representing the internal cell state and the external hidden state of the LSTM cell. When defining the LSTM computational operation, we define these to be updated with the latest cell state and hidden state values we compute, using the `tf.control_dependencies(...)` function.

```
# Variables saving state across unrollings.
# Hidden state
saved_output = tf.Variable(tf.zeros([batch_size, num_nodes]),
trainable=False, name='train_hidden')
# Cell state
saved_state = tf.Variable(tf.zeros([batch_size, num_nodes]),
trainable=False, name='train_cell')
# Same variables for validation phase
saved_valid_output = tf.Variable(tf.zeros([1, num_
nodes]),trainable=False, name='valid_hidden')
saved_valid_state = tf.Variable(tf.zeros([1, num_
nodes]),trainable=False, name='valid_cell')
```

Finally, we will define a softmax layer to get the actual predictions out:

```
# Softmax Classifier weights and biases.
w = tf.Variable(tf.truncated_normal([num_nodes, vocabulary_size],
stddev=0.02))
b = tf.Variable(tf.random_uniform([vocabulary_size],-0.02,0.02))
```

Note that we're using the normal distribution with zero mean and a small standard deviation. This is fine as our model is a simple single LSTM cell. However, when the network gets deeper (that is, multiple LSTM cells stacked on top of each other), more careful initialization techniques are required. One such initialization technique is known as **Xavier initialization**, proposed by Glorot and Bengio in their paper *Understanding the difficulty of training deep feedforward neural networks, Proceedings of the 13th International Conference on Artificial Intelligence and Statistics, 2010*. This is available as a variable initializer in TensorFlow, as shown here: `https://www.tensorflow.org/api_docs/python/tf/contrib/layers/xavier_initializer`.

# Defining an LSTM cell and its operations

With the weights and the bias defined, we can now define the operations within an LSTM cell. These operations include the following:

- Calculating the outputs produced by the input and forget gates
- Calculating the internal cell state

- Calculating the output produced by the output gate
- Calculating the external hidden state

The following is the implementation of our LSTM cell:

```
def lstm_cell(i, o, state):

    input_gate = tf.sigmoid(tf.matmul(i, ix) +
                            tf.matmul(o, im) + ib)
    forget_gate = tf.sigmoid(tf.matmul(i, fx) +
                             tf.matmul(o, fm) + fb)
    update = tf.matmul(i, cx) + tf.matmul(o, cm) + cb
    state = forget_gate * state + input_gate * tf.tanh(update)
    output_gate = tf.sigmoid(tf.matmul(i, ox) +
                             tf.matmul(o, om) + ob)
    return output_gate * tf.tanh(state), state
```

# Defining inputs and labels

Now we will define training inputs (unrolled) and labels. The training inputs is a list with the `num_unrolling` batches of data (sequential), where each batch of data is of the `[batch_size, vocabulary_size]` size:

```
train_inputs, train_labels = [], []

for ui in range(num_unrollings):
    train_inputs.append(tf.placeholder(tf.float32,
                        shape=[batch_size,vocabulary_size],
                        name='train_inputs_%d'%ui))
    train_labels.append(tf.placeholder(tf.float32,
                        shape=[batch_size,vocabulary_size],
                        name = 'train_labels_%d'%ui))
```

We also define placeholders for validation inputs and outputs, which will be used to compute the validation perplexity. Note that we do not use unrolling for validation-related computations.

```
# Validation data placeholders
valid_inputs = tf.placeholder(tf.float32, shape=[1,vocabulary_size],
                name='valid_inputs')
valid_labels = tf.placeholder(tf.float32, shape=[1,vocabulary_size],
                name = 'valid_labels')
```

# Defining sequential calculations required to process sequential data

Here we will calculate the outputs produced by a single unrolling of the training inputs in a recursive manner. We will also use dropout (refer to *Dropout: A Simple Way to Prevent Neural Networks from Overfitting, Srivastava, Nitish, and others, Journal of Machine Learning Research 15 (2014): 1929-1958*), as this gives a slightly better performance. Finally we compute the logit values for all the hidden output values computed for the training data:

```
# Keeps the calculated state outputs in all the unrollings
# Used to calculate loss
outputs = list()

# These two python variables are iteratively updated
# at each step of unrolling
output = saved_output
state = saved_state

# Compute the hidden state (output) and cell state (state)
# recursively for all the steps in unrolling
for i in train_inputs:
    output, state = lstm_cell(i, output, state)
    output = tf.nn.dropout(output,keep_prob=1.0-dropout)
    # Append each computed output value
    outputs.append(output)

# calculate the score values
logits = tf.matmul(tf.concat(axis=0, values=outputs), w) + b
```

Next, before calculating the loss, we have to make sure that the output and the external hidden state are updated to the most current value we calculated earlier. This is achieved by adding a tf.control_dependencies condition and keeping the logit and loss calculation within the condition:

```
with tf.control_dependencies([saved_output.assign(output),
                              saved_state.assign(state)]):
    # Classifier.
    loss = tf.reduce_mean(
      tf.nn.softmax_cross_entropy_with_logits_v2(
        logits=logits, labels=tf.concat(axis=0,
                                         values=train_labels)))
```

We also define the forward propagation logic for validation data. Note that we do not use dropout during validation, but only during training:

```
# Validation phase related inference logic

# Compute the LSTM cell output for validation data
valid_output, valid_state = lstm_cell(
    valid_inputs, saved_valid_output, saved_valid_state)

# Compute the logits
valid_logits = tf.nn.xw_plus_b(valid_output, w, b)
```

# Defining the optimizer

Here we will define the optimization process. We will use a state-of-the-art optimizer known as **Adam**, which is one of the best stochastic gradient-based optimizers to date. Here in the code, gstep is a variable that is used to decay the learning rate over time. We will discuss the details in the next section. Furthermore, we will use gradient clipping to avoid the exploding gradient:

```
# Decays learning rate everytime the gstep increases
tf_learning_rate = tf.train.exponential_decay(0.001,gstep,
                    decay_steps=1, decay_rate=0.5)
# Adam Optimizer. And gradient clipping.
optimizer = tf.train.AdamOptimizer(tf_learning_rate)
gradients, v = zip(*optimizer.compute_gradients(loss))
gradients, _ = tf.clip_by_global_norm(gradients, 5.0)
optimizer = optimizer.apply_gradients(
    zip(gradients, v))
```

# Decaying learning rate over time

As mentioned earlier, I use a decaying learning rate instead of a constant learning rate. Decaying the learning rate over time is a common technique used in deep learning for achieving better performance and reducing overfitting. The key idea here is to step-down the learning rate (for example, by a factor of 0.5) if the validation perplexity does not decrease for a predefined number of epochs. Let's see how exactly this is implemented, in more detail:

First we define `gstep` and an operation to increment `gstep`, called `inc_gstep` as follows:

```
# learning rate decay
gstep = tf.Variable(0,trainable=False,name='global_step')
# Running this operation will cause the value of gstep
# to increase, while in turn reducing the learning rate
inc_gstep = tf.assign(gstep, gstep+1)
```

With this defined, we can write some simple logic to call the `inc_gstep` operation whenever validation loss does not decrease, as follows:

```
# Learning rate decay related
# If valid perplexity does not decrease
# continuously for this many epochs
# decrease the learning rate
decay_threshold = 5
# Keep counting perplexity increases
decay_count = 0
min_perplexity = 1e10

# Learning rate decay logic
def decay_learning_rate(session, v_perplexity):
  global decay_threshold, decay_count, min_perplexity
  # Decay learning rate
  if v_perplexity < min_perplexity:
    decay_count = 0
    min_perplexity= v_perplexity
  else:
    decay_count += 1

  if decay_count >= decay_threshold:
    print('\t Reducing learning rate')
    decay_count = 0
    session.run(inc_gstep)
```

Here we update `min_perplexity` whenever we experience a new minimum validation perplexity. Also, `v_perplexity` is the current validation perplexity.

# Making predictions

Now we can make predictions, simply by applying a softmax activation to the logits we calculated previously. We also define prediction operation for validation logits as well:

```
train_prediction = tf.nn.softmax(logits)
# Make sure that the state variables are updated
# before moving on to the next iteration of generation
with tf.control_dependencies([saved_valid_output.assign(valid_output),
                            saved_valid_state.assign(valid_state)]):
    valid_prediction = tf.nn.softmax(valid_logits)
```

# Calculating perplexity (loss)

We defined what perplexity is in *Chapter 7, Long Short-Term Memory Networks*. To review, perplexity is a measure of how *surprised* the LSTM is to see the next n-gram, given the current n-gram. Therefore, a higher perplexity means poor performance, whereas a lower perplexity means a better performance:

```
train_perplexity_without_exp = tf.reduce_sum(
    tf.concat(train_labels,0)*-tf.log(tf.concat(
        train_prediction,0)+1e-10))/(num_unrollings*batch_size)
# Compute validation perplexity
valid_perplexity_without_exp = tf.reduce_sum(valid_labels*-tf.
log(valid_prediction+1e-10))
```

# Resetting states

We employ state resetting, as we are processing multiple documents. So, at the beginning of processing a new document, we reset the hidden state back to zero. However, it is not very clear whether resetting the state helps or not in practice. On one hand, it sounds intuitive to reset the memory of the LSTM cell at the beginning of each document to zero, when starting to read a new story. On the other hand, this creates a bias in state variables toward zero. We encourage you to try running the algorithm both with and without state resetting and see which method performs well.

```
# Reset train state
reset_train_state = tf.group(tf.assign(saved_state,
                            tf.zeros([batch_size, num_nodes])),
                            tf.assign(saved_output, tf.zeros(
                            [batch_size, num_nodes])))
```

```
# Reset valid state
reset_valid_state = tf.group(tf.assign(saved_valid_state,
                                 tf.zeros([1, num_nodes])),
                             tf.assign(saved_valid_output,
                                 tf.zeros([1, num_nodes]))))
```

# Greedy sampling to break unimodality

This is quite a simple technique where we can stochastically sample the next prediction out of the *n* best candidates found by the LSTM. Furthermore, we will give the probability of picking one candidate to be proportional to the likelihood of that candidate being the next bigram:

```
def sample(distribution):

    best_inds = np.argsort(distribution)[-3:]
    best_probs = distribution[best_inds]/
    np.sum(distribution[best_inds])
    best_idx = np.random.choice(best_inds,p=best_probs)
    return best_idx
```

# Generating new text

Finally, we will define the placeholders, variables, and operations required for generating new text. These are defined similarly to what we did for the training data. First, we will define an input placeholder and variables for state and output. Next, we will define state resetting operations. Finally, we will define the LSTM cell calculations and predictions for the new text to be generated:

```
# Text generation: batch 1, no unrolling.
test_input = tf.placeholder(tf.float32, shape=[1, vocabulary_size],
name = 'test_input')

# Same variables for testing phase
saved_test_output = tf.Variable(tf.zeros([1,
                                 num_nodes]),
                                 trainable=False, name='test_hidden')
saved_test_state = tf.Variable(tf.zeros([1,
                                 num_nodes]),
                                 trainable=False, name='test_cell')

# Compute the LSTM cell output for testing data
test_output, test_state = lstm_cell(
test_input, saved_test_output, saved_test_state)
```

```
# Make sure that the state variables are updated
# before moving on to the next iteration of generation
with tf.control_dependencies([saved_test_output.assign(test_output),
                              saved_test_state.assign(test_state)]):
    test_prediction = tf.nn.softmax(tf.nn.xw_plus_b(test_output,
                              w, b))


# Reset test state
reset_test_state = tf.group(
    saved_test_output.assign(tf.random_normal([1,
                              num_nodes],stddev=0.05)),
    saved_test_state.assign(tf.random_normal([1,
                              num_nodes],stddev=0.05)))
```

# Example generated text

Let's take a look at some of the data generated by the LSTM after 50 steps of learning:

```
they saw that the birds were at her bread, and threw behind him a comb
which
made a great ridge with a thousand times thousands of spikes.  that
was a
collier.
the nixie was at church, and thousands of spikes, they were flowers,
however, and had hewn through the glass, the children had formed a
hill of mirrors, and was so slippery that it was impossible for the
nixie to cross it.  then she thought, i will go home quickly and
fetch my axe, and cut the hill of glass in half.  long before she
returned, however, and had hewn through the glass, the children saw
her from afar,
and he sat down close to it,
and was so slippery that it was impossible for the
nixie to cross it.
```

As you can see, the text looks much better than the text we saw being generated from RNNs. There actually exists a story about a water-nixie in our training corpus. However, our LSTM does not merely output that text, but it adds more color to that story by introducing new things, such as talking about a church and flowers, which are not found in the original text. Next we will investigate how the text generated from standard LSTMs compares to other models, such as LSTMs with peepholes and GRUs.

# Comparing LSTMs to LSTMs with peephole connections and GRUs

Now we will compare LSTMs to LSTMs with peepholes and GRUs in the text generation task. This will help us to compare how well different models (LSTMs with peepholes and GRUs) perform in terms of perplexity as well as the quality of the generated text. This is available as an exercise in `lstm_extensions.ipynb` located in the `ch8` folder.

# Standard LSTM

First, we will reiterate the components of a standard LSTM. We will not repeat the code for standard LSTMs as it is identical to what we discussed previously. Finally, we will see some text generated by an LSTM.

## Review

Here we will revisit what a standard LSTM looks like. As we already mentioned, an LSTM consists of the following:

- **Input gate**: This decides how much of the current input is written to the cell state
- **Forget gate**: This decides how much of the previous cell state is written to the current cell state
- **Output gate**: This decides how much information from the cell state is exposed to output into the external hidden state

In *Figure 8.1*, we will illustrate how each of these gates, input, cell state, and the external hidden states are connected:

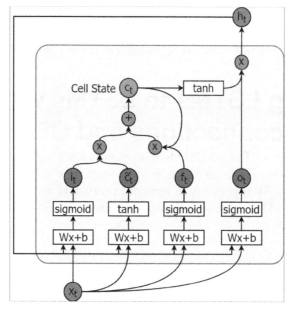

Figure 8.1: An LSTM cell

# Example generated text

Here we will show the text produced by a standard LSTM after a single step of training and 25 steps of training on our dataset.

Text produced at step 1:

```
emy that then the to they the the to and and and then there the to
the to the withe there the the to, and ther, and ther tthe the the the
withe the the the the wid the th to e the there to, and the the the
the the wid the the the to, the and to the was and and was the when
hind the whey the the to and was the whe wous thout hit the to hhe was
they his up the was was the wou was and and wout the the ous to hhe
the was and was they hind and and then the the the wit to the wther
thae wid the and the the wit the ther, the there the to the wthe wit
the the the the wit up the they og a and the whey the the ous th the
wthe the ars to and the whey it a and whe was they the ound the was
whe was and and to ther then the and ther the wthe art the the and and
the the the to and when the the wie to the wthe wit up the whe wou
wout hit hit the the the to the whe was aou was to t the out and the
and hit the the the with then the wie the to then the the to, the to a
t to the the wit up he the wit there
```

Text produced at step 25:

```
there, said the father for a while, and her trouble she was to carry
the mountain.  then they were all the child, and they were once and
only sighed, but they said, i am as
old now as the way and drew the child, and he began and wife looked at
last and said, i have the child, fath-turn, and
hencefore they were to himself, and then they trembled, hand all three
days with him.  when the king of the golden changeling, and his wife
looked at last and only one lord, and then he was laughing, wished
himself, and then he said
nothing and only sighed.  then they had said, all the changeling
laugh, and he said, who was still done, the bridegroom, and he went
away to him, but he did not trouble to the changeling away, and then
they were over this, he was all to the wife, and she said,
has the wedding did gretel give her them, and said, hans in a place.
in her trouble shell into the father.  i am you.
the king had said, how he was to sweep.  then the spot on hand but the
could give you doing there,
```

We can see that at step 25, there is quite a dramatic increase in the quality of the text compared to step 1. Furthermore, this text looks much better than the text we saw in the *Chapter 6, Recurrent Neural Networks* examples, when 100 stories were used to train the model.

# Gated Recurrent Units (GRUs)

Here we will first briefly delineate what a GRU is composed of, followed by the code for implementing a GRU cell. Finally, we look at some code generated by a GRU cell.

## Review

In order to review, let's briefly go through what a GRU is. A GRU is an elegant simplification of the operations of an LSTM. A GRU introduces two different modifications to an LSTM (see *Figure 8.2*):

- It connects the internal cell state and the external hidden state into a single state

- Then it combines the input gate and the forget gate into one update gate

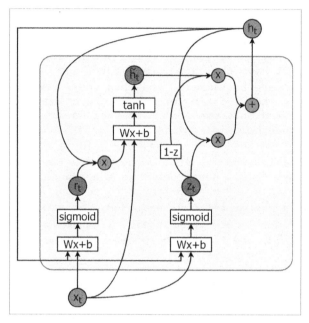

Figure 8.2: A GRU cell

# The code

Here we will define a GRU cell:

```
def gru_cell(i, o):
    """Create a GRU cell."""
    reset_gate = tf.sigmoid(tf.matmul(i, rx) + tf.matmul(o, rh)
                            + rb)
    h_tilde = tf.tanh(tf.matmul(i,hx) + tf.matmul(
        reset_gate * o, hh) + hb)
    z = tf.sigmoid(tf.matmul(i,zx) + tf.matmul(o, zh) + zb)
    h = (1-z)*o + z*h_tilde

    return h
```

Then we will call this method as we did earlier in our example:

```
for i in train_inputs:
    output = gru_cell(i, output)
    output = tf.nn.dropout(output,keep_prob=1.0-dropout)
    outputs.append(output)
```

# Example generated text

Here we will show text produced by a GRU after a single step of training and 25 steps of training on our dataset.

Text produced at step 1:

```
          hing ther that ther her to the was shen andmother to to her the
cake, and the caked the woked that the wer hou shen her the the the
that her her, and to ther to ther her that the wer the wer ther the
wong are whe was the was so the the caked her the wong an the woked
the wolf the soought and was the was he grandmred the wolf sas shen
that ther to hout her the the cap the wolf so the wong the soor ind
the wolf the when that, her the the wolf to and the wolf sher the the
cap the cap.  the wolf so ther the was her her, the the the wong and
whe her the was her he grout the ther, and the cap., and the caked the
the ther the were cap and the would the the wolf the was the whe wher
cad-the cake the was her her, he when the ther, the wolf so the that,
and the wolf so and her the the the cap.  the the wong to the wolf,
andmother the cap. the so to ther ther, the woked he was the was the
when the caked her cad-ing and the cake, and
```

Text produced at step 25:

```
you will be sack, and the king's son, the king continued, and he was
about to them all, and that she was strange carry them to somether,
and who was there, but when the shole before the king, and the king's
daughter was into such into the six can dish of this wine before the
said, the king continued, and said to the king, when he was into the
castle to so the king.
then the king was stranged the king.
then she said, and said that he saw what the sack, but the king, and
the king content up the king.
the king had the other, and said, it is not down to the king was in
the blower to be took them.  then the king sack, the king, and the
other, there, and
said to the other, there, and the king, who had been away, the six
content the six conved the king's strong one, they were not down the
king.
then she said to her, and saw the six content until there, and the
king content until the six convered the
```

We can see that in terms of the quality of text, GRUs do not demonstrate a significant quality improvement compared to standard LSTMs. However, the output of GRUs seems to have more repetitions (for example, the word *king*) in text more frequently than the LSTMs. This is possibly due to compromising of long-term memory caused by the simplification of the model (that is, having only a single state, compared to the two states in a standard LSTM).

# LSTMs with peepholes

Here we will discuss LSTMs with peepholes and how they are different from a standard LSTM. Next we will discuss their implementation, followed by the text generated by the LSTM with peepholes model.

## Review

Now, let's briefly look at LSTMs with peepholes. Peepholes are essentially a way for the gates (input, forget, and output) to directly see the cell state, instead of waiting for the external hidden state (see *Figure 8.3*):

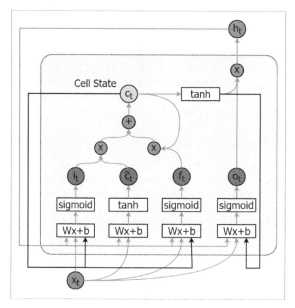

Figure 8.3: An LSTM with peepholes

## The code

Note that we're keeping the peep connections diagonal. We found that nondiagonal peephole connections (proposed by Gers and Schmidhuber in their paper *Recurrent Nets that Time and Count, Neural Networks, 2000*) hurt performance more than they help, for this language modeling task. Therefore, we adopted a different variation that uses diagonal peephole connections, as used by Sak, Senior, and Beaufays in their paper *Long Short-Term Memory Recurrent Neural Network Architectures for Large Scale Acoustic Modeling, Proceedings of the Annual Conference of the International Speech Communication Association, INTERSPEECH, 2014: 338-342.*

The following is the code implementation:

```
def lstm_with_peephole_cell(i, o, state):

    input_gate = tf.sigmoid(tf.matmul(i, ix) + state*ic +
                            tf.matmul(o, im) + ib)
    forget_gate = tf.sigmoid(tf.matmul(i, fx) + state*fc +
                             tf.matmul(o, fm) + fb)
    update = tf.matmul(i, cx) + tf.matmul(o, cm) + cb
    state = forget_gate * state + input_gate * tf.tanh(update)
    output_gate = tf.sigmoid(tf.matmul(i, ox) + state*oc +
                             tf.matmul(o, om) + ob)

    return output_gate * tf.tanh(state), state
```

Then we will call this method for each batch of inputs for spanning across all time steps (that is, the num_unrollings time steps), as in this code:

```
for i in train_inputs:
    output, state = lstm_with_peephole_cell(i, output, state)
    output = tf.nn.dropout(output,keep_prob=1.0-dropout)
    outputs.append(output)
```

# Example generated text

Here we show text produced by a standard LSTM after a single step of training and 25 steps of training on our dataset.

The following is the text produced at step 1:

```
our oned he the the hed the the the he here hed he he e e and her and
the ther her the then hed and her and her her the hed her and the the
he he ther the hhe the he ther the whed hed her he hthe and the the
the ther the to e and the the the ane and and her and the hed ant and
the and ane hed and ther and and he e the th the hhe ther the the and
the the the the the the the hed and ther hhe wher the her he he and he
hthe the the the he the then the he he e and the the the and and the
the the ther to he hhe wher ant the her and the hed the he he the and
ther and he the and and the ant he he e the and ther he e and ther
here th the whed
```

The following is the text produced at step 25:

```
will, it was there, and it was me, and i trod on the stress and there
is a stone and the went and said, klink, and that the princess and
they said, i will not stare
it, the wedding and that the was of little the sun came in the sun
came out, and then the wolf is took a little coat and i were at little
hand and beaning therein and said, klink, and broke out of the shoes
he had the wolf of the were to patches a little put into the were, and
they said, she was to pay the bear said, "ah, that they come to the
well and there is a stone and the wolf were of the light, and that the
two old were of glass there is a little that his
well as well and wherever a stone
and they were the went to the well, and the went the sun came in the
seater hand, and they said, klink, and broke in his sead, and i were
my good one
the wedding and said, that the two of slapped to said to said, "ah,
that his store once the worl's said, klink, but the went out of a
patched on his store, and the wedding and said, that
```

The text produced by LSTMs with peepholes appears to be grammatically poor compared to text produced by LSTMs or GRUs. Let's now see how each method compares quantitatively in terms of the perplexity measure.

# Training and validation perplexities over time

In *Figure 8.4*, we will plot the behavior of perplexity over time for LSTMs, LSTMs with peepholes, and GRUs. First, we can see that not having dropout gives a significant reduction in training perplexity. However, we should not conclude that dropout adversely affects performance, as this appealing performance is due to the overfitting training data. This is evident from the validation perplexity graph. Although LSTM's train perplexity appears to be competitive with the models that use dropout, the validation perplexity is much higher than these models. This shows us that dropout in fact helps us in the language generation task.

Also, from all the methods that use dropout, we can see that LSTM and GRUs deliver the best performance. One surprising observation is that LSTMs with peepholes produce the worst training perplexity and a slightly worse validation perplexity. This means that peephole connections do not add any value to solving our problem, but instead make the optimization difficult by introducing more parameters to the model. Following this analysis, we will use LSTMs from here on. We leave experimenting with GRUs as an exercise for the readers:

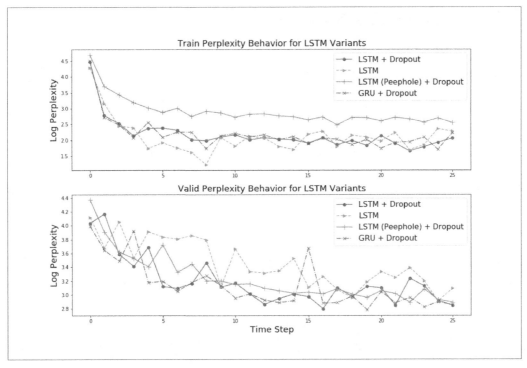

Figure 8.4: Perplexity change for training data over time (LSTMs, LSTM (peephole), and GRUs)

The current literature suggests that among LSTMs and GRUs, there is no clear winner and a lot depends on the task (refer to the paper *Empirical Evaluation of Gated Recurrent Neural Networks on Sequence Modeling, Chung and others, NIPS 2014 Workshop on Deep Learning, December 2014*).

# Improving LSTMs – beam search

As we saw earlier, the generated text can be improved. Now let's see if beam search, which we discussed in *Chapter 7, Long Short-Term Memory Networks*, might help to improve the performance. In beam search, we will look ahead a number of steps (called a **beam**) and get the beam (that is, a sequence of bigrams) that has the highest joint probability calculated separately for each beam. The joint probability is calculated by multiplying the prediction probabilities of each predicted bigram in a beam. Note that this is a greedy search, meaning that we will calculate the best candidates at each depth of the tree iteratively, as the tree grows. It should be noted that this search will not result in the globally best beam.

# Implementing beam search

To implement beam search, we only have to change the text generation technique. Training and validation operations stay the same. However the code will be more complicated than the text generation operation flow we saw earlier. This code is available to the end of the `lstm_for_text_generation.ipynb` exercise file in the `ch8` folder.

First, we will define the beam length (that is, the number of steps we look into the future) and `beam_neighbors` (that is, the number of candidates we compare at each time step):

```
beam_length = 5
beam_neighbors = 5
```

We will define the `beam_neighbor` number of placeholders to maintain the best candidates at each time step:

```
sample_beam_inputs = [tf.placeholder(tf.float32, shape=[1, vocabulary_
size]) for _ in range(beam_neighbors)]
```

Next, we will define two placeholders to hold the best greedily found global beam index and the locally maintained best candidate beam indices, which we will use to continue our predictions for the next stage of predictions:

```
best_beam_index = tf.placeholder(shape=None, dtype=tf.int32)
best_neighbor_beam_indices = tf.placeholder(shape=[beam_neighbors],
dtype=tf.int32)
```

Then we will define state and output variables for each beam candidate as we did for a single prediction earlier:

```
saved_sample_beam_output = [tf.Variable(tf.zeros([1, num_nodes])) for
_ in range(beam_neighbors)]
saved_sample_beam_state = [tf.Variable(tf.zeros([1, num_nodes])) for _
in range(beam_neighbors)]
```

We will also define state reset operations:

```
reset_sample_beam_state = tf.group(
    *[saved_sample_beam_output[vi].assign(tf.zeros([1, num_nodes]))
for vi in range(beam_neighbors)],
    *[saved_sample_beam_state[vi].assign(tf.zeros([1, num_nodes])) for
vi in range(beam_neighbors)]
)
```

Also, we will need cell output and prediction calculations for each beam:

```
# We calculate lstm_cell state and output for each beam
sample_beam_outputs, sample_beam_states = [],[]
for vi in range(beam_neighbors):
    tmp_output, tmp_state = lstm_cell(
        sample_beam_inputs[vi], saved_sample_beam_output[vi],
        saved_sample_beam_state[vi]
    )
    sample_beam_outputs.append(tmp_output)
    sample_beam_states.append(tmp_state)

# For a given set of beams, outputs a list of prediction vectors of
size beam_neighbors
# each beam having the predictions for full vocabulary
sample_beam_predictions = []
for vi in range(beam_neighbors):
    with tf.control_dependencies([saved_sample_beam_output[vi].
assign(sample_beam_outputs[vi]),
                                  saved_sample_beam_state[vi].
assign(sample_beam_states[vi])]):
        sample_beam_predictions.append(tf.nn.softmax(tf.nn.xw_
plus_b(sample_beam_outputs[vi], w, b)))
```

Next, we will define a new set of operations for updating the state and output variables of each beam with the best beam candidate indices found at each step. This is important for each step, as the best beam candidates will not uniformly branch out from each tree at a given depth. *Figure 8.5* shows an example. We will indicate the best beam candidates with bold font and arrows:

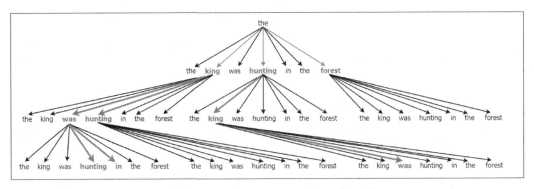

Figure 8.5: A beam search illustrating the requirement for updating beam states at each step

As seen here, candidates are not uniformly sampled, having always one candidate from a subtree (a set of arrows starting from the same point) at a given depth. For example, at depth two, there are no candidates spawning from the *hunting* → *king* path, so the state update we calculated for that path is not useful anymore. So the state we maintained for that path must be replaced with the state update we had for the *king* → *was* path, as there are now two paths sharing the parent *king* → *was*. We will use the following code to make such replacements to the states:

```
stacked_beam_outputs = tf.stack(saved_sample_beam_output)
stacked_beam_states = tf.stack(saved_sample_beam_state)


update_sample_beam_state = tf.group(
    *[saved_sample_beam_output[vi].assign(tf.gather_nd(stacked_beam_
outputs,[best_neighbor_beam_indices[vi]])) for vi in range(beam_
neighbors)],
    *[saved_sample_beam_state[vi].assign(tf.gather_nd(stacked_beam_
states,[best_neighbor_beam_indices[vi]])) for vi in range(beam_
neighbors)]
)
```

# Examples generated with beam search

Let's see how our LSTM performs with beam search. It looks better than before:

```
and they sailed to him and said,
        oh, queen.  where heavens, she went to her, and thumbling
where the whole kingdom likewis, and that she had given him as that
he had to eat, and they gave him the money, hans took his head that
he had been the churchyar, and they gave him the money, hans took his
head that he had been the world, and, however do that, he have begging
his that he was
placed where they were brought in the mouse's horn again.  where
have, you come?  then thumbling where the world, and when they came to
them, and that he was soon came back, and then the will make that they
hardled the world, and, however do that heard him, they have gone out
through the room, and said the king's son was again and said,
        ah, father, i have been in a dream, for his horse again,
answered the door.  when they saw
each other that they had been.  then they saw they had been.
```

Compared to the text produced by the LSTM, this text seems to have more variation in the text while keeping the text grammatically consistent as well. So, in fact, beam search helps to produce quality predictions compared to predicting one word at a time. Also, we see that the LSTM interestingly combines different elements from stories to come up with interesting concepts (for example, mouse's horn, bringing Thumbling, a character, and Hans, a character from a different story, together). But still, there are instances where words together don't make much sense. Let's see how we can improve our LSTM further.

# Improving LSTMs – generating text with words instead of n-grams

Here we will discuss ways to improve LSTMs. First, we will discuss how the number of model parameters grows if we use one-hot-encoded word features. This motivates us to use low-dimensional word vectors instead of one-hot-encoded vectors. Finally, we will discuss how we can employ word vectors in the code to generate better-quality text compared to using bigrams. The code for this section is available in `lstm_word2vec.ipynb` in the ch8 folder.

## The curse of dimensionality

One major limitation stopping us from using words instead of n-grams as the input to our LSTM is that this will drastically increase the number of parameters in our model. Let's understand this through an example. Consider that we have an input of size *500* and a cell state of size *100*. This would result in a total of approximately *240K* parameters (excluding the softmax layer), as shown here:

$$=\sim 4x\left(500x100 + 100x100 + 100\right) =\sim 240K$$

Let's now increase the size of the input to *1000*. Now the total number of parameters would be approximately *440K*, as shown here:

$$=\sim 4x\left(1000x100 + 100x100 + 100\right) =\sim 440K$$

As you can see, for an increase of 500 units of the input dimensionality, the number of parameters has grown by 200,000. This not only increases the computational complexity, but also increases the risk of overfitting due to the large number of parameters. So, we need ways of restricting the dimensionality of the input.

## Word2vec to the rescue

As you will remember, not only can Word2vec give a lower-dimensional feature representation of words compared to one-hot encoding, but it also gives semantically sound features. To understand this, let's consider three words: *cat*, *dog*, and *volcano*. If we one-hot encode just these words and calculate the Euclidean distance between them, it would be the following:

$$distance(cat, volcano) = distance(cat, dog)$$

However, if we learn word embeddings, it would be the following:

$$distance(cat,volcano) > distance(cat,dog)$$

We would like our features to represent the latter, where similar things have a lower distance than dissimilar things. Consequently, the model will be able to generate better-quality text.

# Generating text with Word2vec

Here, our LSTM gets a bit more complex than the standard LSTM, as we are plugging in an embedding layer in the middle of the input and the LSTM. *Figure 8.6* depicts the overall architecture of LSTM-Word2vec. This is available as an exercise in the `lstm_word2vec.ipynb` file located in the `ch8` folder.

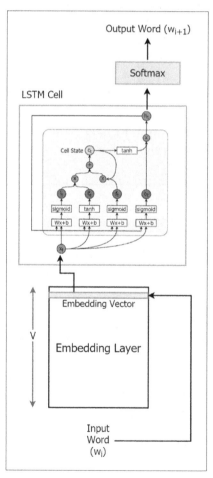

Figure 8.6: The structure of a language modeling LSTM using word vectors

We will first learn word vectors using the **Continuous Bag-of-Words (CBOW)** model. The following are some of the best relationships learned by our Word2vec model:

```
Nearest to which: what
Nearest to not: bitterly, easily, praying, unseen
Nearest to do: did
Nearest to day: evening, sunday
Nearest to two: many, kinsmen
Nearest to will: may, shall, 'll
Nearest to pick-axe: ladder
Nearest to stir: bestir, milk
```

Now we can feed the embeddings — instead of one-hot-encoded vectors — to the LSTM. For this, we incorporate the `tf.nn.embedding_lookup` function, as follows:

```
for ui in range(num_unrollings):
    train_inputs.append(tf.placeholder(tf.int32, shape=[batch_
size],name='train_inputs_%d'%ui))
    train_inputs_embeds.append(tf.nn.embedding_
lookup(embeddings,train_inputs[ui]))
```

For a more general-purpose language modeling task, we can use already available pretrained word vectors. Word vectors found by learning from text corpus with billions of words are freely available to be downloaded and used. Here we will list several such repositories that are readily available word vectors:

- **Word2vec**: `https://code.google.com/archive/p/word2vec/`
- **Pretrained GloVe word vectors**: `https://nlp.stanford.edu/projects/glove/`
- **fastText word vectors**: `https://github.com/facebookresearch/fastText/blob/master/pretrained-vectors.md`

However, as we are working with a very limited-size vocabulary, we will learn our own word vectors. It will be a computational overhead if we try to use these massive word vector repositories for a vocabulary of a few thousand words. Moreover, since we are outputting stories, certain unique words (for example, elves and water-nixie) might not even have been used during learning.

The rest of the code will be similarly used for LSTM cell computations, loss, optimization, and predictions we discussed earlier. However, remember that our input size is not the vocabulary size anymore, but the embedding size.

# Examples generated with LSTM-Word2vec and beam search

The following text is generated by LSTM-Word2vec (after applying a simple preprocessing step involving removing redundant spaces). Now the text looks quite realistic:

```
i am in a great castle. the king's son. the king 's son. "you are
mine  with the dragon , and  a glass mountain and she gave it to you.
"the king's son. "i  have not". "no," said the  king's son , and  a
great lake, and in its little dish, which was much larger than do you
want to have  not. the king. if i had a great lake, but it was not
long before it. then the king's son. the king's son, however, drank
only the milk.  then the king 's son said, "you are not". then the
wedding was celebrated, and when she got to the king's son. "you are
mine, and a glass mountain and the king 's son, however. they gave
him to see her heart, and went away, and the old king's son, who was
sitting by the town, and when they went to the king's boy. she was in
its little head against it as long as it had strength to do so, until
at last it was standing in the kitchen and heard the crown, which are
so big. when she got into a carriage, and slept in the whole night,
and the wedding was celebrated, and when she got to the glass mountain
they thrust the princess remained, the child says, come out.  when
she got into a great lake, but the king's son, and there was a great
lake before the paddock came to a glass mountain, and there were full
of happiness. when the bride, she got to sleep in a great castle, and
as soon as it was going to be put to her house, but the wedding was
celebrated, and when she got to the old woman, and a glass of wine.
when it was evening, she began to cry in the whole night, and the
wedding was celebrated, and after this the king's boy. and when she
had washed up, and when the bride, who came to her, but when it was
evening, when the king 's son. the king 's son. the king 's son. "i
will follow it. then the king". if i had a great lake, and a glass
mountain, and there were full dress, i have not. "thereupon the king's
son as the paddock had to put in it. she felt a great lake, so she is
mine. then the king 's son's son".
```

You can see that there are no repetitions of text, as we saw with standard RNNs, and the text looks grammatically correct in most cases, and there are very few spelling mistakes.

So far we have analyzed how the generated text looks like for standard LSTMs, LSTMs with peepholes, GRUs, LSTMs with beam search, and LSTMs with beam search using Word2vec. Now we will see how these methods compare to each other quantitatively again.

# Perplexity over time

Here in *Figure 8.7*, we will plot the behavior of perplexity over time for all the methods we saw so far: LSTMs, LSTMs with peepholes, GRUs, and LSTMs using the Word2vec features. To make the comparison interesting, we will also compare one of the best models we can think of: a three-layer deep LSTM that uses word vectors and dropout. We can see that from the methods that use dropout (that is, the methods that reduce overfitting), LSTMs with the Word2vec features show promising results. I am not stating that LSTMs with Word2vec deliver good performance based on just numerical values, but also considering the difficulty of the problem. In the Word2vec settings, the atomic unit we use for learning are words, unlike the other models that use bigrams. Language generation at the word level can be challenging compared to that at the bigram level due to the large size of the vocabulary. Therefore, achieving a training perplexity at the word level that is comparable to that of the bigram-based models can be thought of as good performance. Looking at the validation perplexity, we can see that the word-vector-based methods exhibit a higher validation perplexity. This is understandable as the task is more challenging due to the large vocabulary. Another interesting observation I'd like to draw your attention to is, comparing the single layer LSTM and the deep LSTMs. You can see that the deep LSTM shows a much lower and a stable validation perplexity over time, which lead us to believe that deep models often deliver better. Note that we don't report the results of using beam search, as beam search only affects the prediction and has no effect on the training perplexity:

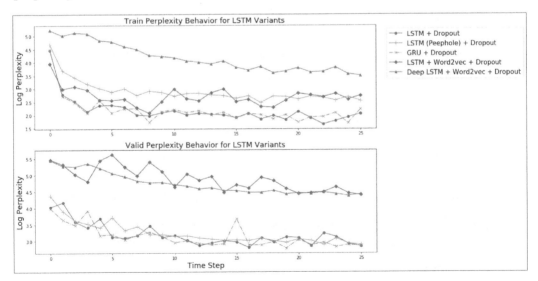

Figure 8.7: Perplexity change for training data over time (LSTMs, LSTM (Peephole) and GRUs, and LSTMs + Word2vec)

# Using the TensorFlow RNN API

We will now examine how we can use the TensorFlow RNN API to make the code simpler. The TensorFlow RNN API contains a variety of RNN-related functions that help us to implement RNNs faster and easier. We will now see how the same example we discussed in the preceding sections can be implemented using the TensorFlow RNN API. However, to make things exciting, we will implement a deep LSTM network with three layers that we talked about in the comparisons. The full code for this is available in the `lstm_word2vec_rnn_api.ipynb` file in the `Ch8` folder.

First, we will define the placeholders for holding inputs, labels, and corresponding embedding vectors for the inputs. We ignore the validation data related computations as we have already discussed them:

```
# Training Input data.
train_inputs, train_labels = [],[]
train_labels_ohe = []
# Defining unrolled training inputs
for ui in range(num_unrollings):
    train_inputs.append(tf.placeholder(tf.int32,
        shape=[batch_size],name='train_inputs_%d'%ui))
    train_labels.append(tf.placeholder(tf.int32,
        shape=[batch_size], name = 'train_labels_%d'%ui))
    train_labels_ohe.append(tf.one_hot(train_labels[ui],
        vocabulary_size))

# Defining embedding lookup operations for all the unrolled
# trianing inputs
train_inputs_embeds = []
for ui in range(num_unrollings):
    # We use expand_dims to add an additional axis
    # As this is needed later for LSTM cell computation
    train_inputs_embeds.append(tf.expand_dims(
                               tf.nn.embedding_lookup(
                               embeddings,train_inputs[ui]),0))
```

Thereafter, we will define a list of LSTM cells from the LSTM cell from the RNN API:

```
# num_nodes here is a sequence of hidden layer sizes
cells = [tf.nn.rnn_cell.LSTMCell(n) for n in num_nodes]
```

We will also define `DropoutWrapper` for all the LSTM cells, that performs the dropout operation on the inputs/states/outputs of the LSTM cell:

```
# We now define a dropout wrapper for each LSTM cell
dropout_cells = [
```

```
rnn.DropoutWrapper(
    cell=lstm, input_keep_prob=1.0,
    output_keep_prob=1.0-dropout, state_keep_prob=1.0,
    variational_recurrent=True,
    input_size=tf.TensorShape([embeddings_size]),
    dtype=tf.float32
) for lstm in cells
]
```

The parameters provided to this function are as follows:

- `cell`: This is the type of the RNN cell we're using in the computations
- `input_keep_prob`: This is the amount of units of the input to keep activated when performing dropout (between 0 and 1)
- `output_keep_prob`: This is the amount of units of the output to keep activated when performing dropout
- `state_keep_prob`: This is the amount of units of the cell state to keep activated when performing dropout
- `variational_recurrent`: This is a special type of dropout for RNNs introduced by Gal and Ghahramani in *A Theoretically Grounded Application of Dropout in Recurrent Neural Networks, Data-Efficient Machine Learning workshop, ICML (2016)*.

Then we will define a tensor called `initial_state` (initialized with zeros), which will contain the iteratively updated states (both the hidden state and the cell state) of the LSTM:

```
# Initial state of the LSTM memory.
initial_state = stacked_dropout_cell.zero_state(batch_size, dtype=tf.float32)
```

With the list of LSTM cells defined, we can now define a `MultiRNNCell` object that encapsulates the list of LSTM cells as follows:

```
# We first define a MultiRNNCell Object that uses the
# Dropout wrapper (for training)
stacked_dropout_cell = tf.nn.rnn_cell.MultiRNNCell(dropout_cells)
# Here we define a MultiRNNCell that does not use dropout
# Validation and Testing
stacked_cell = tf.nn.rnn_cell.MultiRNNCell(cells)
```

Next we will calculate the output of the LSTM cell using the `tf.nn.dynamic_rnn` function as follows:

```
# Defining the LSTM cell computations (training)
train_outputs, initial_state = tf.nn.dynamic_rnn(
    stacked_dropout_cell, tf.concat(train_inputs_embeds,axis=0),
    time_major=True, initial_state=initial_state
)
```

For this function, we will provide several parameters, as shown here:

- `cell`: This is the type of the sequential model that will be used to compute the output. In our case, this would be the LSTM cell we defined earlier.
- `inputs`: These are the inputs for the LSTM cell. The inputs need to have a shape of [num_unrollings, batch_size, embeddings_size]. Therefore, we have all the batches of data for all the time steps in this tensor. We will call this type of data *time major*, as the time axis is the $0^{th}$ axis.
- `time_major`: We are saying that our inputs are *time major*.
- `initial_state`: An LSTM needs an initial state to start with.

With the final hidden state and cell state of the LSTM calculated, we will now define the logits (unnormalized scores obtained from the softmax layer for each word) and predictions (normalized scores of the softmax layer for each word):

```
# Reshape the final outputs to [num_unrollings*batch_size, num_nodes]
final_output = tf.reshape(train_outputs, [-1,num_nodes[-1]])

# Computing logits
logits = tf.matmul(final_output, w) + b
# Computing predictions
train_prediction = tf.nn.softmax(logits)
```

Then we will make our logits and labels time major. This is necessary for the loss function we will be using:

```
# Reshape logits to time-major fashion [num_unrollings, batch_size,
vocabulary_size]
time_major_train_logits = tf.reshape(logits, [num_unrollings,batch_
size,-1])

# We create train labels in a time major fashion [num_unrollings,
batch_size, vocabulary_size]
# so that this could be used with the loss function
time_major_train_labels = tf.reshape(tf.concat(train_
labels,axis=0), [num_unrollings,batch_size])
```

Now we will arrive at defining the loss between the outputs computed from the LSTM and the softmax layer and the actual labels. For this, we will use the `tf.contrib.seq2seq.sequence_loss` function. This function is widely used in machine translation tasks to compute the difference between the model output translation and the actual translation, which are sequences of words. Therefore, the same concept can be extended to our problem because we are essentially outputting a sequence of words:

```
# We use the sequence-to-sequence loss function to define the loss
# We calculate the average across the batches
# But get the sum across the sequence length
loss = tf.contrib.seq2seq.sequence_loss(
    logits = tf.transpose(time_major_train_logits,[1,0,2]),
    targets = tf.transpose(time_major_train_labels),
    weights= tf.ones([batch_size, num_unrollings], dtype=tf.float32),
    average_across_timesteps=False,
    average_across_batch=True
)


loss = tf.reduce_sum(loss)
```

Let's take a look at the arguments we are providing to this `loss` function:

- `logits`: These are the unnormalized scores of predictions we computed earlier. However, this function accepts the logits ordered to the following shape: `[batch_size, num_unrollings, vocabulary_size]`. For this, we use the `tf.transpose` function.

- `targets`: These are the actual labels for the batch or sequence of inputs. These need to be in the `[batch_size, num_unrollings]` shape.

- `weights`: These are the weights we give to each position in the time axis as well as the batch axis. We are not discriminating inputs by their position, so we will set it to 1 for all the positions.

- `average_across_timesteps`: We don't average the loss across time steps. We need the sum across time steps, so we will set this to `False`.

- `average_across_batch`: We need to average the loss over the batch, so we will set this to `True`.

Next we will define the optimizer, just like we did before:

```
# Used for decaying learning rate
gstep = tf.Variable(0, trainable=False)

# Running this operation will cause the value of gstep
# to increase, while in turn reducing the learning rate
```

```
inc_gstep = tf.assign(gstep, gstep+1)

# Adam Optimizer. And gradient clipping.
tf_learning_rate = tf.train.exponential_decay(0.001,gstep,decay_
steps=1, decay_rate=0.5)

print('Defining optimizer')
optimizer = tf.train.AdamOptimizer(tf_learning_rate)
gradients, v = zip(*optimizer.compute_gradients(loss))
gradients, _ = tf.clip_by_global_norm(gradients, 5.0)
optimizer = optimizer.apply_gradients(
    zip(gradients, v))

inc_gstep = tf.assign(gstep, gstep+1)
```

With all the functions defined, you can now run the code as shown in the exercise file.

# Summary

In this chapter, we looked at the implementations of the LSTM algorithm and other various important aspects to improve LSTMs beyond standard performance. As an exercise, we trained our LSTM on the text of stories by the Brothers Grimm and asked the LSTM to output a fresh new story. We discussed how to implement an LSTM with code examples extracted from exercises.

Next, we had a technical discussion about how to implement LSTMs with peepholes and GRUs. Then we did a performance comparison between a standard LSTM and its variants. We saw that the LSTMs performed the best compared to LSTMs with peepholes and GRUs. We made the surprising observation of peepholes actually hurting the performance rather than helping for our language modeling task.

Then we discussed some of the various improvements possible for enhancing the quality of outputs generated by an LSTM. The first improvement was beam search. We looked at an implementation of beam search and covered how to implement it step by step. Then we looked at how we can use word embeddings to teach our LSTM to output better text.

In conclusion, LSTMs are very powerful machine learning models that can capture both long-term and short-term dependencies. Moreover, beam search in fact helps to produce more realistic-looking textual phrases compared to predicting one at a time. Also, we saw that we obtained the best performance using word vectors as inputs instead of using the one-hot-encoded feature representation.

In the next chapter, we will look at another interesting task involving both feed-forward networks and LSTMs: generating image captions.

# 9
# Applications of LSTM – Image Caption Generation

In the previous chapter, we saw how we can use LSTMs to generate text. In this chapter, we will use an LSTM to solve a more complex task: generating suitable captions for given images. This task is more complex in the sense that solving it involves multiple subtasks, such as training/using a CNN to generate encoded vectors of images, learning word embeddings, and training an LSTM to generate captions. So this is not as straightforward as the text generation task, where we simply input text and output text in a sequential manner.

Automated image captioning or image annotation has a wide variety of applications. One of the most prominent application is image retrieval in search engines. Automated image captioning can be used to retrieve all the images belonging to a certain concept (for example, a cat) as per the user's request. Another application can be in social media, where, when an image is uploaded by a user, the image is automatically captioned so that either the user can refine the generated caption or post it as it is.

For generating captions for images, we will use a popular dataset for image captioning tasks known as **Microsoft Common Objects in Context (MS-COCO)**. We will first process images from the dataset (MS-COCO) to obtain an encoding of the images with a pretrained **Convolutional Neural Network (CNN)**, which is already good at classifying images. The CNN will take a fixed-size image as the input and output the class the image belongs to (for example, cat, dog, bus, and tree). Using this CNN, we can obtain compressed encoded vectors describing images.

Then we will process the captions of the images to learn the word embeddings of the words found in captions. We can also use pretrained word vectors for this task. Finally, having obtained both the image and word encodings, we will feed them into an LSTM and train it on the images and their respective captions. Then we will ask to generate a caption for a set of unseen images (that is, the validation set).

We will use a pretrained CNN to generate image encodings. Then we will first implement our own word embedding learning algorithm and LSTMs from scratch. Finally, we will see how we can use pretrained word vectors along with the LSTM modules available in the TensorFlow RNN API to achieve this. Using pretrained word vectors and the RNN API reduces the amount of coding we have to do otherwise, significantly.

# Getting to know the data

Let's first understand the data we are working with both directly and indirectly. There are two datasets we will rely on:

- The ILSVRC ImageNet dataset (http://image-net.org/download)
- The MS-COCO dataset (http://cocodataset.org/#download)

We will not engage the first dataset directly, but it is essential for caption learning. This dataset contains images and their respective class labels (for example, cat, dog, and car). We will use a CNN that is already trained on this dataset, so we do not have to download and train on this dataset from scratch. Next we will use the MS-COCO dataset, which contains images and their respective captions. We will directly learn from this dataset by mapping the image to a fixed-size feature vector, using the CNN, and then map this vector to the corresponding caption using an LSTM (we will discuss the process in detail later).

# ILSVRC ImageNet dataset

ImageNet is an image dataset that contains a large set of images (~1 million) and their respective labels. These images belong to 1,000 different categories. This dataset is very expressive and contains almost all the objects found in the images we want to generate captions for. Therefore, I consider ImageNet to be a good dataset to train on, in order to obtain image encodings that are required for caption generation. We say we use this dataset indirectly because we will use a pretrained CNN that is trained on this dataset. Therefore we will not be downloading, nor training the CNN on this dataset, by ourselves. *Figure 9.1* shows some of the classes available in the ImageNet dataset:

Figure 9.1: A small sample of the ImageNet dataset

# The MS-COCO dataset

Now we will move on to the dataset that we will actually be using, which is called **MS-COCO** (short for, **Microsoft - Common Objects in COntext**). We will use the dataset from the year 2014. As described earlier, this dataset consists of images and their respective descriptions. The dataset is quite large (for example, the training dataset consists of ~120,000 samples and can measure over 15 GB). Datasets are updated every year, and a competition is then held to recognize the team that achieves state-of-the-art performance. Using the full dataset is important when the objective is to achieve state-of-the-art performance. However, in our case, we want to learn a reasonable model that is able to suggest what is in an image generally. Therefore, we will use a smaller dataset (~40,000 images and ~200,000K captions) to train our model on. *Figure 9.2* includes some of the samples available:

A pink and green marker, next to another object.
A pair of red scissors on top of a desk.
A close up image of the finger holes on a pair of scissors and sharpie markers.
A close up of a red pair of scissors and a green sharpie marker.
A very close up view of some scissors and markers.

A bathroom that has magazine rack and small cabinet.
Compact bathroom area, tub, toilet, magazine area and sink.
Small residential bath room decorated in wood tones
A tissue box on top of a toilet in a bathroom.
an image of a clean full bathroom

A woman exercising a brown horse in a riding ring.
A woman is in a barn with a brown horse.
A woman training her beautiful brown horse.
A woman with a brown horse in a dirt area of building.
A woman and a horse in a barn with dirt floor.

Man in mid air reaching between his legs to reach a frisbee.
A man is doing tricks with a frisbee
A person is jumping with a Frisbee in the air.
a person jumping in the air while playing with a frisbee
A man in mid air attempting to catch a frisbee.

A grey motorcycle on dirt road next to a building.
A motorcycle is parked on a dirt road in front of an old farm truck selling produce.
there is a bike on a dirt road
Motorcycle sitting on a dirt road in front of a farm house advertising produce.
A motorcycle that is sitting in the dirt.

Figure 9.2: A small sample of the MS-COCO dataset

For learning with and testing our end-to-end image caption generation model, we will use the 2014 validation dataset, provided on the official MS-COCO dataset website. The dataset consists of ~41,000 images and ~200,000 captions. We will use the initial set of 1,000 samples as the validation set and the rest as the training set.

 In practice, you should use separate datasets for testing and validation. However, as we are using limited data, to maximize the learning, we consider the same dataset for both testing and validation.

In *Figure 9.3*, we can see some of the images found in the validation set. These are some hand-picked examples from the validation set representing a variety of different objects and scenes. We will use these for visually inspecting results, as it is infeasible to visually inspect all the 1,000 samples in the validation set:

Figure 9.3: An unseen image we use to test image caption generation capability of our algorithm

# The machine learning pipeline for image caption generation

Here we will look at the image caption generation pipeline at a very high level and then discuss it piece by piece until we have the full model. The image caption generation framework consists of three main components and one optional component:

- A CNN generating encoded vectors for images
- An embedding layer learning word vectors
- (Optional) An adaptation layer that can transform a given embedding dimensionality to an arbitrary dimensionality (details will be discussed later)
- An LSTM taking the encoded vectors of the images, and outputting the corresponding caption

First, let's look at the CNN generating the encoded vectors for images. We can achieve this by first training a CNN on a large classification dataset, such as ImageNet, and using that knowledge to generate compressed vectorized representations of images.

One might ask, why not input the image as it is to the LSTM? Let's go back to a simple calculation we did in the previous chapter:

> *"An increase of 500 units in the input layer resulted in an increase of 200,000 parameters."*

The images we deal with here are around 224 × 224 × 3 ~ 150,000. This should give you an idea of the increase in the number of parameters this would result in for the LSTM. Therefore, finding a compressed representation is crucial. Another reason why LSTMs are not suitable for directly processing raw image data is that it is not very straightforward compared to using a CNN to process image data.

There exist convolutional variants of LSTMs called Convolution LSTMs. Convolution LSTMs are capable of working with image inputs by using the convolution operation, instead of fully connected layers. Such networks are heavily used for spatiotemporal problems (for example, weather data or video prediction) that has both spatial and temporal dimensions to the data. You can read more about convolutional LSTMs in *Long-term Recurrent Convolutional Networks for Visual Recognition and Description, Jeff Donahue, and others, Proceedings of the IEEE conference on Computer Vision and Pattern Recognition (2015).*

Although the training procedure is completely different, our goal for this training process is similar to what we achieve after we learn word embeddings. For word embeddings, we would like similar words to have similar vectors (that is, high similarity) and different words to have different vectors (that is, low similarity). In other words, if $Image_x$ represents the encoded vector obtained for image $x$, then we should have this:

$$Distance\left(Image_{cat}, Image_{volcano}\right) > Distance\left(Image_{cat}, Image_{dog}\right)$$

Next we will learn the word embeddings for the text corpus created by extracting all the words from all the captions available in the MS-COCO dataset. Again, learning the word embeddings helps us to reduce the dimensionality of the input to the LSTM, and it also helps us to produce more meaningful features as the input to the LSTM. However, this also serves another crucial purpose in the pipeline.

When we used an LSTM to generate text, we used either the one-hot-encoded representation of the words or word embeddings/vectors. Therefore, the input to the LSTM was always of a fixed size. If the input sizes were dynamic, we couldn't handle it with standard LSTMs. However, we didn't have to worry about this as we dealt only with text.

In this case, however, we are working with both images and text, and we need to make sure that the encoded image vectors and the representation of each word corresponding to the caption of that image are all of same dimensionality. Also, with word vectors, we can create an arbitrary fixed-length feature representation for all the words. Therefore, we use word vectors to match the image encoding vector length.

Finally, we will create a sequence of data for each image, where the first element of the sequence is the vectorized representation of the image, followed by the word vectors for each word in the caption of the image, in that order. We will then use this sequence of data to train the LSTM as we did earlier.

This approach is similar to the approach found in *Show, Attend and Tell: Neural Image Caption Generation with Visual Attention, Xu and others, Proceedings of the 32nd International Conference on Machine Learning (2015)*. The process is depicted in *Figure 9.4*:

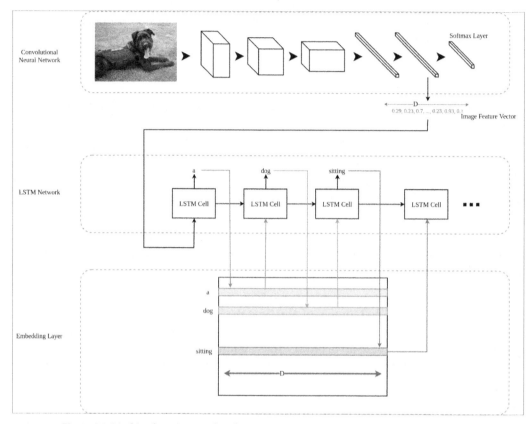

Figure 9.4: Machine learning pipeline for training on the task of generating image captions

# Extracting image features with CNNs

With a high level understanding of the overall pipeline, we will now discuss in detail how we can use CNNs to extract feature vectors for images. In order to get good feature vectors, we first need to either train the CNN with the images and its corresponding classes or use a pretrained CNN freely available on the internet. We will be *reinventing the wheel* if we train a CNN from scratch, as there are pretrained models available for free download. We also need to keep in mind that if the CNN needs to be capable of describing many objects, it needs to be trained on a set of classes corresponding to a variety of objects. This is why a model trained on a large dataset such as ImageNet (for example, compared to training on a small dataset having only 10 different classes) is important. As we saw earlier, ImageNet contains 1,000 object categories. This is more than adequate for the task we are trying to solve.

Keep in mind, however, that ImageNet contains ~1 M images. Also, since there are 1,000 classes, we cannot use a small CNN with a simple structure (for example, a CNN with few layers) to learn well. We need more powerful and deeper CNNs, but with the complexity of the CNN and the complexity of the dataset itself, it can take days (even weeks) on GPUs to train such a network. For example, VGG (a well-known CNN that has produced exceptionally good classification accuracy on ImageNet) can take 2-3 weeks to train.

Therefore, we need smarter ways to solve this issue. Fortunately, CNNs such as VGG are readily available to download, so we can use them without any additional training. These are called **pretrained models**. Using pretrained models allows us to save several weeks of computational time. This is quite easy, as all we need is the learned weights and the actual structure of the CNN to recreate the network and use it immediately for inference.

In this exercise, we will use the VGG CNN (available at `http://www.cs.toronto. edu/~frossard/post/vgg16/`). VGG architecture won the second place in the 2014 ImageNet competition. VGG has several variants to it: a 13-layer deep network (VGG-13), a 16-layer deep network (VGG-16), and a 19-layer deep network (VGG-19). We will use the 16-layer deep VGG-16. *Figure 9.5* displays the VGG-16 network:

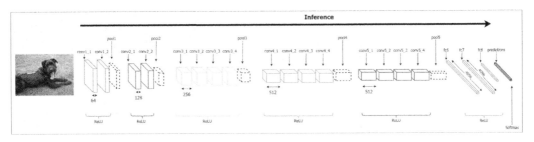

Figure 9.5: A 16-layer VGG architecture

# Implementation – loading weights and inferencing with VGG-16

The website `http://www.cs.toronto.edu/~frossard/post/vgg16/` provides the weights as a dictionary of NumPy arrays. There are 16 weight values and 16 bias values corresponding to the 16 layers of VGG-16. They are saved under the keys as follows:

```
conv1_1_W, conv1_1_b, conv1_2_W, conv1_2_b, conv2_1_W, conv2_1_b...
```

First, download the file from the website and place it in the `ch9/image_caption_data` folder. Now we will discuss the implementation, from loading the downloaded CNN to making predictions with the pretrained CNN we'll use. First, we will discuss how to create necessary TensorFlow variables and load them with the downloaded weights. Next, we will define an input reading pipeline to read in images as inputs to the CNN and also several preprocessing steps. Then we will define the inference operations for the CNN to get predictions for the inputs. Then we will define calculations to get the class, along with the prediction for that class which the CNN thinks that it suits the best for a given input. The last operation is not required to generate captions for images; however, it is important to ensure that we have configured the pretrained CNN correctly.

# Building and updating variables

We will first load the dictionary of NumPy arrays containing the weights of the CNN to the memory with the following:

```
weight_file = os.path.join('image_caption_data', 'vgg16_weights.npz')
weights = np.load(weight_file)
```

Then we will create TensorFlow variables and assign them actual weights. Also, this can take up quite a bit of memory. So, to avoid crashes, we will specifically ask TensorFlow to save this on CPU rather than on GPU. We will outline the code for building and loading the TensorFlow variables with correct weights here. We will first define all the dictionary keys (denoting different layer IDs of the CNN) in a Python list, `TF_SCOPES`. Then, we will iterate through each layer ID while using the corresponding weight matrix and the bias vector, as initializers, to specific TensorFlow variables named according to the respective layer ID:

```
def build_vgg_variables(npz_weights):
    '''
    Build the required tensorflow variables to
    populate the VGG-16 model
    and populate them with actual weights
    :param npz_weights: loaded weights as a dictionary
    :return:
    '''

    params = []
    print("Building VGG Variables (Tensorflow)...")

    with tf.variable_scope('CNN'):
        # Iterate through each convolution and fully connected layer
        # and create TensorFlow variables using variable scoping
        for si,scope in enumerate(TF_SCOPES):
            with tf.variable_scope(scope) as sc:
                weight_key, bias_key = TF_SCOPES[si]+'_W',
                                       TF_SCOPES[si]+'_b'

                with tf.device('/cpu:0'):
                    weights = tf.get_variable(TF_WEIGHTS_STR,
                            initializer= npz_weights[weight_key])
                    bias = tf.get_variable(TF_BIAS_STR,
                            initializer = npz_weights[bias_key])

                params.extend([weights,bias])

    return params
```

# Preprocessing inputs

Next, we will define an input pipeline to input image to VGG-16. VGG-16 has the following requirements for the input images in order for the predictions to be correct:

- Inputs should be of size [224,224,3]
- Inputs should have zero-mean (but not unit variance)

The following code creates a pipeline that reads straight from a set of given filenames, applies the preceding transformations, and creates a batch of such transformed images. This procedure is defined in the preprocess_inputs_with_tfqueue function in the exercise file.

First, we will define a queue of filenames. This holds the filenames we should be reading (that is, the filenames of the images):

```
# FIFO Queue of file names
# creates a FIFO queue until the reader needs them
filename_queue = tf.train.string_input_producer(filenames,
                    capacity=10, shuffle=False)
```

Next we will define a reader, which takes the filename queue as the input and outputs a buffer which holds the images obtained by reading the filenames produced by the queue at any given time:

```
# Reader which takes a filename queue and read()
# which outputs data one by one
reader = tf.WholeFileReader()
_, image_buffer = reader.read(filename_queue,
                    name='image_read_op')


# Read the raw image data and return as uint8
dec_image = tf.image.decode_jpeg(contents=
                image_buffer,channels=3,name='decode_jpg')
# Convert uint8 data to float32
float_image = tf.image.convert_image_dtype(dec_image,
                dtype=tf.float32,name= 'float_image')
```

Next we will do the aforementioned preprocessing:

```
# Resize image to 224x224x3
resized_image = tf.image.resize_images(float_
                image,[224,224])*255.0


# For VGG, images are only zero-meaned
# (not standardized to unit variance)
std_image = resized_image - tf.reduce_mean(resized_
image,axis=[0,1], keepdims=True)
```

After the preprocessing pipeline is defined, we will ask TensorFlow to produce a batch of preprocessed images at a time, without shuffling:

```
image_batch = tf.train.batch([std_image],
                batch_size = batch_size, capacity = 10,
                allow_smaller_final_batch=False,
                name='image_batch')
```

# Inferring VGG-16

So far, we have created our CNN and we have defined a pipeline for reading images and creating a batch by reading image files saved on the disk. Now we would like to infer the CNN with the images read from the pipeline. **Inferring** refers to passing an input (that is, image) and obtaining the prediction (that is, the probabilities of an image belonging to some class) as outputs. For this we will start from the first layer and iterate until we reach the softmax layer. This process is defined in the function `inference_cnn` in the exercise file.

At each layer, we will get the weights and the bias as follows:

```
def inference_cnn(tf_inputs, device):

    with tf.variable_scope('CNN'):
        for si, scope in enumerate(TF_SCOPES):
            with tf.variable_scope(scope,reuse=True) as sc:
                weight, bias = tf.get_variable(TF_WEIGHTS_STR),
                               tf.get_variable(TF_BIAS_STR)
```

Then for the first convolution layer we compute the output:

```
h = tf.nn.relu(tf.nn.conv2d(tf_inputs,weight,strides=[1,1,1,1],
               padding='SAME')+bias)
```

For the rest of the convolution layers we compute the output, where the input is the previous layer's output:

```
h = tf.nn.relu(tf.nn.conv2d(h, weight, strides=[1, 1, 1, 1],
               padding='SAME') + bias)
```

And for the pooling layers, the output is computed as follows:

```
h = tf.nn.max_pool(h, [1,2,2,1], [1,2,2,1],padding='SAME')
```

Then, for the first fully connected layer found immediately after the last convolution pooling layer, we will define the layer output as follows. We need to reshape the input from last convolution/pooling layer of the [batch_size, height, width, channels] to [batch_size, height*width*channels] size as this is a fully connected layer:

```
h_shape = h.get_shape().as_list()
h = tf.reshape(h, [h_shape[0], h_shape[1] * h_shape[2] * h_shape[3]])
h = tf.nn.relu(tf.matmul(h, weight) + bias)
```

For the next set of fully connected layers except for the last layer, we get the output as follows:

```
h = tf.nn.relu(tf.matmul(h, weight) + bias)
```

Finally, for the last fully connected layer, we do not apply any type of activations. This will be the image feature representation which we will be feeding into the LSTM. This will be a 1,000 dimensional vector:

```
out = tf.matmul(h,weight) + bias
```

# Extracting vectorized representations of images

The most important information we extract from the CNN is the image feature representations. As the image representations, we will obtain the network output of the very last layer before applying softmax. Therefore, a vector corresponding to a single image is of length 1,000:

```
tf_train_logit_prediction = inference_cnn(train_image_batch, device)
tf_test_logit_prediction = inference_cnn(test_image_batch, device)
```

# Predicting class probabilities with VGG-16

Next, we will define the operations required to get feature representations of the images and also the actual softmax predictions to make sure that our model is actually correct. We will define these for both the training data and the test data:

```
tf_train_softmax_prediction = tf.nn.softmax(tf_train_logit_prediction)
tf_test_softmax_prediction = tf.nn.softmax(tf_test_logit_prediction)
```

Now let's run these operations and see if they work properly (see *Figure 9.6*):

Figure 9.6: Class prediction for our test images with VGG

It seems that our CNN knows what it is doing. Of course, there are misclassified samples (for example, giraffe identified as a llama), but most of the time it is correct.

 When running the preceding defined operations to obtain the feature vectors and the predictions, be mindful of the `batch_size` variable. Increasing this will make the code run quickly. However, it also might lead to a system crash if large enough RAM memory (> 8 GB) is not available. It is recommended that you keep this less than 10 if you do not have a high end machine.

# Learning word embeddings

We will next discuss how we can learn word embeddings for the words found in the captions. First we will preprocess the captions in order to reduce the vocabulary:

```
def preprocess_caption(capt):
    capt = capt.replace('-',' ')
    capt = capt.replace(',','')
    capt = capt.replace('.','')
    capt = capt.replace('"','')
    capt = capt.replace('!','')
    capt = capt.replace(':','')
    capt = capt.replace('/','')
    capt = capt.replace('?','')
    capt = capt.replace(';','')
    capt = capt.replace('\' ',' ')
    capt = capt.replace('\n',' ')

    return capt.lower()
```

For example, consider the following sentence:

*A living room and dining room have two tables, couches, and multiple chairs.*

This will be transformed to the following:

*a living room and dining room have two tables couches and multiple chairs*

Then we will use the **Continuous Bag-of-Words (CBOW)** model to learn the word embeddings as we did in *Chapter 3, Word2vec – Learning Word Embeddings*. A crucial condition we have to keep in mind while learning word embeddings is that **the dimensionality of the embedding should match the dimensionality of the feature representations obtained for the images**, as standard LSTMs cannot handle dynamic-sized inputs.

If we are to use pretrained word embeddings, it is most likely that the dimensionality of the embeddings is different from the size of the image feature representations. In that case, we can use adaptation layers (similar to a layer of a neural network) to match the word vector dimensionality to the image feature representation dimensionality. We will see an exercise doing just that, later.

Now let's look at some of the word embeddings learnt after running 100,000 steps:

```
Nearest to suitcase: woman
Nearest to girls: smart, racket
Nearest to barrier: obstacle
Nearest to casings: exterior
Nearest to normal: lady
Nearest to developed: natural
Nearest to shoreline: peninsula
Nearest to eating: table
Nearest to hoodie: bonnet
Nearest to prepped: plate, timetable
Nearest to regular: signs
Nearest to tie: pants, button
```

# Preparing captions for feeding into LSTMs

Now, before feeding word vectors along with image feature vectors, we need to perform a few more preprocessing steps on the caption data.

Before the preprocessing, let's look at a few basic statistics about the captions. A caption has approximately ten words on average, with a standard deviation of approximately two words. This information is important for us to truncate captions which are unnecessarily long.

First, following the preceding statistics, let's set the maximum caption length allowed to be 12.

Next, let's introduce two new word tokens, SOS and EOS. **SOS** denotes the **start of a sentence**, whereas **EOS** denotes the **end of a sentence**. These help the LSTM to identify both the start and end of a sentence easily.

Next, we will append captions with length less than 12 with EOS tokens such that their length is 12.

So, consider the following caption:

*a man standing on a tennis court holding a racquet*

This would appear as follows:

*SOS a man standing on a tennis court holding a racquet EOS*

Consider this caption:

*a cat sitting on a desk*

It would become the following:

*SOS a cat sitting on a desk EOS EOS EOS EOS EOS*

However, consider the following caption:

*a well lit and well decorated living room shows a glimpse of a glass front door through the corridor*

This would become the following:

*SOS a well lit and well decorated living room shows a EOS*

Note that even after being truncated, the context of the image is still mostly preserved.

Bringing all the captions to the same length is important so that we can process a batch of images and captions instead of processing them one by one.

# Generating data for LSTMs

Here we will define how to extract a batch of data to train the LSTM. Whenever we process a fresh batch of data, the first input should be the image feature vector and the label should be SOS. We will define a batch of data, where, if the first_sample Boolean is True, then the input is extracted from the image feature vectors, and if first_sample is False, the input is extracted from the word embeddings. Also, after generating a batch of data, we will move the cursor by one, so we get the next item in the sequence next time we generate a batch of data. This way we can unroll a sequence of batches of data for the LSTM where the first batch of the sequence is the image feature vectors, followed by the word embeddings of the captions corresponding to that batch of images.

```
# Fill each of the batch indices
for b in range(self._batch_size):

    cap_id = cap_ids[b] # Current caption id
    # Current image feature vector
    cap_image_vec = self._image_data[self._fname_caption_tuples[
                                     cap_id][0]]

    # Current caption
```

```
cap_text = self._fname_caption_tuples[cap_id][1]

# If the cursor exceeds the length of the caption, reset
if self._cursor[b]+1>=self._cap_length:
    self._cursor[b] = 0

# If we're processing a fresh set of cap IDs
# The first sample should be the image feature vector
if first_sample:
    batch_data[b] = cap_image_vec
    batch_labels[b] = np.zeros((vocabulary_size),
                    dtype=np.float32)
    batch_labels[b,cap_text[0]] = 1.0
# If we're continuing from an already processed batch
# Keep producing the current word as the input and
# the next word as the output
else:
    batch_data[b] = self._word_embeddings[
                    cap_text[self._cursor[b]],:]
    batch_labels[b] = np.zeros((vocabulary_size),
                    dtype=np.float32)
    batch_labels[b,cap_text[self._cursor[b]+1]] = 1.0

# Increment the cursor
self._cursor[b] = (self._cursor[b]+1)%self._cap_length
```

We visualize the data generation process as shown in the following figure, for a `batch_size=1` and `num_unrollings=5`. To have a larger batch size, you can perform this for the `batch_size` number of such sequences in parallel.

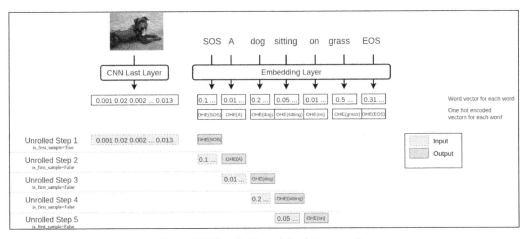

Figure 9.7: Visualization of the data generation

# Defining the LSTM

Now that we have defined the data generator to output a batch of data, starting with a batch of image feature vectors followed by the caption for the respective images word by word, we will define the LSTM cell. The definition of the LSTM and the training procedure is similar to what we observed in the previous chapter.

We will first define the parameters of the LSTM cell. Two sets of weights and a bias for input gate, forget gate, output gate, and for calculating the candidate value:

```
# Input gate (i_t) - How much memory to write to cell state
# Connects the current input to the input gate
ix = tf.Variable(tf.truncated_normal([embedding_size, num_nodes],
stddev=0.01))
# Connects the previous hidden state to the input gate
im = tf.Variable(tf.truncated_normal([num_nodes, num_nodes],
stddev=0.01))
# Bias of the input gate
ib = tf.Variable(tf.random_uniform([1, num_nodes],0.0, 0.01))


# Forget gate (f_t) - How much memory to discard from cell state
# Connects the current input to the forget gate
fx = tf.Variable(tf.truncated_normal([embedding_size, num_nodes],
stddev=0.01))
# Connects the previous hidden state to the forget gate
fm = tf.Variable(tf.truncated_normal([num_nodes, num_nodes],
stddev=0.01))
# Bias of the forget gate
fb = tf.Variable(tf.random_uniform([1, num_nodes],0.0, 0.01))


# Candidate value (c~_t) - Used to compute the current cell state
# Connects the current input to the candidate
cx = tf.Variable(tf.truncated_normal([embedding_size, num_nodes],
stddev=0.01))
# Connects the previous hidden state to the candidate
cm = tf.Variable(tf.truncated_normal([num_nodes, num_nodes],
stddev=0.01))
# Bias of the candidate
cb = tf.Variable(tf.random_uniform([1, num_nodes],0.0,0.01))


# Output gate - How much memory to output from the cell state
# Connects the current input to the output gate
ox = tf.Variable(tf.truncated_normal([embedding_size, num_nodes],
stddev=0.01))
# Connects the previous hidden state to the output gate
```

```
om = tf.Variable(tf.truncated_normal([num_nodes, num_nodes],
stddev=0.01))
# Bias of the output gate
ob = tf.Variable(tf.random_uniform([1, num_nodes],0.0,0.01))
```

Then we will define the softmax weights:

```
# Softmax Classifier weights and biases.
w = tf.Variable(tf.truncated_normal([num_nodes, vocabulary_size],
stddev=0.01))
b = tf.Variable(tf.random_uniform([vocabulary_size],0.0,0.01))
```

We will now define the state and output variables to maintain the state and output of the LSTM for both training and validation data:

```
# Variables saving state across unrollings.
# Hidden state
saved_output = tf.Variable(tf.zeros([batch_size, num_nodes]),
trainable=False, name='test_cell')
# Cell state
saved_state = tf.Variable(tf.zeros([batch_size, num_nodes]),
trainable=False, name='train_cell')

# Hidden and cell state variables for test data
saved_test_output = tf.Variable(tf.zeros([batch_size, num_
nodes]),trainable=False, name='test_hidden')
saved_test_state = tf.Variable(tf.zeros([batch_size, num_
nodes]),trainable=False, name='test_cell')
```

Next we will define the LSTM cell computations:

```
def lstm_cell(i, o, state):
    input_gate = tf.sigmoid(tf.matmul(i, ix) + tf.matmul(o, im) +
                        ib)
    forget_gate = tf.sigmoid(tf.matmul(i, fx) + tf.matmul(o, fm) +
                        fb)
    update = tf.matmul(i, cx) + tf.matmul(o, cm) + cb
    state = forget_gate * state + input_gate * tf.tanh(update)
    output_gate = tf.sigmoid(tf.matmul(i, ox) + tf.matmul(o, om) +
                        ob)
    return output_gate * tf.tanh(state), state
```

Then we will iteratively calculate the state and output of the LSTM cell for num_ unrollings steps at each training step:

```
# These two python variables are iteratively updated
# at each step of unrolling
output = saved_output
state = saved_state

# Compute the hidden state (output) and cell state (state)
# recursively for all the steps in unrolling
for i in train_inputs:
    output, state = lstm_cell(i, output, state)
    # Append each computed output value
    outputs.append(output)

# Calculate the score values
logits = tf.matmul(tf.concat(axis=0, values=outputs), w) + b

# Predictions.
train_prediction = tf.nn.softmax(logits)
```

Then, after saving the output and state of the LSTM to the variables we defined earlier, we will calculate loss, by summing across unrolled axis and taking the average over the batch axis:

```
# State saving across unrollings.
with tf.control_dependencies([saved_output.assign(output),
                             saved_state.assign(state)]):
    # When define the loss we need to sum accross all time steps
    # But average across the batch axis
    loss = 0
    split_logits = tf.split(logits,num_or_size_splits=num_unrollings)

    for lgt,lbl in zip(split_logits, train_labels):
        loss += tf.reduce_mean(
            tf.nn.softmax_cross_entropy_with_logits_v2(logits=lgt,
            labels=lbl)
        )
```

Finally, we will define an optimizer to optimize the weights of the LSTM and the softmax layer with respect to the loss:

```
optimizer = tf.train.AdamOptimizer(learning_rate)
gradients, v = zip(*optimizer.compute_gradients(loss))
gradients, _ = tf.clip_by_global_norm(gradients, 5.0)
optimizer = optimizer.apply_gradients(
    zip(gradients, v))
```

Having generated the image feature vectors, prepared data to be fed to the LSTM, and defined calculations required to learn the LSTM defined, we will now discuss the evaluation metrics that we can use to evaluate the captions generated for our validation dataset.

# Evaluating the results quantitatively

There are many different techniques for evaluating the quality and the relevancy of the captions generated. We will briefly discuss several such metrics we can use to evaluate the captions. We will discuss four metrics: BLEU, ROGUE, METEOR, and CIDEr. All these measures share a key objective, to measure the adequacy (meaning of generated text) and fluency (grammatical correctness of text) in the generated text. To calculate all these measures, we will use a candidate sentence and a reference sentence, where a candidate sentence is the sentence/phrase predicted by our algorithm and the reference sentence is the true sentence/phrase we want to compare with.

# BLEU

**Bilingual Evaluation Understudy (BLEU)** was proposed by Papineni and others in *BLEU: A Method for Automatic Evaluation of Machine Translation, Proceedings of the 40th Annual Meeting of the Association for Computational Linguistics (ACL), Philadelphia, July (2002): 311-318*. It measures the n-gram similarity between reference and candidate phrases, in a position-independent manner. This means that a given n-gram from the candidate is present anywhere in the reference sentence and is considered to be a match. BLEU calculates the n-gram similarity in terms of precision. BLEU comes in several variations (BLEU-1, BLEU-2, BLEU-3, and so on), denoting the value of $n$ in the n-gram.

$$BLEU\left(\text{candidate},\text{ref}\right)=\frac{\sum_{\forall n-gram\ in\ candidate}Count_{clip}\left(n-gram\right)}{\sum_{n-gram\ in\ candidate}Count\left(n-gram\right)}\times BP$$

Here, *Count(n-gram)* is the number of total occurrences of a given n-gram in the candidate sentence. *Count$_{clip}$ (n-gram)* is a measure that calculates *Count(n-gram)* for a given n-gram and clips that value by a maximum value. The maximum value for an n-gram is calculated as the number of occurrences of that n-gram in the reference sentence. For example, consider these two sentences:

Candidate: **the** the the the the the the
Reference: **the** cat sat on **the** mat

$$Count("the") = 7$$
$$Count_{clip}("the") = 2$$

Note that the entity, $\dfrac{\sum_{\forall n\text{-}gram\ in\ candidate} Count_{clip}(n-gram)}{\sum_{\forall n\text{-}gram\ in\ candidate} Count(n-gram)}$ , is a form of precision. In fact, it is called the modified n-gram precision. When multiple references are present, the BLEU is considered to be the maximum:

$$BLEU = \max\left(BLEU\left(candidate, ref_i\right)\right)$$

However, the modified n-gram precision tends to be higher for smaller candidate phrases because this entity is divided by the number of n-grams in the candidate phrase. This means that this measure will incline the model to produce shorter phrases. To avoid this, a penalty term, *BP* is added to the preceding term that penalizes short candidate phrases as well. BLEU possesses several limitations such as BLEU ignores synonyms when calculating the score and does not consider recall, which is also an important metric to measure accuracy. Furthermore, BLEU appears to be a poor choice for certain languages. However, this is a simple metric that has been found to correlate well with human judgement as well in most situations. We will discuss BLEU in more detail in the next chapter.

# ROUGE

**Recall-Oriented Understudy for Gisting Evaluations (ROUGE)** proposed by Chin-Yew Lin in *ROUGE: A Package for Automatic Evaluation of Summaries, Proceedings of the Workshop on Text Summarization Branches Out (2004),* can be identified as a variant of BLEU, and uses recall as the basic performance metric. ROGUE metric looks like the following:

$$ROUGE - N = \frac{Count_{match}}{Count_{ref}}$$

Here, $Count_{match}$ is the number of n-grams from candidates that were present in the reference, and $Count_{ref}$ is the total n-grams present in the reference. If there exist multiple references, *ROUGE-N* is calculated as follows:

$$ROUGE - N = \max\left(ROUGE - N\left(ref_i, candidate\right)\right)$$

Here, $ref_i$ is a single reference from the pool of available references. There are numerous variants of ROGUE measure that introduce various improvements to the standard ROGUE metric. ROGUE-L computes the score based on the longest common subsequence found between the candidate and reference sentence pairs. Note that the longest common subsequence does not need to be continuous in this case. Next, ROGUE-W calculates the score based on the longest common subsequence, which is penalized by the amount of fragmentation present within the subsequence. ROGUE also suffers from limitations such as not considering precision in the calculations of the score.

# METEOR

**Metric for Evaluation of Translation with Explicit ORdering (METEOR)**, proposed by Michael Denkowski and Alon Lavie in *Meteor Universal: Language Specific Translation Evaluation for Any Target Language, Proceedings of the Ninth Workshop on Statistical Machine Translation (2014): 376-380*, is a more advanced evaluation metric that performs alignments for a candidate and a reference sentence. METEOR is different from BLEU and ROUGE in the sense that METEOR takes the position of words into account. When computing similarities between a candidate sentence and a reference sentence, the following cases are considered as matches:

- **Exact**: The word from the candidate exactly matches the word from the reference sentence
- **Stem**: A stemmed word (for example, walk of the word walked) matches the word from reference sentence
- **Synonym**: The word from a candidate sentence is a synonym for the word from the reference sentence

To calculate the METEOR score, the matches between a reference sentence and a candidate sentence can be shown as in Figure 9.8, with the help of a table. Then, precision ($P$) and recall ($R$) values are calculated based on the number of matches present in the candidate and reference sentences. Finally, the harmonic mean of $P$ and $R$ is used to compute the METEOR score:

$$F_{mean} = \frac{P.R}{\alpha P + \left(1 - \alpha\right)R}\left(1 - \gamma \times \text{frag}^{\beta}\right)$$

Here, α, β, and γ are tunable parameters, and *frag* penalizes fragmented matches, in order to prefer candidate sentences that have less gaps in matches as well as closely follow the order of words of the reference sentence. The *frag* is calculated by looking at the number of crosses in the final unigram mapping (*Figure 9.8*):

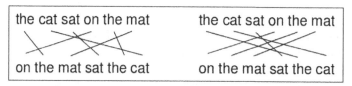

Figure 9.8: Different possible alignments for two strings

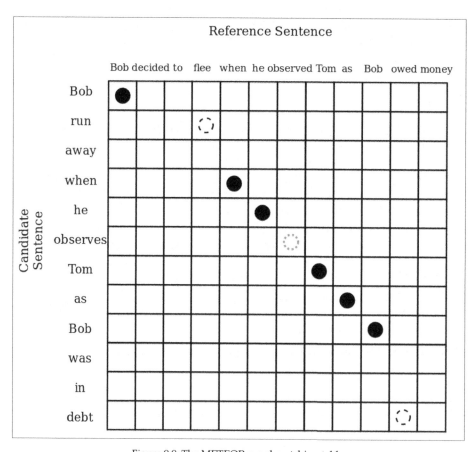

Figure 9.9: The METEOR word matching table

You can see that we denoted matches between the candidate sentence and the reference sentence in circles and ovals. For example, we denote exact matches with a solid black circle, synonyms with a dashed hollow circle, and stemmed matches with dotted circles.

METEOR is computationally more complex, but has been often found to correlate with the human judgement more than BLEU, suggesting that METEOR is a better evaluation metric than BLEU.

# CIDEr

**Consensus-based Image Description Evaluation (CIDEr)**, proposed by *Ramakrishna Vedantam and others* in *CIDEr: Consensus-based Image Description Evaluation, IEEE Conference on Computer Vision and Pattern Recognition (CVPR), 2015*, is another measure that evaluates the consensus of a candidate sentence to a given set of reference statements. CIDEr is defined to measure the grammaticality, saliency, and accuracy (that is, precision and recall) of a candidate sentence.

First, CIDEr weighs each n-gram found in both the candidate and reference sentences by means of TF-IDF, so that more common n-grams (for example, if words considered for example, *a* and *the*) will have a smaller weight, whereas rare words will have a higher weight. Finally, CIDEr is calculated as the cosine similarity between the vectors formed by TF-IDF weighed n-grams found in the candidate sentence and the reference sentence:

$$\text{CIDEr}\left(\text{cand}, \text{ref}\right) = \frac{1}{m} \sum_{j} \frac{TF-IDF_{vec}\left(cand\right).TF-IDF_{vec}\left(ref_j\right)}{\left\|TF-IDF_{vec}\left(cand\right)\right\| \left\|TF-IDF_{vec}\left(ref_j\right)\right\|}$$

Here, *cand* is the candidate sentence, *ref* is the set of reference sentences, $ref_j$ is the $j^{th}$ sentence of *ref*, and *m* is the number of reference sentences for a given candidate. Most importantly, $TF-IDF_{vec}\left(cand\right)$ is the TF-IDF values calculated for all the n-grams in the candidate sentence and formed as a vector. $TF-IDF_{vec}\left(ref_j\right)$ is the same vector for the reference sentence, $ref_j$. $\left\|TF-IDF_{vec}\left(.\right)\right\|$ denotes the magnitude of the vector.

Overall, it should be noted that there is no clear-cut winner that is able to perform well across all the different tasks that are found in natural language processing. These metrics are significantly task-dependent and should be carefully chosen depending on the task.

# BLEU-4 over time for our model

In *Figure 9.10*, we report the evolution of the BLEU-4 value for our experiment. We can see that the score goes up over time and reaches close to 0.3. Note that the current state of the art (at the time of writing) for the MS-COCO dataset is around 0.369 (*Bottom-Up and Top-Down Attention for Image Captioning and Visual Question Answering, Anderson and others, 2017*), which is obtained with much more complex models as well as more advanced regularization being employed. In addition, the actual full training set of MS-COCO is almost three times the size of the training set we used. So, a BLEU-4 score of 0.3 with limited training data, a single LSTM cell and no special regularization is quite a good result:

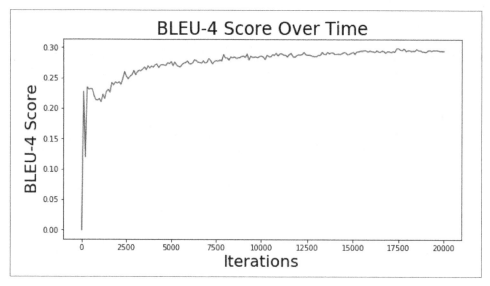

Figure 9.10: BLEU-4 for the image caption generation example over time

# Captions generated for test images

Let's see what sort of captions are generated for the test images.

After 100 steps, the only thing that our model has learned is that the caption starts with an sos token, and there are some words followed by a bunch of EOS tokens (see *Figure 9.11*):

Figure 9.11: Captions generated after 100 steps

After 1,000 steps, our model knows to generate slightly semantic phrases and recognizes objects in some images correctly (for example, a man holding a tennis racket, shown in *Figure 9.12*). However, the text seems to be short and vague, and in addition, several images are described incorrectly:

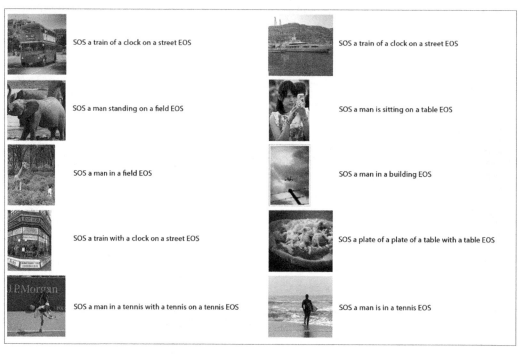

Figure 9.12: Captions generated after 1,000 steps

After 2,000 steps, our model has become quite good at generating expressive phrases composed of proper grammar (see *Figure 9.13*). Images are not described with small and vague phrases as we saw in step 1,000 before:

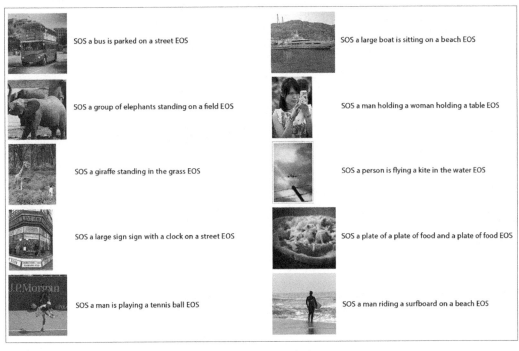

SOS a bus is parked on a street EOS

SOS a large boat is sitting on a beach EOS

SOS a group of elephants standing on a field EOS

SOS a man holding a woman holding a table EOS

SOS a giraffe standing in the grass EOS

SOS a person is flying a kite in the water EOS

SOS a large sign sign with a clock on a street EOS

SOS a plate of a plate of food and a plate of food EOS

SOS a man is playing a tennis ball EOS

SOS a man riding a surfboard on a beach EOS

Figure 9.13: Captions generated after 2,000 steps

After 5,000 steps, our model now recognizes most of the images correctly (see *Figure 9.14*). Also, it can generate very relevant and grammatically correct phrases, explaining what is happening in the image. However, note that it is not perfect. For example, our algorithm gets the fourth image quite wrong. The image is actually a building, whereas our algorithm knows that it's something urban, but is unable to distinguish the building, mistaking it for a clock. The eighth image is also recognized incorrectly. The image depicts an airplane in the sky, but the algorithm mistakes it for a person flying a kite:

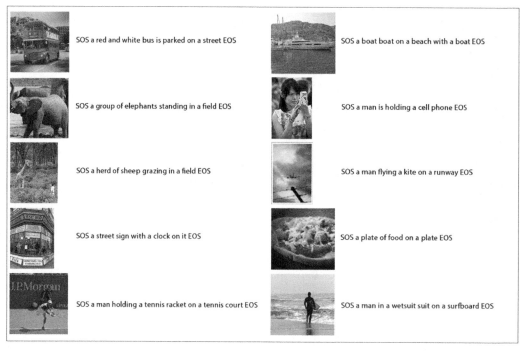

Figure 9.14: Captions generated after 5,000 steps

After 10,000 steps, our algorithm is quite good at describing images. It correctly describes most of the images, but still it gets ninth image wrong. The image shows a pizza, and the algorithm seems to think this is a sandwich (see *Figure 9.15*). Another observation is that the seventh image is actually a woman holding a cell phone, but the algorithm seems to think that it is a man. However, we can see that there are people in the background of that image, so the algorithm might be mistaking the person in the foreground for that of the background. From this point, the algorithm generates different variations of what is happening in the image, as each image has multiple captions for training:

Figure 9.15: Captions generated after 10,000 steps

Remember that these are the results obtained using approximately only one third of the full training data available. Furthermore, we are using a simple single cell LSTM. We encourage you to try to maximize the performance by employing the full set of training data as well as to use multilayered LSTMs (or GRUs) with better regularization (dropout).

# Using TensorFlow RNN API with pretrained GloVe word vectors

So far, we have implemented everything from scratch in order to understand the exact underlying mechanisms of such a system. Here we will discuss how to use the TensorFlow RNN API along with pretrained GloVe word vectors in order to reduce both the amount of code and learning for the algorithm. This will be available as an exercise in the `lstm_image_caption_pretrained_wordvecs_rnn_api.ipynb` notebook found in the `ch9` folder.

We will first discuss how to download the word vectors and then discuss how to load only the relevant word vectors from the downloaded file, as the vocabulary size of the pretrained GloVe vectors is around 400,000 words, whereas ours is just 18,000. Next, we will perform some elementary spelling correction of the captions, as there seems to be a lot of spelling mistakes present. Then we will discuss how we can process the cleaned data using a `tf.nn.rnn_cell.LSTMCell` module found in the RNN API.

# Loading GloVe word vectors

First, download the GloVe embedding file available at `https://nlp.stanford.edu/projects/glove/` and place it in the `ch9` folder. Next, we will define a NumPy array to hold the loaded relevant word vectors from GloVe:

```
pret_embeddings = np.empty(shape=(vocabulary_size,50),
                           dtype=np.float32)
```

Then we will open the ZIP file containing the downloaded GloVe word vectors and read line by line. The ZIP file contains several different variations of GloVe having different embedding sizes (for example, 50, 100). We will use the `glove.6B.50d.txt` file found in the ZIP file as this is the smallest and is adequate for the problem we are trying to solve. Each line in the file will be of the following format (each value in a line separated by a space):

```
dog 0.11008 -0.38781 -0.57615 -0.27714 0.70521 ...
```

In the following code, we show how to extract relevant word embeddings from the file. First, we will open the ZIP file and read the text file we identified (`glove.6B.50d.txt`):

```
with zipfile.ZipFile('glove.6B.zip') as glovezip:
    with glovezip.open('glove.6B.50d.txt') as glovefile:
```

Next we will enumerate each line in the text file and read the word that `line` corresponds to (that is, the first element of the line), and also read the corresponding word vector for that word:

```
for li, line in enumerate(glovefile):
    # Decode the line to get rid of any
    # unparsable symbols
    line_tokens = line.decode('utf-8').split(' ')

    # Get the word
    word = line_tokens[0]

    # Get the vector
    vector = [float(v) for v in line_tokens[1:]]
```

Then, if the word is found in our dataset, we will save that vector in the NumPy array we defined previously that holds the word vectors. We will save a given vector in the row given by our `dictionary` variable that holds a mapping of words to a unique ID. At the same time, in addition to the given word, we will also process the word produced by adding an apostrophe and s to the end of the word (for example, *cat* → *cat's*). We initialize both these variations with the `word` vector corresponding to the original word (for example, *cat*) as the GloVe file doesn't contain words denoting possession (for example, *cat's*). We will also save all the words from the captions that matched some word in GloVe into the `words_in_glove` list. This will be used in the next step:

```
if word in dictionary.keys():
    words_in_glove.append(word)
    pret_embeddings[dictionary[word],:] = vector
    words_found += 1
    found_word_ids.append(dictionary[word])

    word_with_s = word + '\'s'
    if word_with_s in dictionary.keys():
        pret_embeddings[dictionary[word_with_s],:] =
            vector
        words_found += 1
        found_word_ids.append(dictionary[word_with_s])
```

# Cleaning data

Now we have to deal with an issue that we ignored when we had to learn word vectors from scratch. There are many spelling mistakes (in the captions) present in the MS-COCO dataset. Therefore, to utilize the pretrained word vectors maximally, we need to correct these spelling mistakes to make sure that these words will have the correct word vector assigned to them. In order to correct the spellings, we use the following procedure.

First, we will compute the IDs of the words that were not found in the GloVe file (possibly due to wrong spellings):

```
notfound_word_ids = list(set(list(range(0,vocabulary_size))) -
                    set(found_word_ids))
```

Then, if any of these words were found in a caption, we will correct the spellings of those words using the following logic.

First, calculate the similarity between the incorrect word (denoted by `cw`) and all words in the `words_in_glove` list (each identified by `gw`), using string matching:

```
# for each word not found in pretrained embeddings
# we find most similar spellings
                for gw in words_in_glove:
                        cor, found_sim = correct_spellings.correct_
wrong_word(cw,gw,cap)
```

If this similarity is greater than `0.9` (heuristically chosen), we will replace the incorrect word with the following logic. We had to correct some words manually as there were multiple highly similar words to some words (for example, *stting* was similar to both *setting* and *sitting*):

```
def correct_wrong_word(cw,gw,cap):

    '''
    Spelling correction logic
    This is a very simple logic that replaces
    words with incorrect spelling with the word that highest
    similarity. Some words are manually corrected as the words
    found to be most similar semantically did not match.
    '''

    correct_word = None
    found_similar_word = False
    sim = string_similarity(gw,cw)
    if sim>0.9:
        if cw != 'stting' and cw != 'sittign' and \
            cw != 'smilling' and \
            cw!='skiies' and cw!='childi' and cw!='sittion' and \
            cw!='peacefuly' and cw!='stainding' and \
            cw != 'staning' and cw!='lating' and cw!='sking' and \
            cw!='trolly' and cw!='umping' and cw!='earing' and \
            cw !='baters' and cw !='talkes' and cw !='trowing' and \
            cw !='convered' and cw !='onsie' and cw !='slying':
            print(gw,' ',cw,' ',sim,' (',cap,')')
            correct_word = gw
            found_similar_word = True
        elif cw == 'stting' or cw == 'sittign' or cw == 'sittion':
            correct_word = 'sitting'
```

```
                found_similar_word = True
            elif cw == 'smilling':
                correct_word = 'smiling'
                found_similar_word = True
            elif cw == 'skiies':
                correct_word = 'skis'
                found_similar_word = True
            elif cw == 'childi':
                correct_word = 'child'
                found_similar_word = True
                .

                .

                .

            elif cw == 'onsie':
                correct_word = cw
                found_similar_word = True
            elif cw =='slying':
                correct_word = 'flying'
                found_similar_word = True
            else:
                raise NotImplementedError

        else:
            correct_word = cw
            found_similar_word = False
    return correct_word, found_similar_word
```

Although not all the spelling mistakes will be captured by the preceding code, most of them will be. Also, this is adequate for our exercise.

# Using pretrained embeddings with TensorFlow RNN API

After we preprocess the caption data, we will move on to learning how to use the RNN API with the pretrained GloVe embeddings. We will first discuss how we can make the embedding size of GloVe vectors (50) to match the size of the image feature vectors (1,000). Thereafter, we will explore how we can use the off-the-shelf LSTM modules from TensorFlow RNN API to learn from the data. Finally, we will learn how we can feed data with different modalities (images and text) to the model, as images and text have to be processed differently. We will now discuss the details, step by step. We depict the full learning model as a diagram in *Figure 9.16*:

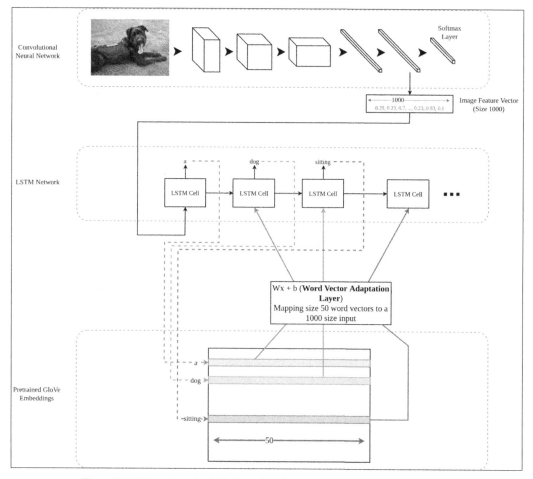

Figure 9.16: Using pretrained GloVe embeddings with the TensorFlow RNN API

# Defining the pretrained embedding layer and the adaptation layer

We will first define a TensorFlow variable to contain the pretrained embeddings. We'll leave this as a trainable variable as we only did a crude initialization for some words (that is, we used the same word vectors for the `'s` extension of the words). So the word vectors will improve as the training continues:

```
embeddings = tf.get_variable(
        'glove_embeddings',shape=[vocabulary_size, 50],
        initializer=tf.constant_initializer(pret_embeddings,
        dtype=tf.float32)
)
```

We will then define the weights and biases for the adaptation layer. The adaptation layer takes an input of the `[batch_size, 50]` size, which is a batch of GloVe word vectors, and we'll convert it to a batch of vectors of the `[batch_size, 1000]` size. This will act as a linear layer that adapts the GloVe word vectors to the correct input size (to match the size of image feature vectors):

```
with tf.variable_scope('embeddings'):
    # We need to match the size of the input to the LSTM to
    # be same as input_size always
    # For that we use a dense layer that will take the input
    # of size 50 and produce inputs of size 1000 (input size)
    embedding_dense = tf.get_variable('embedding_dense',
                    shape=[50,1000],
                    dtype=tf.float32,
            initializer=tf.contrib.layers.xavier_initializer())
    embedding_bias = tf.get_variable('embedding_bias',
                    dtype=tf.float32,
                    initializer=tf.random_uniform(
                        shape=[1000],
                        minval=-0.1,
                        maxval=0.1))
```

# Defining the LSTM cell and softmax layer

Next we will define the LSTM cell that learns to model an image followed by a sequence of words, and a softmax layer which converts the LSTM cell output to a probabilistic prediction. We will use `DropoutWrapper` (similar to that in *Chapter 8, Applications of LSTM – Generating Text*) to improve performance:

```
# LSTM cell and Dropout Cell
with tf.variable_scope('rnn'):
```

```
lstm = tf.nn.rnn_cell.LSTMCell(num_nodes)
# We use dropout to improve the performance
dropout_lstm = rnn.DropoutWrapper(
    cell=lstm, input_keep_prob=0.8,
    output_keep_prob=0.8, state_keep_prob=1.0,
    dtype=tf.float32
)
```

Here, we will define the weights and biases of the softmax layer:

```
# Defining the softmax weights and biases
with tf.variable_scope('rnn'):
    w = tf.Variable(tf.truncated_normal([num_nodes, vocabulary_size],
                    stddev=0.01),
                    name='softmax_weights',
                    trainable=True)
    b = tf.Variable(tf.random_uniform([vocabulary_size],0.0,0.01),
                    name='softmax_bias',trainable=True)
```

# Defining inputs and outputs

We will now define the input and output placeholders that will hold the inputs and outputs required to train our model. We will have three important placeholders feeding values in:

- `is_train_text`: This is a `num_unrollings` long list of placeholders, where each placeholder contains a Boolean value representing if we are currently feeding in the image feature vector or the text at a given time step. This is essential as we will later define a conditional input processing operation (that is, if the Boolean is `false`, return the image feature as is; if the Boolean is `true`, perform `tf.nn.embedding_lookup` on the inputs).

- `train_inputs`: This is a list of placeholders having the `num_unrollings` placeholders, where each placeholder contains an input of the `[batch_size, 1000]` size (where `1000` is the `input_size`). For images, we will feed in the image feature vector, and for text we will feed in a batch of word IDs (as returned by the `dictionary` variable containing a mapping from a word to a unique ID) from the captions. However, we will append each word ID with 999 zeros to make the input size 1,000 (where the 999 zeros are discarded at processing).

- `train_labels`: This is a list of placeholders having the `num_unrollings` placeholders that will contain the corresponding output to a given input (that is, SOS, if the input is image feature vectors, or the next word in the caption, if the input is a word in the caption).

The code will be as shown here:

```
is_train_text, train_inputs, train_labels = [],[],[]

for ui in range(num_unrollings):
    is_train_text.append(tf.placeholder(tf.bool,
        shape=None, name='is_train_text_data_%d'%ui))
    train_inputs.append(tf.placeholder(tf.float32,
        shape=[batch_size,input_size],name='train_inputs_%d'%ui))
    train_labels.append(tf.placeholder(tf.int32,
        shape=[batch_size], name = 'train_labels_%d'%ui))
```

# Processing images and text differently

Here we will understand one of the most crucial differences we make when using pretrained embeddings, compared with when we learned embeddings from scratch. When we were learning embeddings from scratch, we had the flexibility of making the embedding size match the image feature vector size. Having the same dimensionality of inputs is a must, as LSTMs cannot handle inputs with arbitrary dimensionality. However, since now we are using pretrained embeddings, and they do not match the input size we have specified, we need to use an adaptation layer that maps the 50-dimensional inputs to a 1,000-dimensional input. Also, we need to say to TensorFlow that we do not need the previous transformation for the image feature vectors. We will see in detail how to implement this.

First, we will use the `tf.cond` operation to differentiate between the two different processing mechanisms. The `tf.cond(pred, true_fn, false_fn)` operation can switch between different operations (that is, `true_fn` and `false_fn`), depending on whether the Boolean `pred` is `true` or `false`. We need to achieve the following:

- If data is image feature vectors (that is, `is_train_text` is `false`), we need no additional processing. We will simply forward data as it is using the `tf.identity` operation.

- If data is text (word IDs) (that is, `is_train_text` is `true`), we first need to perform the `tf.nn.embedding_lookup` operation on the batch of word IDs (found in the zeroth column). Next, we will pass the returned word vectors (of size `[batch_size, 50]`) through the adaptation layer to make the word vectors `[batch_size, 1000]` using `embedding_dense` and `embedding_bias` (this performs similar to a typical layer of a fully connected neural network without the nonlinear activation).

We write the processed inputs to `train_inputs_processed`:

```
train_inputs_processed = []
for ui in range(num_unrollings):

    train_inputs_processed.append(
        tf.cond(is_train_text[ui],
            lambda: tf.add(
                tf.matmul(tf.nn.embedding_lookup(
                    embeddings, tf.reduce_sum(tf.cast(
                                train_inputs[ui],tf.int32),
                    axis=1)
                ),embedding_dense),embedding_bias),
            lambda: tf.identity(train_inputs[ui]))
    )
```

We also need to set the shape of each tensor found in the `train_inputs_processed` list because, after performing the `tf.cond` operation, the shape information is lost. Also, the shape information is required for LSTM cell calculations:

```
[t_in.set_shape([batch_size,input_size]) for t_in in train_inputs_
processed]
```

# Defining the LSTM output calculation

Next, we will define the initial state of the LSTM cell:

```
initial_state = lstm.zero_state(batch_size, dtype=tf.float32)
```

Then, using the `tf.nn.dynamic_rnn` function, we will calculate the output for all the time steps in the `num_unrollings` window, which we will calculate LSTM output in a single step:

```
# Gives a [num_unrolling, batch_size, num_nodes] size output
train_outputs, initial_state = tf.nn.dynamic_rnn(
    dropout_lstm, tf.concat([tf.expand_dims(t_in,axis=0) for t_in in
train_inputs_processed],axis=0),
    time_major=True, initial_state=initial_state
)
```

# Defining the logits and predictions

The previously calculated `train_output` will be of the [num_unrollings, batch_ size, vocabulary_size] size. This is known as a **time-major format**. Then, to calculate the logits and predictions from the LSTM output in a single go for all the num_unrollings time steps, we will reshape the final output as follows:

```
final_output = tf.reshape(train_outputs, [-1,num_nodes])
logits = tf.matmul(final_output, w) + b
train_prediction = tf.nn.softmax(logits)
```

# Defining the sequence loss

Then we will reshape the logits and labels back to the time-major format, as this is required by the loss function we're using:

```
time_major_train_logits = tf.reshape(logits, [
    num_unrollings,batch_size,vocabulary_size])

time_major_train_labels = tf.reshape(tf.concat(
    train_labels,axis=0), [num_unrollings,batch_size])
```

We now calculate the loss using the `tf.contrib.seq2seq.sequence_loss` function. We will need the loss averaged across the batch, but summed over the time steps:

```
loss = tf.contrib.seq2seq.sequence_loss(
    logits = tf.transpose(time_major_train_logits, [1,0,2]),
    targets = tf.transpose(time_major_train_labels),
    weights= tf.ones([batch_size, num_unrollings],
                    dtype=tf.float32),
    average_across_timesteps=False,
    average_across_batch=True
)
loss = tf.reduce_sum(loss)
```

# Defining the optimizer

Finally, we will define the optimizer that will optimize the pretrained embeddings, the adaptation layer, the LSTM cell, and the softmax weights with respect to the loss defined earlier. We will use `AdamOptimizer` and the learning rate decay over time to improve performance. We also decay the learning rate as we did in *Chapter 8, Applications of LSTM – Generating Text*:

```
# This variable and operation are used to decay the learning rate
# as we saw in chapter 8
global_step = tf.Variable(0, trainable=False)
```

```
inc_gstep = tf.assign(global_step,global_step + 1)

# We define a decaying learning rate
learning_rate = tf.train.exponential_decay(
    0.001, global_step, decay_steps=1, decay_rate=0.75,
    staircase=True)
# We define Adam Optimizer
optimizer = tf.train.AdamOptimizer(learning_rate)

# Gradient clipping
gradients, v = zip(*optimizer.compute_gradients(loss))
gradients, _ = tf.clip_by_global_norm(gradients, 5.0)
optimizer = optimizer.apply_gradients(
    zip(gradients, v))
```

After defining all the necessary TensorFlow operations, you can run the optimization process for a predefined number of steps, interleaved by calculation of the BLEU score on test data as well as predictions for several test image. The exact process can be found in the exercise file.

# Summary

In this chapter, we focused on a very interesting task that involves generating captions for given images. Our learning model was a complex machine learning pipeline, which included the following:

- Inferring feature vectors for a given image using a CNN
- Learning word embeddings for the words found in the captions
- Training an LSTM with the image feature vectors and their corresponding captions

We discussed each component in detail. First, we talked about how we can use a pretrained CNN model on a large classification dataset (that is, ImageNet) to extract good feature vectors without training a model from scratch. For this, we used a VGG with 16 layers. Next we discussed step by step how we can create TensorFlow variables, load the weights into them, and create the network. Finally, we ran a few of the test images through the model to make sure the model is actually capable of recognizing objects in the image.

Then we used the CBOW algorithm to learn good word embeddings of the words found in the captions. We made sure that we matched the dimensionality of the word embeddings with the image feature vectors, as standard LSTMs cannot handle inputs with dynamic dimensionality.

Finally, we used a simple LSTM network, where we input a sequence of data, in which the first element is the image feature vector preceded by the word embeddings corresponding to each word in the caption belonging to that image. First we preprocessed the captions by introducing two tokens to denote the beginning and end of each caption and then by truncating the captions, so that all of them were of the same length.

Thereafter, we discussed several different metrics (BLEU, ROUGE, METEOR, and CIDEr), which we can use to quantitatively evaluate the generated captions, and we saw that as we ran our algorithm through the training data, the BLEU-4 score increased over time. Additionally, we visually inspected the generated captions and saw that our ML pipeline progressively gets better at captioning images.

Finally, we discussed how we can use the pretrained GloVe embeddings and the TensorFlow RNN API to perform the same task with less code and more efficiency.

In the next chapter, we will learn how we can implement a machine translation system that takes a sentence/phrase in a source language as an input, and output a sentence/phrase that is the corresponding translation of a different language.

# 10
# Sequence-to-Sequence Learning – Neural Machine Translation

Sequence-to-sequence learning is the term used for tasks that require mapping an arbitrary length sequence to another arbitrary length sequence. This is one of the most sophisticated tasks that involves learning many-to-many mappings. Examples of this task include **Neural Machine Translation (NMT)** and creating chatbots. NMT is where we translate a sentence from one language (source language) to another (target language). Google Translate is an example of an NMT system. Chatbots (that is, software that can communicate with/answer a person) are able to converse with humans in a realistic manner. This is especially useful for various service providers, as chatbots can be used to find answers for easily solvable questions which customers might have, instead of redirecting them to human operators.

In this chapter, we will learn how to implement a NMT system. However, before diving directly into such recent advances, we will first briefly visit some of the **Statistical Machine Translation (SMT)** methods, which preceded NMT and were the state-of-the-art systems until NMT caught up. Next, we will walk through the steps required for building an NMT. Finally, we will learn how to implement a real NMT system that translates from German to English, step by step.

# Machine translation

Humans often communicate with each other by means of a language, compared to other communication methods (for example, gesturing). Currently, more than 5,000 languages are spoken worldwide. Furthermore, learning a language to a level where it is easily understandable for a native speaker of that language is a difficult task to master. However, communication is essential for sharing knowledge, socializing and expanding your network. Therefore, language acts as a barrier for communicating with different parts of the world. This is where **machine translation** (**MT**) comes in. MT systems allow the user to input a sentence in his own tongue (known as the source language) and output a sentence in a desired target language.

The problem with MT can be formulated as follows. Say, we are given a sentence (or a sequence of words) belonging to a source language $S$, defined by the following:

$$W_s = \{w_1, w_2, w_3, \ldots, w_L\}$$

Here, $W_s \in S$.

The source language would be translated to a sentence $W_T$, where $T$ is the target language and is given by the following:

$$W_T = \{w_1', w_2', w_3', \ldots, w_M'\}$$

Here, $W_T \in T$.

$W_T$ is obtained through the MT system, which outputs the following:

$$p(W_T \mid W_s) \forall W_T \in W^*_T$$

Here, $W^*_T$ is the pool of possible translation candidates found by the algorithm for the source sentence. Also, the best candidate from the pool of candidates is given by the following equation:

$$W_T^{best} = argmax_{W_T \in W^*_T} \left( p(W_T \mid W_S); \theta \right)$$

Here, $\theta$ is the model parameters. During training, we optimize the model with to maximize the probability of some known target translations for a set of corresponding source translations (that is, training data).

So far, we discussed the formal setup of the language translation problem that we're interested in solving. Next, we will walk through the history of MT to get a feel of how people tried solving this in the early days.

# A brief historical tour of machine translation

Here we will discuss the history of MT. The inception of MT involved rule-based systems. Then, more statistically sound MT systems emerged. An **Statistical Machine Translation (SMT)** used various measures of statistics of a language to produce translations to another language. Then came the era of NMT. NMT currently holds the state of the art performance in most machine learning tasks compared with other methods.

## Rule-based translation

NMT came long after statistical machine learning, and statistical machine learning has been around for more than half a century now. The inception of SMT methods dates back to 1950-60, when during one of the first recorded projects, the *Georgetown-IBM experiment*, more than 60 Russian sentences were translated to English.

One of the initial techniques for MT was word-based machine translation. This system performed word-to-word translations using bilingual dictionaries. However, as you can imagine, this method has serious limitations. The obvious limitation is that word-to-word translation is not a one-to-one mapping between different languages. In addition, word-to-word translation may lead to incorrect results as it does not consider the context of a given word. The translation of a given word in the source language can change depending on the context in which it is used. To understand this with a concrete example, let's look at the translation example from English to French in *Figure 10.1*. You can see that in the given two English sentences a single word changes. However this creates drastic changes in the translation:

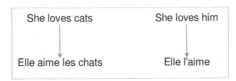

Figure 10.1: Translations (English to French) between languages are not one-to-one mappings between words

In the 1960s, the **Automatic Language Processing Advisory Committee (ALPAC)** released a report, *Languages and machines: computers in translation and linguistics, National Academy of the Sciences (1966)*, on MT's prospects. The conclusion was this:

*There is no immediate or predictable prospect of useful machine translation.*

This was because MT was slower, less accurate, and more expensive than human translation at the time. This delivered a huge blow to MT advancements, and almost a decade passed in silence.

Next came corpora-based MT, where an algorithm was trained using tuples of source sentence, and the corresponding target sentence was obtained through a parallel corpus, that is, the parallel corpus will be of format, ([(<*source_sentence_1*>, <*target_sentence_1*>), (<*source_sentence_2*>, <*target_sentence_2*>), ...]). The parallel corpus is a large text corpus formed as tuples, consisting of text from the source language and the corresponding translation of that text. An illustration of this is shown in *Table 10.2*. It should be noted that building a parallel corpus is much easier than building bilingual dictionaries and more accurate because the training data is richer than word-to-word training data. Furthermore, instead of directly relying on manually created bilingual dictionaries, the bilingual dictionary (that is, the transition models) of two languages can be built using the parallel corpus. A transition model shows how likely a target word/phrase is to be the correct translation, given the current source word/phrase. In addition to learning the transition model, corpora based MT also learn the word alignment models. A word alignment model can represent how words in a phrase from the source language corresponds to the translation of that phrase. An example of a parallel corpora and a word alignment model is depicted in *Figure 10.2*.

An illustration of an example parallel corpora is shown in *Table 10.2*:

| Source language sentences (English) | Target language sentences (French) |
|---|---|
| I went home | Je suis allé à la maison |
| John likes to play guitar | John aime jouer de la guitare |
| He is from England | Il est d'Angleterre |
| ... | .... |

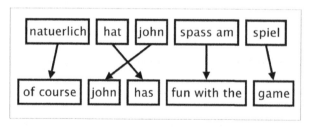

Figure 10.2: Word alignment between two different languages

Another popular approach was interlingual machine translation, which involved translating the source sentence to an language neutral *interlingua* (that is, a metalanguage), and then generating the translated sentence out of the interlingua. More specifically, an interlingual machine translation system consists of two important components, an analyzer and a synthesizer. The analyzer will take the source sentence and identify agents (for example, nouns), actions (for example, verb), and so on, and also how they interact with each other. Next, these identified elements are represented by means of an interlingual lexicon. An example of an interlingual lexicon can be made with the synsets (that is, the group of synonyms sharing a common meaning) available in WordNet. Then, from this interlingual representation, the synthesizer will create the translation. Since the synthesizer knows the nouns, verbs, and so on through the interlingual representation, it can generate the translation in the target language by incorporating language-specific grammar rules.

# Statistical Machine Translation (SMT)

Next, more statistically sound systems started emerging. One of the pioneering models of this era was IBM Models 1-5 that did word-based translation. However, as we discussed earlier, word translations are not one-to-one from the source language to a target language (for example, compound words and morphology). Eventually, researchers started experimenting with phrase-based translation systems which made some notable advances in machine translation.

Phrase-based translation works in a similar way to word-based translation, except that it uses phrases of a language as the atomic units of translation instead of individual words. This is a more sensible approach as it makes modeling the one-to-many, many-to-one, or many-to-many relationships between words easier. The main goal of phrase-based translation is to learn a *phrase-translation model* that contains a probability distribution of different candidate target phrases for a given source phrase. As you can imagine, this method involves maintaining huge databases of various phrases in two languages. A reordering step for phrases is also performed as there is no monotonic ordering of words between a sentence from one language and one in another. An example of this is shown in *Figure 10.2*. If the words are monotonically ordered between languages, there should not be crosses between word mappings.

One of the limitations of this approach is that the decoding process (finding the best target phrase for a given source phrase) is expensive. This is due to the size of the phrase-database as well as a source phrase that often contains multiple target language phrases. To alleviate the burden, syntax-based translations arose.

In syntax-based translation, the source sentence is represented by a syntax tree. In *Figure 10.3*, **NP** represents a noun phrase, **VP** a verb phrase, and **S** a sentence. Then a **reordering phase** takes place, where the tree nodes are reordered to change the order of subject, verb, and object, depending on the target language. This is because the sentence structure can change depending on the language (for example, in English it is *subject-verb-object*, whereas in Japanese it is *subject-object-verb*). The reordering is decided according to something known as the **r-table**. The r-table contains the likelihood probabilities for the tree nodes to be changed to some other order:

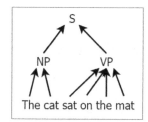

Figure 10.3. Syntax tree for a sentence

An **insertion phase** then takes place. In the insertion phase, we stochastically insert a word into each node of the tree. This is due to the assumption that there is an invisible NULL word, and it generates target words at the random positions of the tree. Also, the probability of inserting a word is determined by something called the **n-table**, which is a table that contain probabilities of inserting a particular word into the tree.

Next the **translation phase** occurs, where each leaf node is translated to the target word in a word-by-word manner. Finally, the translated sentence is read off the syntax tree, to construct the target sentence.

# Neural Machine Translation (NMT)

Finally, around the year 2014, NMT systems were introduced. NMT is an end-to-end system that takes a full sentence as an input, performs certain transformations, and then outputs the translated sentence for the corresponding source sentence. Therefore, NMT eliminates the need for the feature engineering required for machine translation, such as building phrase translation models and building syntax trees, which is a big win for the NLP community. Also, NMT has outperformed all the other popular MT techniques in a very short period, just two to three years. In *Figure 10.4*, we depict the results of various MT systems reported in the MT literature. For example, 2016 results are obtained from Sennrich, and others in their paper, *Edinburgh Neural Machine Translation Systems for WMT 16, Association for Computational Linguistics, Proceedings of the First Conference on Machine Translation, August 2016: 371-376*, and from Williams and others in their paper, *Edinburgh's Statistical Machine Translation Systems for WMT16, Association for Computational Linguistics, Proceedings of the First Conference on Machine Translation, August 2016: 399-410*. All the MT systems are evaluated with the BLEU score. As we discussed in *Chapter 9, Applications of LSTM – Image Caption Generation*, the BLEU score denotes the number of n-grams (for example, unigrams and bigrams) of candidate translation that matched in the reference translation. So the higher the BLEU score, the better the MT system is. We'll discuss BLEU metric in detail later in the chapter. There is no need to highlight that NMT is a clear-cut winner:

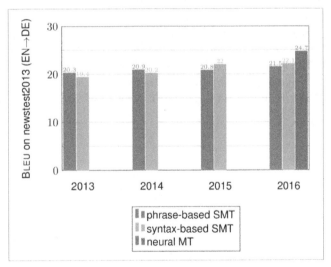

Figure 10.4. Comparison of statistical machine translation system to NMT systems.
Courtesy of Rico Sennrich.

A case study assessing the potential of NMT systems is available in *Is Neural Machine Translation Ready for Deployment? A Case Study on 30 Translation Directions, Junczys-Dowmunt, Hoang* and *Dwojak, Proceedings of the Ninth International Workshop on Spoken Language Translation, Seattle (2016).* The study looks at the performance of different systems on several translation tasks between various languages (English, Arabic, French, Russian, and Chinese). The results also support that NMT systems (NMT 1.2M and NMT 2.4M) perform better than SMT systems (PB-SMT and Hiero).

*Figure 10.5* shows several statistics for a set from a 2017 current state-of-the-art machine translator. This is from a presentation, *State of the Machine Translation, Intento, Inc, 2017,* produced by Konstantin Savenkov, cofounder and CEO at Intento. We can see that the performance of the MT produced by DeepL (`https://www.deepl.com`) appears to be competing closely with other MT giants, including Google. The comparison includes MT systems such as DeepL (NMT), Google (NMT), Yandex (NMT-SMT hybrid), Microsoft (has both SMT and NMT), IBM (SMT), Prompt (rule-based), and SYSTRAN (rule-based/SMT hybrid). The graph clearly shows that NMT systems are leading the current MT advancements. The LEPOR score is used to assess different systems. LEPOR is a more advanced metric than BLEU, and it attempts to solve the *language bias problem*. The language bias problem refers to the phenomenon that some evaluation metrics (such as, BLEU) perform well for certain languages, but perform poorly for some others.

However, it should also be noted that the results do contain some bias due to the averaging mechanism used in this comparison. For example, Google Translator has been averaged over a larger set of languages (including difficult translation tasks), whereas DeepL has been averaged over a smaller and relatively easier subset of languages. Therefore, we should not conclude that the DeepL MT system is better than the Google MT system. Nevertheless, the overall results provide a general comparison of the performance of the current NMT and SMT systems:

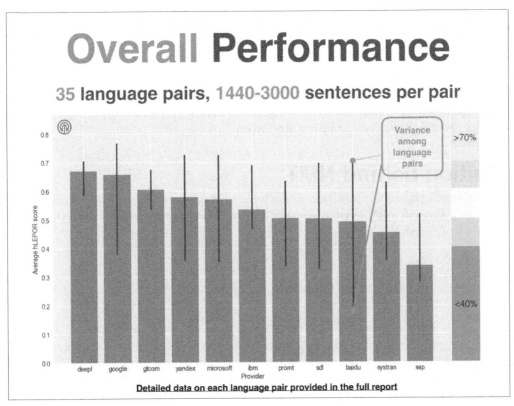

Figure 10.5: Performance of various MT systems. Courtesy of Intento, Inc.

We saw that NMT has already outperformed SMT systems in very few years, and it is the current state of the art. We will now move onto discussing details and the architecture of an NMT system. Finally, we will be implementing an NMT system from scratch.

# Understanding Neural Machine Translation

Now that we have an appreciation for how machine translation has evolved over time, let's try to understand how state-of-the-art NMT works. First, we will take a look at the model architecture used by neural machine translators and then move on to understanding the actual training algorithm.

# Intuition behind NMT

First, let's understand the intuition underlying an NMT system's design. Say, you are a fluent English and German speaker and were asked to translate the following sentence to English:

*Ich ging nach Hause*

This sentence translates to the following:

*I went home*

Although it might not have taken more than few seconds for a fluent person to translate this, there is a certain process involved in the translation. First, you read the German sentence, and then you create a thought or concept about what this sentence represents or implies. And finally, you translate the sentence to English. The same idea is used for building NMT systems (see *Figure 10.6*). The encoder reads the source sentence (that is, similar to you reading the German sentence). Then the encoder outputs a context vector (the context vector corresponds to the thought/ concept you imagined after reading the sentence). Finally, the decoder takes in the context vectors and outputs the translation in English:

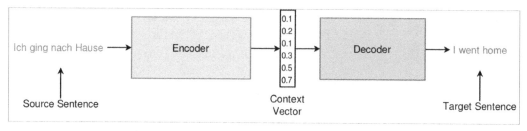

Figure 10.6. Conceptual architecture of an NMT system

# NMT architecture

Now we will look at the architecture in more detail. The sequence-to-sequence approach discussed here was proposed by Sutskever, Vinyals, and Le in their paper, *Sequence to Sequence Learning with Neural Networks, Proceedings of the 27th International Conference on Neural Information Processing Systems - Volume 2: 3104-3112*. From the diagram in *Figure 10.6*, we can see that there are two major components in the NMT architecture. These are called the encoder and decoder. In other words, NMT can be seen as an encoder-decoder architecture. The **encoder** converts a sentence from a given source language to a *thought*, and the **decoder** decodes or translates the *thought* to a target language. As you can see, this shares some features with the interlingual machine translation method we briefly talked about. This is illustrated in *Figure 10.7*. The left-hand side of the context vector denotes the encoder (which takes a source sentence in word by word to train a time-series model). The right-hand side denotes the decoder that outputs word by word (while using the previous word as the current input) the corresponding translation of the source sentence. We will also use embedding layers (for both source and target languages) to provide word vectors as inputs to the models:

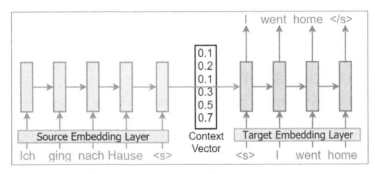

Figure 10.7: Unrolling the source and target sentences over time

With a basic understanding of what NMT looks like, let's formally define the objective of the NMT. The ultimate objective of an NMT system is to maximize the log likelihood, given a source sentence $x_s$ and its corresponding $y_T$, that is, to maximize the following:

$$\frac{1}{N} \sum_{i=1}^{N} logP\left(y_T \mid x_s\right)$$

Here, $N$ refers to the number of source and target sentence tuples we have as training data.

Then, during inference, for a given source sentence, $x_s^{infer}$, we will find the $y_T^{best}$ translation using the following:

$$y_T^{best} = argmax_{y \in Y_T} P\left(y_T \mid x_s^{infer}\right) = argmax_{y \in Y_T} \prod_{i=1}^{M} P\left(y_T^i \mid x_s^{infer}\right)$$

Here, $Y_T$ is the set of possible candidate sentences.

Before we examine each part of the NMT architecture, let's define the mathematical notation to understand the system more concretely.

Let's define the encoder LSTM as $LSTM_{enc}$ and the decoder LSTM as $LSTM_{dec}$. At the time step $t$, let's define the cell state of the LSTM as $c_t$ and the external hidden state as $h_t$. Therefore, feeding in the input $x_t$ into the LSTM produces $c_t$ and $h_t$:

$$c_t, h_t = LSTM\left(x_t \mid x_1, x_2, \ldots, x_{t-1}\right)$$

Now, we will talk about the embedding layer, the encoder, the context vector, and finally, the decoder.

## The embedding layer

In both *Chapter 8, Applications of LSTM – Generating Text* and *Chapter 9, Applications of LSTM – Image Caption Generation*, we discussed in detail the benefit of using word embedding instead of one-hot-encoded representations of words, especially when the vocabulary is large. Here as well, we are using a two-word embedding layer, $Emb_s$, for the source language and $Emb_T$ for the target language. So, instead of feeding $x_t$ directly into the $LSTM$, we will be getting $Emb(x_t)$. However, to avoid unnecessarily increasing the notation, we will assume $x_t = Emb(x_t)$.

## The encoder

As mentioned earlier, the encoder is responsible for generating a *thought vector* or a context vector that represents what is meant by the source language. For this, we will use an LSTM network (see *Figure 10.8*):

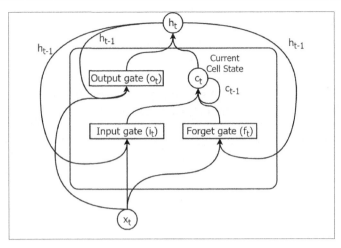

Figure 10.8: An LSTM cell

The encoder is initialized with $c_0$ and $h_0$ as zero vectors. The encoder takes a sequence of words, $x_s = \left\{ x_s^{\,1}, x_s^{\,2}, \ldots, x_s^{\,L} \right\}$, as the input and calculates a context vector, $v = \left\{ v_c, v_h \right\}$, where $v_c$ is the final cell state and $v_h$ is the final external hidden state obtained after processing the final element, $x_T^{\,L}$, of the sequence, $x_T$. We represent this as the following:

$$c_L, h_L = LSTM_{enc}\left( x_s^{\,L} \mid x_s^{\,1}, x_s^{\,2}, \ldots, x_s^{\,L-1} \right)$$

$$v_c = c_L$$

$$v_h = h_L$$

# The context vector

The idea of the context vector ($v$) is to represent a sentence of a source language concisely. Also, in contrast to how the encoder's states are initialized (that is, they are initialized with zeros), the context vector becomes the initial state for the decoder LSTM. In other words, the decoder LSTM doesn't start with an initial state of zeros, but with the context vector as its initial state. We will talk about this in more detail next.

# The decoder

The decoder is responsible for decoding the context vector into the desired translation. Our decoder is an LSTM network as well. Though it is possible for the encoder and decoder to share the same set of weights, it is usually better to use two different networks for the encoder and the decoder. This increases the number of parameters in our model, allowing us to learn the translations more effectively.

First, the decoder's states are initialized with the context vector, $v = \{v_c, v_h\}$, as shown here:

$$c_0 = v_c$$

$$h_0 = v_h$$

Here, $c_0, h_0 \in LSTM_{dec}$.

This ($v$) is the crucial link that connects the encoder with the decoder to form an end-to-end computational chain (see in *Figure 10.6* that the only thing shared by the encoder and decoder is $v$). Also, this is the only piece of information that is available to the decoder about the source sentence.

Then we will compute the $m^{th}$ prediction of the translated sentence with the following:

$$c_m, h_m = LSTM_{dec}\left(y_T^{m-1} \mid v, y_T^{1}, y_T^{2}, \ldots, y_T^{m-2}\right)$$

$$y_T^{m} = \text{softmax}\left(w_{softmax} \times h_m + b_{softmax}\right)$$

The full NMT system with the details of how the LSTM cell in the encoder connects to the LSTM cell in the decoder and how the softmax layer is used to output predictions is shown in *Figure 10.9*:

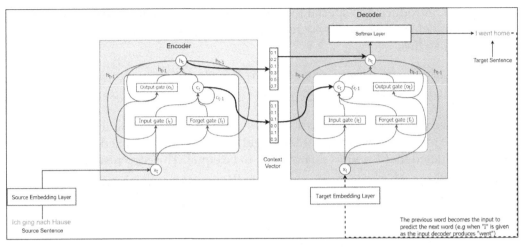

Figure 10.9: The encoder-decoder architecture with the LSTMs

# Preparing data for the NMT system

In this section, we will talk about the exact process for preparing data for training and predicting from the NMT system. First, we talk will about how to prepare training data (that is, the source sentence and target sentence pairs) to train the NMT system followed by inputting a given source sentence to produce the translation of the source sentence.

# At training time

The training data consists of pairs of source sentences and corresponding translations to the target language. An example might look like this:

- *( Ich ging nach Hause , I went home)*
- *( Sie hat in der Schule gewartet , She was waiting at school)*

We have $N$ such pairs in our dataset. If we are to implement a fairly good translator, $N$ needs to be in the scale of millions. An increase of training data as such, also implies prolonged training times.

Next, we will introduce two special tokens: <s> and </s>. The <s> token represents the start of a sentence, whereas </s> represents the end of a sentence. Now, the data would look like this:

- *(<s> Ich ging nach Hause </s> , <s> I went home </s>)*
- *(<s> Sie hat in der Schule gewartet </s> , <s> She was waiting at school </s>)*

Thereafter, we will pad the sentences with the </s> tokens such that the source sentences are of a fixed length $L$ and the target sentences are of a fixed length $M$. It should be noted that $L$ and $M$ do not need to be equal. This step results in the following:

- *(<s> Ich ging nach Hause </s> </s> </s> , <s> I went home </s> </s> </s>)*
- *(<s> Sie hat in der Schule gewartet </s> , <s> She was waiting at school </s>)*

If a sentence has a length greater than $L$ or $M$, it is truncated to fit the length. Then the sentences are passed through a tokenizer to get the tokenized words out. Here I'm ignoring the second tuple (that is, a pair of sentences), as both are processed similarly:

*(['<s>' , 'Ich' , 'ging' , 'nach' , 'Hause' , '</s>' , '</s>' , '</s>'] , ['<s>' , 'I' , 'went' , 'home' , '</s>' , '</s>' , '</s>'])*

It should be noted that bringing sentences to a fixed length is not essential, as LSTMs are capable of handling dynamic sequence sizes. However, bringing them to a fixed length helps us to process sentences as batches instead of processing them one by one.

# Reversing the source sentence

Next we will perform a special trick on the source sentences. Say, we have the sentence, $ABC$ in the source language, which we want to translate to $\alpha\beta\gamma\phi$ in the target language. We will first reverse the source sentences so that the sentence, $ABC$ would be read as $CBA$. This means that in order to translate $ABC$ to $\alpha\beta\gamma\phi$, we need to feed in $CBA$. This improves the performance of our model significantly, especially when the source and target languages share the same sentence structure (for example, subject-verb-object).

Let's try to understand why this helps. Mainly, it helps to build good *communication* between the encoder and the decoder. Let's start from the previous example. We will concatenate the source and target sentence:

$$ABC\alpha\beta\gamma\phi$$

If you calculate the distance (that is, the number of words separating two words) from $A$ to $\alpha$ or $B$ to $\beta$, they will be the same. However, consider this when you reverse the source sentence, as shown here:

$$CBA\alpha\beta\gamma\phi$$

Here, $A$ is very close to $\alpha$ and so on. Also, to build good translations, building good communications at the very start is important. This can possibly help NMT systems to improve their performance with this simple trick.

Now, our dataset becomes this:

$(['</s>', '</s>', '</s>', 'Hause', 'nach', 'ging', 'Ich', '<s>'], ['<s>', 'I', 'went', 'home', '</s>', '</s>', '</s>'])$

Next, using the learned embeddings, $Emb_s$ and $Emb_T$, we replace each word with its corresponding embedding vector.

The other good news is that our source sentence ends with a <s> token and the target sentence starts with a <s> token, so during training, we do not have to do any special processing to build the link between the end of the source sentence and the beginning of the target sentence.

> Note that the source sentence reversing step is a subjective preprocessing step. This might not be necessary for some translational tasks. For example, if your translation task is to translate from Japanese (that is, often written subject-object-verb format) to Filipino (often written verb-subject-object), then reversing the source sentence might actually cause harm rather than helping. This is because by reversing the text in the Japanese language, you are increasing the distance between the starting element of the target sentence (that is, the verb (Japanese)) and the corresponding source language entity (that is, the verb (Filipino)).

# At testing time

At testing time, we only have the source sentence, but not the target sentence. Also, we prepare our source data as we did for the training phase. Next, we get the translated output word by word by feeding in the last predicted word by the decoder as the next input. The prediction process is first triggered by feeding in an <s> token to the decoder first.

We will talk about the exact training procedure and the predicting procedure for a given source sentence.

# Training the NMT

Now that we have defined the NMT architecture and preprocessed training data, it is quite straightforward to train the model. Here we will define and illustrate (see *Figure 10.10*) the exact process used for training:

1. Preprocess $(x_S, y_T)$ as explained previously

2. Feed $x_s$ into the $LSTM_{enc}$ and calculate $v$ conditioned on $x_s$

3. Initialize $LSTM_{dec}$ with $v$

4. Predict $\hat{y}_T = \{\hat{y}_T^{\,1}, \hat{y}_T^{\,2}, \ldots, \hat{y}_T^{\,M}\}$ corresponding to the input sentence $x_s$ from $LSTM_{dec}$, where the $m^{th}$ prediction, out of the target vocabulary $V$ is calculated as follows:

$$\hat{y}_T^{\,m} = softmax\left(\mathrm{w}_{softmax}\mathrm{h}^m + \mathrm{b}_{softmax}\right)$$

$$\mathrm{w}_T^m = \mathrm{argmax}_{w^m \in V}\,\mathrm{P}\left(\hat{y}_T^{(m,w^m)} \mid v, \hat{y}_T^{\,1}, \ldots, \hat{y}_T^{\,m-1}\right)$$

Here, $\mathrm{w}_T^m$ denotes the best target word for $m^{th}$ position.

5. Calculate the loss: categorical cross-entropy between the predicted word, $\hat{y}_T^{\,m}$, and the actual word at the $m^{th}$ position, $y_T^{\,m}$

6. Optimize both the $LSTM_{enc}$, $LSTM_{dec}$, and *softmax* layer with respect to the loss

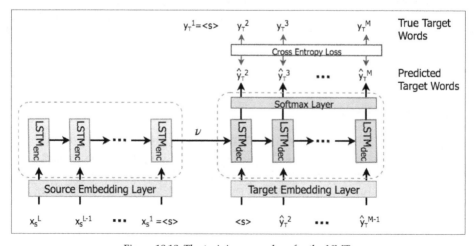

Figure 10.10: The training procedure for the NMT

# Inference with NMT

Inferencing is slightly different from the training process for NMT (*Figure 10.11*). As we do not have a target sentence at the inference time, we need a way to trigger the decoder at the end of the encoding phase. This shares similarities with the image captioning exercise we did in *Chapter 9, Applications of LSTM – Image Caption Generation*. In that exercise, we appended the *<SOS>* token to the beginning of the captions to denote the start of the caption and *<EOS>* to denote the end.

We can simply do this by giving *<s>* as the first input to the decoder, then by getting the prediction as the output, and by feeding in the last prediction as the next input to the NMT:

1. Preprocess $x_s$ as explained previously

2. Feed $x_s$ into $LSTM_{enc}$ and calculate $v$ conditioned on $x_s$

3. Initialize $LSTM_{dec}$ with $v$

4. For the initial prediction step, predict $\hat{y}_T^2$ by conditioning the prediction on $\hat{y}_T^1 = <s>$ and $v$

5. For subsequent time steps, while $\hat{y}_T^i \neq </s>$, predict $\hat{y}_T^{m+1}$ by conditioning the prediction on $\{\hat{y}_T^m, \hat{y}_T^{m-1}, ..., <s>\}$ and $v$

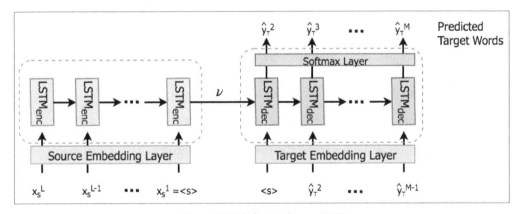

Figure 10.11: Inferring from a NMT

# The BLEU score – evaluating the machine translation systems

**BLEU** stands for **Bilingual Evaluation Understudy** and is a way of automatically evaluating machine translation systems. This metric was first introduced in the paper, *BLEU: A Method for Automatic Evaluation of Machine Translation, Papineni and others, Proceedings of the 40th Annual Meeting of the Association for Computational Linguistics (ACL), Philadelphia, July 2002: 311-318*. We will be implementing the BLEU score calculation algorithm and is available as an exercise in `bleu_score_example.ipynb`. Let's understand how this is calculated.

Let's consider an example to learn the calculations of the BLEU score. Say, we have two candidate sentences (that is, a sentence predicted by our MT system) and a reference sentence (that is, corresponding actual translation) for some given source sentence:

- Reference 1: The cat sat on the mat
- Candidate 1: The cat is on the mat

To see how good the translation is, we can use one measure, *precision*. Precision is a measure of how many words in the candidate are actually present in the reference. In general, if you consider a classification problem with two classes (denoted by negative and positive), precision is given by the following formula:

$$Precision = \frac{number\ of\ samples\ correctly\ classified\ as\ positive}{all\ the\ samples\ classified\ as\ positive}$$

Let's now calculate the precision for candidate 1:

*Precision = # of times each word of candidate appeared in reference/ # of words in candidate*

Mathematically, this can be given by the following formula:

$$Precision = \frac{\sum_{unigram \in Candidate} IsFoundInRef(unigram)}{|Candidate|}$$

*Precision for candidate 1 = 5/6*

This is also known as the 1-gram precision since we consider a single word at a time.

Now let's introduce a new candidate:

Candidate 2: The the the cat cat cat

It is not hard for a human to see that candidate 1 is far better than candidate 2. Let's calculate the precision:

*Precision for candidate 2 = 6/6 = 1*

As we can see, the precision score disagrees with the judgment we made. Therefore, precision alone cannot be trusted to be a good measure of the quality of a translation.

# Modified precision

To address the precision limitation, we can use a modified 1-gram precision. The modified precision clips the number of occurrences of each unique word in the candidate by the number of times that word appeared in the reference:

$$p_1 = \frac{\sum_{unigram \in \{Candidate\}} Min\left(Occurences\left(unigram\right), unigram_{max}\right)}{|Candidate|}$$

Therefore, for candidates 1 and 2, the modified precision would be as follows:

*Mod-1-gram-Precision Candidate 1 = (1 + 1 + 1 + 1 + 1)/ 6 = 5/6*

*Mod-1-gram-Precision Candidate 2= (2 + 1) / 6 = 3/6*

We can already see that this is a good modification as the precision of candidate 2 is reduced. This can be extended to any n-gram by considering *n* words at a time instead of a single word.

# Brevity penalty

Precision naturally prefers small sentences. This raises a question in evaluation, as the MT system might generate small sentences for longer references and still have a higher precision. Therefore, *brevity penalty* is introduced to avoid this. Brevity penalty is calculated by the following:

$$BP = \begin{cases} 1 & if\ c > r \\ e^{(1-r/c)} & if\ c \leq r \end{cases}$$

Here, $c$ is the candidate sentence length and $r$ is the reference sentence length. In our example, we calculate as shown here:

BP for candidate 1 = $e^{(1-(6/6))} = e^0 = 1$

BP for candidate 2 = $e^{(1-(6/6))} = e^0 = 1$

# The final BLEU score

Next, to calculate the BLEU score, we first calculate several different modified n-gram precisions for a bunch of different $n = 1, 2, ..., N$ values. We will then calculate the weighted geometric mean of the n-gram precisions:

$$BLEU = BP \times exp\left(\sum_{i=1}^{N} w_n p_n\right)$$

Here, $w_n$ is the weight for the modified n-gram precision $p_n$. By default, equal weights are used for all n-gram values. In conclusion, BLEU calculates a modified-n-gram precision and penalizes the modified-n-gram precision with a brevity penalty. The modified n-gram precision avoids potential high precision values given to meaningless sentences (for example, candidate 2).

# Implementing an NMT from scratch – a German to English translator

Now we will implement an actual neural machine translator. We will be implementing the NMT using raw TensorFlow operations variables. The exercise is available in `ch10/neural_machine_translation.ipynb`. However, there is a sublibrary in TensorFlow, known as the `seq2seq` library. You can read more information about `seq2seq` as well as, learn to implement an NMT with `seq2seq` in the *Appendix, Mathematical Foundations and Advanced TensorFlow*.

The reason why we use raw TensorFlow is because, once you learn to implement a machine translator from scratch without using any helper functions, you will be able to quickly learn to use the `seq2seq` library. Furthermore, online resources are very scarce for learning to implement sequence-to-sequence models using raw TensorFlow. However, there are numerous resources/tutorials on how to use the `seq2seq` library for machine translation.

TensorFlow provides very informative sequence to sequence learning tutorials focused on NMT at `https://www.tensorflow.org/tutorials/seq2seq`.

# Introduction to data

We use English-German sentence pairs available at `https://nlp.stanford.edu/projects/nmt/`. There are ~4.5 million sentence pairs available. However, we will use only 250,000 sentence pairs due to computational feasibility. The vocabulary consists of the 50,000 most common English words and 50,000 most common German words, and the words not found in the vocabulary will be replaced with a special token, <unk>. Here, we will list example sentences found in the dataset:

```
DE:  Das Großunternehmen sieht sich einfach die Produkte des kleinen
Unternehmens an und unterstellt so viele Patentverletzungen , wie es
nur geht .

EN:  The large corporation will look at the products of the small
company and bring up as many patent infringement assertions as
possible .

DE:  In der ordentlichen Sitzung am 22. September 2008 befasste
sich der Aufsichtsrat mit strategischen Themen aus den einzelnen
Geschäftsbereichen wie der Positionierung des Kassamarktes im
Wettbewerb mit außerbörslichen Handelsplattformen , den Innovationen
im Derivatesegment und verschiedenen Aktivitäten im Nachhandelsbereich
.

EN:  At the regular meeting on 22 September 2008 , the Supervisory
Board dealt with strategic issues from the various business areas ,
such as the positioning of the cash market in competition with OTC
trading platforms , innovation in the derivatives segment and various
post ##AT##-##AT## trading activities .
```

# Preprocessing data

After you download the training data (`train.en` and `train.de`) as instructed in the exercise file, let's look at what's in these files. The `train.en` file contains English sentences, whereas `train.de` contains the corresponding German sentences. Next, we will select 250,000 sentence pairs from the large corpus that we have as data. We will also collect 100 sentences held out from the training data as our test data. Finally, the vocabularies for the two languages are found in `vocab.50K.en.txt` and `vocab.50K.de.txt`.

Then we will preprocess this data as explained earlier in the chapter. Reversing the sentences is optional for the word embedding learning (if performed separately), as reversing a sentence would not change the context of a given word. We will use the following simple tokenizing algorithm for tokenizing sentences into words. Essentially, we are introducing spaces before various punctuation marks so they can be tokenized to individual elements. Then for any word that is not found in the vocabulary, we will replace it with a special <unk> token. The is_source parameter tells if we're processing source sentences (is_source = True) or target sentences (is_source = False):

```
def split_to_tokens(sent,is_source):
    '''
    This function takes in a sentence (source or target)
    and preprocess the sentency with various steps
    (e.g. removing punctuation)
    '''

    global src_unk_count, tgt_unk_count

    # Remove punctuation and new-line chars
    sent = sent.replace(',',' ,')
    sent = sent.replace('.',' .')
    sent = sent.replace('\n',' ')

    sent_toks = sent.split(' ')
    for t_i, tok in enumerate(sent_toks):
        if is_source:
            # src_dictionary contain the word ->
            # word ID mapping for source vocabulary
            if tok not in src_dictionary.keys():
                if not len(tok.strip())==0:
                    sent_toks[t_i] = '<unk>'
                    src_unk_count += 1
        else:
            # tgt_dictionary contain the word ->
            # word ID mapping for target vocabulary
            if tok not in tgt_dictionary.keys():
                if not len(tok.strip())==0:
                    sent_toks[t_i] = '<unk>'
                    # print(tok)
                    tgt_unk_count += 1
    return sent_toks
```

# Learning word embeddings

Next we will move onto learning the word embeddings. To learn the word embeddings, we will use the **Continuous Bag-of-Words (CBOW)** model. However, you are welcome to experiment with other word embedding learning methods such as GloVe. We will not go through the code (found in the `word2vec.py` file), but share some of the learned word embeddings:

*German Word Embeddings*

```
Nearest to In: in, Aus, An, Neben, Bei, Mit, Trotz, Auf,
Nearest to war: ist, hat, scheint, wäre, hatte, bin, waren, kam,
Nearest to so: verbreitet, eigentlich, ausserdem, ziemlich, Rad-,
zweierlei, wollten, ebenso,
Nearest to Schritte: Meter, Minuten, Gehminuten, Autominuten, km,
Kilometer, Fahrminuten, Steinwurf,
Nearest to Sicht: Aussicht, Ausblick, Blick, Kombination, Milde,
Erscheinung, Terroranschläge, Ebenen,
```

*English Word Embeddings*

```
Nearest to more: cheaper, less, easier, better, further, greater,
bigger, More,
Nearest to States: Kingdom, Nations, accross, attrition, Efex,
Republic, authoritative, Sorbonne,
Nearest to Italy: Spain, Poland, France, Switzerland, Madrid,
Portugal, Fuengirola, 51,
Nearest to island: shores, Principality, outskirts, islands, skyline,
ear, continuation, capital,
Nearest to 2004: 2005, 2001, 2003, 2007, 1996, 2006, 1999, 1995,
```

It is possible to learn the embeddings simultaneously while training the machine translation system. Another alternative is to use the pretrained word embeddings. We will talk about how to do that later in the chapter.

# Defining the encoder and the decoder

We will use two separate LSTMs as the encoder and the decoder.

First, we will define hyperparameters:

- `batch_size`: You will have to be very careful when setting the batch size. Our NMT can take quite an amount of memory when running.
- `num_nodes`: This is the number of hidden units in the LSTM. A large `num_nodes` hyperparameter will result in better performance and a high computational cost.

- enc_num_unrollings: We set this to be the number of words in a source sentence. We will be unrolling the LSTM for the full length of the sentence at a single computation. The higher enc_num_unrollings is, the better your model will perform. However, this will slow down the algorithm.

- dec_num_unrollings: This is set to be the number of words in the target sentence. Higher dec_num_unrollings will also result in a better performance, but a large computational cost.

- embedding_size: This is the dimensionality of the vectors we learn. An embedding size of 100-300 will be adequate for most of the real-world problems that use word vectors.

Here we will define the hyperparameters:

```
# We set the input size by loading the saved word embeddings
# and getting the column size
tgt_emb_mat = np.load('en-embeddings.npy')
input_size = tgt_emb_mat.shape[1]

num_nodes = 128
batch_size = 10

# We unroll the full length at one go
# both source and target sentences
enc_num_unrollings = 40
dec_num_unrollings = 60
```

If you have a large batch size (on a standard laptop more than 20), you can run into issues such as the following:

Resource exhausted: OOM when allocating tensor with ...

In this case, you should reduce the batch size and rerun the code.

Next, we will define the weights and biases for the LSTMs and the softmax layer. We will use an encoder and decoder variable scope to make the naming of variables more intuitive. This is a standard LSTM cell, and we will not reiterate the weight definition.

Then we will define four TensorFlow placeholders for training:

- `enc_train_inputs`: This is a list of the `enc_num_unrollings` placeholder, where each placeholder is of the `[batch_size, input_size]` size. This is used to feed a batch of source language sentence to the encoder.

- `dec_train_inputs`: This is a list of the `dec_num_unrollings` placeholders, where each placeholder is of the `[batch_size, input_size]` size. This is used to feed the corresponding batch of the target language sentence.

- `dec_train_labels`: This is a list of the `dec_num_unrollings` placeholders, where each placeholder is of the `[batch_size, vocabulary_size]` size. This contains words of the `dec_train_inputs` offset by 1. So that two placeholders from `dec_train_inputs` and `dec_train_labels` with the same index in the list would have the $i^{th}$ word and the $i+1^{th}$ word.

- `dec_train_masks`: This is of the same size as `dec_train_inputs` and masks any element that has a `</s>` label from the loss calculation. This is important as there are many data points with the `</s>` token, as that is used for padding sentences to a fixed length:

```
for ui in range(dec_num_unrollings):
    dec_train_inputs.append(tf.placeholder(tf.float32,
        shape=[batch_size,input_size],
        name='dec_train_inputs_%d'%ui))
    dec_train_labels.append(tf.placeholder(tf.float32,
        shape=[batch_size,vocabulary_size],
        name = 'dec_train_labels_%d'%ui))
    dec_train_masks.append(tf.placeholder(tf.float32,
        shape=[batch_size,1],
        name='dec_train_masks_%d'%ui))

for ui in range(enc_num_unrollings):
    enc_train_inputs.append(tf.placeholder(tf.float32,
        shape=[batch_size,input_size],
        name='train_inputs_%d'%ui))
```

To initialize the weights of both the LSTM cells and the softmax layers, we will be using **Xavier initialization**, introduced by Glorot and Bengio in 2010 in their paper, *Understanding the difficulty of training deep feedforward neural networks, Proceedings of the 13th International Conference on Artificial Intelligence and Statistics (2010).* This is a principled initialization technique designed to alleviate the vanishing gradient problem in very deep networks. This is available through the `tf.contrib.layers.xavier_initializer()` variable initializer provided in TensorFlow. Specifically, in Xavier initialization, the weights of the $j^{th}$ layer of the neural network are initialized according to the uniform distribution, $U[a,b]$, where $a$ is the minimum value and $b$ is the maximum value:

$$W \sim U\left[-\frac{\sqrt{6}}{\sqrt{n_j + n_{j+1}}}, \frac{\sqrt{6}}{\sqrt{n_j + n_{j+1}}}\right]$$

Here, $n_j$ is the size of the $j^{th}$ layer.

# Defining the end-to-end output calculation

Here, with the variables and input/output placeholders defined, we will move onto defining output calculations from the encoder to the decoder and the loss function as well.

For the output, we will first calculate the LSTM cell state and the hidden state for all the words in a given batch of sentences. This is achieved by running a `for` loop, where in the $i^{th}$ iteration, we feed in the $i^{th}$ placeholder in `enc_train_inputs`, and the cell state and the output hidden state from the $i-1^{th}$ iteration. The `enc_lstm_cell` function works similarly to the `lstm_cell` function we saw in *Chapter 8, Applications of LSTM – Generating Text* and *Chapter 9, Applications of LSTM – Image Caption Generation*:

```
# Update the output and state of the encoder iteratively
for i in enc_train_inputs:
    output, state = enc_lstm_cell(i, output,state)
```

Next, we will calculate the output of the decoder for the whole target sentence similarly. However, in order to do that we should finish the calculations shown in the preceding code snippet so that we can obtain $v$ to initialize the decoder states with. This is achieved with the `tf.control_dependencies(...)` statement. So the nested commands within the `with` statement will only execute after the encoder output is fully calculated:

```
# With the computations of the enc_lstm_cell done,
# calculate the output and state of the decoder
with tf.control_dependencies([saved_output.assign(output),
                              saved_state.assign(state)]):
    # Calculate the decoder state and output iteratively
    for i in dec_train_inputs:
        output, state = dec_lstm_cell(i, output, state)
        outputs.append(output)
```

Then, after the decoder outputs are calculated, we will calculate the logits of the softmax layer using the hidden state of the LSTM as the input to the layer:

```
# Calculate the logits of the decoder for all unrolled steps
logits = tf.matmul(tf.concat(axis=0, values=outputs), w) + b
```

Now, with the logits calculated, we can calculate the loss. Note that we are using mask to mask out the elements that should not be contributing to the loss (that is, the </s> elements we append to make the sentence of fixed length):

```
loss_batch = tf.concat(axis=0,values=dec_train_masks) *
            tf.nn.softmax_cross_entropy_with_logits_v2(
                logits=logits, labels=tf.concat(axis=0,
                values=dec_train_labels))
loss = tf.reduce_mean(loss_batch)
```

Thereafter, unlike in previous chapters, we will use two optimizers: Adam and standard stochastic gradient descent. This is because using Adam in long run gave undesired results (for example, sudden large fluctuations of the BLEU score). We also use gradient clipping to avoid any gradient explosions.

```
# We use two optimizers: Adam and naive SGD
# using Adam in the long run produced undesirable results
# (e.g.) sudden fluctuations in BLEU
# Therefore we use Adam to get a good starting point for optimizing
# and then switch to SGD from that point onwards
with tf.variable_scope('Adam'):
    optimizer = tf.train.AdamOptimizer(learning_rate)
with tf.variable_scope('SGD'):
    sgd_optimizer = tf.train.GradientDescentOptimizer(sgd_learning_
rate)

# Calculates gradients with clipping for Adam
gradients, v = zip(*optimizer.compute_gradients(loss))
gradients, _ = tf.clip_by_global_norm(gradients, 5.0)
optimize = optimizer.apply_gradients(zip(gradients, v))
```

```
# Calculates gradients with clipping for SGD
sgd_gradients, v = zip(*sgd_optimizer.compute_gradients(loss))
sgd_gradients, _ = tf.clip_by_global_norm(sgd_gradients, 5.0)
sgd_optimize = optimizer.apply_gradients(zip(sgd_gradients, v))
```

We will use the following statement to ensure that the gradient flows correctly from the decoder to the encoder by making sure the gradient exists for all the trainable variables:

```
for (g_i,v_i) in zip(gradients,v):
    assert g_i is not None, 'Gradient none for %s'%(v_i.name)
```

Note that running the NMT will be much slower compared to previous exercises, and on a single GPU it can take more than 12 hours to run fully.

# Some translation results

These are results that we obtained after 10,000 steps:

```
DE:  &#124; Ferienwohnungen 1 Zi &#124; Ferienhäuser &#124; Landhäuser
&#124; Autovermietung &#124; Last Minute Angebote ! !

EN (TRUE):&#124; 1 Bedroom Apts &#124; Holiday houses &#124; Rural
Homes &#124; Car Rental &#124; Last Minute Offers !

EN (Predicted): Casino Tropez &#124; Club &#124; Club &#124;
Aparthotels Hotels &#124; Club &#124; Last Minute Offers &#124; Last
Minute Offers &#124; Last Minute Offers &#124; Last Minute Offers
&#124; Last Minute Offers ! </s>

DE: Wie hilfreich finden Sie die Demo ##AT##-##AT## CD ?

EN (TRUE): How helpful do you find the demo CD ##AT##-##AT## ROM ?

EN (Predicted): How to install the new version of XLSTAT ? </s>

DE:  Das „ Ladino di Fassa " ist jedoch mehr als ein Dialekt - es ist
eine richtige Sprache .

EN (TRUE):This is Ladin from Fassa which is more than a dialect : it
is a language in its own right .

EN (Predicted): The <unk> <unk> <unk> <unk> <unk> <unk> <unk> <unk>
<unk> <unk> <unk> <unk> <unk> <unk> <unk> <unk> <unk> <unk> <unk>
<unk> <unk> <unk> <unk> <unk> <unk> <unk> <unk> <unk> <unk> <unk>
<unk> <unk> <unk> <unk> <unk> <unk> <unk> <unk> <unk> <unk> <unk>
```

```
<unk> <unk> <unk> <unk> <unk> <unk> <unk> <unk> <unk> <unk> <unk>
<unk> <unk> <unk> <unk> <unk> <unk> <unk>
```

DE: **In der Hotelbeschreibung im Internet müßte die Zufahrt beschrieben werden .**

EN (TRUE): There are no adverse comments about this hotel at all .

EN (Predicted): The <unk> <unk> is a bit of the <unk> <unk> . </s>

We can see that the first sentence is recognized quite well. However, the second sentence is very poorly translated.

Also, here are the results obtained after 100,000 steps:

DE: **Das Hotel Opera befindet sich in der Nähe des Royal Theatre , Kongens Nytorv , ' Stroget ' und Nyhavn .**

EN (TRUE): Hotel Opera is situated near The Royal Theatre , Kongens Nytorv , " Strøget " and fascinating Nyhavn .

EN (Predicted): Best Western Hotel <unk> <unk> , <unk> , <unk> , <unk> , <unk> , <unk> , <unk> , <unk> , <unk> , <unk> , <unk> , <unk> , <unk> , <unk> , <unk> , <unk> , <unk> , <unk> , <unk> , <unk> , <unk> , <unk> , <unk> , <unk> , <unk> , <unk> , <unk> ,

DE: **Alle älteren Kinder oder Erwachsene zahlen EUR 32,00 pro Übernachtung und Person für Zustellbetten .**

EN (TRUE):All older children or adults are charged EUR 32.00 per night and person for extra beds .

EN (Predicted): All older children or adults are charged EUR 15 <unk> per night and person for extra beds . </s>

DE: **Im Allgemeinen basieren sie auf Datenbanken , Templates und Skripts .**

EN (TRUE):In general they are based on databases , template and scripts .

EN (Predicted): The user is the most important software of the software . </s>

DE: **Tux Racer wird Ihnen helfen , die Zeit totzuschlagen und sie können OpenOffice zum Arbeiten verwenden .**

```
EN (TRUE): Tux Racer will help you pass the time while you wait ,
and you can use OpenOffice for work .

EN (Predicted): <unk> .com we have a very friendly and helpful
staff . </s>
```

We can see that, even though the translations are not perfect, it most of the time captures the context of the source sentence, and our NMT is quite good at generating grammatically correct sentences.

*Figure 10.12* depicts the BLEU score over time for the NMT. There is a clear increase in the BLEU score for both train and test datasets over time:

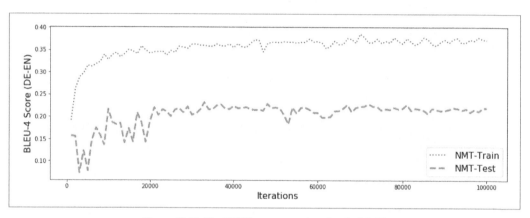

Figure 10.12: The BLEU score over time for the NMT

# Training an NMT jointly with word embeddings

Here we will discuss how we can train an NMT jointly with word embeddings. We will be covering two concepts in this section:

- Training an NMT jointly with a word embedding layer
- Using pretrained embeddings instead of randomly initializing the embeddings layer

There are several multilingual word embedding repositories available:

- Facebook's fastText: `https://github.com/facebookresearch/fastText/blob/master/pretrained-vectors.md`

- CMU multilingual embeddings: `http://www.cs.cmu.edu/~afm/projects/multilingual_embeddings.html`

From these, we will use the CMU embeddings (~200 MB) as it's much smaller compared with fastText (~5 GB). We first need to download the German (`multilingual_embeddings.de`) and English (`multilingual_embeddings.en`) embeddings. This is available as an exercise in `nmt_with_pretrained_wordvecs.ipynb` in the `ch10` folder.

# Maximizing matchings between the dataset vocabulary and the pretrained embeddings

We will first have to get a subset of the pretrained word embeddings that are relevant for the problem we're interested in solving. This is important as the vocabulary of pretrained word embeddings can be large and might contain lots of words that are not found in the dataset vocabulary. The pretrained word embeddings are a set of lines, where a line is a word and the word vector separated by spaces. An example line from pretrained embeddings might look like this:

```
door 0.283259492301 0.198089365764 0.335635845187 -0.385702777914
0.491404970211 ...
```

One obvious and naïve way of achieving this is to run through the pretrained dataset vocabulary line by line, and if the word in the current line matches any word in the dataset vocabulary, we will save that word embedding to be used in the future. However, this will be highly inefficient as usually a vocabulary tends to be biased toward various design decisions made by the creator. For example, some might consider *cat's*, *cat*, and *Cat* to be the same word, whereas others might consider them to be separate words. If we naïvely match pretrained word embedding vocabulary and the dataset vocabulary, we might miss many words. Therefore, will we use the following logic to make sure that we get most out of the pretrained word vectors.

First, we will define two NumPy arrays to hold the relevant word embeddings for both the source and target languages:

```
de_embeddings = np.random.uniform(size=(vocabulary_size, embeddings_
size),low=-1.0, high=1.0)
en_embeddings = np.random.uniform(size=(vocabulary_size, embeddings_
size),low=-1.0, high=1.0)
```

Then we will open the text file containing word vectors as shown here. The `filename` parameter is `multilingual_embeddings.de` for German and `miltilingual_embeddings.en` for English:

```
with open(filename,'r',encoding='utf-8') as f:
```

Next we will separate the word and the word vector by splitting the line by spaces:

```
line_tokens = line.split(' ')
lword = line_tokens[0]
vector = [float(v) for v in line_tokens[1:]]
```

We will also ignore if a word is empty (that is, has only spaces, tabs, or new line characters):

```
if len(lword.strip())==0:
    continue
```

We will also strip out any accents present in the words (especially in German words) to make sure that we will get the most chances of resulting in a match:

```
lword = unidecode.unidecode(lword)
```

Thereafter, we will use the following logic to check for matches. We will write a set of cascading conditions to check for matches, for both source and target languages:

1. First check whether the word from the pretrained embeddings (`lword`) is in the dataset vocabulary as it is

2. If not, check whether the first letter is capitalized (that is, *cat* becomes *Cat*), if found in the dataset vocabulary

3. If not, check whether the word from the pretrained embeddings (`lword`) is similar to any of the word results by removing special characters (for example, accents) from the dataset vocabulary words

If one of these conditions is satisfied, we will get that word embedding vector and assign it to the row indexed by the ID of that word (*word → ID*) mapping is stored in `src_dictionary` and `tgt_dictionary` for the two languages. We will do this for both the languages:

```
# Update the randomly initialized
# matrix for the embeddings
# Update the number of words
# matched with pretrained embeddings
try:
    dword = dictionary[lword]
    words_found_ids.append(dictionary[lword])
```

```
        embeddings[dictionary[lword],:] = vector
        words_found += 1

    # If a given word is not found in our vocabulary,
    except KeyError:
        try:
            # First try to match the same
            # with first letter capitalized
            # capitalized
            if len(lword)>0:
                firt_letter_cap = lword[0].upper()+lword[1:]

            else:
                continue

            # Update the word embeddings matrix
            dword = dictionary[firt_letter_cap]
            words_found_ids.append(dictionary[
                                firt_letter_cap])
            embeddings[dictionary[firt_letter_cap],:] = vector
            words_found += 1

        except KeyError:
            # If not found try to match the word with
            # the unaccented word
            try:
                dword = unaccented_dict[lword]
                words_found_ids.append(dictionary[lword])
                embeddings[dictionary[lword],:] = vector
                words_found += 1
            except KeyError:

                continue
```

# Defining the embeddings layer as a TensorFlow variable

We will define two trainable TensorFlow variables, for embedding layers (that is, `tgt_word_embeddings` and `src_word_embeddings`), as follows:

```
tgt_word_embeddings = tf.get_variable(
    'target_embeddings',shape=[vocabulary_size,
        embeddings_size],
    dtype=tf.float32, initializer = tf.constant_initializer(
```

```
        en_embeddings)
)
src_word_embeddings = tf.get_variable(
    'source_embeddings',shape=[vocabulary_size,
        embeddings_size],
    dtype=tf.float32, initializer = tf.constant_initializer(
        de_embeddings)
)
```

Then we will first change the dimensionality of the placeholders in `dec_train_inputs` and `enc_train_inputs` to be `[batch_size]` and the data type to `tf.int32`. This is so that we can use them to perform the embeddings lookup (`tf.nn.embedding_lookup(...)`) for each unrolled input as follows:

```
# Defining unrolled training inputs as well as embedding lookup
(Encoder)
for ui in range(enc_num_unrollings):
    enc_train_inputs.append(tf.placeholder(tf.int32,
                            shape=[batch_size],
                            name='train_inputs_%d'%ui))
    enc_train_input_embeds.append(tf.nn.embedding_lookup(
                            src_word_embeddings,
                            enc_train_inputs[ui]))


# Defining unrolled training inputs, embeddings,
# outputs, and masks (Decoder)
for ui in range(dec_num_unrollings):      dec_train_inputs.append(tf.
placeholder(tf.int32,
                            shape=[batch_size],
                            name='dec_train_inputs_%d'%ui))
    dec_train_input_embeds.append(tf.nn.embedding_lookup(
                            tgt_word_embeddings,
                            dec_train_inputs[ui]))
    dec_train_labels.append(tf.placeholder(tf.float32,
                            shape=[batch_size,vocabulary_size],
                            name = 'dec_train_labels_%d'%ui))
    dec_train_masks.append(tf.placeholder(tf.float32,
                            shape=[batch_size,1],
                            name='dec_train_masks_%d'%ui))
```

Then the LSTM cell computations for the encoder and decoder changes as shown here In this part, we first calculate the encoder LSTM cell output with the source sentence inputs. Next by using the final state information from the encoder as the initialization state for the decoder (that is, using `tf.control_dependencies(...)`) we compute the decoders output as well as the softmax logits and predictions:

```
# Update the output and state of the encoder iteratively
for i in enc_train_inputs:
    output, state = enc_lstm_cell(i, output,state)


print('Calculating Decoder Output')
# With the computations of the enc_lstm_cell done,
# calculate the output and state of the decoder
with tf.control_dependencies([saved_output.assign(output),
                            saved_state.assign(state)]):
    # Calculate the decoder state and output iteratively
    for i in dec_train_inputs:
        output, state = dec_lstm_cell(i, output, state)
        outputs.append(output)
```

Note that, the exercise file has a slightly different output calculation than shown here. Instead of feeding in the previous prediction as input, we feed in the true word as the input. This tends to deliver better performance than feeding in the previous prediction, and will be discussed in detail in the next section. However the overall idea remains the same.

The final steps include, computing the loss for the decoder and defining an optimizer to optimize the model parameters, as we saw earlier.

Finally we outline the computational graph for the implementation of our NMT. Here we visualize the computational graph for our model.

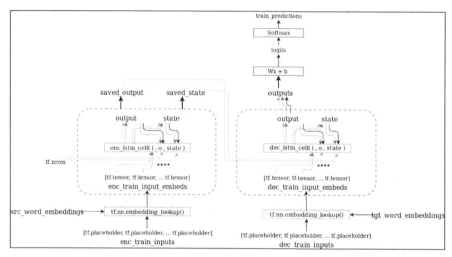

Figure: 10.13: Computational graph of the NMT system with pretrained embeddings

# Improving NMTs

As you can see from the preceding results, our translation model is not behaving ideally. These results were obtained by running the optimization for more than 12 hours on a single NVIDIA 1080 Ti GPU. Also note that this is not even the full dataset, we only used 250,000 sentence pairs for training. However, if you type something into Google Translate, which uses the **Google Neural Machine Translation (GNMT)** system, the translation almost always looks very realistic with only minor mistakes. So it is important to know how we can improve the model so that it can produce better results. In this section, we will discuss several ways of improving NMTs such as teacher forcing, deep LSTMs, and attention mechanism.

# Teacher forcing

As we discussed in the *Training the NMT* section, we do the following to train the NMT:

- First, we fed the full encoder sentence to obtain the final state outputs of the encoder
- We then set the final states of the encoder to be the initial state of the decoder
- We also asked the decoder to predict the full target sentence without any additional information except for the last state output of the encoder

This can be too difficult of a task for the model. We can understand this phenomenon as follows. Say, a teacher asks a kindergarten student to complete the following sentence, given just the first word:

*I ___ ___ ___ ___ ___ ___*

This means that the child needs to pick a subject; verb; and an object, know the syntax of the language, understand the grammar rules of the language, and so on. Therefore, the tendency for the child to produce an incorrect sentence is high.

However, if we ask the child to produce it word-by-word they might do a better job at coming up with a sentence. In other words, we ask the child to produce the next word given the following:

*I ___*

Then we ask them to fill the blank given:

*I like ___*

And continue in the same fashion:

*I like to ___, I like to fly ___, I like to fly kites ___*

This way, the child can do a better job at producing a correct and meaningful sentence. This phenomenon is known as **teacher forcing**. We can adopt the same approach to alleviate the difficulty of the translation task, as shown in *Figure 10.13*:

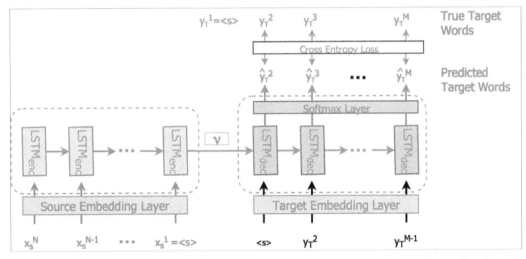

Figure 10.14: The teacher forcing mechanism. The darker arrows in the inputs depict newly introduced input connections to the decoder. The right-hand side figure shows how the decoder LSTM cell changes.

As shown in bold in the figure, the inputs to the decoder have been replaced with actual target words in the training data. Therefore NMT decoder no longer has to carry the burden of predicting a whole target sentence given the source sentence. Rather, the decoder only has to predict the current word correctly, given the previous word. Something worth noting is that, we discussed the training procedure without any details about teacher forcing, in the previous discussion. However, we actually use teacher forcing in all the exercises for this chapter.

# Deep LSTMs

One obvious improvement we can do is to increase the number of layers by stacking LSTMs on top of each other, thereby creating a *deep LSTM* (see *Figure 10.14*). For example, the Google NMT system uses eight LSTM layers stacked upon each other (*Google's Neural Machine Translation System: Bridging the Gap between Human and Machine Translation, Wu and others, Technical Report (2016)*). Though this hampers the computational efficiency, having more layers greatly improves the neural network's ability to learn the syntax and other linguistic characteristics of the two languages.

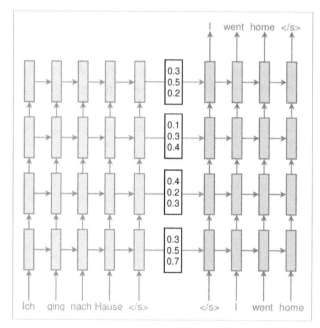

Figure 10.15: An illustration of a deep LSTM

# Attention

Attention is one of the key breakthroughs in machine translation that gave rise to better working NMT systems. Attention allows the decoder to access the full state history of the encoder, leading to creating a richer representation of the source sentence, at the time of translation. Before delving into the details of an attention mechanism, let's understand one of the crucial bottlenecks in our current NMT system and the benefit of attention in dealing with it.

# Breaking the context vector bottleneck

As you have probably already guessed, the bottleneck is the context vector, or thought vector, that resides between the encoder and the decoder (see *Figure 10.15*):

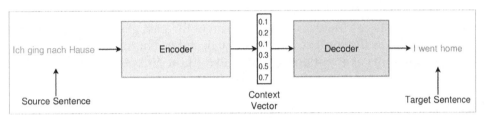

Figure 10.16: The encoder-decoder architecture

To understand why this is a bottleneck, let's imagine translating the following English sentence:

*I went to the flower market to buy some flowers*

This translates to the following:

*Ich ging zum Blumenmarkt, um Blumen zu kaufen*

If we are to compress this into a fixed length vector, the resulting vector needs to contain these:

- Information about the subject (*I*)
- Information about the verbs (*buy* and *went*)
- Information about the objects (*flowers* and *flower market*)
- Interaction of the subjects, verbs, and objects with each other in the sentence

Generally, the context vector has a size of 128 or 256 elements. This is a very impractical and an extremely difficult requirement for the system. Therefore, most of the time, the context vector fails to provide the complete information required to make a good translation. This results in an underperforming decoder that suboptimally translates a sentence.

Furthermore, during the decoding, the context vector is observed only in the beginning. Thereafter, the decoder LSTM must memorize the context vector until the end of the translation. Though LSTMs are good at long-term memorizing, practically they are limited. This will heavily affect outcomes, especially for long sentences.

This is where attention comes in handy. With the attention mechanism, the decoder will have access to the full state history of the encoder for each decoding time step. This allows the decoder to have access to a very rich representation of the source sentence. Furthermore, the attention mechanism introduces a softmax layer that allows the decoder to calculate a weighted mean of the past observed encoder states, which will be used as the context vector for the decoder. This allows the decoder to pay different amounts of attention to different words at different decoding steps.

# The attention mechanism in detail

Now let's investigate the actual implementation of the attention mechanism in detail. We will use the attention mechanism detailed in the paper, *Neural Machine Translation by Learning to Jointly Align and Translate, Bahdanau, Cho,* and *Bengio, arXiv:1409.0473 (2014)*. For consistency with the paper, we will use the following notations:

- Encoder's hidden state: $h_i$
- Target sentence words: $y_i$
- Decoder's hidden state: $s_i$
- Context vector: $c_i$

So far, our decoder LSTM was composed of an input $y_i$ and a hidden state $s_{i-1}$. We will ignore the cell state as this is an internal part of the LSTM. This can be represented as follows:

$$LSTM_{dec} = f\left(y_i, s_{i-1}\right)$$

Here, $f$ represents the actual update rules used to calculate $y_{i+1}$ and $s_i$. With the attention mechanism, we are introducing a new time-dependent context vector $c_i$ for the $i^{th}$ decoding step. The $c_i$ vector is a weighted mean of the hidden states of all the unrolled encoder steps. A higher weight will be given to the $j^{th}$ hidden state of the encoder if the $j^{th}$ word is more important for translating the $i^{th}$ word in the target language. Now the decoder LSTM becomes this:

$$LSTM_{dec} = f\left(y_i, s_{i-1}, c_i\right)$$

Conceptually, attention mechanism can be thought of as a separate layer and illustrated as in *Figure 10.16*. As shown, the attention functions as a layer. The attention layer is responsible for producing $c_i$ for the $i^{th}$ time step of the decoding process:

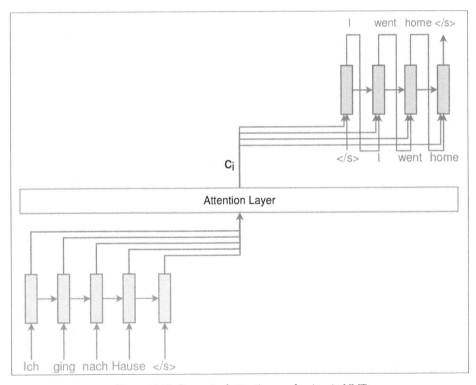

Figure 10.17: Conceptual attention mechanism in NMT

Let's now see how to calculate $c_i$:

$$c_i = \sum_{j=1}^{L} \alpha_{ij} h_j$$

Here, $L$ is the number of words in the source sentence, and, $\alpha_{ij}$ is a normalized weight representing the importance of the $j^{th}$ encoder hidden state for calculating the $i^{th}$ decoder prediction. This is calculated using a softmax layer. $L$ is the length of the encoder sentence:

$$\alpha_{ij} = \frac{exp\left(e_{ij}\right)}{\sum_{k=1}^{L} exp\left(e_{ik}\right)}$$

Here, $e_{ij}$ is the *energy* or *importance* measuring how much the $j^{th}$ hidden state of the encoder and to the previous decoder state $s_{i-1}$ contributes to calculating $s_i$:

$$e_{ij} = v_a^T tanh\left(W_a s_{i-1} + U_a h_j\right)$$

This essentially means that $e_{ij}$ is calculated with a multilayer perceptron whose weights are $v_a$, $W_a$, and $U_a$ and $s_{i-1}$ and $h_j$ are the inputs to the network. The attention mechanism is shown in *Figure 10.17*:

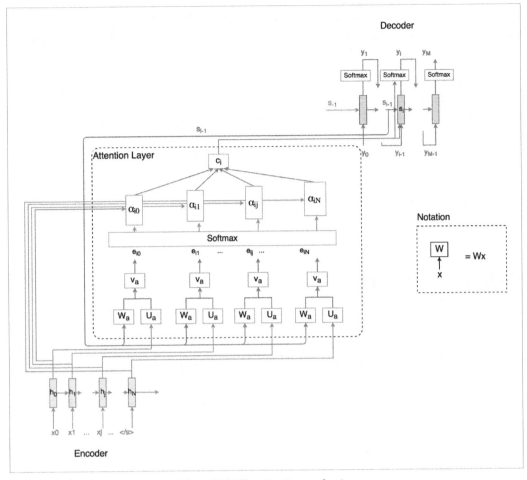

Figure 10.18: The attention mechanism

# Implementing the attention mechanism

Here we will discuss how we can implement the attention mechanism. Two major changes the system will go through are as follows:

- More parameters (that is, weights) will be introduced (for calculating attention and using attention as an input to the decoder LSTM cell)

- A new function for attention related computations will be introduced (that is, `attn_layer`)

- Changes to decoder LSTM cell computation to take the attention-weighted sum of all the encoder LSTM cell outputs as an input

We will only be discussing the additional things introduced compared to the standard NMT model. You can find the full exercise for NMT with attention in the `neural_machine_translation_attention.ipynb`.

# Defining weights

Three new sets of weights will be introduced to implement the attention mechanism. All these weights are used to calculate the *energy* term (that is, $e_{ij}$) we discussed earlier:

```
W_a = tf.Variable(tf.truncated_normal([num_nodes,num_nodes],
    stddev=0.05),name='W_a')
U_a = tf.Variable(tf.truncated_normal([num_nodes,num_nodes],
    stddev=0.05),name='U_a')
v_a = tf.Variable(tf.truncated_normal([num_nodes,1],
    stddev=0.05),name='v_a')
```

Also, we will define a new set of weights that will be used to take $c_i$ as an input to the $i^{th}$ step of unrolling of the decoder:

```
dec_ic = tf.get_variable('ic',shape=[num_nodes, num_nodes],
    initializer = tf.contrib.layers.xavier_initializer())
dec_fc = tf.get_variable('fc',shape=[num_nodes, num_nodes],
    initializer = tf.contrib.layers.xavier_initializer())
dec_cc = tf.get_variable('cc',shape=[num_nodes, num_nodes],
    initializer = tf.contrib.layers.xavier_initializer())
dec_oc = tf.get_variable('oc',shape=[num_nodes, num_nodes],
    initializer = tf.contrib.layers.xavier_initializer())
```

# Computing attention

For computing attention values for each position of the encoder and decoder, we will define a function that does that for us, attn_layer(...). This method calculates attention for all the positions (that is,the num_enc_unrollings) of the encoder, for a single unrolling step of the decoder. The attn_layer(...) method takes two arguments as parameters to the function:

```
attn_layer(h_j_unrolled, s_i_minus_1)
```

The parameters are as follows:

- h_i_unrolled: These are the num_enc_unrolling encoder LSTM cell outputs we calculated during feeding in the source sentence to the encoder. This will be a list of the num_enc_unrolling tensors, where each tensor is [batch_size, num_nodes] sized.

- s_i_minus_1: The pervious decoder's LSTM cell output. This will be a tensor of the [batch_size, num_nodes] size.

First we will create a single tensor with the list of unrolled encoder outputs of the [num_enc_unrollings * batch_size, num_nodes] size:

```
enc_logits = tf.concat(axis=0,values=h_j_unrolled)
```

Then we will calculate $W_a s_{i-1}$ with the following operation:

```
# of size [enc_num_unroll x batch_size, num_nodes]
w_a_mul_s_i_minus_1 = tf.matmul(enc_outputs,W_a)
```

Next we will calculate $U_a h_j$:

```
# of size [enc_num_unroll x batch_size, num_nodes]
u_a_mul_h_j = tf.matmul(tf.tile(s_i_minus_1,[enc_num_
unrollings,1]), U_a)
```

Now we will calculate *energy* as $e_{ij} = v_a^T tanh\left(W_a s_{i-1} + U_a h_j\right)$. This is a tensor of the [enc_num_unroll * batch_size ,1] size:

```
e_j = tf.matmul(tf.nn.tanh(w_a_mul_s_i_minus_1 +
    u_a_mul_h_j),v_a)
```

We can now first break the large `e_j` to the `enc_num_unrolling` long list of tensors with `tf.split(...)`, where each tensor is of the `[batch_size, 1]` size. Thereafter, we concatenate this list along axis 1 to produce a tensor of the `[batch_size, enc_num_unrollings]` size (that is, `reshaped_e_j`). Therefore, a single row of `reshaped_e_j` will correspond to the attention values for all the positions of the encoder's unrolled timesteps:

```
# list of enc_num_unroll elements, each
# element [batch_size, 1]
batched_e_j = tf.split(axis=0,
    num_or_size_splits=enc_num_unrollings,value=e_j)
# of size [batch_size, enc_num_unroll]
reshaped_e_j = tf.concat(axis=1,values=batched_e_j)
```

We can now easily calculate the normalized attention values for `reshaped_e_j`. The values will be normalized across the unrolled time steps (axis 1 of `reshaped_e_j`):

```
# of size [batch_size, enc_num_unroll]
alpha_i = tf.nn.softmax(reshaped_e_j)
```

This is followed by breaking `alpha_i` into a list of `enc_num_unroll` tensors, each of the `[batch_size,1]` size:

```
alpha_i_list = tf.unstack(alpha_i,axis=1)
```

Afterwards, we will calculate the weighted sum of each of the encoder outputs (that is, `h_j_unrolled`) and assign this to `c_i`, which will be used as an input to the $i^{th}$ time step of unrolling, of the decoder LSTM cell:

```
c_i_list =  [tf.reshape(alpha_i_list[e_i],
    [-1,1])*h_j_unrolled[e_i] for e_i in range(enc_num_
unrollings)]
    c_i = tf.add_n(c_i_list) # of size [batch_size, num_nodes]
```

Then to take `c_i` as an input to the $i^{th}$ step of unrolling of the decoder LSTM cell, the decoder LSTM cell computation changes as follows:

```
# Definition of the cell computation (Decoder)
def dec_lstm_cell(i, o, state, c):
    """Create a LSTM cell"""
    input_gate = tf.sigmoid(tf.matmul(i, dec_ix) + tf.matmul(o, dec_
im) +
                tf.matmul(c, dec_ic) + dec_ib)
    forget_gate = tf.sigmoid(tf.matmul(i, dec_fx) + tf.matmul(o, dec_
fm) +
                tf.matmul(c, dec_fc) + dec_fb)
    update = tf.matmul(i, dec_cx) + tf.matmul(o, dec_cm) +
```

```
                tf.matmul(c, dec_cc) +dec_cb
        state = forget_gate * state + input_gate * tf.tanh(update)
        output_gate = tf.sigmoid(tf.matmul(i, dec_ox) + tf.matmul(o, dec_
om) +
                    tf.matmul(o, dec_oc) + dec_ob)
        return output_gate * tf.tanh(state), state
```

# Some translation results – NMT with attention

Here are the results we obtained after 10,000 steps:

**DE: &#124; Ferienwohnungen 1 Zi &#124; Ferienhäuser &#124; Landhäuser &#124; Autovermietung &#124; Last Minute Angebote ! !**

EN (TRUE):&#124; 1 Bedroom Apts &#124; Holiday houses &#124; Rural Homes &#124; Car Rental &#124; Last Minute Offers !

EN (Predicted): &#124; Apartments &#124; Hostels &#124; Hostels &#124; Last Minute Offers ! </s>

**DE: Wie hilfreich finden Sie die Demo ##AT##-##AT## CD ?**

EN (TRUE): How helpful do you find the demo CD ##AT##-##AT## ROM ?

EN (Predicted): How can you find the XLSTAT ##AT##-##AT## MX ? </s>

**DE: Das „ Ladino di Fassa " ist jedoch mehr als ein Dialekt - es ist eine richtige Sprache .**

EN (TRUE):This is Ladin from Fassa which is more than a dialect : it is a language in its own right .

EN (Predicted): The <unk> " is a very important role in the world . </s>

**DE: In der Hotelbeschreibung im Internet müßte die Zufahrt beschrieben werden .**

EN (TRUE): There are no adverse comments about this hotel at all .

EN (Predicted): The <unk> <unk> is the <unk> of the Internet . </s>

Similar to what we observed earlier, the NMT with attention is good at translating some sentences, but poor at translating others.

Also, these are the results obtained after 100,000 steps:

```
DE: Das Hotel Opera befindet sich in der Nähe des Royal Theatre ,
Kongens Nytorv , &apos; Stroget &apos; und Nyhavn .

EN (TRUE): Hotel Opera is situated near The Royal Theatre , Kongens
Nytorv , &quot; Strøget &quot; and fascinating Nyhavn .

EN (Predicted): Best Western Hotel <unk> <unk> , <unk> , <unk> ,
<unk> , <unk> , <unk> , <unk> , <unk> , <unk> , <unk> , <unk> , <unk>
, <unk> , <unk> , <unk> , <unk> , <unk> , <unk> , <unk> , <unk> ,
<unk> , <unk> , <unk> , <unk> , <unk> , <unk> , <unk> , <unk> ,

DE:  Alle älteren Kinder oder Erwachsene zahlen EUR 32,00 pro
Übernachtung und Person für Zustellbetten .

EN (TRUE):All older children or adults are charged EUR 32.00 per night
and person for extra beds .

EN (Predicted): All older children or adults are charged EUR 15 <unk>
per night and person for extra beds . </s>

DE:  Im Allgemeinen basieren sie auf Datenbanken , Templates und
Skripts .

EN (TRUE):In general they are based on databases , template and
scripts .

EN (Predicted): The user is the most important software of the
software . </s>

DE: Tux Racer wird Ihnen helfen , die Zeit totzuschlagen und sie
können OpenOffice zum Arbeiten verwenden .

EN (TRUE): Tux Racer will help you pass the time while you wait ,
and you can use OpenOffice for work .

EN (Predicted): <unk> .com we have a very friendly and helpful
staff . </s>
```

We have used the same set of test sentences we used to evaluate the standard NMT for easier comparison. We can see that the NMT with attention model provides much better translations compared to the standard NMT. But still there is the possibility of getting some translations wrong, as we use limited amount of data.

*Figure 10.18* depicts the BLEU score over time for the NMT and NMT with attention, side by side. We can clearly see that the NMT with attention gives a better BLEU score in both training and test data:

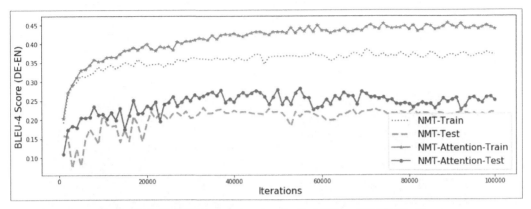

Figure 10.19: The BLEU score over time for the NMT and NMT+Attention

 According to 2017 results, the current state of the art BLEU score for German to English translation is 35.1 (*The University of Edinburgh's Neural MT Systems for WMT17 by Rico Sennrich and others arXiv preprint arXiv:1708.00726 (2017)*)

# Visualizing attention for source and target sentences

In *Figure 10.19*, we can visualize how the attention values look for different source words for a given target word for several source to target translation pairs. If you remember, when calculating attention, we had the `enc_num_unrollings` attention values for a given position of the decoder. Therefore, if you concatenate all the attention vectors for all the positions in the decoder, you can create an **attention matrix**.

In the attention matrix, we have target words as rows and source words as columns. A higher (lighter) value for some rows and columns indicates that when predicting the target word found in that row, the decoder mostly paid attention to the source word given by the column. For example, you can see that `Hotel` in the target sentence is highly correlated with `Hotel` in the source sentence:

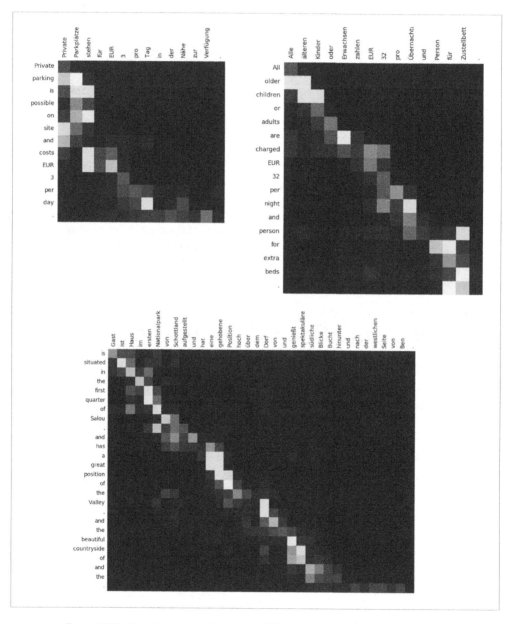

Figure 10.20: Attention matrices for several different source-target translation pairs

This brings us to the end of our discussion about NMT. We discussed the basic encoder-decoder architecture used in NMT as well as discussing how to evaluate NMT systems. Then we discussed several ways to improve NMT systems such as teacher forcing, using deep LSTMs, and the attention mechanism.

It is important to understand that NMT has a wide variety of use cases in the real world. One of the obvious use cases is for international businesses having branches spread out in many countries. In such businesses, employees from different countries need to have faster ways of communicating without making language a barrier. Therefore, automatically translating emails from one language to another can be very useful for such a company. Next, in manufacturing, MT can be used to produce multilingual product descriptions/user-manuals of products. Then experts can perform light post-processing to make sure the translations are accurate. Finally, MT can come in handy for day-to-day tasks, such as multilingual translations. Say, the user is not a native English speaker and needs to search for something that they don't know how to fully describe in English. In that case, the user can write a multilingual search query. Then the MT system can translate the query to different languages and search resources on the internet that matches the user's search request.

# Other applications of Seq2Seq models – chatbots

One other popular application of sequence to sequence models is in creating chatbots. A chatbot is a computer program that is able to make a realistic conversation with a human. Such applications are very useful for companies with a huge customer base. Responding to the customers asking basic questions for which answers are obvious accounts for a significant portion of customer support requests. A chatbot can serve customers with basic concerns when it is able to find an answer. Also, if the chatbot is unable to answer a question, the request gets redirected to a human operator. Chatbots can save lot of the time that human operators spend answering basic concerns and let them attend to more difficult tasks.

# Training a chatbot

So, how can we use a sequence-to-sequence model to train a chatbot? The answer is quite straightforward as we have already learned about the machine translation model. The only difference would be how the source and target sentence pairs are formed.

In the NMT system, the sentence pairs consist of a source sentence and the corresponding translation in a target language for that sentence. However, in training a chatbot, the data is extracted from the dialogue between two people. The source sentences would be the sentences/phrases uttered by person A, and the target sentences would be the replies to person A made by person B. Here is an example of this. This data consists of movie dialogues between people and is found at https://www.cs.cornell.edu/~cristian/Cornell_Movie-Dialogs_Corpus.html.

> BIANCA: *They do not!*
>
> CAMERON: *They do to!*
>
> BIANCA: *I hope so.*
>
> CAMERON: *She okay?*
>
> BIANCA: *Let's go.*
>
> CAMERON: *Wow*
>
> BIANCA: *Okay -- you're gonna need to learn how to lie.*
>
> CAMERON: *No*
>
> BIANCA: *I'm kidding. You know how sometimes you just become this "persona"? And you don't know how to quit?*
>
> BIANCA: *Like my fear of wearing pastels?*
>
> CAMERON: *The "real you".*

Here are links to several other datasets for training conversational chatbots:

- Reddit comments dataset: `https://www.reddit.com/r/datasets/comments/3bxlg7/i_have_every_publicly_available_reddit_comment/`
- Maluuba dialogue dataset: `https://datasets.maluuba.com/Frames`
- Ubuntu dialogue corpus: `http://dataset.cs.mcgill.ca/ubuntu-corpus-1.0/`
- NIPS conversational intelligence challenge: `http://convai.io/`
- Microsoft research social media text corpus: `https://tinyurl.com/y7ha9rc5`

*Figure 10.20* shows the similarity of a chatbot system to an NMT system. For example, we train a chatbot with a dataset consisting of dialogues between two people. The encoder takes in the sentences/phrases spoken by one person, where the decoder is trained to predict the other person's response. After training in such a way, we can use the chatbot to provide a response to a given question:

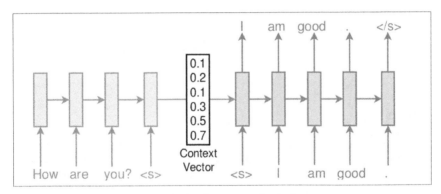

Figure 10.21: Illustration of a chatbot

# Evaluating chatbots – Turing test

The Turing test was invented by Alan Turing in the 1950s as a way of measuring the intelligence of a machine. The experiment settings are well-suited for evaluating chatbots. The experiment is set up as follows.

There are three parties involved: an evaluator (that is, a human) (**A**), another human (**B**), and a machine (**C**). The three of them sit in three different rooms so that none of them can see the others. The only communication medium is text, which is typed into a computer by one party, and the receiver sees the text on a computer on their side. The evaluator communicates with both the human and the machine. And at the end of the conversation, the evaluator is to distinguish the machine from the human. If the evaluator cannot make the distinction, the machine is said to have passed the Turing test. This setup is illustrated in *Figure 10.21*:

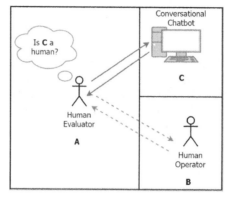

Figure 10.22: The Turing test

# Summary

In this chapter, we talked in detail about NMT systems. Machine translation is the task of translating a given text corpus from a source language to a target language. First we talked about the history of machine translation briefly to build a sense of appreciation for what has gone into machine translation, to become what it is today. We saw that today the highest performing machine translation systems are actually NMT systems. Next we talked about the fundamental concept of these systems and decomposed the model into the embedding layer, the encoder, the context vector, and the decoder. We first established the benefit of having an embedding layer as it gives semantic representations of words compared to one-hot-encoded vectors. Then we understood the objective of the encoder, which is to learn a good fixed dimensional vector that represents the source sentence. Next, once the fixed dimensional context vector was learned, we used this to initialize the decoder. The decoder is responsible for producing the actual translation of the source sentence. Then we discussed how the training and the inference work in the NMT systems.

Then we looked at an actual implementation of an NMT system that translates sentences from German to English to understand the internal mechanisms of the NMT system. Here we looked at an NMT system implemented using basic TensorFlow operations, as this gives us an in-depth understanding of the step-by-step execution of the system, compared with using off-the-shelf libraries such as seq2seq in TensorFlow. Then we learned that the context vector causes a bottleneck in the system as the system is forced to embed all the knowledge in the source sentence to a fixed dimensional (comparatively small) vector. Due to the difficulty of the task the system underperforms, we moved on to learning a technique that avoids this bottleneck: the attention mechanism. Instead of depending solely on the fixed-dimensional vector for learning translations, the attention mechanism, allows the decoder to observe full state history of the encoder at each decoding step, allowing the decoder to form a rich context vector. We saw that this technique allows NMT systems to perform much better.

Finally, we talked about another popular application of sequence-to-sequence learning: chatbots. Chatbots are machine learning applications that are able to make realistic conversation with a human and even answer questions. We saw that NMT systems and chatbots work similarly, and only the training data is the difference. We also discussed the Turing test, which is a qualitative test that can be used to evaluate chatbots.

In the next chapter, we will discuss the various future trends in NLP.

# 11

# Current Trends and the Future of Natural Language Processing

In this chapter, we will discuss the latest trends in NLP and what the future will be like. In the first section, we will talk about the latest trends in NLP. Improving the existing models is a key part of the latest trends. This includes improving the performance of existing models (for example, the word embeddings and machine translation systems).

The rest of the chapter is about the novel areas emerging recently in the field of NLP. We will be driving our discussion into five different subareas, drawing on unique and instructive papers from the discipline. First we will see how NLP has ventured into other research fields, such as computer vision and reinforcement learning. Next we will discuss several novel attempts that have been made to achieve **Artificial General Intelligence** (**AGI**) in NLP, by training a single model to perform several NLP tasks. We will also look at some of the new tasks emerging in the realm of NLP, such as detecting sarcasm and language grounding. Then we will see how NLP is being used in social media, especially in mining social media for information. Finally, we will learn about some new time-series learning models that have appeared recently, such as Phased LSTMs. For example, Phased LSTMs are much better at identifying specific events happening over very long periods of time.

To summarize, we will be talking about the latest NLP trends, and then, the most important emerging innovations:

- Current trends in NLP
- Penetration of NLP into other fields
- Advances in AGI in terms of NLP

- Emerging Novel NLP tasks
- NLP for social media
- Better time-series models

> Most of the material in this chapter pertaining to current trends and new directions is based on scholarly papers from within the discipline. We have referenced all the primary sources to credit the authors and provide resources for further reading. In-text references include a bracketed number that correlates with the numbering in the *References* section at the end of the chapter.

# Current trends in NLP

In this section, we will talk about current trends in NLP. These trends are from the NLP research conducted between 2012 and early 2018. First let's talk about the current states of word embeddings. Word embeddings is a crucial topic as we have already seen many interesting tasks that rely on word embeddings to perform well. We will then look at important improvements in NMT.

# Word embeddings

Many variants of word embeddings have emerged over time. With the inception of high-quality word embeddings (refer to *Distributed representations of words and phrases and their compositionality, Mikolov and others* [1]) in NLP, it can be said that NLP had a resurgence, where many took an interest in using word embeddings in various NLP tasks (for example, sentiment analysis, machine translation, and question answering). Also, there have been many attempts to improve word embeddings, leading to even better embeddings. The four models that we'll introduce are in the areas of region embedding, probabilistic word embedding, meta-embedding, and topic embedding.

# Region embedding

The **tv-embedding** (short for, **two-view embedding**) model was introduced in Rie Johnson and Tong Zhang's paper, *Semi-supervised Convolutional Neural Networks for Text Categorization via Region Embedding* [2]. This approach is different from word embeddings, as these are region-embeddings where they embed a region of a text into a fixed dimensional vector. For example, unlike in word embedding, where we had a vector for each word (for example, *cat*), with tv-embedding, we have embeddings for phrases (for example, *the cat sat on a mat*). An embedding is called a two-view embedding if it preserves the information required to predict a view (that is, a word or a region) from another view (that is, a context word or context region).

# Input representation

Let's now look at the details of this approach. A tv-embedding system would look like *Figure 11.1*. First, a numerical representation of regions of words is found. For example, consider the following phrase:

*very good drama*

This can be represented as shown here:

*very good drama* | *very good drama* | *very good drama*

| 1 | 0 | 0 | 0 | 1 | 0 | 0 | 0 | 1 |

This is called a **sequence one-hot-encoded vector**. Alternatively, it can be represented as shown here:

*very good drama*

| 1 | 1 | 1 |

This is called the **Bag-of-Words (BOW)** representation. We can see that the BOW representation is more compact and does not grow with the phrase size. However, note that this representation loses contextual information. Note that BOW is the feature representation we use to represent words or text phrases. This is not related to the CBOW word embedding learning algorithm we discussed in *Chapter 3, Word2vec – Learning Word Embeddings*.

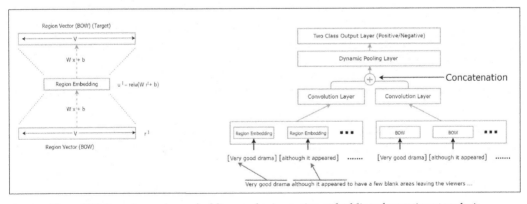

Figure 11.1: Learning region embeddings and using region embeddings for sentiment analysis

# Learning region embeddings

We learn region embeddings the same way we learned word embeddings. We feed in an input containing a text region and ask the model to predict the target context region. For example, we use a region size of three for the phrase:

*very good drama I enjoyed it*

Then, for the input we use this:

*very good drama*

The output (target) will be as follows:

*I enjoyed it*

As an exercise, we will see if the learned region embeddings help to improve sentiment analysis tasks. For this, we will use the dataset found at http://ai.stanford.edu/~amaas/data/sentiment/. This is a text corpus containing IMDB movie reviews. We will first learn useful region embeddings by training an embedding layer to predict the context region correctly for a given input text region. Then we will use these embeddings as an *additional* input to the sentiment analysis network. This is available as an exercise in tv_embeddings.ipynb in the ch11 folder.

# Implementation – region embeddings

For this example, we will use 400 positive and 400 negative samples from the dataset as our training data. We will also set up a held-out validation set consisting of roughly 150 positive and 150 negative samples. We will only gloss over this implementation and not discuss the specific details. You can refer to the exercise file for more details.

First, for learning region embeddings, we will define a fully connected set of weights and a bias:

```
w1 = tf.get_variable('w1', shape=[vocabulary_size,500],
    initializer = tf.contrib.layers.xavier_initializer_conv2d())
b1 = tf.get_variable('b1',shape=[500],
    initializer = tf.random_normal_initializer(stddev=0.05))
```

Next, using the weights and bias, we will calculate the hidden value that has rectified linear units, which is a type of nonlinearity we use in neural networks:

```
h = tf.nn.relu(
    tf.matmul(train_dataset,w1) + b1
)
```

Then we will define another set of weights and bias, which acts as the top regression layer. The top layer predicts the BOW representation of the context region, for a given text region:

```
w = tf.get_variable('linear_w', shape=[500, vocabulary_size],
    initializer= tf.contrib.layers.xavier_initializer())
b = tf.get_variable('linear_b', shape=[vocabulary_size],
    initializer= tf.random_normal_initializer(stddev=0.05))
```

We will next calculate the final output:

```
out =tf.matmul(h,w)+b
```

We will now define loss. Loss is a mean squared error between the predicted context region BOW and the true context BOW. We will use `train_mask` to mask some of the nonexisting words (*0s* in the true BOW representation), similar to the negative sampling method we discussed in *Chapter 3, Word2vec – Learning Word Embeddings*.

```
loss = tf.reduce_mean(tf.reduce_sum(train_mask*(
    out - train_labels)**2,axis=1))
```

Finally, we will use the optimizer to optimize the defined loss:

```
optimizer = tf.train.AdamOptimizer(
        learning_rate = 0.0005).minimize(loss)
```

Then we will use the learned embeddings as an additional input to classify text, as shown in *Figure 11.1*. For this, we will concatenate region embeddings sequentially for all the text regions found in a given review. We will do the same for the BOW inputs. Then we will convolve over the concatenated vectors (that is, the region embedding and BOW vectors) in parallel and concatenate the convolution outputs. Next we will feed the concatenated convolution output into the top classification layer, which outputs whether the movie review was positive or negative.

## Classification accuracy

When performance is measured against a held-out validation dataset, the model with tv-embeddings seems to slightly outperform the model that does not use tv-embeddings (see *Figure 11.2*). This difference can be improved by employing regularization techniques such as dropout and training for a longer time. Therefore, we can conclude that tv-embeddings in fact contribute to better performance with text classification tasks, compared with just using a simple representation such as BOW:

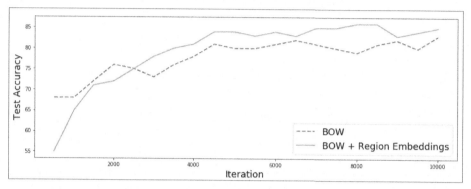

Figure 11.2: Sentiment classification accuracy for a model using BOW inputs and a model using BOW and region embeddings

# Probabilistic word embedding

The probabilistic word embedding models are another novel development in the word embedding area. *A Generative Word Embedding Model and Its Low Rank Positive Semidefinite Solution* [3], by Shaohua Li and others, introduces a word embedding technique called **PSDVec**, which produces embeddings that are different and more informative than the deterministic word vector models we saw earlier in the book (for example, skip-gram, CBOW, and GloVe). PSDVecs will provide for an embedding distribution for each word embedding instead of an exact numerical vector. As an example, if we assume a word vector has an embedding size of 1, and GloVe says that the word vector for the word *dog* is 0.5, PSDVec will provide a distribution over all the possible values that might look as shown in *Figure 11.3*. PSDVec might say that the embedding value for *dog* can be 0.5 with a higher probability (for example, 0.3), and it can be 0.1 with a lower probability (for example, 0.05):

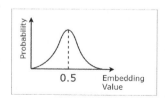

Figure 11.3: What PSDVec gives for a one-dimensional embedding

The probabilistic models have a richer interpretation than the deterministic models, such as Word2vec. To learn such probabilistic distributions of word vectors, they use a technique known as **variational inference**. In their work, they learn an embedding layer as well as a residual layer that captures noisy and nonlinear relationships between words. The authors show that PSDVec provides competitive performance compared with standard Word2vec and GloVe.

# Ensemble embedding

In their paper, *Learning Word Meta-Embeddings* [4], Wenpeng Yin and Hinrich Schütze propose an approach to learning *meta-embeddings*, an ensemble embedding model from several publicly available embedding sets. Two key benefits of this approach are (1) enhanced performance as they leverage multiple word embedding sets and (2) higher vocabulary coverage due to using multiple word embedding sets.

# Topic embedding

Topic embedding is also gaining interest in the NLP community. It allows any document to be represented by a set of topics (for example, information technology, medicine, and entertainment), and for a given document, we will compute weights for each topic, representing how relevant the document is to that topic. For example, a document about using machine learning for healthcare will have higher weights for topics such as *information technology* and *medicine*, but a low weight for the topic, *law*.

The paper *Topical Word Embeddings* [5], by Yang Liu and others, takes this approach for learning word embeddings. **Topical Word Embeddings** (TWE) learns multi-prototype embeddings. Multi-prototype embeddings are different from standard word embeddings as they give different embedding values depending on the context in which the word is used. For example, in the context of **information technology** (**IT**), *Windows* will give a different embedding value, compared to what it provides in the context of *home*. They learn the topics by a process known as **Latent Dirichlet Allocation** (**LDA**), a popular method used for topic modeling. The authors evaluate their method in a multiclass text classification task from a news group, which contains various topics such as IT, medicine, and politics. TWE outperforms other topic modeling methods, such as BOW and LDA used alone.

# Neural Machine Translation (NMT)

NMT has already proven its versatility, and many companies and researchers are investing in improving NMT systems. NMTs offer the current state-of-the-art translation performance that has been demonstrated by an autonomous translation system. However, these systems still haven't reached human translation capability. Therefore, a lot of effort is underway for improving NMT systems. As we discussed in *Chapter 10, Sequence-to-Sequence Learning – Neural Machine Translation* MT has potential in various domains such as manufacturing and business. Another use case of real-time machine translation can be found in the domain of tourism, where tourists can obtain English translations of various languages (through photos/ speech/text), while visiting some other country.

# Improving the attention mechanism

We already talked about the *attention mechanism* that eliminates the notorious performance bottleneck limit vanilla encoder-decoder style NMTs. With the attention mechanism, the decoder was given freedom to look at the complete source sentence at each decoding step. However, the improvements don't stop there. One improvement that has been suggested is the *input feeding* approach found in *Effective Approaches to Attention-based Neural Machine Translation* [6], *Minh-Thang Luong and others*. With this method, we feed the previous attention vector as an input to the current time step of the decoder. This measure is taken to make the decoder aware of the previous word alignment information, as this increases the performance of the MT system.

The paper *CKY-based Convolutional Attention for Neural Machine Translation* [7], by Taiki Watanabe and others, introduces an approach which uses a sophisticated **Convolution Neural Network (CNN)** for learning where to attend in the source sentence. This tends to deliver better results as CNNs are good at collecting spatial information compared with multilayer perceptrons, which have been used in the original attention mechanism.

# Hybrid MT models

As we saw in the results of the NMT system we implemented in *Chapter 10, Sequence-to-Sequence Learning – Neural Machine Translation*, the predictions often include the <unk> token. This is to replace rare words occurring in the predictions. However, we do not want this behavior. So there should be a way to replace these rare words in the source and target sentences with some meaningful words.

However, it is not practical to have all the possible words in a language in the vocabulary, as this would result in a gigantic database. Currently, the *Oxford English Dictionary* contains more than 150,000 distinct words. However, adding various tenses of verbs, names, and objects in the world, this quickly reaches unmanageable numbers.

This is where the hybrid models come in handy (see *Figure 11.4*). In the hybrid models, we do not replace rare words with the <unk> token. Instead, we keep the word in the sentence, and when a rare word is encountered in the source sentence, we delegate the task of processing the word to a character level encoder. Since there is a very small set of possible characters, this approach is quite feasible. Then the last state of the character level encoder is returned to a word-based machine translator and continues through the sentence normally. Also, the same process is used for the decoder when the decoder outputs an <unk> token. This was introduced in *Minh-Thang Luong's thesis Neural Machine Translation* [8]. You can find an implementation of a hybrid NMT model at `https://github.com/lmthang/nmt.hybrid.`

Here, for clarity, we will show the prediction method used in hybrid NMTs in pseudocode style.

For each word in the source sentence, it is as follows:

```
If word != <unk>
    encode the word with the word-based encoder
Else
    For each character in actual rare word
        Encode with the character-based encoder
    Return last hidden state of the char-based encoder as the input to
the word-based encoder, instead of the <unk> token
```

For each word predicted by the decoder, the prediction is as follows:

```
If word != <unk>
    Decode with the word-based decoder
If word == <end>
    Stop prediction
Else
    Initialize the character level decoder with the word-based decoder
hidden state
    Output a sequence of characters using the character level decoder
until <end> is output
```

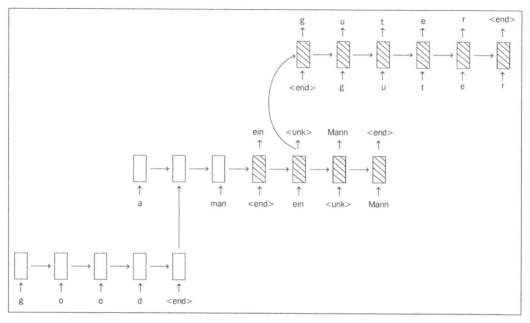

Figure 11.4: A hybrid neural machine translation model

Now let's look at some of the promising NLP directions that we will see in the future. These directions include combining NLP with other established research areas, such as reinforcement learning and **Generative Adversarial Models (GANs)**.

# Penetration into other research fields

Next we will discuss three different areas, which have blended with NLP to produce some interesting machine learning tasks. We will be discussing three specific areas:

- NLP and computer vision
- NLP and reinforcement learning
- NLP and generative adversarial networks

# Combining NLP with computer vision

First we will discuss two applications where NLP is combined with various computer vision applications to process multimodal data (that is, images and text).

# Visual Question Answering (VQA)

VQA is a novel research area, where the focus is to produce an answer to a textual question about an image. For example, consider these questions about *Figure 11.5*:

Q1: What color is the sofa?

Q2: How many black chairs are there?

Figure 11.5: The image about which we've asked questions

With this type of information provided to the system, the system should output the following (preferably):

Answer Q1: The color of the sofa is black

Answer Q2: There are two black chairs in the room

The learning model for this type of task would be quite similar to the architecture we used for image caption generation in *Chapter 9, Applications of LSTM – Image Caption Generation*. The dataset will consist of images and questions and answers corresponding to the image.

The process during training would be as follows:

1. Feed the images through a CNN (for example, pretrained on ImageNet) to obtain a context vector, representing the image

2. Create a sequence of data, where the sequence is composed of `(image encoding, <s>, question, </s>, <s>, answer, </s>)`, and `<s>` denotes the start and `</s>` is a special token marking the end of question

3. Use this sequence to train an LSTM on the answers for the corresponding question

During prediction, the process is as follows:

1. Feed the images through a CNN (for example, pretrained on ImageNet) to obtain a context vector, representing the image.

2. Create a sequence of data, where the sequence is composed of `(image encoding, <s>, question, </s>, <s>)`.

3. Feed the sequence to the LSTM and once the last `<s>` is fed, it iteratively predicts words by feeding in the last predicted word as the input to the next step until the LSTM outputs `</s>`. The newly predicted words will compose the answer.

One of the early CNN- and LSTM-based models successfully used for answering questions about images is explained in *Exploring Models and Data for Image Question Answering* [8], *Mengye Ren and others*. Another more advanced method is proposed in *Hierarchical Question-Image Co-Attention for Visual Question Answering* [9], *Jiasen Lu and others*.

The code for a VQA system written in TensorFlow is available at `https://github.com/tensorflow/models/tree/master/research/qa_kg`. This code contains the method described in the paper *Learning to Reason: End-to-End Module Networks for Visual Question Answering* [10], *Ronghang Hu and others*.

A good dataset for training and testing the VQA models (dataset with images, and question and answers corresponding to each image) is found at `http://www.visualqa.org/vqa_v1_download.html`, which was introduced in *VQA: Visual Question Answering* [11], *Stanislaw Antol and others*.

# Caption generation for images with attention

A paper titled *Show, Attend and Tell: Neural Image Caption Generation with Visual Attention* [12], *Kelvin Xu and others*, describes interesting research, where the focus was to learn where to look in an image to generate a caption. The main contribution here is that, unlike the standard image caption generation models that use a fully connected layer of the CNN to extract feature vectors, this method uses a lower convolution layer as the feature representation of the image. Then, on top of the convolution layer, it uses a 2D attention layer (similar to the one-dimensional attention layer we used in *Chapter 10, Sequence-to-Sequence Learning – Neural Machine Translation*) that represents the part of the image on which the model should focus while generating the word. For example, given an image of a *dog sitting on a carpet*, when generating the word *dog*, the image caption generator can pay more attention to the part of the image where the dog is than to the rest of the image.

# Reinforcement learning

Another field of research leveraged by NLP is **reinforcement learning (RL)**. NLP and RL had no interaction with each other for decades, and it is quite interesting to see how NLP problems are formulated through an RL lens and solved by RL techniques. Let's quickly understand what RL is. In RL, an agent interacts with an environment. The agent can observe the environment (completely or partially), which is fed to the agent as a state. Then, depending on the state, the agent will take an action sampled from some action space. Finally, after the execution of the action, a reward will be provided to the agent. The goal of the agent is to maximize the long-term reward it accumulates.

Next we will discuss how RL is used to solve various NLP tasks. First, we will discuss how RL is used to teach several agents a "language" that they use to communicate about data. This will be followed by RL being used to train agents to fulfill a user's request better by asking questions about the information the user didn't specify.

# Teaching agents to communicate using their own language

In *Multi-agent cooperation and the emergence of (natural) language* [13], *Angeliki Lazaridou and others* teach several agents to learn a unique language for communication. This is specifically done by selecting two agents from the group—a sender and a receiver. The sender is given a pair of images (where one image is the target), and the sender should send a small message for the receiver. The message is composed of symbols chosen from a fixed vocabulary that has no semantic meaning between symbols initially. The receiver sees the images, but does not know the target and is supposed to identify the target from the message received. The ultimate goal would be for the agent to activate the same symbol for similar-looking images. If the receiver predicts the target image correctly, both agents will receive a reward of 1; if it fails, both receive a reward of 0. This is depicted in *Figure 11.6*:

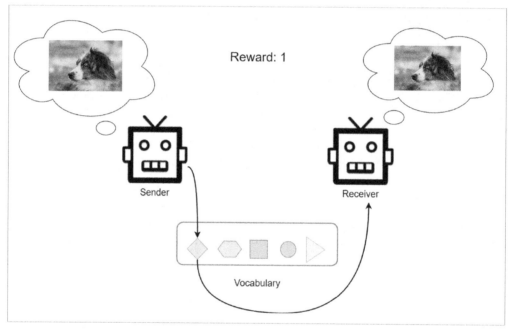

Figure 11.6: Agents learning to use the vocabulary to communicate about images, where only a single image is provided at a time. If the receiver identifies the image correctly, both the sender and receiver will get positive rewards.

# Dialogue agents with reinforcement learning

The following two papers use RL to train end-to-end deep learning-based dialogue systems: *Towards End-to-End Reinforcement Learning of Dialogue Agents for Information Access* [14], *Bhuwan Dhingra and others* and *A Network-based End-to-End Trainable Task-oriented Dialogue System* [15], *Tsung-Hsien Wen and others*. A dialogue system converses with a human in natural language and tries to accomplish the task implied by the phrase uttered by the human. For example, a human might ask this:

*What are some of the French restaurants in Sydney?*

Then the agent should convert the question to a system desired feature vector, which is achieved through a system called a **belief tracker**. A belief tracker maps the free-form natural language request to a fixed feature vector. This also could be viewed as a semantic parser. Then the feature vector is used to query a structured knowledge base to find the answer.

However, there can be tricky situations, where the human provides partial information in the request. For example, the human might ask the following:

*What are the best restaurants in town?*

Then the system might ask this:

*Which town?*

To this, the human answers the following:

*Sydney.*

Then the system might ask this:

*Which cuisine?*

To this, the human answers the following:

*French.*

After obtaining all the information needed to complete the request, the system will query the knowledge base and find the answer. A reward function can be designed to give positive reward whenever the system finds the correct answer. This will motivate the agent to ask correct relevant questions that are required to fill the missing information of the user's request.

# Generative Adversarial Networks for NLP

Generative models are a family of models that are able to generate new samples from some observed sample distribution. We already saw an example of a generative model when we used an LSTM to generate text. Another example of this would be to generate images. A model is trained on handwritten digits, and the model is asked to generate new handwritten digits. For generating images, we can use **Generative Adversarial Models (GANs)**, a popular generative method. A GAN looks as shown in *Figure 11.7*:

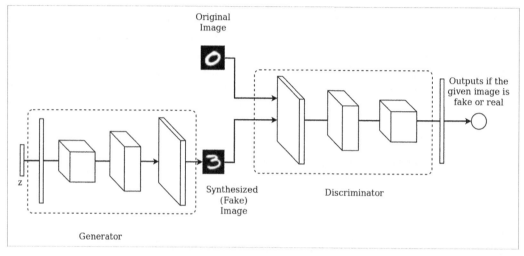

Figure 11.7. A Generative Adversarial Network (GAN)

There are two different components in the system: a generator and a discriminator. The generator's objective is to generate images that look like the real image. The discriminator tries to distinguish real (for example, true handwritten images) and fake images (generated by the generator) correctly. We will provide the generator with some noise (that is, sample values generated from a normal distribution), and it generates an image. The generator is an *inverse* CNN, where it takes a vector as an input and outputs an image. This contrasts with a standard CNN, which takes an image as an input and outputs a prediction vector. The discriminator tries to discriminate between real images and the ones generated by the generator. So at the beginning, it is easy for the discriminator to distinguish between real ones and the fake ones. The generator is optimized in a way that it becomes more difficult for the discriminator to identify fake ones from the real one. With this process, the generator becomes good at generating images that look like real images.

GANs were originally designed to generate realistic images. However, there have been several attempts to adapt GANs for generating sentences. *Figure 11.8* illustrates the general approach to using a GAN to generate sentences. Next, let's look at the specifics of this approach:

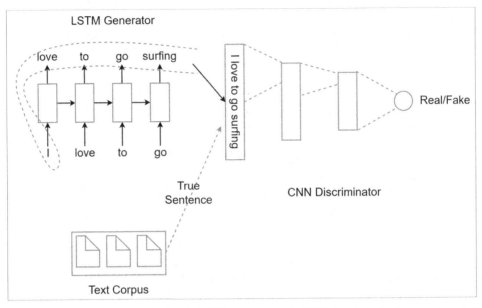

Figure 11.8: The general concept of using an LSTM generator and a CNN discriminator to generate sentences

In *Generating Text via Adversarial Training* [16], *Yizhe Zhang and others* use a modified GAN for generating text. In their work, there are significant differences to the convolutional GAN we discussed earlier. First, they use an LSTM generator, which takes some random item from the vocabulary as the input and generates an arbitrarily long sentence. Next, the discriminator is a CNN that is trained to classify a given sentence into one of two classes (that is, fake or real). The data is fed to the CNN and trained, similar to the sentence classification CNN we discussed in *Chapter 5, Sentence Classification with Convolutional Neural Networks*. First, the CNN will be very good at discriminating between real sentences and fake sentences. Over time, the LSTM will be optimized to produce more and more realistic looking sentences to fool the classifier.

In *SeqGAN: Sequence Generative Adversarial Nets with Policy Gradient* [17], *Lantao Yu and others* show another approach for generating text using a generative model. In this case also, the generator is an LSTM network and the discriminator is a CNN network (for example, similar to *Generating Text via Adversarial Training* [16], *Zhang and others*). However, unlike the approach in that work, the training process is formulated as a reinforcement learning problem.

The state is the currently generated text string by the generator, and the action space is the vocabulary to choose words from. This process is continued until the full text is generated for a given step. The reward is obtained only at the end of the full sequence. The output of the discriminator is used as the reward. Therefore, the reward will be high if the output of the discriminator is close to 1 (that is, the discriminator thinks data is real) and low if the output is close to 0. Then with the reward defined, the authors use *policy gradient* to train the generator through backpropagation. Specifically, the policy gradient calculates the gradients for the parameters (that is, weights) in the generator with respect to the reward produced by the discriminator. A TensorFlow implementation of SeqGAN is available at

```
https://github.com/LantaoYu/SeqGAN.
```

# Towards Artificial General Intelligence

**Artificial General Intelligence (AGI)** enables machines to perform cognitive or intellectual tasks that a human can perform. It is a different or a more difficult concept than AI, as AGI involves achieving general intelligence beyond asking a machine to perform a task given necessary data. For example, let's say we put a robot in a novel environment (say, a house that robot has never visited) and ask it to make coffee. If it can actually navigate the house, find the machine, learn how to operate it, execute the correct sequence of actions needed to make coffee and bring the coffee to a human, then we can say that robot has achieved AGI. We are still far from achieving AGI, but steps are being made in that direction. Also, NLP will play a great role in this as the most natural way for humans to interact is vocal communication.

The papers that will be discussed here are single models that try to learn to do many tasks. In other words, a single end-to-end model will be able to classify images, detect objects, recognize speech, translate between languages, and so on. We can think of machine learning models that are capable of doing many tasks as a step towards AGI.

## One Model to Learn Them All

In *One Model To Learn Them All* [18], *Lukasz Kaiser and others* introduce a single deep learning model that is capable of learning many tasks (for example, image classification, image caption generation, language translation, and speech recognition). Specifically, this model (which is called the **MultiModel**) consists of several modules: subnetworks, an encoder, an input/output mixer, and a decoder.

First, the MultiModel comprises several subnetworks or *modality-nets*. A modality-net converts inputs belonging to some specific modality (for example, images) to a unified representation. This way, all the inputs having different modalities can be processed by a single deep network. Note that modality-nets are not task specific; they are only input-modality specific. This means that several tasks having the same input modality will share a single modality-net. Next we will list the roles performed by the encoder, I/O mixer, and the decoder.

The encoder processes the inputs produced by the modality networks using computational elements such as convolution blocks, attention blocks, and a mixture of experts blocks. We will describe the tasks achieved by each of these elements later.

The I/O mixer combines (or mixes) the encoded input with the previously observed outputs to produce encoded outputs. This module processes the inputs and the previously observed outputs as an *autoregressive model*. To understand what an autoregressive model is, let's consider a time series denoted by $y = \{y_0, y_1, y_2, \ldots, y_{t-1}\}$. In its simplest form, an autoregressive model predicts $y_t$ as a function of $y_{t-1}$ (that is, $y_t = \beta_1 y_{t-1} + \beta_0 + \in$, where $\beta_0$ and $\beta_1$ are learnable coefficients and $\in$ captures noise present in $y$. However, this can be generalized to arbitrary number of previous $y$ values, for example, $y_t = \beta_2 y_{t-2} + \beta_1 y_{t-1} + \beta_0 + \in$. This is useful as the MultiModel processes many types of time-series data such as speech and text.

The decoder takes in both the encoded outputs and the encoded inputs and produces a decoded output using convolution and attention blocks and a mixture of experts blocks. We will describe these blocks here:

- **The convolutional block**: The convolutional block detects local and spatial patterns and converts them to feature maps.
- **The attention block**: The attention block decides what to pay attention to in the input, when encoding/decoding.
- **The mixture of experts block**: The mixture of experts block is a way to increase the model capacity at a negligible extra computational cost. A mixture of experts is a collection of several feed-forward networks (that is, experts) with a trainable (and differentiable) gating mechanism that chooses different networks depending on the inputs.

Though the details vastly differ, you should be able to see a resemblance to the NMT system we studied in *Chapter 10, Sequence-to-Sequence Learning – Neural Machine Translation*. The MultiModel first encodes the input, as we encoded the source sentence through the NMT encoder. Finally, the MultiModel decodes and produces a human-readable output, just as the NMT decoder produced a target sentence.

The MultiModel is trained to perform various tasks with the following datasets, which are laid out in the paper *One Model To Learn Them All, Kaiser and others*:

1. Wall Street Journal (WSJ) speech corpus: WSJ speech corpus is a large dataset containing utterances (~ 73 hours of speech) by various people (including journalists with varying experience). This dataset is found at `https://catalog.ldc.upenn.edu/ldc93s6a`.

2. ImageNet dataset: The ImageNet dataset is the image dataset we discussed in *Chapter 9, Applications of LSTM – Image Caption Generation*. It contains more than a million images belonging to 1,000 different classes. The dataset is found at `image-net.org/download`.

3. MS-COCO image captioning dataset: MS-COCO data was also used in *Chapter 9, Applications of LSTM – Image Caption Generation*. This contains images and image descriptions generated by humans. This dataset can be found at `http://cocodataset.org/#download`.

4. WSJ parsing dataset: Parsing is the process of identifying nouns, determinants, verbs, noun phrases, verb phrases, and so on, in a sentence and constructing a parse tree for that sentence. A dataset constructed by parsing a corpus of WSJ material is found in the WSJ parsing dataset. The dataset is found at `https://catalog.ldc.upenn.edu/ldc99t42`.

5. WMT English-German translation corpus: This is a bilingual text corpus, having English sentences and corresponding German translations, similar to the dataset we used in *Chapter 10, Sequence-to-Sequence Learning – Neural Machine Translation*. Datasets are found at `http://www.statmt.org/wmt14/translation-task.html`.

6. The reverse of 5: This is the German-English translation.

7. WMT English-French translation corpus: This is a bilingual text corpus, having English sentences and corresponding French translation, similar to the dataset we used in *Chapter 10, Sequence-to-Sequence Learning – Neural Machine Translation*. Datasets are found at `http://www.statmt.org/wmt14/translation-task.html`.

8. The reverse of 7: This is the French-English translation. In *One Model To Learn Them All*, the authors actually say *German-French* here, which we take to be an inadvertent error, as the preceding corpus is English with French translations.

After training on these datasets, the model is expected to perform the following tasks with a good accuracy:

- Converting speech to text
- Generating captions for a given image
- Identifying objects in a given image
- Translating from English to German or French
- Building parse trees for English

A TensorFlow implementation is found at `https://github.com/tensorflow/tensor2tensor`.

# A joint many-task model – growing a neural network for multiple NLP tasks

In *A Joint Many-Task Model – Growing a Neural Network for Multiple NLP Tasks* [19], *Kazuma Hashimoto and others* train an end-to-end model on a variety of NLP tasks. However, this method formulation is different from the previously discussed approach. In this case, the lower layers of the model learn simpler tasks, and higher (or deeper) layers learn more advanced tasks. To achieve this, the required labels (for example, **part-of-speech** (POS) tags) for training are provided to individual levels of the network. These tasks are categorized into three different types in this order (that is, lower to higher in the network): word-level tasks, syntactic tasks, and semantic tasks. When organized in this fashion, higher layers can use the knowledge of completing simpler tasks to perform more advanced tasks (for example, identifying dependencies of a sentence can benefit from the POS tags). This concept is illustrated in *Figure 11.9*.

## First level – word-based tasks

The first two layers perform word-level tasks. Given a sentence, the first layer performs POS tagging for each word in the sentence. The next layer performs chunking, a process where tags are again assigned to each word.

## Second level – syntactic tasks

The next layer performs dependency parsing on the sentence. Dependency parsing is the task of analyzing the grammar structure of a sentence and identifying relationships between words.

# Third level – semantic-level tasks

The next layer encodes the relatedness information of sentences. However, relatedness is measured between two sentences. To process two sentences in parallel, we have two parallel stacks of what we described earlier. Therefore, we have two different networks encoding two sentences with respect to their relatedness. The final layer performs textual entailment. Textual entailment is the task of analyzing whether the premise sentence (second sentence) entails the hypothesis sentence (first sentence). The output can be entailment, contradiction, or neutral. Here we will list examples of positive/negative and neutral textual entailments:

- Positive:

  Hypothesis: *cloudy skies lead to rain*

  Premise: *If it is cloudy, it will rain*

- Negative:

  Hypothesis: *cloudy skies don't lead to rain*

  Premise: *If it is cloudy, it will rain*

- Neutral:

  Hypothesis: *cloudy skies lead to rain*

  Premise: *if it is cloudy, your dog will bark*

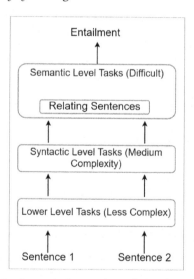

Figure 11.9: Solving increasingly complex tasks in a bottom to top manner

# NLP for social media

Now we will discuss how NLP has influenced social media mining. Here we will discuss findings presented in several papers. These findings include detecting rumors from truth and detecting emotions and identifying manipulations of words by politicians, for example, to gain more support (that is, political framing).

# Detecting rumors in social media

In *Detect Rumors Using Time Series of Social Context Information on Microblogging Websites* [20], *Jing Ma and others* propose a way to detect rumors in microblogs. Rumors are stories or statements that are either deliberately false or for which the truth is not verified. Identifying rumors in their early phases is important to prevent false/invalid information being delivered to people. In this paper, an event is defined as a set of microblogs relevant to that event. A time-sensitive context feature is derived for each microblog and they are binned into time intervals depending on the time the microblog appeared. Thereafter, they use a **Dynamic-Series Time Structure (DSTS)** to learn a "shape" of the time series of the evolution context-features. More specifically, given a series of temporal context features, DSTS represents the shape of the time-series with a combination of feature vectors over time $(f_0, f_1, f_2, ..., f_t)$ and a function of the slope between consecutive context features over time $(0, f_1-f_0, f_2-f_1 ...)$. This can help to identify rumors as these patterns tend to behave differently for rumors and nonrumors. For example, the number of question marks in microblogs related to a nonrumor event goes down with time, whereas for rumors, it does not.

# Detecting emotions in social media

*EmoNet: Fine-Grained Emotion Detection with Gated Recurrent Neural Networks* [21], *Muhammad Abdul-Mageed and Lyle Ungar*, shows an approach for detecting emotions in social media posts (for example, tweets). Detecting emotions in social media posts plays an important role as the emotions help to determine one's physical and mental health. Ability to detect emotions also provides customer insights, which are valuable for businesses. Therefore, correctly mining the emotions from social media posts can provide parents with their children's physical/mental status or can help businesses grow. However, technical barriers exist for automatic emotion detection approaches as there is limited amount of data due to the controversial nature of the emotions themselves. For example, when one says, *I love Mondays*, it could be a sarcastic remark indicating the loathing of a working person. On the contrary, it also could be someone actually being happy about Mondays because of some weekly celebration that takes place on Mondays.

The authors use Plutchik's wheel of emotions (see *Figure 11.10*) to categorize emotions, from which they end up with 24 different categories. However, tweets might be using various synonyms to mean the same thing (for example, happy can be expressed with joyful, blissful, and excited). Therefore, the authors used Google synonyms and other resources and found 665 different emotion hashtags belonging to the 24 main categories.

Next, to collect data, they crawled through tweet posts dating back to 2009 and collected about 0.5 billion tweets. Then they performed preprocessing on the raw data, mainly to remove duplicates and tweets with multiple emotions and ended up with around 1.5 million tweets. Finally, a gated recurrent network (that is, a network of GRUs) was used to classify the tweets and predict what type of an emotion a given tweet is expressing:

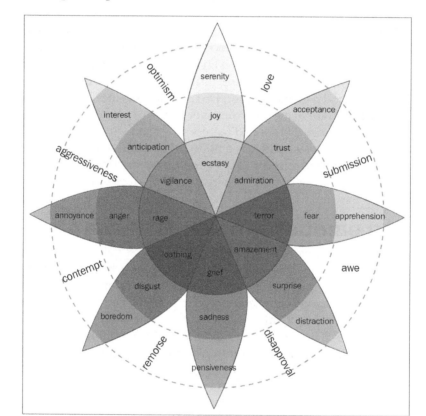

Figure 11.16: Plutchik's wheel of emotion

# Analyzing political framing in tweets

Social media is widely being used as a platform for various tasks in politics. In recent U.S. elections, candidates heavily leveraged Twitter to advertise their agendas, expand their supporter bases, and attack and retaliate against opposing candidates. This highlights the importance of such political posts for mining important information. Identifying *political framing* is one such important and difficult task. Political framing refers to careful manipulation of words to control public perception.

In *Leveraging Behavioral and Social Information for Weakly Supervised Collective Classification of Political Discourse on Twitter* [22], *Kristen Johnson and others* develop a labeled dataset that consists of tweets by 40 members of Congress chosen randomly. First, the tweets were extracted and labeled using a *policy framing codebook* to annotate the tweets. Next, due to the dynamic nature of the problem, weakly supervised models were used to learn the tweets. Weakly supervised models are designed to learn with a limited amount of data (unlike deep learning models).

# New tasks emerging

Now we will investigate several novel areas that have emerged in the recent past. These areas include detecting sarcasm, language grounding (that is, the process of eliciting common sense from natural language), and skimming text.

# Detecting sarcasm

Sarcasm is when a person utters something which actually means the opposite of the utterance (for example, *I love Mondays!*). Detecting sarcasm can even be difficult for humans sometimes, and detecting sarcasm through NLP is an even harder task. *Sarcasm SIGN: Interpreting Sarcasm with Sentiment Based Monolingual Machine Translation* [23], *Lotem Peled and Roi Reichart*, uses NLP for detecting sarcasm in Twitter posts. They first create a dataset of 3,000 tweet pairs, where one tweet is the sarcastic tweet and the other tweet is the decrypted nonsarcastic tweet. The decrypted tweets were created by five human judges who looked at the tweet and came up with the actual meaning. Then they used a *monolingual* machine translation mechanism to learn sarcasm. This is a sequence-to-sequence model as we discussed in an earlier chapter. Instead of giving a pair of sentences belonging to two different languages, here we provide the sarcastic and nonsarcastic sentence pair.

# Language grounding

Language grounding is the task of deriving common sense from the natural language. For example, when we use language, often there is a strong conceptual idea of objects and actions we want to explain. This allows us to draw various conclusions about objects, even when the conclusions are not directly present in the sentence. However, this is not the case for machines. Machines do not learn the natural language by relating it to actual conceptual entities they represent. However, this is an essential part if we want to build true AI. Language grounding is the task of achieving this property. For example, when we say *the car entered the garage*, it implies that the garage is bigger than the car. However, it is not necessarily learned by a machine learning algorithm, unless given a reward for learning that. In *Verb Physics: Relative Physical Knowledge of Actions and Objects* [24], Maxwell Forbes and Yejin Choi propose an approach for learning language grounding.

In this paper, the authors focus on five different properties or dimensions for grounding: size, weight, strength, rigidness, and speed. Finally, a factor graph model is used to learn various properties of the objects appearing in a conversation. The factor graph contains subgraphs consisting of two subgraphs for each attribute — object subgraph and verb subgraph.

Next, each subgraph contains nodes. There are two types of nodes:

- **Object-pair nodes (nodes found in the object subgraph)**: These capture the relative strength of an attribute for two objects (for example, denoted by $O^{size}_{(human, berry)}$ : *probability of size(human) > size(berry)*)
- **Action frame nodes (nodes found in the verb subgraph)**: These capture how verbs are related to attributes (that is, denoted by $F^{size}_{threw}$ : for sentence *x threw y*, what is the probability that *size(x) > size(y)*)

Then it is possible to create connections (that is, binary factors) between two object pair nodes, or two action frame nodes, depending on how likely a given pair of nodes to appear in a similar context. For example, $O^{size}_{(human, ball)}$ and $O^{size}_{(human, stone)}$ should have high binary factor, where $O^{size}_{(human, ball)}$ and $O^{size}_{(human, car)}$ should have a low binary factor. Then the most crucial connections (that is, connections between action frame nodes and object pair nodes) are established by learning from unstructured natural language.

Finally with this graph, if we need to know the relationship between *weight(human)* and *weight(ball)*, we can infer the connection strength connecting $F^{weight}_{threw}$ with $O^{weight}_{(human, ball)}$ . This is performed via something known as *loopy belief propagation*.

# Skimming text with LSTMs

Skimming text plays an important role in many NLP activities. For example, if an LSTM is designed to answer questions from a book, it probably shouldn't be reading the full text, but read only the relevant parts that contain information that helps answering the questions. Another use might be for document retrieval, where a set of relevant documents containing some text need to be fetched from an existing large document base. In *Learning to Skim Text* [25], *Adams Wei Yu and others* propose a model called LSTM-Jump that does exactly this.

There are three important hyperparameters:

- $N$: This is the total number of jumps allowed
- $R$: This is the number of tokens to be read between two jumps
- $K$: This is the maximum jump size allowed (in a step)

Next, an LSTM is created with a softmax layer with $K$ nodes on top of the LSTM. This softmax layer decides how many jumps to make at a given time step. This functioning of this softmax layer is somewhat similar to the attention mechanism. The jumping or skimming stops if one of the following conditions is encountered:

- Jump softmax samples a 0
- The LSTM reaches the end of the text
- The number of jumps exceeds $N$

# Newer machine learning models

Now we will discuss several newer machine learning models that have emerged to resolve various limitations of the current models (for example, standard LSTMs). One such model is Phased LSTMs that allow us to pay attention to very specific events that happen in future during learning. Another model is **Dilated RNNs (DRNNs)**, which provides a way to model complex dependencies present in the inputs. DRNNs also enable parallel computation of unrolled RNNs, compared with naïvely iterating through the unrolled RNNs.

# Phased LSTM

Current LSTM networks have shown a remarkable performance in many of the sequential learning tasks. However, they are not well-suited for processing irregularly timed data, such as data provided by event-driven sensors. This is mainly because no matter whether an event is transpired or not, an LSTM's cell state and the hidden states are continuously updated. This behavior can cause the LSTM to ignore special events that might rarely or irregularly happen.

Phased LSTMs are introduced in *Phased LSTM: Accelerating Recurrent Network Training for Long or Event-based Sequences* [26], *Daniel Neil and others*, and they try to solve this issue by introducing a new *time gate*. Updates to the cell state and the hidden state are only allowed when the time gate is open. Therefore, unless an event occurs, the time gate would be closed causing the cell state and the hidden state to remain the same. This behavior helps to preserve information for a longer time and pay attention to the event that occurred. *Figure 11.11* illustrates the general concept.

This timing gate operation is achieved through three newly introduced parameters:

- $\tau$: This controls the real-time oscillation period
- $r_{on}$: This controls the time the gate is open to the full duration
- $s$: This controls the phase shift of the oscillations of the gate

These variables can be learned jointly with the rest of the parameters of the LSTM. TensorFlow already has released an implementation of Phased LSTMs, which is found at https://www.tensorflow.org/api_docs/python/tf/contrib/rnn/ PhasedLSTMCell:

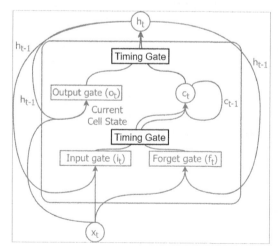

Figure 11.11: The general concept of a timing gate. The hidden state and the cell state are allowed to be updated only if the timing gate is on.

# Dilated Recurrent Neural Networks (DRNNs)

Current RNNs have several limitations in learning long-term dependencies, such as the following:

- Complex dependencies present in the inputs
- The vanishing gradient
- Effective parallelization of the learning

DRNNs are introduced in *Dilated Recurrent Neural Networks* [27], *Shiyu Chang and others*. They attempt to resolve all these limitations at once.

DRNNs solve the issue of learning complex dependencies by ensuring that a given state is connected to older hidden states, not just the immediate previous hidden state. This by design helps to learn long-term dependencies more effectively.

This architecture solves the issue of the vanishing gradient as one hidden state sees the past beyond the immediate previous hidden state, so it is easy to propagate the gradient through time to longer distances.

If you compress the DRNN architecture, it represents a standard RNN that processes multiple inputs at the same time. Therefore, again by design, DRNNs allow greater parallelization compared with standard RNNs. *Figure 11.12* shows how DRNNs differ from standard RNNs. An implementation of this is available at `https://github.com/code-terminator/DilatedRNN`.

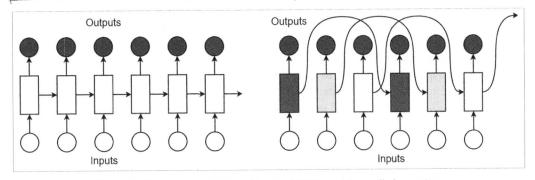

Figure 11.12: A standard RNN (left) and a DRNN (right) unrolled over time.
The differently shaded unrolled RNNs can be processed in parallel because
they don't have any shared connections.

# Summary

This chapter was aimed at learning the current trends in NLP and learning the future directions that NLP is being driven to. Though it is a very broad topic, we discussed some of the very recent advancements that have been made in NLP. As current trends, we first looked at the advancements being made with regard to word embeddings. We saw that much more accurate embeddings with richer interpretations (for example, probabilistic) are emerging. Then we looked into improvements that have been made in machine translation, as it is one of the most sought after areas in NLP. We saw that better attention mechanisms and better MT models capable of producing increasingly more realistic translations are both emerging.

We then looked at some of the novel research in NLP that is taking place (mostly in 2017). First we investigated the penetration of NLP into other fields: computer vision, reinforcement learning, and the generative adversarial models. We looked at how NLP systems are being improved so that they come closer to achieving GAI. Next we looked at what type of progress NLP has made in social media, such as how NLP is being used to detect and debunk rumors, detect emotions, and analyze political situations.

We also looked into some of the more recent and interesting tasks that are gaining more popularity among the NLP community, such as learning to detect sarcasm using an encoder-decoder learning model, language grounding that has gained thorough insights into what is implied by some utterance, and learning to skim text instead of reading it fully from end-to-end. We discussed some of the latest machine learning models that have been recently introduced. Phased LSTMs are an advance type of LSTMs that have more control over how to update the cell state and the hidden state. This behavior allows LSTMs to learn longer-term dependencies with irregularities. Finally, we discussed another type of model called DRNNs. DRNNs introduce a simple modification to how standard RNNs are unrolled over time. With this modification, DRNNs are able to model complex dependencies, solve the vanishing gradient problem, and enable more parallelization for processing data.

# References

[1] *Distributed representations of words and phrases and their compositionality*, T. Mikolov, I. Sutskever, K. Chen, G. S. Corrado, and J. Dean, *Advances in Neural Information Processing Systems,pp. 3111–3119, 2013.*

[2] *Semi-supervised convolutional neural networks for text categorization via region embedding, Johnson, Rie and Tong Zhang, Advances in Neural Information Processing Systems, pp. 919-927, 2015.*

[3] *A Generative Word Embedding Model and Its Low Rank Positive Semidefinite Solution*, Li, Shaohua, Jun Zhu, and Chunyan Miao, Proceedings of the 2015 Conference on Empirical Methods in Natural Language Processing, pp. 1599-1609, 2015.

[4] *Learning Word Meta-Embeddings*, Wenpeng Yin and Hinrich Schütze, Proceedings of the 54th Annual Meeting of the Association for Computational Linguistics, vol. 1, pp. 1351-1360, 2016.

[5] *Topical Word Embeddings*, Yang Liu, Zhiyuan Liu, Tat-Seng Chua, and Maosong Sun, AAAI, pp. 2418-2424, 2015.

[6] *Effective Approaches to Attention-based Neural Machine Translation*, Thang Luong, Hieu Pham, and Christopher D. Manning, Proceedings of the 2015 Conference on Empirical Methods in Natural Language Processing, pp. 1412-1421, 2015.

[7] *CKY-based Convolutional Attention for Neural Machine Translation*, Watanabe, Taiki, Akihiro Tamura, and Takashi Ninomiya, Proceedings of the Eighth International Joint Conference on Natural Language Processing (Volume 2: Short Papers), vol. 2, pp. 1-6, 2017.

[8] *Neural Machine Translation*, Minh-Thang Luong. Stanford University, 2016.

[9] *Exploring Models and Data for Image Question Answering*, Ren, Mengye, Ryan Kiros, and Richard Zemel, Advances in Neural Information Processing Systems, pp. 2953-2961, 2015.

[10] *Learning to Reason: End-to-End Module Networks for Visual Question Answering*, Hu, Ronghang, Jacob Andreas, Marcus Rohrbach, Trevor Darrell, and Kate Saenko, CoRR, abs/1704.05526 3, 2017.

[11] *VQA: Visual Question Answering*, Antol, Stanislaw, Aishwarya Agrawal, Jiasen Lu, Margaret Mitchell, Dhruv Batra, C. Lawrence Zitnick, and Devi Parikh, Computer Vision (ICCV), 2015 IEEE International Conference on, pp. 2425-2433, IEEE, 2015.

[12] *Show, Attend and Tell: Neural Image Caption Generation with Visual Attention*, Xu, Kelvin, Jimmy Ba, Ryan Kiros, Kyunghyun Cho, Aaron Courville, Ruslan Salakhudinov, Rich Zemel, and Yoshua Bengio, International Conference on Machine Learning, pp. 2048-2057, 2015.

[13] *Multi-agent cooperation and the emergence of (natural) language*, Lazaridou, Angeliki, Alexander Peysakhovich, and Marco Baroni, International Conference on Learning Representations, 2016.

[14] *Towards End-to-End Reinforcement Learning of Dialogue Agents for Information Access*, Dhingra, Bhuwan, Lihong Li, Xiujun Li, Jianfeng Gao, Yun-Nung Chen, Faisal Ahmed, and Li Deng, Proceedings of the 55th Annual Meeting of the Association for Computational Linguistics (Volume 1: Long Papers), vol. 1, pp. 484-495, 2017.

[15] *A Network-based End-to-End Trainable Task-oriented Dialogue System, Wen, Tsung-Hsien, David Vandyke, Nikola Mrksic, Milica Gasic, Lina M. Rojas-Barahona, Pei-Hao Su, Stefan Ultes,* and *Steve Young, arXiv:1604.04562v3, 2017.*

[16] *Generating Text via Adversarial Training, Zhang, Yizhe, Zhe Gan,* and *Lawrence Carin, NIPS workshop on Adversarial Training, vol. 21, 2016.*

[17] *SeqGAN: Sequence Generative Adversarial Nets with Policy Gradient, Yu, Lantao, Weinan Zhang, Jun Wang,* and *Yong Yu, AAAI, pp. 2852-2858, 2017.*

[18] *One Model To Learn Them All, Kaiser, Lukasz, Aidan N. Gomez, Noam Shazeer, Ashish Vaswani, Niki Parmar, Llion Jones,* and *Jakob Uszkoreit, arXiv:1706.05137v1, 2017.*

[19] *A Joint Many-Task Model: Growing a Neural Network for Multiple NLP Tasks, Hashimoto, Kazuma, Yoshimasa Tsuruoka,* and *Richard Socher, Proceedings of the 2017 Conference on Empirical Methods in Natural Language Processing, pp. 1923-1933, 2017.*

[20] *Detect Rumors Using Time Series of Social Context Information on Microblogging Websites, Ma, Jing, Wei Gao, Zhongyu Wei, Yueming Lu,* and *Kam-Fai Wong, Proceedings of the 24th ACM International on Conference on Information and Knowledge Management, pp. 1751-1754, ACM, 2015.*

[21] *Emonet: Fine-Grained Emotion Detection with Gated Recurrent Neural Networks, Abdul-Mageed, Muhammad,* and *Lyle Ungar, Proceedings of the 55th Annual Meeting of the Association for Computational Linguistics (Volume 1: Long Papers), vol. 1, pp. 718-728, 2017.*

[22] *Leveraging Behavioral and Social Information for Weakly Supervised Collective Classification of Political Discourse on Twitter, Johnson, Kristen, Di Jin,* and *Dan Goldwasser, Proceedings of the 55th Annual Meeting of the Association for Computational Linguistics (Volume 1: Long Papers), vol. 1, pp. 741-752, 2017.*

[23] *Sarcasm SIGN: Interpreting Sarcasm with Sentiment Based Monolingual Machine Translation, Peled, Lotem,* and *Roi Reichart, Proceedings of the 55th Annual Meeting of the Association for Computational Linguistics (Volume 1: Long Papers), vol. 1, pp. 1690-1700, 2017.*

[24] *Verb Physics: Relative Physical Knowledge of Actions and Objects, Forbes, Maxwell,* and *Yejin Choi, Proceedings of the 55th Annual Meeting of the Association for Computational Linguistics (Volume 1: Long Papers), vol. 1, pp. 266-276, 2017.*

[25] *Learning to Skim Text, Yu, Adams Wei, Hongrae Lee,* and *Quoc Le, Proceedings of the 55th Annual Meeting of the Association for Computational Linguistics (Volume 1: Long Papers), vol. 1, pp. 1880-1890, 2017.*

[26] *Phased LSTM: Accelerating Recurrent Network Training for Long or Event-based Sequences, Neil, Daniel, Michael Pfeiffer,* and *Shih-Chii Liu, Advances in Neural Information Processing Systems, pp. 3882-3890, 2016.*

[27] *Dilated recurrent neural networks, Chang, Shiyu, Yang Zhang, Wei Han, Mo Yu, Xiaoxiao Guo, Wei Tan, Xiaodong Cui, Michael Witbrock, Mark A. Hasegawa-Johnson,* and *Thomas S. Huang, Advances in Neural Information Processing Systems, pp. 76-86, 2017.*

# Mathematical Foundations and Advanced TensorFlow

Here we will discuss some of the concepts that will be useful to understand details provided in the chapters. First we will discuss several mathematical data structures found throughout the book, followed by a description about various operations performed on those data structures. Next, we will discuss the concept of probabilities. Probabilities play a vital role in machine learning, as they usually give insights to how uncertain a model is about its prediction. Thereafter, we discuss a high-level library known as Keras in TensorFlow, as well as how to implement a neural machine translator with the seq2seq sublibrary in TensorFlow. Finally we conclude this section with a guide on how to use the TensorBoard as a visualization tool for word embeddings.

## Basic data structures

## Scalar

A scalar is a single number unlike a matrix or a vector. For example, 1.3 is a scalar. A scalar can be mathematically denoted as follows:

$$n \in R$$

Here, $R$ is the real number space.

# Vectors

A vector is an array of numbers. Unlike a set, where there is no order to elements, a vector has a certain order to the elements. An example vector is [1.0, 2.0, 1.4, 2.3]. Mathematically, it can be denoted as follows:

$$a = \left( a_0, a_1, \ldots, a_{\{n-1\}} \right)$$

$$a \in R^n$$

Alternatively, we can write this as:

$$a \in R^{n \times 1}$$

Here, $R$ is the real number space and $n$ is the number of elements in the vector.

# Matrices

A matrix can be thought of as a two-dimensional arrangement of a collection of scalars. In other words, a matrix can be thought of as a vector of vectors. An example matrix would be as shown here:

$$A = \begin{pmatrix} 1 & 4 & 2 & 3 \\ 2 & 7 & 7 & 1 \\ 5 & 6 & 9 & 0 \end{pmatrix}$$

A more general matrix of size $m \times n$ can be mathematically defined like this:

$$A = \begin{pmatrix} a_{0,0} & a_{0,1} & \cdots & a_{0,n-1} \\ a_{1,0} & a_{1,1} & \cdots & a_{1,n-1} \\ \vdots & \vdots & \ddots & \vdots \\ a_{m-1,0} & a_{m-1,1} & \cdots & a_{m-1,n-1} \end{pmatrix}$$

And:

$$A \in R^{m \times n}$$

Here, $m$ is the number of rows of the matrix, $n$ is the number of columns in the matrix, and $R$ is the real number space.

# Indexing of a matrix

We will be using zero-indexed notation (that is, indexes start with 0).

To index a single element from a matrix at $(i, j)^{th}$ position, we use the following notation:

$$A_{i,j} = a_{i,j}$$

Referring to the previously defined matrix, we get the following:

$$A = \begin{pmatrix} 1 & 4 & 2 & 3 \\ 2 & 7 & 7 & 1 \\ 5 & 6 & 9 & 0 \end{pmatrix}$$

We index an element from $A$ like this:

$$A_{1,0} = 2$$

We denote a single row of any matrix $A$ as shown here:

$$A_{i,:} = \left( a_{i,0}, a_{i,1}, \ldots, a_{i,n} \right)$$

For our example matrix, we can denote the second row (indexed as 1) of the matrix as shown here:

$$A_{1,:} = (2, 7, 7, 1)$$

We denote the slice starting from the $(i, k)^{th}$ index to the $(j, l)^{th}$ index of any matrix $A$ as shown here:

$$A_{1:j,k:l} = \begin{pmatrix} a_{i,k} & \cdots & a_{i,l} \\ \vdots & \ddots & \vdots \\ a_{j,k} & \cdots & a_{j,l} \end{pmatrix}$$

In our example matrix, we can denote the slice from first row third column to second row fourth column as shown here:

$$A_{0:1,2:3} = \begin{pmatrix} 2 & 3 \\ 7 & 1 \end{pmatrix}$$

# Special types of matrices

## Identity matrix

An identity matrix is where it is equal to 1 on the diagonal of the matrix and 0 everywhere else. Mathematically, it can be shown as follows:

$$I_{i,j} = \begin{pmatrix} 1 & if\ i = j \\ 0 & otherwise \end{pmatrix}$$

This would look like the following:

$$A = \begin{pmatrix} 1 & 0 & \cdots & 0 \\ 0 & 1 & \cdots & 0 \\ \vdots & \vdots & \ddots & \vdots \\ 0 & 0 & \cdots & 1 \end{pmatrix}$$

Here, $I \in R^{n \times n}$.

The identity matrix gives the following nice property when multiplied with another matrix $A$:

$$AI = A$$

# Diagonal matrix

A diagonal matrix is a more general case of the identity matrix, where the values along the diagonal can take any value and the off-diagonal values are zeros:

$$A = \begin{pmatrix} a_{0,0} & 0 & \cdots & 0 \\ 0 & a_{1,1} & \cdots & 0 \\ \vdots & \vdots & \ddots & \vdots \\ 0 & 0 & \cdots & a_{n-1,n-1} \end{pmatrix}$$

# Tensors

An $n$-dimensional matrix is called a **tensor**. In other words, a matrix with an arbitrary number of dimensions is called a tensor. For example, a four-dimensional tensor can be denoted as shown here:

$$T \in R^{k \times l \times m \times n}$$

Here, $R$ is the real number space.

# Tensor/matrix operations

# Transpose

Transpose is an important operation defined for matrices or tensors. For a matrix, the transpose is defined as follows:

$$\left(A_{i,j}\right)^T = A_{j,i}$$

Here, $A^T$ denotes the transpose of $A$.

An example of the transpose operation can be illustrated as follows:

$$A = \begin{pmatrix} 1 & 4 & 2 & 3 \\ 2 & 7 & 7 & 1 \\ 5 & 6 & 9 & 0 \end{pmatrix}$$

After the transpose operation:

$$A^T = \begin{pmatrix} 1 & 2 & 5 \\ 4 & 7 & 6 \\ 2 & 7 & 9 \\ 3 & 1 & 0 \end{pmatrix}$$

For a tensor, transpose can be seen as permuting the dimensions order. For example, let's define a tensor $S$, as shown here:

$$S \in R^{d_1, d_2, d_3, d_4}$$

Now a transpose operation (out of many) can be defined as follows:

$$S^T \in R^{d_4, d_3, d_2, d_1}$$

# Multiplication

Matrix multiplication is another important operation that appears quite frequently in linear algebra.

Given the matrices $A \in R^{m \times n}$ and $B \in R^{n \times p}$, the multiplication of $A$ and $B$ is defined as follows:

$$C = AB$$

Here, $C \in R^{m \times p}$.

Consider this example:

$$A = \begin{pmatrix} 1 & 2 \\ 4 & 5 \\ 7 & 8 \end{pmatrix}$$

$$B = \begin{pmatrix} 8 & 5 & 2 \\ 9 & 6 & 3 \end{pmatrix}$$

This gives $C = AB$, and the value of $C$ is as follows:

$$C = \begin{pmatrix} 26 & 17 & 8 \\ 77 & 50 & 23 \\ 128 & 83 & 38 \end{pmatrix}$$

# Element-wise multiplication

Element-wise matrix multiplication (or the Hadamard product) is computed for two matrices that have the same shape. Given the matrices $A \in R^{m \times n}$ and $B \in R^{m \times n}$, the element-wise multiplication of $A$ and $B$ is defined as follows:

$$C = A \circ B$$

Here, $C \in R^{m \times n}$

Consider this example:

$$A = \begin{bmatrix} 2 & 3 \\ 1 & 2 \\ 6 & 1 \end{bmatrix} B = \begin{bmatrix} 3 & 2 \\ 1 & 3 \\ 3 & 5 \end{bmatrix}$$

This gives $C = A \circ B$, and the value of $C$ is as follows:

$$C = \begin{bmatrix} 6 & 6 \\ 1 & 6 \\ 18 & 5 \end{bmatrix}$$

# Inverse

The inverse of the matrix $A$ is denoted by $A^{-1}$, where it satisfies the following condition:

$$A^{-1}A = I$$

Inverse is very useful if we are trying to solve a system of linear equations. Consider this example:

$$Ax = b$$

We can solve for $x$ like this:

$$A^{-1}(Ax) = A^{-1}b$$

This can be written as, $(A^{-1}A)x = A^{-1}b$ using the associative law (that is, $A(BC) = (AB)C$).

Next, we will get $Ix = A^{-1}b$ because $A^{-1}A = I$, where $I$ is the identity matrix.

Lastly, $x = A^{-1}b$ because $Ix = x$.

For example, polynomial regression, one of the regression techniques, uses a linear system of equations to solve the regression problem. Regression is similar to classification, but instead of outputting a class, regression models output a continuous value. Let's look at an example problem: given the number of bedrooms in a house, we'll calculate the real-estate value of the house. Formally, a polynomial regression problem can be written as follows:

$$y_i = \beta_0 + \beta_1 x_i + \beta_2 x_i^2 + \cdots + \beta_m x_i^m + \varepsilon_i \ (i = 1, 2, \ldots, n)$$

Here, $(x_i, y_i)$ is the $i^{th}$ data input, where $x_i$ is the input, $y_i$ is the label, and $\varepsilon$ is noise in data. In our example, $x$ is the number of bedrooms and $y$ is the price of the house. This can be written as a system of linear equations as follows:

$$
\begin{bmatrix} y_1 \\ y_2 \\ y_3 \\ \vdots \\ y_n \end{bmatrix} =
\begin{bmatrix}
1 & x_1 & x_1^2 & \cdots & x_1^m \\
1 & x_2 & x_2^2 & \cdots & x_2^m \\
1 & x_3 & x_3^2 & \cdots & x_3^m \\
\vdots & \vdots & \vdots & \ddots & \vdots \\
1 & x_n & x_n^2 & \cdots & x_n^m
\end{bmatrix}
\begin{bmatrix} \beta_0 \\ \beta_1 \\ \beta_2 \\ \vdots \\ \beta_m \end{bmatrix} +
\begin{bmatrix} \varepsilon_1 \\ \varepsilon_2 \\ \varepsilon_3 \\ \vdots \\ \varepsilon_n \end{bmatrix}
$$

However, $A^{-1}$ does not exist for all $A$. There are certain conditions that need to be satisfied in order for the inverse to exist for a matrix. For example, to define the inverse, $A$ needs to be a square matrix (that is, $R^{n \times n}$). Even when the inverse exists, we cannot always find it in the closed form; sometimes it can only be approximated with finite-precision computers. If the inverse exists, there are several algorithms for finding it, which we will be discussing here.

When it is said that $A$ needs to be a square matrix for the inverse to exist, I refer to the standard inversion. There exists variants of inverse operation (for example, Moore-Penrose inverse, also known as pseudoinverse) that can perform matrix inversion on general $m \times n$ matrices.

# Finding the matrix inverse – Singular Value Decomposition (SVD)

Let's now see how we can use SVD to find the inverse of a matrix $A$. SVD factorizes $A$ into three different matrices, as shown here:

$$A = UDV^T$$

Here the columns of $U$ are known as left singular vectors, columns of $V$ are known as right singular vectors, and diagonal values of $D$ (a diagonal matrix) are known as singular values. Left singular vectors are the eigenvectors of $AA^T$ and the right singular vectors are the eigenvectors of $A^T A$. Finally, the singular values are the square roots of the eigenvalues of $AA^T$ and $A^T A$. Eigenvector $v$ and its corresponding eigenvalue $\lambda$ of the square matrix $A$ satisfies the following condition:

$$Av = \lambda v$$

Then if the SVD exists, the inverse of $A$ is given by this:

$$A^{-1} = VD^{-1}U^T$$

Since $D$ is diagonal, $D^{-1}$ is simply the element-wise reciprocal of the nonzero elements of $D$. SVD is an important matrix factorization technique that appears in many occasions in machine learning. For example, SVD is used for calculating **Principal Component Analysis (PCA)**, which is a popular dimensionality reduction technique for data (a purpose similar to that of t-SNE that we saw in *Chapter 4, Advanced Word2vec*). Another, more NLP-oriented application of SVD is document ranking. That is, when you want to get the most relevant documents (and rank them by relevance to some term, for example, *football*), SVD can be used to achieve this.

# Norms

Norm is used as a measure of the *size* of the matrix (that is, of the values in the matrix). The $p^{th}$ norm is calculated and denoted as shown here:

$$\|A\|_p = \left(\sum_i |A_i|^p\right)^{1/p}$$

For example, the L2 norm would be this:

$$\|A\|_2 = \sqrt{\sum_i |A_i|^2}$$

# Determinant

The determinant of a square matrix, denoted by $det(A)$, is the product of all the eigenvalues of the matrix. Determinant is very useful in many ways. For example, $A$ is invertible if and only if the determinant is nonzero. The following equation shows the calculations for the determinant of a $3\times3$ matrix:

$$\begin{vmatrix} a & b & c \\ d & e & f \\ g & h & i \end{vmatrix} = a\begin{vmatrix} e & f \\ h & i \end{vmatrix} - b\begin{vmatrix} d & f \\ g & i \end{vmatrix} + c\begin{vmatrix} d & e \\ g & h \end{vmatrix}$$

$$= a(ei - fh) - b(di - fg) + c(dh - eg)$$

$$= aei + bfg + cdh - ceg - bdi - afh$$

# Probability

Next, we will discuss the terminology related to probability theory. Probability theory is a vital part of machine learning, as modeling data with probabilistic models allows us to draw conclusions about how uncertain a model is about some predictions. Consider the example, where we performed sentiment analysis in *Chapter 11, Current Trends and the Future of Natural Language Processing* where we had an output value (positive/negative) for a given movie review. Though the model output some value between 0 and 1 (0 for negative and 1 for positive) for any sample we input, the model didn't know how *uncertain* it was about its answer.

Let's understand how uncertainty helps us to make better predictions. For example, a deterministic model might incorrectly say the positivity of the review, *I never lost interest*, is 0.25 (that is, more likely to be a negative comment). However, a probabilistic model will give a mean value and a standard deviation for the prediction. For example, it will say, this prediction has a mean of 0.25 and a standard deviation of 0.5. With the second model, we know that the prediction is likely to be wrong due to the high standard deviation. However, in the deterministic model, we don't have this luxury. This property is especially valuable for critical machine systems (for example, terrorism risk assessing model).

To develop such probabilistic machine learning models (for example, Bayesian logistic regression, Bayesian neural networks, or Gaussian processes) you should be familiar with the basic probability theory. Therefore, we provide some basic probability information here.

# Random variables

A random variable is a variable that can take some value at random. Also, random variables are represented as $x_1$, $x_2$, and so on. Random variables can be of two types: discrete and continuous.

# Discrete random variables

A discrete random variable is a variable that can take discrete random values. For example, trials of flipping a coin can be modeled as a random variable, that is, the side of the coin it lands on when you flip a coin is a discrete variable as the values can only be *heads* or *tails*. Alternatively, the value you get when you roll a die is discrete, as well, as the values can only come from the set, *{1,2,3,4,5,6}*.

# Continuous random variables

A continuous random variable is a variable that can take any real value, that is, if $x$ is a continuous random variable:

$$x \in R$$

Here, $R$ is the real number space.

For example, the height of a person is a continuous random variable as it can take any real value.

# The probability mass/density function

The **probability mass function (PMF)** or the **probability density function (PDF)** is a way of showing the probability distribution over different values a random variable can take. For discrete variables, a PMF is defined and for continuous variables, a PDF is defined. *Figure A.1* shows an example PMF:

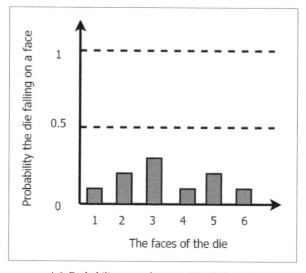

A.1: Probability mass function (PMF) discrete

The preceding PMF might be achieved by a *biased* die. In this graph, we can see that there is a high probability of getting a **3** with this die. Such a graph can be obtained by running a number of trials (say, 100) and then counting the number of times each face fell on top. Finally, divide each count by the number of trials to obtain the normalized probabilities. Note that all the probabilities should add up to 1, as shown here:

$$P\left(X \in \{1,2,3,4,5,6\}\right) = 1$$

The same concept is extended to a continuous random variable to obtain a PDF. Say that we are trying to model the probability of a certain height given a population. Unlike the discrete case, we do not have individual values to calculate the probability for, but rather a continuous spectrum of values (in the example, it extends from 0 to 2.4 m). If we are to draw a graph for this example like the one in *Figure A.1*, we need to think of it in terms of infinitesimally small bins. For example, we find out the probability density of a person's height being between 0.0 m-0.01 m, 0.01-0.02 m, ..., 1.8 m-1.81 m, ..., and so on. The probability density can be calculated using the following formula:

$$\text{probability density for bin}_i = \frac{probability\ of\ person's\ height\ being\ in\ bin_i}{bin_i size}$$

Then, we will plot those bars close to each other to obtain a continuous curve, as shown in *Figure A.2*. Note that the probability density for a given bin can be greater than 1 (since it's density), but the area under the curve must be 1:

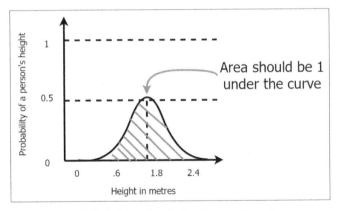

Figure A.2: Probability density function (PDF) continuous

The shape shown in *Figure A.2* is known as the normal (or Gaussian) distribution. It is also called the *bell curve*. We previously gave just an intuitive explanation of how to think about a continuous probability density function. More formally, a continuous PDF of the normal distribution has an equation and is defined as follows. Let's assume that a continuous random variable $X$ has a normal distribution with mean $\mu$ and standard deviation $\sigma$. The probability of $X = x$ for any value of $x$ is given by this formula:

$$P(X = x) = \frac{1}{\sqrt{2\pi\sigma^2}} e^{-\frac{(x-\mu)^2}{2\sigma^2}}$$

You should get the area (which needs to be 1 for a valid PDF) if you integrate this quantity over all possible infinitesimally small $dx$ values, as denoted by this formula:

$$\int_{-\infty}^{\infty} \frac{1}{\sqrt{2\pi\sigma^2}} e^{-\frac{(x-\mu)^2}{2\sigma^2}} dx$$

The integral of the normal for the arbitrary $a$, $b$ values is given by the following formula:

$$\int_{-\infty}^{\infty} e^{-a(x+b)^2} dx = \sqrt{\frac{\pi}{a}}$$

(You can find more information at http://mathworld.wolfram.com/GaussianIntegral.html, or for a less complex discussion, refer to https://en.wikipedia.org/wiki/Gaussian_integral.)

Using this, we can get the integral of the normal distribution, where $a = 1/2\sigma^2$ and $b = -\mu$:

$$\int_{-\infty}^{\infty} \frac{1}{\sqrt{2\pi\sigma^2}} e^{-\frac{(x-\mu)^2}{2\sigma^2}} dx = \frac{1}{\sqrt{2\pi\sigma^2}} \sqrt{\frac{\pi}{1/2\sigma^2}} = \frac{1}{\sqrt{2\pi\sigma^2}} \sqrt{2\pi\sigma^2} = 1$$

This gives the accumulation of all the probability values for all the values of $x$ and gives you a value of 1.

# Conditional probability

Conditional probability represents the probability of an event happening, given the occurrence of another event. For example, given two random variables, $X$ and $Y$, the conditional probability of $X = x$, given that $Y = y$, is denoted by this formula:

$$P(X = x \mid Y = y)$$

A real-world example of such a probability would be as follows:

$$P(Bob\ going\ to\ school = Yes \mid It\ rains = Yes)$$

# Joint probability

Given two random variables, $X$ and $Y$, we will refer to the probability of $X = x$ together with $Y = y$ as the joint probability of $X = x$ and $Y = y$. This is denoted by the following formula:

$$P(X = x, Y = y) = P(X = x)P(Y = y \mid X = x)$$

If $X$ and $Y$ are mutually exclusive events, this expression reduces to this:

$$P(X = x, Y = y) = P(X = x)P(Y = y)$$

A real-world example of this is as follows:

$$P(It\ Rains = yes, Play\ Golf = yes) = P(It\ Rains = Yes)P(Play\ Golf = yes \mid It\ Rains = Yes)$$

# Marginal probability

Marginal probability distribution is the probability distribution of a subset of random variables, given the joint probability distribution of all variables. For example, consider that two random variables, $X$ and $Y$ exist, and we already know $P(X = x, Y = y)$ and we want to calculate $P(x)$:

$$P(X = x) = \sum_{\forall y'} P(X = x, Y = y')$$

Intuitively, we will take the sum over all possible values of $Y$, effectively making the probability of $Y = 1$. This gives us $P(X = x, Y = 1) = P(X = x)$.

# Bayes' rule

Bayes, rule gives us a way to calculate $P(Y = y \mid X = x)$ if we already know $P(X = x \mid Y = y), P(X = x)$, and $P(Y = y)$. We can easily arrive at Bayes' rule as follows:

$$P(X = x, Y = y) = P(X = x)P(Y = y \mid X = x) = P(Y = y)P(X = x \mid Y = y)$$

Now let's take the middle and right parts:

$$P(X = x)P(Y = y \mid X = x) = P(Y = y)P(X = x \mid Y = y)$$

$$P(Y = y \mid X = x) = \frac{P(X = x \mid Y = y)P(Y = y)}{P(X = x)}$$

This is Bayes' rule. Let's put it simply, as shown here:

$$P(y \mid x) = \frac{P(x \mid y)P(y)}{P(x)}$$

# Introduction to Keras

Here we will provide a brief introduction to Keras, which is a sublibrary of TensorFlow that provides more high-level functions for implementing deep learning algorithms. Keras uses basic TensorFlow operations, underneath; however, it exposes a higher level, beginner-friendly API for users. To see how to use Keras, we will look at a quick example. We will outline how one might create a CNN using Keras. Full exercise can be found at `keras_cnn.ipynb` located in the `appendix` folder.

We will first determine what type of a model we will be defining. Keras has two different APIs: sequential and functional. The sequential API is simpler and allows designing a model, layer by layer. However, the sequential API has limited flexibility in designing the organization and connections between layers of the network. On the other hand, the functional API has much more flexibility and allows the user to design the specific details of the neural network. For demonstration purposes, we will implement a CNN using the sequential API in Keras. A sequential model in this case is a sequence of stack of layers (for example, input layer, convolution layer, and pooling layer):

```
model = Sequential()
```

Next, we will define the layers of our CNN one by one. First, we will define a convolution layer with 32 filters, a kernel size of 3 × 3 and *ReLU* nonlinearity. This layer will be taking an input of size 28 × 28 × 1 (that is, the size of an MNIST image):

```
model.add(Conv2D(32, 3, activation='relu', input_shape=[28, 28, 1]))
```

Next, we will define a max-pooling layer. If the kernel size and stride are not defined, they default to 2 (kernel size) and 1 (stride):

```
model.add(MaxPool2D())
```

Then we will add a batch normalization layer:

```
model.add(BatchNormalization())
```

A batch normalization layer (refer to *Batch Normalization: Accelerating Deep Network Training by Reducing Internal Covariate Shift, Ioffe* and *Szegedy, International Conference on Machine Learning, 2015*) normalizes (that is, make activations zero-mean and unit-variance) the outputs of the previous layer. This is an additional step used to improve the performance of the CNN, especially in computer vision applications. Note that we did not use batch normalization in the chapter exercises, as the batch normalization has not been used heavily for NLP tasks, compared to the amount it is used for computer vision applications.

Next, we will add two more convolution layers, followed by a max-pooling layer and a batch normalization layer:

```
model.add(Conv2D(64, 3, activation='relu'))
model.add(MaxPool2D())
model.add(BatchNormalization())
model.add(Conv2D(128, 3, activation='relu'))
model.add(MaxPool2D())
model.add(BatchNormalization())
```

Next, we will flatten the input as this is required to feed the output into a fully connected layer:

```
model.add(Flatten())
```

Then we will add a fully connected layer with 256 hidden units, a *ReLU* activation, and a final softmax output layer with 10 softmax units (that is, for the 10 different classes of MNIST):

```
model.add(Dense(256, activation='relu'))
model.add(Dense(10, activation='softmax'))
```

Finally, we will *compile* the model, when we also tell Keras to use *Adam* as the optimizer and categorical cross-entropy loss and output metric to be the accuracy of the model:

```
model.compile(optimizer='adam', loss='categorical_crossentropy',
metrics=['accuracy'])
```

Once the model, the loss and an optimizer is defined, we can run the Keras model as follows.

To train the model you can use the following command:

```
model.fit(x_train, y_train, batch_size = batch_size)
```

Here, x_train and y_train are the training data. And batch_size defines the batch size. When you run this, the training progress will be shown below.

Then to evaluate the model, use the following:

```
test_acc = model.evaluate(x_test, y_test, batch_size=batch_size)
```

This line will again output a progress bar as well as the test loss and accuracy of each epoch.

# Introduction to the TensorFlow seq2seq library

We used the raw TensorFlow API for all our implementations in this book for better transparency of the actual functionality of the models and for a better learning experience. However, TensorFlow has various libraries that hide all the fine-grained details of the implementations. This allows users to implement sequence-to-sequence models like the **Neural Machine Translation (NMT)** model we saw in *Chapter 10, Sequence-to-Sequence Learning – Neural Machine Translation* with fewer lines of code and without worrying about more specific technical details about how they work. Knowledge about these libraries is important as they provide a much cleaner way of using these models in production code or researching beyond the existing methods. Therefore, we will go through a quick introduction of how to use the TensorFlow seq2seq library. This code is available as an exercise in the seq2seq_nmt.ipynb file.

# Defining embeddings for the encoder and decoder

We will first define the encoder inputs, decoder inputs, and decoder output placeholders:

```
enc_train_inputs = []
dec_train_inputs, dec_train_labels = [],[]
for ui in range(source_sequence_length):
    enc_train_inputs.append(tf.placeholder(tf.int32, shape=[batch_
size],name='train_inputs_%d'%ui))

for ui in range(target_sequence_length):
    dec_train_inputs.append(tf.placeholder(tf.int32, shape=[batch_
size],name='train_inputs_%d'%ui))
    dec_train_labels.append(tf.placeholder(tf.int32, shape=[batch_
size],name='train_outputs_%d'%ui))
```

Next, we will define the embedding lookup function for all the encoder and decoder inputs, to obtain the word embeddings:

```
encoder_emb_inp = [tf.nn.embedding_lookup(encoder_emb_layer, src) for
src in enc_train_inputs]
encoder_emb_inp = tf.stack(encoder_emb_inp)

decoder_emb_inp = [tf.nn.embedding_lookup(decoder_emb_layer, src) for
src in dec_train_inputs]
decoder_emb_inp = tf.stack(decoder_emb_inp)
```

# Defining the encoder

The encoder is made with an LSTM cell as its basic building block. Then, we will define `dynamic_rnn`, which takes the defined LSTM cell as the input, and the state is initialized with zeros. Then, we will set the `time_major` parameter to `True` because our data has the time axis as the first axis (that is, axis 0). In other words, our data has the `[sequence_length, batch_size, embeddings_size]` shape, where time-dependent `sequence_length` is in the first axis. The benefit of `dynamic_rnn` is its ability to handle dynamically sized inputs. You can use the optional `sequence_length` argument to define the length of each sentence in the batch. For example, consider you have a batch of size `[3,30]` with three sentences having lengths of [10, 20, 30] (note that we pad the short sentences up to 30 with a special token). Passing a tensor that has values [10, 20, 30] as `sequence_length` will zero out LSTM outputs that are computed beyond the length of each sentence. For the cell state, it will not zero out, but take the last cell state computed within the length of the sentence and copy that value beyond the length of the sentence, until 30 is reached:

```
encoder_cell = tf.nn.rnn_cell.BasicLSTMCell(num_units)

initial_state = encoder_cell.zero_state(batch_size, dtype=tf.float32)

encoder_outputs, encoder_state = tf.nn.dynamic_rnn(
    encoder_cell, encoder_emb_inp, initial_state=initial_state,
    sequence_length=[source_sequence_length for _ in range(batch_
size)],
    time_major=True, swap_memory=True)
```

The `swap_memory` option allows TensorFlow to swap the tensors produced during the inference process between GPU and CPU, in case the model is too complex to fit entirely in the GPU.

# Defining the decoder

The decoder is defined similar to the encoder, but has an extra layer called, `projection_layer`, which represents the softmax output layer for sampling the predictions made by the decoder. We will also define a `TrainingHelper` function that properly feeds the decoder inputs to the decoder. We also define two types of decoders in this example: a `BasicDecoder` and `BahdanauAttention` decoders. (The attention mechanism is discussed in *Chapter 10, Sequence-to-Sequence Learning – Neural Machine Translation*.) Many other decoders exist in the library, such as `BeamSearchDecoder` and `BahdanauMonotonicAttention`:

```
decoder_cell = tf.nn.rnn_cell.BasicLSTMCell(num_units)

projection_layer = Dense(units=vocab_size, use_bias=True)

helper = tf.contrib.seq2seq.TrainingHelper(
    decoder_emb_inp, [target_sequence_length for _ in range(batch_
size)], time_major=True)

if decoder_type == 'basic':
    decoder = tf.contrib.seq2seq.BasicDecoder(
        decoder_cell, helper, encoder_state,
        output_layer=projection_layer)

elif decoder_type == 'attention':
    decoder = tf.contrib.seq2seq.BahdanauAttention(
        decoder_cell, helper, encoder_state,
        output_layer=projection_layer)
```

We will use dynamic decoding to get the outputs of the decoder:

```
outputs, _, _ = tf.contrib.seq2seq.dynamic_decode(
    decoder, output_time_major=True,
    swap_memory=True
)
```

Next, we will define the logits, cross-entropy loss, and train prediction operations:

```
logits = outputs.rnn_output

crossent = tf.nn.sparse_softmax_cross_entropy_with_logits(
    labels=dec_train_labels, logits=logits)
loss = tf.reduce_mean(crossent)

train_prediction = outputs.sample_id
```

Then, we will define two optimizers, where we use `AdamOptimizer` for the first 10,000 steps and vanilla stochastic `GradientDescentOptimizer` for the rest of the optimization process. This is because, using Adam optimizer for a long term gives rise to some unexpected behaviors. Therefore, we will use Adam to obtain a good initial position for the SGD optimizer and then use SGD from then on:

```
with tf.variable_scope('Adam'):
    optimizer = tf.train.AdamOptimizer(learning_rate)
with tf.variable_scope('SGD'):
    sgd_optimizer = tf.train.GradientDescentOptimizer(learning_rate)
```

```
gradients, v = zip(*optimizer.compute_gradients(loss))
gradients, _ = tf.clip_by_global_norm(gradients, 25.0)
optimize = optimizer.apply_gradients(zip(gradients, v))

sgd_gradients, v = zip(*sgd_optimizer.compute_gradients(loss))
sgd_gradients, _ = tf.clip_by_global_norm(sgd_gradients, 25.0)
sgd_optimize = optimizer.apply_gradients(zip(sgd_gradients, v))
```

 A rigorous evaluation on how optimizers perform in NMT training is found in a paper by Bahar and others, called, *Empirical Investigation of Optimization Algorithms in Neural Machine Translation, The Prague Bulletin of Mathematical Linguistics, 2017.*

# Visualizing word embeddings with TensorBoard

When we wanted to visualize word embedding in *Chapter 3, Word2vec – Learning Word Embeddings,* we manually implemented the visualization with the t-SNE algorithm. However, you also could use TensorBoard for visualizing word embeddings. TensorBoard is a visualization tool provided with TensorFlow. You can use TensorBoard to visualize the TensorFlow variables in your program. This allows you to see how various variables behave over time (for example, model loss/accuracy), so you can identify potential issues in your model.

TensorBoard enables you to visualize scalar values and vectors as histograms. Apart from this, TensorBoard also allows you to visualize word embeddings. Therefore, it takes all the required code implementation away from you, if you need to analyze what the embeddings look like. Next we will see how we can use TensorBoard to visualize word embeddings. The code for this exercise is provided in `tensorboard_word_embeddings.ipynb` in the `appendix` folder.

## Starting TensorBoard

First, we will list the steps for starting TensorBoard. TensorBoard acts as a service and runs on a specific port (by default, on `6006`). To start TensorBoard, you will need to follow the following steps:

1. Open up Command Prompt (Windows) or Terminal (Ubuntu/macOS).

2. Go into the project home directory.

3. If you are using `python` virtuanenv, activate the virtual environment where you have installed TensorFlow.

4. Make sure that you can see the TensorFlow library through Python. To do this, follow these steps:

    1. Type in `python3`, you will get a `>>>` looking prompt

    2. Try `import tensorflow as tf`

    3. If you can run this successfully, you are fine

    4. Exit the `python` prompt (that is, `>>>`) by typing `exit()`

5. Type in `tensorboard --logdir=models`:

    ◦ The `--logdir` option points to the directory where you will create data to visualize

    ◦ Optionally, you can use `--port=<port_you_like>` to change the port TensorBoard runs on

6. You should now get the following message:

    ```
    TensorBoard 1.6.0 at <url>;:6006 (Press CTRL+C to quit)
    ```

7. Enter the `<url>:6006` in to the web browser. You should be able to see an orange dashboard at this point. You won't have anything to display because we haven't generated data.

# Saving word embeddings and visualizing via TensorBoard

First, we will download and load the 50-dimensional GloVe embeddings we used in *Chapter 9, Applications of LSTM – Image Caption Generation*. For that first download the GloVe embedding file (`glove.6B.zip`) from `https://nlp.stanford.edu/projects/glove/` and place it in the `appendix` folder. We will load the first 50,000 word vectors in the file and later use these to initialize a TensorFlow variable. We will also record the word strings of each word, as we will later provide these as labels for each point to display on TensorBoard:

```
vocabulary_size = 50000
pret_embeddings = np.empty(shape=(vocabulary_size,50),dtype=np.float32)

words = []

word_idx = 0
with zipfile.ZipFile('glove.6B.zip') as glovezip:
    with glovezip.open('glove.6B.50d.txt') as glovefile:
        for li, line in enumerate(glovefile):
            if (li+1)%10000==0: print('.',end='')
```

```
line_tokens = line.decode('utf-8').split(' ')
word = line_tokens[0]

vector = [float(v) for v in line_tokens[1:]]
assert len(vector)==50
words.append(word)
pret_embeddings[word_idx, :] = np.array(vector)
word_idx += 1
if word_idx == vocabulary_size:
    break
```

Now, we will define TensorFlow-related variables and operations. Before this, we will create a directory called models, which will be used to store the variables:

```
log_dir = 'models'

if not os.path.exists(log_dir):
    os.mkdir(log_dir)
```

Then, we will define a variable that will be initialized with the word embeddings we copied from the text file earlier:

```
embeddings = tf.get_variable('embeddings',shape=[vocabulary_size, 50],
                        initializer=tf.constant_initializer(pret_
embeddings))
```

We will next create a session and initialize the variable we defined earlier:

```
session = tf.InteractiveSession()
tf.global_variables_initializer().run()
```

Thereafter, we will create a tf.train.Saver object. The Saver object can be used to save TensorFlow variables to the memory, so that they can later be restored if needed. In the following code, we will save the embedding variable to the models directory under the name, model.ckpt:

```
saver = tf.train.Saver({'embeddings':embeddings})
saver.save(session, os.path.join(log_dir, "model.ckpt"), 0)
```

We also need to save a metadata file. A metadata file contains labels/images or other types of information associated with the word embeddings, so that when you hover over the embedding visualization the corresponding points will show the word/label they represent. The metadata file should be of the `.tsv` (tab separated values) format and should contain `vocabulary_size + 1` rows in it, where the first row contains the headers for the information you are including. In the following code, we will save two pieces of information: word strings and a unique identifier (that is, row index) for each word:

```
with open(os.path.join(log_dir,'metadata.tsv'), 'w',encoding='utf-8')
as csvfile:
    writer = csv.writer(csvfile, delimiter='\t',
                        quotechar='|', quoting=csv.QUOTE_MINIMAL)
    writer.writerow(['Word','Word ID'])
    for wi,w in enumerate(words):
      writer.writerow([w,wi])
```

Then, we will need to tell TensorFlow where it can find the metadata for the embedding data we saved to the disk. For this, we need to create a `ProjectorConfig` object, which maintains various configuration details about the embedding we want to display. The details stored in the `ProjectorConfig` folder will be saved to a file called `projector_config.pbtxt` in the `models` directory:

```
config = projector.ProjectorConfig()
```

Here, we will populate the required fields of the `ProjectorConfig` object we created. First, we will tell it the name of the variable we're interested in visualizing. Next, we will tell it where it can find the metadata corresponding to that variable:

```
embedding_config = config.embeddings.add()
embedding_config.tensor_name = embeddings.name
embedding_config.metadata_path = 'metadata.tsv'
```

We will now use a summary writer to write this to the `projector_config.pbtxt` file. TensorBoard will read this file at startup:

```
summary_writer = tf.summary.FileWriter(log_dir)
projector.visualize_embeddings(summary_writer, config)
```

Now if you load TensorBoard, you should see something similar to *Figure A.3*:

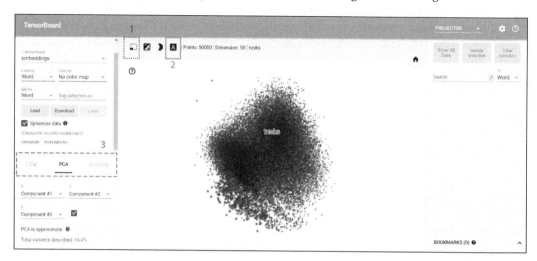

Figure A.3: Tensorboard view of the embeddings

When you hover over the displayed point cloud, it will show the label of the word you're currently hovering over, as we provided this information in the metadata. tsv file. Furthermore, you have several options. The first option (shown with a dotted line and marked as **1**) will allow you to select a subset of the full embedding space. You can draw a bounding box over the area of the embedding space you're interested in, and it will look as shown in *Figure A.4*. I have selected the embeddings at the bottom right corner:

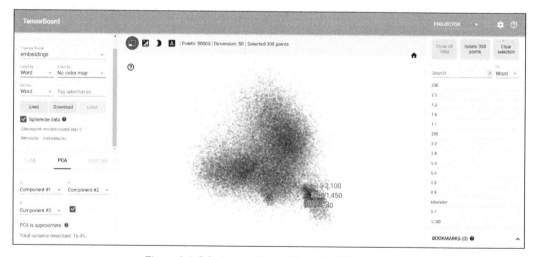

Figure A.4: Selecting a subset of the embedding space

Another option you have is the ability to view words themselves, instead of dots. You can do this by selecting the second option in *Figure A.3* (show inside a solid box and marked as **2**). This would look as shown in *Figure A.5*. Additionally, you can pan/zoom/rotate the view to your liking. If you click on the help button (shown within a solid box and marked as **1** in *Figure A.5*), it will show you a guide for controlling the view:

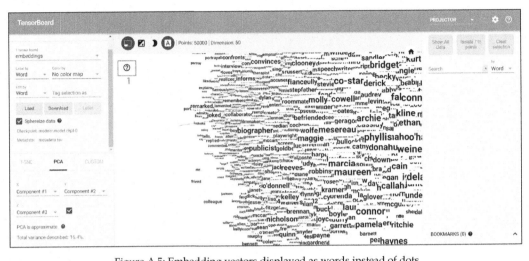

Figure A.5: Embedding vectors displayed as words instead of dots

Finally, you can change the visualization algorithm from the panel on the left-hand side (shown with a dashed line and marked with **3** in *Figure A.3*).

# Summary

Here we discussed some of the mathematical background as well as some implementations we did not cover in the other sections. First we discussed the mathematical notation for scalars, vectors, matrices and tensors. Then we discussed various operations performed on these data structures, such as, matrix multiplication and inversion. Next, we discussed various terminology that is useful for understanding probabilistic machine learning such as, probability density functions, joint probability, marginal probability and Bayes rule. Afterwards, we moved our discussion to cover various implementations that we did not visit in the other chapters. We learnt how to use Keras; a high-level TensorFlow library to implement a CNN. Then we discussed how we can efficiently implement a neural machine translator with the seq2seq library in TensorFlow, compared to the implementation we discussed in *Chapter 10, Sequence-to-Sequence Learning – Neural Machine Translation*. Finally, we ended this section with a guide that teaches you to visualize word embeddings using the TensorBoard; a visualization platform that comes with TensorFlow.

# Other Books You May Enjoy

If you enjoyed this book, you may be interested in these other books by Packt:

**Deep Learning with TensorFlow - Second Edition**
Giancarlo Zaccone, Md. Rezaul Karim

ISBN: 978-1-78883-110-9

- Apply deep machine intelligence and GPU computing with TensorFlow
- Access public datasets and use TensorFlow to load, process, and transform the data
- Discover how to use the high-level TensorFlow API to build more powerful applications
- Use deep learning for scalable object detection and mobile computing
- Train machines quickly to learn from data by exploring reinforcement learning techniques
- Explore active areas of deep learning research and applications

**Python Machine Learning - Second Edition**
Sebastian Raschka, Vahid Mirjalili

ISBN: 978-1-78712-593-3

- Understand the key frameworks in data science, machine learning, and deep learning

- Harness the power of the latest Python open source libraries in machine learning

- Master machine learning techniques using challenging real-world data

- Master deep neural network implementation using the TensorFlow library

- Ask new questions of your data through machine learning models and neural networks

- Learn the mechanics of classification algorithms to implement the best tool for the job

- Predict continuous target outcomes using regression analysis

- Uncover hidden patterns and structures in data with clustering

- Delve deeper into textual and social media data using sentiment analysis

**IPython Interactive Computing and Visualization Cookbook - Second Edition**
Cyrille Rossant

ISBN: 978-1-78588-863-2

- Master all features of the Jupyter Notebook
- Code better: write high-quality, readable, and well-tested programs; profile and optimize your code; and conduct reproducible interactive computing experiments
- Visualize data and create interactive plots in the Jupyter Notebook
- Write blazingly fast Python programs with NumPy, ctypes, Numba, Cython, OpenMP, GPU programming (CUDA), parallel IPython, Dask, and more
- Analyze data with Bayesian or frequentist statistics (Pandas, PyMC, and R), and learn from actual data through machine learning (scikit-learn)
- Gain valuable insights into signals, images, and sounds with SciPy, scikit-image, and OpenCV
- Simulate deterministic and stochastic dynamical systems in Python
- Familiarize yourself with math in Python using SymPy and Sage: algebra, analysis, logic, graphs, geometry, and probability theory

**Python Interviews**
Mike Driscoll

ISBN: 978-1-78839-908-1

- How successful programmers think
- The history of Python
- Insights into the minds of the Python core team
- Trends in Python programming

# Leave a review - let other readers know what you think

Please share your thoughts on this book with others by leaving a review on the site that you bought it from. If you purchased the book from Amazon, please leave us an honest review on this book's Amazon page. This is vital so that other potential readers can see and use your unbiased opinion to make purchasing decisions, we can understand what our customers think about our products, and our authors can see your feedback on the title that they have worked with Packt to create. It will only take a few minutes of your time, but is valuable to other potential customers, our authors, and Packt. Thank you!

# Index

Made in the USA
Columbia, SC
25 October 2018